D1412492

THE GENIUS

And music's voice, and lo! the cup o'erflows! (1)
I love you well, sweet guests, and pray that you
Enjoy the moment fully, holding close
And tenderly your dear ones (2) Ah! make use
Of this fair hour with all your faculties–
With hands and eyes and hearts and kissing mouths (3)
Let me not need entreat you more, dear guests!
And you, beloved cousin: sing to us!

FAT COUSIN:

Alack! alas! my skinny brother's called!
Now comes the eternal song about "cold snow!"

(They sing with laughter.)

THIN COUSIN

(Sings.)

"Dear Mrs. Love, hast thou no concern?
I'm in misery: feel me burn! (4)
Cold, cold snow indeed thou art,
To melt with the fire of my choking heart!
Dear Mrs. Love, come along with me,
And all that heart shall be full of glee! (5)

(All sing. The dull tolling of a bell is heard. Everyman pushes his glass away.)

EVERYMAN:

What bell is that? (6) It can mean nothing good,
Methinks, so loud and fearsome is the sound! (7)
Now terror strikes my heart! (8) Why toll that bell,
And at this hour?

A GUEST:

I hear none, far or near.

Grumbling cousin: <u>Such a feast is a general exertion to make existence as repelling as possible. When my cousins start singing a climax is reached.</u>

① ist so überglücklich, dass er immer wieder nach neuen Worten sucht
② Allgemeine Umarmung
③ In der Umarmung

① is so overjoyed, that he trys to find news words over and over aga
° ② General embracing

③ In the embrace

Grumbl. Cousin
So ein Fest ist eine allgemeine Anstrengung, das Dasein so widerwärtig wie möglich zu machen. Wenn meine Vettern anfangen zu singen, ist das Ziel erreicht.

④ Dear Mrs Love Alack Alas
⑤ Dear Mrs Love Alack Alas
Man lacht über ihn, wirft ihm Blumen zu.

④ Dear Mrs. Love Alack Alas
⑤ Dear Mrs. Love Alack Alas
One laughs at him, throws flowers to him.

5a Thin Cousin, schwingt seine Guitarre wie eine Glocke und beginnt einen Canon, der von den anderen aufgenommen wird:
Canon: Ach wie wohl ist mir am Abend, mir am Abend, mir am Abend
wenn zur Ruh die Glocken läuten Bimbam Bimbam Bimbam Bimbam Bum

⑥ bang: Param.: Welche Glocke?
⑦ fasst sich wieder ans Herz
⑧ ruft laut. Der Canon wird abgebrochen. Alle starren auf Jedermann. Das Läuten ist in der zunehmenden Stille deutlich vernehmbar, nur denen am Tisch nicht. Paramour sucht ihn zu beruhigen. Er wehrt ab.

(Alle lehnen sich schliesslich im Singen zurück) Mitten im Singen entsteht ein himmlisches fernes Glockenläuten, das streng und mahnend anschwillt. Es wird von niemand gehört, nur von Jedermann, der sein Glas auf den Tisch stellt und entsetzt aufhorcht. Er steht auf, sieht erst auf die Anderen, ob sie den Klang auch vernehmen, dann fragt er Paramour und ruft schrecklich durchdringend.

5a Thin cousin, begins a canon, which is being taken up by the others, while he swings his guitar like a bell:

Canon: <u>Oh, how well I feel at nightfall, feel at nightfall, feel at nightfall,</u>
<u>When the bells toll rest and quiet, Bimbam, Bimbam, Bimbam Bimbam, Bum.</u>

⑥ anxious: Param.: <u>What bell?</u>

⑦ again with his hand on his heart

⑧ cries loudly. The canon is interrupted. Everybody stares at Everyman. The tolling of the bell is to be heard distinctly in the growing silence. Paramour tries to calm him. He wards her off.

(Everybody finally leans back while singing) In the midst of the singing a celestial tolling of bells is heard from a distance, sounding from high above, increasing severe and warning. Nobody hears it but Everyman, who sets his glass on the table and listens terrified. He gets up, first looking at the others, whether they also hear the sound, then he asks Paramour and finally cries piercingly.

° clutches her without warning and kisses her on her mouth. She frees herself and gives him resolutely a clashing box on the ear. He is painfully astonished, holds his cheek. Laughing about him. □ old song. ▯ Floret silva undique Floret silva undique ⊞ has emptied ... looks around merrily. ↕ gets up, lifts the glass. △ strongly ⩓ overflowing, almost jubilant, points at everyone in the circle and embraces Paramour. ◊ exulting.

THE GENIUS

A MEMOIR OF

MAX REINHARDT

BY HIS SON

GOTTFRIED REINHARDT

ALFRED A. KNOPF NEW YORK 1979

THIS IS A BORZOI BOOK
PUBLISHED BY ALFRED A. KNOPF, INC.

Published in the United States by Alfred A. Knopf, Inc., New York,
and simultaneously in Canada by Random House of Canada Limited, Toronto.
Distributed by Random House, Inc., New York. Originally published in Germany as
Der Liebhaber: Erinnerungen seines Sohnes Gottfried Reinhardt an Max Reinhardt
by Droemer Knaur, Munich.

Grateful acknowledgment is made to the following for permission to reprint
previously published material:

S. Fischer Verlag: Excerpts from two letters of Thomas Mann. Thomas Mann to Walter Opitz, copyright © S. Fischer Verlag, Frankfurt am Main, 1961, and Thomas Mann to Agnes E. Meyer, copyright © 1963, Katja Mann. By permission of S. Fischer Verlag, Frankfurt am Main.

Alfred A. Knopf, Inc.: Excerpt from *Unfinished Journey: The Autobiography of Yehudi Menuhin*. Copyright © 1976 by Yehudi Menuhin and Patrick Sale and Associates, Ltd. Reprinted by permission of Alfred A. Knopf, Inc.

Methuen, Inc: Excerpt from "Hollywood" by Bertolt Brecht, from *Bertolt Brecht Poems 1913-1956* copyright © 1978. Reprinted by arrangement with Eyre Methuen, Ltd., London, and Methuen, Inc., New York.

The Nation: Review of *The Eternal Road* by Joseph Wood Krutch, *The Nation*, January 23, 1937. Copyright 1937, The Nation.

The New York Times Company: Phillip Carr interview with Reinhardt in Leopoldskron in 1927; Summary of the engagement of the Reinhardt Company in New York by Brooks Atkinson in late 1927–early 1928; Review of the Reinhardt production of *A Midsummer Night's Dream* by Brooks Atkinson in late 1927–early 1928; and Review of *The Eternal Road* by Brooks Atkinson, 1937. Copyright © 1927/28/37 by The New York Times Company. Reprinted by permission.

Kurt Wolff Verlag: Excerpt from *Aus dem Alten Europa, Menschen and Städte* by Helene von Nostitz, published 1933 by Kurt Wolff Verlag, Berlin.

Christiane Zimmer: Excerpts from the personal correspondence of Hugo von Hoffmannsthal. Permission to reprint granted by Christiane Zimmer.

Library of Congress Cataloging in Publication Data
Reinhardt, Gottfried.
The genius : a memoir of Max Reinhardt.
Translation of Der Liebhaber.
Includes index.
1. Reinhardt, Max, 1873–1943. 2. Theatrical
producers and directors—Germany—Biography. I. Title.
PN2658.R4R413 792'.0233'0924 [B] 78-20600
ISBN 0-394-49085-1

Manufactured in the United States of America
First American Edition

To
faithful lovers of
the theatre

Contents

Illustrations

FOLLOWING PAGE 204

All photographs, unless otherwise credited, courtesy of the Max Reinhardt Archive, State University of New York, Binghamton, New York.

ACKNOWLEDGMENTS

A memoir, dealing with things so long ago and mostly so far away—yet addressing itself, inevitably, to the here and now—is not solely dependent on recall, research and a will to expression. It feeds on encouragement (when the will is flagging), on aid in maintaining perspective, on discriminating guidance in selecting the essentials from an embarrassment of riches, and on an ever-watchful attention to the balancing of a style that must be contemporary and yet reflect the essence of its subject. In all these regards I am deeply obligated to my wife, Silvia, without whose moral and collaborative support I would have floundered many times, if not foundered altogether. I owe an equally large debt to my editor, Carol Janeway, who not only understood my problems but was instrumental in solving them. I was lucky to find in her someone with one foot firmly in the Old World and the other as firmly in the New—a requisite for a sufficient grasp of the subject to give effective counsel to the author. Though belonging to a newer generation, her empathy with both matched her well-known professionalism and proved positively co-productive. A colleague of hers, Fritz Bolle, the editor of the book's German version, a springboard for the English, should not be forgotten. Between flights of paternal and filial fancy he regularly brought me down to earth—in particular, to the earth that nourished my father: that of the Mark Brandenburg. In collecting the mass of pertinent data, I am grateful to two institutions: the Max Reinhardt Archive at the State University of New York at Binghamton, and especially to its founder and former director, Professor Alfred Brooks; and the Max Reinhardt-Forschungs-und-Gedenkstätte in Salzburg, Austria, whose directress, Dr. Gisela Prossnitz, was equally cooperative. Finally, I would like to pay tribute to the verbal and epistolary contributors, too numerous to list by name here, of surviving kin, friends, collaborators and eyewitnesses who kindly and generously supplied me with invaluable background information.

THE GENIUS

Walks, Legends and Monuments

A PROLOGUE

FOR THE LAST THIRTY YEARS I have been walking a dog daily. Mocha, a large black poodle, was a New Yorker by birth. In his nineteenth year, we had to have him put to sleep. His place was taken by Berry, a German shepherd of Californian origin, who was also black. He died at the age of fourteen. Berry's successor is a shepherd too, but only partially black. He is a citizen of Salzburg, Austria. On these walks I never fail to think of my father—of how he too loved taking long walks with a dog at his side. Just as mine, his last two were black and the penultimate, a Scottie whom he adored, was, like Berry, a Californian.

Together, Micky and master would explore the steep, rugged hills in back of his Hollywood villa and, later, his cliffside house in Pacific Palisades. On one of their expeditions, Micky was bitten by a rattlesnake. He died before a veterinary could be reached. My father was desolate. Then, one day—he had moved to New York in the meantime—an elderly lady admirer surprised him with the gift of another Scottie. At once, the dog, who was christened Micky II, added one more problem to all the others in this sore period of my father's life. No amount of petting, no culinary bribe, not the most artful kind of playing—and who could play more artfully than Max Reinhardt!—made the slightest impression on him. For the first time my father's powers of seduction seemed to fail miserably. In the house, Micky would lie on the floor for hours, his head stuck sullenly under a chair, until a leash was attached to his collar and, snapping and yelping, he was hustled outdoors for his—or rather my father's paced-for-health—daily constitutionals. Except that now it was Micky who set the pace. For no matter what distance he had been pulled along, once set loose he would make a hell-bent dash for home. With my father in dogged pursuit. It always depressed me to watch this trim, sixty-nine-year-old figure scrambling through deep snow (the scene was Larchmont, New York, where he had rented a house), with overcoat billowing, his crystal-clear voice calling, begging obedience and affection from the surly mutt. When the tiny, sadistic black spot finally disappeared into the white wideness and my father stopped to catch his breath—a breath too labored for a man so exuberantly healthy—he would, at sight of my approach, put on the disarming smile of a boy caught in the act of a little devilment. No, over me he had not lost his seductive powers.

Micky was not to remain satisfied with passive resistance for long. Three-quarters of a year later, he caused my father's death.

My peripatetic association is kindled by the company of a dog. The places I visit with Paris (named after Helen of Troy's abductor): He accompanies me over the same ground my father used to tread—in California, on America's East Coast and in Austria. Nowhere I go is he absent. And it is the special character of my present companion that quickens my flood of thought: When I toss him his ball or rubber ring and he catches them with acrobatic adroitness in mid-air; when, once they are clamped between his handsome white teeth, he coquettishly resists returning the props to me, but, after a second or two, deposits them graciously at my feet; when I bend to pick them up and he snatches them away and darts off to lure me into a woodland chase; when, the scenery having changed, he switches, suitably, to ligneous props and abruptly drops the lot to improvise a scene of mastery over a sapling fallen to the ground; when, star-like, he scorns ensemble play and directorial supervision and prances clear across the stage into the wings; when I conceal myself and see him returning, bored without a partner, dejected at the loss of his audience, see how soon he misses my cues, my repartee, my instructions; when he starts looking for me nervously, but, directly he has spotted me, pretends he doesn't see me—that daily tour de force, enchantingly undisciplined as it is, may not be exactly Reinhardt theatre, but it is *primeval* theatre, with Paris incarnating the basic urge to play, the essence of the Reinhardt theatre and its motivating force.

And, by contrast, Paris's antics bring all the more strongly to mind a drama that began as innocently as our games do and, after an almost classical peripeteia, ended tragically. It was a short play lasting from the day Micky II fell upon my father until the early morning, only five weeks later, when he closed his eyes forever. More precisely, it was the last act of the drama *Max Reinhardt*, one that, by its very conciseness, enfolded all the dramas he lived and played in a wondrous, moving way. I recorded it in a diary. Only a small audience watched the protagonist in this last, difficult performance. The intense scenes were played with such control and delicacy they filled our hearts to overflowing—and tore them to shreds.

How different is this image I carry within me from the garbled, contradictory ones that are rampant: Max Reinhardt, the illusionist, the impressionist, the neo-romantic, the baroque, the international impresario, the lighting wizard and manipulator of the revolving stage, the show-off showman, the circus man, the charlatan, the all-around genius; in America, the monument of heroic European heritage; in Europe, the apostle of American commercialism; in Vienna, the exponent of Wilhelmine and Weimar Berlin; in Berlin, the epitome of all things traditionally Austrian; to intellectuals, the sensual; to dogmatists, the eclectic; to revolutionaries, the conservative; to conservatives, the revolutionary; to aesthetes, the man of sweeping, garish effects; to entertainment merchants, the would-be aristocrat toying with muted chamber plays for the elite; to the puritanical linguists, the producer of cloying feasts for the eye; to the visualists, the promoter of dynamic sound; to his co-workers, their lord protector (with all the ambivalence bred by intimate dependence); to the public, the great sorcerer. While all these legends and monuments taken together may reflect something of the man, any single one or arbitrary number of them distort his portrait.

A number of years ago, I lunched with Lord—then Sir Laurence—Olivier at the Ivy Restaurant in London's West End. We were in accord about practically every subject under the sun: the weather in England and in California; Garbo's epochal mistake twenty years before in choosing her former beau, the silent-screen star John Gilbert, to play her lover in *Queen Christina* in preference to the young, rising actor Olivier; a film I had in mind with him in the starring role; and, last but not least, the delicate tang of the lamb's-lettuce we were presently eating, to which Sir Laurence told me he had given top priority over all other salad greens in his garden. How the subject of lamb's-lettuce propelled us with natural ease on to the subject of Max Reinhardt I don't remember. But suddenly there we were--and gone was our palatal affinity.

In Sir Laurence's estimation my father was one of the few true greats in the theatre and he regretted never having had the opportunity of meeting him. One story in particular—as told to him by an actor friend—had captured his imagination. It seems the informant, torn apart by first-night jitters, had finished the première's opening scene (of Reinhardt's second London production of *The Miracle*, at the Lyceum) convinced that he had mangled it, and made a desperate dash for the wings, where, to his mortification, he ran head on into the director at his command post, the famous bottomless blue eyes burning with contempt. I was tempted to interject that those bottomless blue eyes had surely not revealed anything more sinister than their owner's own first-night jitters, but Olivier's enthusiasm was already sweeping him toward the dramatic climax of his story. Which was that my father, presumably so incensed by the abortive debut, grabbed the culprit by the shoulder and spat squarely in his face.

I was struck dumb. How could an actor who had worked with Reinhardt circulate so improbable a tale about him? And, to compound the felony, how could my vis-à-vis sit there smiling his reverential regard for the salivary thrust? In rapid succession, he enumerated his reasons: Reinhardt, with all his sensitivity, was an uncompromising judge, able to retain his presence of mind in a critical situation and apply psychological therapy. Not alone apply, but apply brilliantly. "There is no one," he added wistfully, "up to anything of the sort any more." I did not say so, but I doubted that there ever was.

Uncompromising judge? It is difficult to find two words less typical of Max Reinhardt. What sort of "uncompromising judge" pleads, cajoles, woos shamelessly to gain his ends? Never pronounces sentence, but coddles all miscreants? He was no judge at all. He was much less and much more. He was a one-man court: advocate—of the author; prosecutor—of the hackneyed; accomplice—of the actor; and, finally, jury—more often hung than unanimous. During his "trials"—the rehearsals, where his most telling characteristics were revealed—there was an atmosphere of inventiveness from the first day to the last. He never presided. Whenever feasible, he was on stage, in the midst of his actors, molding, transmuting, a fermenting agent up to the moment the curtain rose on the première. Naturally, actors also received constructive criticism from him, but only for as long as their performances were in work.

Presence of mind in a critical situation? His emotions were held so cautiously in check and so much time was needed by him to gravitate toward a decision that many were led to suspect he was nothing more than vacillating. If anything, he was frozen into *inaction* by a brush with the unexpected. (To be called on for an extemporaneous speech was for him to expire in terror.) Besides which, on opening night it is the actor who is under pressure, not the director, whose job is done—at least to my father's way of thinking. How often I heard him sigh envyingly over the musical director, who continues to hold the reins through every performance, contrary to his opposite number on the stage, who, once his rehearsals are ended, is reduced to impotence. What, then, one might rightfully ask, was this expendable figure doing "at his command post" in the wings? Nothing, I can vouchsafe, nothing more "mortifying" to an actor than hanging on to the illusion that his suddenly superfluous presence in surroundings he had been so active and dominant a part of for a few creational weeks was not superfluous after all.

My father was not a brilliant psychologist. Offstage he was not even a very good one. His ineptitude for "applying" psychology started in his office. I doubt whether any other man of his position and responsibilities misjudged people and misplaced confidence with such disastrous effect as he. Believing what he wanted to believe was both his strength and his weakness. What enabled him to people his stage with characters of delicious or fierce reality can best be defined by Terence's "Homo sum: humani nil a me alienum puto" ("I am human: nothing human I consider alien to me"), a line he often borrowed from the Roman playwright to express his own point of view. He quoted it in 1928, in his speech "About the Actor," to an audience at Columbia University, adding:

> Made as we are in God's image, we have in us something of the godlike creative will. Therefore we create the whole world all over again in the arts, with all the elements, and on the first day of creation, as the crown of our work, we create man in our image.

It was this "creative will" which served him as an instrument to make personalities come to life, not to deal with them shrewdly. He was incapable of a negative approach, even as a detour. His charge was purely positive, in his philosophy as in his mode of living. For him to administer "shock therapy" was out of the question. Admittedly, he had an aggressive mind, but his nature was most pacific, made him shrink from all confrontation. This squeamish man spit into an actor's face?

I realized that Sir Laurence was staring at me severely. It wasn't that I had been sitting there withdrawn, reviewing mentally all my father's personality traits and idiosyncrasies—there was no need for that, as they are embedded in my consciousness, a single, complex polyphonic chord that never loses clarity despite the false notes added to it so often. It was that so accomplished a raconteur had swiftly detected that his audience was held by something other than the piquancy of his narrative.

Then, all at once, the ridiculously simple explanation struck me: my superstitious father had fallen back—as he always did when he wanted to wish someone luck—on the age-old Central European rite of simulating spitting frontally three successive times in the direction of that person. Sir Laurence listened unamused. And when I conjectured that my father's "burning" eyes in all likelihood were burning with tears of joy—he cried very easily—because the actor friend probably had not mangled the scene at all, but carried it off perfectly, Sir Laurence closed up like a sensitive seaflower suddenly exposed to an environmental threat. Now it was his turn to think. Courteous disdain had replaced his expression of unremitting courtesy. But whether his thoughts dwelt solely and commiseratingly on a great man whose own son understood him so little or whether his distant look was merely focused on more pressing matters, I was given no opportunity to determine. His chair was slid back and he was on his feet, begging my pardon for a departure he had no choice but to make courteously—yet at once.

Paris and I have just returned from one of our run-throughs. His performance is over—till tomorrow. In my mind it goes on. I sit down at my desk—as I have done so often, and in so many places—to try telling what I know about my father—and, once again, I hesitate, ask myself whether I am really the one to set the slanted image of him straight. I am neither a biographer, a historian, an author nor a son by profession. Still, I would not be the first son to write about his father. What prompts them to do it? Perhaps, like me, they feel that a lifetime of intimacy equips them to search their parent's mind, psyche and modus operandi better than otherwise more qualified writers. But then, does this very contiguity not make them too subjective for rigorous appraisal? Subjective, surely. *Too* subjective? That depends. It depends on the son, on whether he is conversant with the theme and the environment of his subject. But it also depends on the father, on whether his accomplishments are still tangible or accessible for study and analysis, on whether there is enough material about him extant for more objective biographers to interpret definitively.

My father was a man of the living theatre, a place where art is born anew each time the curtain rises and where it dies with its fall. Therefore, all tangible evidence of his work is gone. Of his personality, one which made him the magnetic pole of an era, there is even less substantial trace. So that whoever attempts to appraise his life and work can do so only on the basis of more or less arbitrary speculation or secondhand information drawn from the memory of a generation rapidly dying out, from theatrical reviews, which not only are as unreliable as most eyewitness accounts are but, in addition—tending, as they do, to literary essay, polemic, censure or panegyric—are clouded by prejudice. Publicity releases and Festschriften make no better source material. A director's prompt books are books, not direction. Scenic designs are designs, not scenes. Memoirs of contemporaries are by their nature biased. He himself put very little on paper. And the fame of his name—one he invented for himself—is blinding.

"Genius" is a big word. Some might question a son's right to apply it to his father. Others might doubt its validity in the performing arts. An obvious defense would be that the overwhelming majority of arbiters in Max Reinhardt's lifetime deemed him to be one and that the son, writing about the man rather than the professional, was merely quoting them. I make no such defense. From the days of my earliest consciousness I was aware of that quality in him. To me, it was never limited to his "profession." It permeated his—and therefore my—most private life. That so many others concurred only seemed to confirm a truth. As did the violence of his detractors. The value *he* attached to a name may be gleaned from the one he gave to his first little theatre. Borrowing from Goethe, he called it Schall und Rauch (Sound and Smoke) after Faust's reply to Marguerite's question about whether he believed in God: "God? Feeling is everything, name is sound and smoke . . ."

Still, where there is smoke there is fire, and where there is sound there is a voice. I have seen the fire and I have heard the voice.

It is now evening. But I don't switch on the light in my Salzburg study. In darkness memories slip quietly into the mind, unsummoned. *Crash.* A workman in lederhosen has entered my study, cursing as he stumbles against a chair. Discovering me, he apologizes for the racket. Something impels me to ask him who founded the Salzburg Festival. He squints at me oddly. All he came for was to repair a leaking radiator. But, proud Salzburger that he is, he gives my question a thought, replies tentatively: "Mozart. . . ."

I turn on my desk lamp and pick up my pen. *Too* subjective? I think not. Although more subjective no writer could ever be. All I hope is that at this première of mine my father is standing in the wings and will "spit" at me three times in succession.

THE DIARY

FRIDAY,
SEPTEMBER 24, 1943

"Sergeant Reinhardt wanted on the phone!" The second call in half an hour. Embarrassing. I've begged my New York friends never to call me at the post. But just because my unit is stationed at the old Paramount Studio in Long Island City and makes motion pictures and because I—illicitly—sleep off the post, they ignore the fact that I'm a soldier. At any rate, they don't take it seriously. Neither do I. But my superiors pretend they do. And all incoming calls must be taken in the major's office and I'm obliged to talk in his nosy presence—usually in German! Not necessarily the most suitable means of communication for a GI these days. My defense that we're not at war with a language—for instance, spoken by the majority of our friends the Swiss—isn't very persuasive.

The first call came from Eleonora. She asked whether she could accompany me to Fire Island tomorrow. Was thrilled as a teen-age Sinatra fan when I said yes. My God, she still loves him as passionately as on the first day! Second call: "Long distance, Sergeant. Fire Island. Kindly make it short." The major hands me the receiver and sneers as he listens unashamedly. My embarrassment tickles him. Soon I'm not only embarrassed but deeply perturbed. It's Papa. He has never called me at the post until now. I can hardly make out what he's saying. He's speaking from a public booth. "When are you coming?" he repeats over and over. My insistent "Tomorrow, just as we said," doesn't satisfy him. "Anything wrong?" I ask. His answer sounds muddled. Only a single word is clear: "Come!" It keeps recurring and then the line is dead. I hang up and explain gratuitously: "It was my father." "Yeah, we really ought to set you up with a nice suite of offices, maybe a coupla phones and a secretary and a bathroom. The whole bit. Like you had at MGM." I apologize for the intrusion. "Skip it, Sergeant. I'm crazy for Kraut dialogue."

I'm not bothered by the silly sarcasm of an unemployed screenwriter, which Herr Major was in civilian life, or he wouldn't have taken advantage of his reserve commission in peacetime. I'm troubled about Papa. What's wrong with him? That he's not in good shape I've sensed for quite a while. Big cities no longer agree with him. The daily struggle for existence, resumed too late in life, enervates him. New York's broiling summer has driven him to Fire Island. True, Rosalinda [Reinhardt's American Fledermaus of 1942] is still a sellout. We both live on it. But somehow he never overcame the subsequent flop of Sons and Soldiers. No matter that it was Irwin Shaw's and not his. Hard as the blow of the Thornton Wilder debacle [The Merchant of Yonkers, 1938] had been to him at the age of sixty-five, the even harder blow at sixty-nine—with only one year's grace until that frightening numeral 70!—proved too much. [For us close to him to ignore his birthday altogether was unthinkable. On the other hand, he always hated formal social functions. So I tried my best to keep the celebration intimate—just a few close friends for dinner at the Hapsburg House, the Austrian restaurant in New York with the Bemelmans frescos. Still, when he got wind of my plans he lost all control: "Do you want to hold a wake for me?!" I can still hear the excitation in his voice. Happily, the evening turned out to be most heartwarming and even he in the end admitted he'd enjoyed it. Everyone agreed he seemed his own self again. Fire Island had done wonders for him.]

Haven't seen him since September 9. Why suddenly this strange telephone call? Obviously something's wrong. But what? He has no immediate money problems. Can it be Helen [the planned production of Offenbach's La Belle Hélène for that fall]? It is an uphill struggle. We still lack twenty thousand dollars to get her off the ground, though we've been schnorring for three whole months. What an insane business. At our last audition, singing our heads off [I and my collaborators—book: Sergeant John Meehan, Jr.; lyrics: Corporal Herbert Baker, gifted son of the well-known vaudevillian Belle Baker; piano: Ignace Strassfogel, chief coach of the Metropolitan Opera; at the apartment of Mr. Balaban, manager of the Roxy], we didn't raise new money, instead succeeded in losing one of our hard-earned backers. Unfortunately he was so carried away with our previous effort he decided to come back for more. [Of this event my father, prophetically, said to my future wife, who was also present: "Tonight I saw the best performance of Helen I'll ever see." Our backer took a contrary view.] Goodbye twenty thousand dollars! Can't possibly face Papa tomorrow without something positive to report. Decide reluctantly to call Bill Paley [president and owner of CBS, the radio—and now television—network]. Didn't want to tap him this time. He has helped so much so often. But I see no other alternative. To my relief I reach him immediately. He asks me to his office this afternoon after retreat.

Doesn't even let me finish my pitch. The twenty thousand dollars are ours. Jupiter be praised, rehearsals for Helen Goes to Troy can begin. Isn't it marvelous that Eleonora and I can greet Papa tomorrow with this surprise?

Dramatis Personae

PAPA. ELEONORA. I.

"I": MEANING SERGEANT GOTTFRIED REINHARDT, age thirty, Serial Number 39020194, U.S. Army, Signal Corps, stationed at the Signal Corps Photographic Center, Long Island City, New York. Naturalized U.S. citizen, single, born on March 20, 1913, in Berlin, Germany, the second (four and a half years younger) son of director-producer Max Reinhardt and actress Else Heims-Reinhardt; through Pressburg-born paternal grandfather a Hungarian national. Became Czechoslovakian citizen when, in 1918, Pressburg became Bratislava. Raised in Berlin, graduated from Collège Royal Français, a humanistic school founded for Huguenot immigrants by the Great Elector of Brandenburg, where, with the exception of mathematics, natural sciences and German, all courses were conducted in French. As a Gymnasium student I presented public performances of French plays, then studied philosophy and history for two semesters at the University of Berlin, and, extracurricularly, directed two plays on the professional stage: the first acclaimed by public and press a brilliant success, the second, with the director in the lead, decried by public and press—and mortified family—as such a dismal flop that the chastened perpetrator deemed it the better part of honor to flee unvalorously to America (October 1932), a move his father, though in less urgent circumstances, had long recommended. This debacle spared nineteen-year-old-me—the only one of my family so fortunate—the trauma of witnessing Hitler's take-over of Germany.

First, one of America's twelve million unemployed, then assistant to film director Ernst Lubitsch at Paramount in Hollywood, thereafter, consecutively, reader, assistant producer, screenwriter, full producer and director at Metro-Goldwyn-Mayer. After Pearl Harbor, drafted into the service. Basic training in Camp Crowder, Missouri; eventually, assigned to SCPC, Long Island City; there, producing propaganda and training films. On-the-side activities: dialogue direction and co-authorship of English libretto for Max Reinhardt's *Rosalinda* on Broadway.

"Eleonora": Meaning Eleonora von Mendelssohn, age forty-three, oldest child of long-deceased Robert von Mendelssohn, head of the family banking house—one of Germany's most prestigious—a Prussian cavalry officer, and his Italian wife, concert pianist Giulietta Cordigliani, a founding mother of the Fascist party. After flight from Hitler Germany, an American resident subsisting partly on the sale of smuggled family art treasures, partly on loans from kind friends and admirers and partly on earnings as an actress. One-eighth Jewish, raised on the princely von Mendelssohn estate in Berlin-Grunewald, with its Rembrandt-, Rubens-, Raphael-bedecked walls, offset by such speculative investments as Manet, Degas and Renoir, amidst a collection of Stradivaris, Guarnieris, Steinways, Bechsteins and Bösendorfers; a multi-linguist and accomplished pianist, turned actress through persevering passion for Max Reinhardt; four times married and, according to her gallant understatement, never once quite a bride: first, to the pianistically puissant, sexually impotent Edwin Fischer; second, to the dashing Hungarian cavalry captain Emmerich von Jessensky, whose concentrated manliness was transmuted, on marriage with the heiress, to concentration on a man's dower rights; third, to the arch-Austrian matinée idol Rudolf Forster, who not only played but was the most tied-in-knots neurasthenic ever to appear on stage or screen; and, fourth, to amateur painter-actor—mainly portrayals of Goebbels in wartime wave of anti-Nazi films—Martin Kosleck, an even greater amateur in waging war—or peace—between the sexes. In her shy superior bearing is manifest Eleonora's derivation from the philosopher, composer, banker dynasty; in every way a relic of a bygone age.

When, exactly two hundred years ago, her great-great-great-grandfather, Moses Mendelssohn, moved from Dessau to Berlin, the collector of customs at Oranienburg Gate registered: ". . . three goats, two bags of flour, four hogs, one Jew . . ." And those were the good old days! Two centuries later, the descendants of the philosopher, who enjoyed the protection of Frederick the Great, do not find it so easy to enter Berlin, let alone to escape it, and in the order of commodities to be ticked off have slid far below the hogs, in keeping with the new practices in Germany's slaughter-houses.

But Eleonora is not only a relic because of her family tree. The Mendelssohn patriciate, after all, did not represent the spirit of *Prussia,* but Prussian *spirit.* Her true nobility Eleonora carries within herself. She is generous to the point of self-sacrifice, art-loving to the point of artistry, with a masculine intelligence lacking practical sense and propelled by the most feminine instincts in the world, a world no longer existing. Clinging tenaciously to the wreckage of this world, she is defenseless against the base currents swirling around her, valiant to the point of self-destruction, sustained only by her own enthusiasm and by continuously being in love, always with the best, the best people and the best ideas—and broken on them. Today, she herself is a wreck, struggling boldly and shrewdly—in true aristocratic fashion—to keep from going under. Still, her ravaged features cannot erase the rare classical beauty which was hers as a young woman. Her radiance choked with adoration the eight-year-old Gottfried standing correctly at the side of his mother and brother to welcome her arrival in their staid Biedermeier drawing room in Berlin. She had come from her mother's Florentine estate to visit them and, without preamble, confided her bursting LOVE: for the train ride, the dancing landscape, the cheeky Berlin taxi driver, the newly built Pergamon Museum across the river from the Reinhardt house, for the Reinhardt house, for all the Reinhardts, for music—with a cascading demonstration on the keyboard—for her godmother, Eleonora Duse, and for her latest liaison: Napoleon Bonaparte, who, she wanted her startled audience to be the first to know, had seduced her body and soul.

In the ensuing years, reality succeeded in bruising, but never in ensnaring her. The men in her love life may have become more contemporary, but seldom more plausible. In any case, none of them made her happy. Always focusing on the utopian, she unfailingly made legendary heroes her mark, so that for different, though always cogent reasons, they remained out of her reach, be it that they were elsewhere spoken for, had one foot—even two—in the grave, were indifferent to sex, preoccupied with their own or committed to a variation which left Eleonora out. Her gallery of never-to-be-attained heroes runs the gamut from the Corsican conqueror through the playwrights Noël Coward and Charles MacArthur, the critic Alexander Woollcott, the general Dwight D. Eisenhower to the musical generalissimo Arturo Toscanini—all, in their turn, insubstantially substituting for the quicksilvery-elusive Max Reinhardt. Having dedicated herself to him with all the fire of her youth, she foundered on the realities of a life whose sights were long firmly set.

Thwarted in her feverish attempts to capture him, she sought the relief of morphine, thus driving even further away a man to whom any artificial intoxicant or stimulus was abhorrent. By an ironic turn of fate, when her addiction had brought her to her nadir, she was to become the only one among her rivals whom he, broken in health and spirit, would turn to for support and tenderness. In this unexpected sunset glow of her misspent existence, she reflects the expiring Europe of that day: shabbily glamorous, faded in beauty, irrational in passion, its inherent strength hopelessly squandered, myopic (Eleonora could not see beyond her nose), obdurate and clutching to tradition (Eleonora could match Joan of Arc in both), decadent, in the grip of knaves (which will lead to Eleonora's ruin), self-lacerating and somnambulating toward cataclysm (Eleonora will commit suicide—with, it has been whispered, a little outside assistance—in a few years).

"Papa": Meaning professor, three times honorary doctor, Max Reinhardt, age seventy, married to actress Helene Thimig (his second wife); legal residence: 15000 Corona del Mar, Pacific Palisades, California; living for the past year at the Hotel Gladstone, 114 East 52nd Street, New York City; at present vacationing on Fire Island, New York. A naturalized American citizen, born, the oldest of seven children, on September 9, 1873, in Baden near Vienna, to Wilhelm and Rosa Goldmann, née Wengraf. His father, a business failure, came from the village of Stompfa, near Pressburg, his mother, stemming from a well-to-do bourgeois family fallen on lean times, from Moravian Brünn (Brno). Shortly after Max's birth, his parents moved to Vienna's commercial Mariahilferstrasse.

Having finished grammar school at the age of fourteen, Max is obliged to contribute to his family's support: first as apprentice in a factory, then in a bank. His first love, the theatre, is frustrated by parental opposition. However, at the age of seventeen, bolstered by the intervention of a gay-blade uncle, he pushes his determination and, under the stage name Reinhardt (legalized in 1904, it will become his and his entire family's permanently), he steps onto the boards of a suburban student theatre as a fledgling actor. Its manager becomes his first drama coach, is soon superseded by another. But Max derives little benefit from lessons. Barely eighteen, he appears for the first time professionally on another suburban stage, and in the same summer joins a strolling company playing Pressburg. The following season finds him an ensemble member of the Salzburg municipal theatre. There, Otto Brahm, manager of the Deutsches Theater in Berlin, sees him and engages him for his distinguished company. For eight years, he remains a member. He falls in love with a young colleague, Else Heims, and, in time, marries her. Under Brahm's guidance, Max develops into a consummate character actor, makes the acquaintance of contemporary literature and meets most of its exponents.

Except for the classics, which are treated in a reverently declamatory manner, the stylistic order of the day is extreme naturalism, in writing, playing and designing. With others of the rising generation, Max joins the insurgents against this "gray on gray" and hollow routine. He takes part in university theatricals and during summer vacations goes on tour. One of the youngest of the group, he gradually becomes its magnetic pole.

De facto, if, for a while, not yet de jure, he begins to function as director. Not in the then customary sense of the term—as a sort of theatrical traffic cop—but in the sense that, through his own efforts, has since become the accepted one.

In a Berlin coffeehouse, young intellectuals and artists, talking excitedly about changes in the air, form a club which Reinhardt soon dominates. On their free evenings, they amuse themselves by performing parodies of what we would today call the "establishment." A benefit for an ailing member becomes the occasion for their first public offering. The club expands into a popular cabaret. Reinhardt acts as organizer, author and performer. Cabaret gradually gives place to drama, its name Schall und Rauch to the Kleines Theater (the Little Theatre). Here, the plays of the day and the morrow are given in a non-naturalistic style which underscores their emphasis on mood and psychology. Reinhardt's own efforts as a dramatist fail. Instead, he becomes the dramatist's creative interpreter: transforming the flat-painted stage into three-dimensional space; operating audaciously with light and color; introducing visual and acoustical dynamism; imbuing acting with a heretofore unknown intensity; expunging bathos from the classics.

The year 1903 brings about the painful but inevitable rupture with Brahm. A large contingent of his actors deserts to Reinhardt. Breaking his long-term contract with the Deutsches Theater, he is at last free to take over officially the management of his Little Theatre. All the good years to follow would not, however, eventuate without the moral and organizational support of his brother Edmund, who, on joining forces with him, gradually takes over all administrative tasks.

The first milestone in Reinhardt's career is reached: the sensational hit of Maxim Gorki's *Lower Depths*, with Reinhardt in the role of Luka (but without officially directing). Overnight, it makes him the first theatre man of Berlin. He takes over a second house: the Neues Theater (the New Theatre, today the home of Brecht's Berliner Ensemble). There, in the same year, he stages—now with credit on the playbill—Maeterlinck's *Pelléas et Mélisande*. His repertoire includes Wedekind, Wilde, Strindberg and Hofmannsthal. He visits an exhibition by the scenic artist and theatrical visionary Gordon Craig, which impresses him deeply and decisively. So much so, he travels to London to learn more about Craig's concepts and, while there, is stimulated by the freer English style of producing Shakespeare. With the result that in 1905 Berlin sees Reinhardt's first *Midsummer Night's Dream*. And once again his career skyrockets overnight: the event makes him the first theatre man of Europe. On this evening, the modern director is born. The fresh currents in the theatre and in the arts feeding it (Reinhardt, before all others, channeling them toward the stage) sweep Brahm, the revolutionary of yesteryear, from his conservative pedestal. He loses the Deutsches Theater. After a short intermezzo, it is offered to Reinhardt. In six months, the lessee is the owner.

There follow years of fruitful management and directorial initiative during which all of Shakespeare and the German classics, in addition to Aristophanes, Molière, Offenbach, Nestroy, Ibsen, Wedekind, Strindberg, Hauptmann, Hofmannsthal and Shaw, all the greats—those neglected, dusty or still waiting for discovery—are brought to life. A peerless ensemble coalesces under Reinhardt's aegis, though he himself gives up acting. Making music for it are the great composers and conductors of their day. Stage designs and costumes come from the drawing boards of the household names of contemporary impressionism and expressionism.

Money pours in, additional real estate is acquired and the beginnings of a fortune made. In 1906 the Kammerspiele (Chamber Playhouse) is built. The architect in Reinhardt has begun to stir (this house being only the first of ten he will build or rebuild).

Gradually the gauge of Reinhardt's tracks widens to include pantomime, ballet, opera, morality plays and theatre of the masses for the masses: his at once compacted and individualistic choral direction evolves. He inaugurates his first festival (in Munich). In 1911 *The Miracle* at London's Olympia Hall brings him still another overnight claim to fame: he is now, at the age of thirty-eight, the first theatre man of the world—which he tours with his rousing, spectacular *Oedipus Rex.* His company has come to be at home on two continents—from New York to Christiania (Oslo), Amsterdam to Odessa. In 1912 and 1913, he shoots two films in Italy.

During World War I, the "enemy" Shakespeare is paid the unprecedented tribute of being presented in cycles. Reinhardt takes over management of the union-affiliated Volksbühne (People's Stage). The Foreign Ministry sends him and his company as cultural propagandists to all neutral countries. He is the Kaiser's lone effective good-will ambassador.

The young actress Helene Thimig makes her debut in Berlin and casts a spell over the "Great Sorcerer." The autocrat turns populist: in 1918, he rebuilds a circus into a three-thousand-seat arena theatre, Das Grosse Schauspielhaus (The Great Playhouse) to accommodate crowds both in the audience and onstage, mingling both by eliminating the proscenium. But devastating press reactions to "Reinhardt's circus antics," in addition to the postwar economic crisis, blast this lifelong, short-lived dream. Combined with his marriage problems, the defeat drives him from Berlin. He moves to Vienna and founds the Salzburg Festival, opening it in 1920 with *Everyman* on the square in front of the Cathedral. The autocrat turns aristocrat: he has bought Leopoldskron Castle near Salzburg and, in his hands, it becomes an artistic and social vortex. In 1924, he takes over Vienna's dilapidated Theater in der Josefstadt, decorates it in rich rococo style and reopens it with commedia dell'arte.

Max Reinhardt's Berlin theatres cannot survive without his animating force. He returns, reanimates them and increases their number: Die Komödie (The Comedy), a playbox on Kurfürstendamm, is built and, shortly thereafter, a larger adjoining one, the Theater am Kurfürstendamm. Additional houses are leased when the need arises to accommodate runs, so that the Reinhardt organization, on occasion, operates ten theatres in Berlin and Vienna simultaneously. Leaving the managerial responsibilities to his brother Edmund, he devotes all his energies to directing and experiences a second golden era with Shaw, Pirandello, Hamsun, Tolstoi, Maugham, Hauptmann, Hofmannsthal, Galsworthy, Goldoni, Goethe, Kleist, Bourdet, Johann Strauss, Offenbach, Büchner, Romain Rolland, Werfel, Tristan Bernard, Gozzi, Schiller and Shakespeare, Shakespeare, Shakespeare. Against the rising competition of ideologically oriented theatre, Reinhardt easily holds his own with the quality of his performances bare of ideology.

In 1924, America sees a revival of *The Miracle*. In 1927, the troupe of the Deutsches Theater pays a visit to Manhattan. In 1928, Reinhardt lectures at Columbia University, makes his widely quoted speech "About the Actor" (later memorialized in the pages of the *Encyclopædia Britannica*).

The black year of 1929 also casts its shadow on Max Reinhardt: In the midst of world depression comes the death of his guardian-angel brother. Burdened with an empire he is neither willing nor able to administer, he runs into debt. His twenty-fifth jubilee as manager of the Deutsches Theater is a glamorous affair: festive performances, testimonials from the worlds of theatre, finance and politics, academic honors, but they cannot keep the rudderless ship afloat in a sea of street fights, breadlines, financial scandals and heinous political intrigues. The tread of the Nazi boot is growing louder. In 1932, he gives up his Berlin theatres for good. He is fifty-nine. His last direction in that city: Hofmannsthal's *Great World Theatre*. Its première nearly coincides with the Reichstag fire—a much greater world theatre.

Forced to leave Germany, Max Reinhardt loses his operational base and most of his possessions. He seeks asylum in tottering Austria. The European tours he organizes are all, suddenly, failures.

1934: Emigration to the United States, where the triumph of his fourteenth *Midsummer Night's Dream,* in California, wins him a three-picture contract with Warner Brothers. However, only one results from it. In 1935, Else Heims, after many years of bitter contest, agrees to a divorce. He marries Helene Thimig. In 1937, in New York, the biblical pageant *The Eternal Road* brings artistic kudos and commercial disaster. It is followed by a Thornton Wilder play that fails. He founds his third drama school, in Los Angeles, from which more talent emerges than tuition is paid in.

The school's insolvency sends him to Broadway once again to try his luck. He succeeds with five hundred-odd performances of his American *Fledermaus* (*Rosalinda*) and flops with thirteen performances of *Sons and Soldiers* by Irwin Shaw. September 9, 1943: Max Reinhardt is seventy years old. At his birthday celebration he is handed a scroll illustrated by the Viennese artist Victor Tischler, inscribed with a handwritten tribute by Franz Werfel and signed by Vicki Baum, S. N. Behrman, Bertolt Brecht, Frank Capra, Marlene Dietrich, Norman Bel Geddes, Olivia de Havilland, Vladimir Horowitz, John Huston, Aldous Huxley, Leopold Jessner, Erich Wolfgang Korngold, Fritz Lang, Charles Laughton, Ernst Lubitsch, Alma Mahler-Werfel, Heinrich Mann, Thomas Mann, Fritzi Massary, Ferenc Molnár, William S. Paley, Gregor Piatigorsky, Luise Rainer, Edward G. Robinson, Arthur Rubinstein, Arnold Schönberg, Josef von Sternberg, Arturo Toscanini, Bruno Walter, Jack Warner, Thornton Wilder, William Wyler, and Carl Zuckmayer. In his message, Werfel congratulates Max Reinhardt on a life of rich, undiminished productivity and closes with this sentence: "For the true artist the sun is always just about to rise. Even in the evening!"

Without a doubt it is evening. Is the sun about to rise?

THE DIARY

SATURDAY,
SEPTEMBER 25, 1943

A beautiful autumn day, crisp but not yet too cold. Ideal weather for a trip to the sea, for a reunion with Papa. Ideally suited for the news I'm bringing. Can hardly wait till twelve o'clock: off with the "military," on with the weekend. Herbie and John as excited as I am. At last we've made it. No more auditions! No more schnorring! Look forward to taking over the direction of dialogue and generally assisting Papa again. But will absolutely have to wangle a furlough. I won't be able to take another Rosalinda. The long day at the post, evening rehearsals in the theatre, late nights with him in the hotel—it's too much. Thank God Darvas [Lili Darvas, onetime beauty and Reinhardt actress, wife of the Hungarian author Ferenc Molnár] is going to help me this time. Called her right after Paley. She too was delirious. Also called Korngold in North Hollywood. [Erich Wolfgang Korngold, noted composer and Reinhardt's musical adaptor and conductor of the Berlin, Vienna and Paris Fledermaus, the Berlin and London La Belle Hélène, the Midsummer Night's Dream film, the New York Rosalinda.] Promises his arrival by end of next week.

Roll call in the "barracks yard." Ludicrous as always: Facing us, not The Smiling Lieutenant [shot on these premises by Ernst Lubitsch in 1930], but our unsmiling company commander and brick-faced top sergeant, with the barracks as backdrop, more of a set than functional dwellings [only the less enterprising of B Company slept in them]. Instead of a Love Parade [another Lubitsch classic produced here], our preposterous formation parades lovelessly past the old sound stages, offices and workshops of the scrapped film studio. "'Ten-shun!" The analphabetic sergeant bellows our names alphabetically: ". . . [Herbert] Baker, [John] Cheever, [George] Cukor, [William] Holden, [Arthur] Laurents, [John] Meehan, [Gottfried] Reinhardt, [William] Saroyan, [Irwin] Shaw, [Irving] Wallace . . ." [Each name even then familiar from film credits, playbills or book covers. Subsequently responsible for such works as: The Wapshot Scandal, My Fair Lady, The Bridge on the River Kwai, West Side Story, The Red Badge of Courage, The Chapman Report, The Young Lions; plus all the former Hollywood cameramen, stunt men, cutters, set designers and animators.]

Following Saturday's uniform inspection the assemblage of masquerading celebrities swarms off into the welcoming arms of publishers, agents and business managers waiting outside. While the lower ranks in their private cars are swallowed up in New York's traffic—street, theatrical and literary—most of the officer corps, having less "rank" off the post, wait for the bus or rush to the subway, unless a "private" ride is offered. [*Junior PFC Laemmle, heir of the founder of Universal Pictures*] *could easily afford a whole fleet of cars. But he can't drive. And a chauffeur would hardly be in the proper style for his present status, even in our bizarre unit. He's lugging a bulging barracks bag, in nervous search of a taxi.* [*His predicament was due to the fact that the majority of his superiors had been fired by him from Universal at least once in the past. Now they availed themselves of the opportunity for revenge by regularly sending him on detached service to the most unattractive regions.*] *I pick him up. "To Grand Central?" "No, first to the Corn Exchange Bank, Fifty-second and Park." "But it's closed!" "I've phoned. They're keeping it open for me." It's comforting to have one's personal Schweik in a war. Another Laemmle story to delight Papa. Everything seems to smile at us today.*

Am fetching Eleonora in my trusty old Buick. It too has seen better days. She can't wait for the moment when she'll look her beloved Max in the eyes. She too has a surprise for him: truffles. And herself. We drive to Bay Shore, Long Island, leave the car at the landing and cross over to Ocean Beach in the all but empty motorboat that now makes the trip only once a day. For the season's over. Shore, sky, water seem to rejoice over that. They look freshly scrubbed. The white crests of the waves flash us special smiles.

I think I discern his outline at the pier. Yes, there he is—straight as a rod, sunburned, his white hair flowing in the breeze, dog at his side. Seventy? He? Nonsense. Eleonora has stood up and begun to wave ecstatically. I have to keep a firm grip on her to prevent her from falling overboard. Actually, she doesn't see him at all. Every day she's more nearsighted, more forlorn. Now he waves back. And I wave to him. What was wrong with him yesterday? "Come!"—it still rings in my ears. Well, we have come! Here we are! We land, embrace, but he doesn't speak. Eleonora presents him with the truffles. He smiles but doesn't thank her. I tell him the good news. It seems to please him, as the truffles do, as our arrival and the beautiful weather do, but he doesn't react as he normally would. Eleonora shoots me surreptitious looks. What's she trying to tell me? I'm confused.

Something's happened to him. But what? Eleonora's of late permanently reddened eyes give me no answer. Give me no peace. I make my report, become hectically expansive about plans for the next days, mention problems which could wait, go into detail out of place here at the landing pier, in the wind, surrounded by luggage. After all, we've a long, pleasant weekend ahead of us!

Have we? For now, unexpectedly, three words struggle from his lips, separated by painfully long pauses: "I-is . . . W-wolf-f-g-gang . . . c-coming?" His eyes are more eloquent: They express an interest so intense, his embarrassed smile manages to cover up the halting speech so deftly, that I cling to its meaning and repress the obvious defect even more than I'm tempted to do anyway. I know he's been worried about my brother for a long time. With good reason. For a long time his beloved problem child has been looking for a job without success. And his last, an excellent one, he lost only because his employer [Jack Warner] and he had different views about what time a producer should get up in the morning, the kind of controversy Papa always warned him against. I tell Papa about Wolfgang's good chances for a new job. And since we can count on money coming in now, we'll be able to invite him to New York. Two weeks ago, for the birthday, this wasn't possible. [Thimig's trip from California had been a present from Korngold.] If only Eleonora would stop throwing me those ominous looks behind his back!

Papa's mouth opens to speak. I curb my loquacity, wink at him in encouragement. He wrinkles his brow pensively, shakes his head and smiles as though wanting to apologize, then looks at me inquiringly. And then once again: "I-is . . . W-wolf-f-g-gang . . . c-coming?"

. . . I can't go on, I'm too tired.

3 o'clock in the morning,
SUNDAY,
SEPTEMBER 26, 1943

I can't sleep. The day was too full, too overwhelming. And this spook house! All the rooms leading to a middle section that cuts through the two stories of the run-down building from its damp foundation to the creaking roof beams. A wide, rectangular shaft bordered by balustraded galleries, branching off into alcoves, little connecting stairs and corridors: an old-fashioned theatre set permitting a numberless variety of entrances and exits. One can follow every move of the others, hear every footstep. Until long after midnight I observed Papa from the second floor as he paced restlessly, tirelessly from his bedroom to the central living room. Back and forth, back and forth. Simultaneously, I saw one flight above me the shadow of the Hungarian housekeeper creeping about. And then, on my own level, Eleonora in a flowing gown, tiptoeing to and fro, peering stealthily over the railing, pale, beautiful, until, ghost-like, she disappeared again. Now it has become still in the house, except for the wind howling outside and the thunderous impact of the ocean throwing itself against the small heap of dunes called Fire Island. I've the feeling that any one of these angry breakers could wash us, house, island, away. Hitchcock couldn't have caught the mood more perfectly. Except that I'm not in the mood for a thriller. I rack my brain about what I must do. It doesn't get me anywhere, just robs me of sleep. Where did I leave off . . . ?

We load the luggage onto a cart available for this purpose—no automobiles are permitted on the island—and start for Papa's summer house at the seaside. He takes up the lead. His gait is as rapid, elastic and determined as ever. I quicken my step to catch up with him. Ask softly what's the matter. Mutely, he points to his mouth. We pass a public telephone booth. He nods toward it and then to the wretched dog straining at the lead. Finally, with enormous difficulty, he manages to articulate that he bit his tongue, summing up with: "T-too ssst-tupid . . ." He's evidently ashamed. For him all infirmities have something to do with guilt. I curse my medical ignorance, which is surpassed only by his. But one thing even I know: biting one's tongue doesn't produce amnesia. For he doesn't only find it agonizing to form words, he didn't even retain, or perhaps never perceived, why Wolfgang isn't coming.

Halfway, a small chapel comes into view, a primitive wooden structure with steeple and bell, standing alone on the long, narrow, sandy ridge between the Atlantic Ocean and the Great South Bay, a relic of cozier times. In its isolation, its daily fight with wind, sand and flood, it is touching proof of human trustfulness. Papa stops and decides: "M-most b-beau-t-tiful b-beach in the w-world!" That's how it's always been with him. Wherever he happens to be, whoever his current collaborator is, whoever he has fallen in love with most recently, is the best, the most gifted, the most beautiful. An enviable talent and, I can't help thinking at this moment, a good omen. Anticipating his wish, Eleonora takes the dog's leash from his hand so that, true to Reinhardt custom, the father may show a church to his son. Eleonora, ever an "adventure," a bewitching outsider, even when she was happy with him—and that was a very long time ago—for the first time belongs. In the patient way she stands there and waits for us, she has simply, quite naturally, become his wife. For how long? She doesn't care.

Twenty minutes of extraordinary circumstances have combined to make her what a whole lifetime wasn't able to bring about. The dread in her eyes has given way to bliss.

Papa's not too fond of Protestant churches. They're too bare for him, too untheatrical—the way he understands the word "theatrical": as something sacred. Yet we enter the chapel as if it were St. Peter's, St. Stephen's in Vienna or Monreale above Palermo. And he doesn't enjoy playing the cicerone one bit less. I'm transported back to my childhood. More so when he seats himself reverently in a pew and the colorful guide yields to—a worshipper? I've often asked myself on these occasions whether he was actually praying. He's no Jewish Christian. Neither a converted one like Klemperer [Otto Klemperer, the conductor] nor a secret, holy one like Werfel [Franz Werfel, the writer from Prague, who told me that only the advent of Hitler and the onus of opportunism stopped him from publicly embracing the Catholic faith], much less an unholy one like L.B. [Louis B. Mayer, the motion-picture mogul who left ten million dollars to Cardinal Spellman]. But as a scene he prefers Catholic churches to synagogues, although all his life he has remained a pious Jew. Anyway, I guess, one can be devout without praying or speak with one's God wherever one may be. I sense that he now is speaking to his God. Moreover, I believe I know what about. I wish I could assist him here too, but unfortunately it's in a language I haven't mastered.

Clouds are gathering in the southeast, the sea grows restless, the mood more autumnal. The bone-white beach is deserted. I doubt that, except for Papa's, more than two or three other houses are still occupied. As darkness sets in, it grows chilly. One feels cut off from the lights and the life on the mainland. The chill is increased by the housekeeper, who maltreats the English language and, indeed, shows little tenderness in any other area. We've literally reached the end of the world.

Evening enhances this feeling. Papa's excessive playing of the gracious host has, I realize, besides the genuine motive, three calculated ones: to prevent Eleonora and me from having a private talk, to keep me and the witch in the kitchen apart and, above all, to avoid having a confrontation with me alone. I manage to outwit him all around.

However, with E. it serves little purpose. She no longer shares my disquietude. She warns me against doing anything rash. Insists we mustn't unsettle him. Her real fear of course is that I'll upset the status quo. She likes it at the end of the world. I don't.

I force the confrontation with him. Learn that shortly before he called me on Friday there was a fight between his Scottie and a boxer near the phone booth. He finally managed to separate them and to find refuge for

Micky and himself in the booth. But the hastily closed door gave him no refuge from Micky. The enraged animal turned its venom on him. In the confined space, he was unable to ward off the vicious assault. He shows me shoes perforated through and through and draws my attention to innumerable red spots—tiny teeth marks—on his chest, arms and legs. In his excitement, he tells me, he bit his tongue and this is what impaired his speech.

As always, we change for dinner. I use the time for a quick visit to the kitchen. Brusquely I'm told that my father must have had a stroke. "He came home with his face all out of shape. And his talk—you couldn't understand a word. In the morning it looked like he was better again. Till I made his bed. He wet it in the night. Me, I'm not staying with this old man any more. I'm quitting."

We sit down to dinner as though we were in some grand-seigneurial hall attended by liveried lackeys and not that slovenly domestic. Papa is as always meticulously groomed, acting with perfect nonchalance. Or rather: acting nonchalance to perfection. Eleonora, resplendent in a long crimson velvet gown, décolleté, wearing antique Russian jewelry, acts a guest at a fête in the D'Annunzio villa on Lake Garda. Worsening of the weather has heightened her euphoria. We're shut off from the outside world even more than before; she has him even more for her own. I'm doing a bit of acting myself: have got myself togged out in civvies for the "soirée."

Watching these two once glamorous figures pretending to each other in the bleak room makes my thoughts travel to remote places and into the past. I think of all the bright hours I had with Papa in the bright rooms—with Eleonora so often present. I think of the elegant "white dining room" in our palais on Kupfergraben [the house in Berlin where I was born], of his Gobelin-hung staterooms in the Hofburg [Vienna's imperial castle], complete with Franz Josef's portable privy in full display, emblazoned with a double eagle in the bottom of the bowl, of the splendors of Schloss Leopoldskron. . . .

Extras

THE GUESTS WERE ARRIVING. For a brief moment, feelings of high anticipation gave way to a twinge of awkwardness. Was there perhaps a misunderstanding? Had the invitation been for a masked ball?

But reassurance came quickly. Everyone else wore formal evening dress. Knowing winks quickly replaced nervous smiles. Was the landlord, after all, not l'homme de théâtre par excellence? So why should one not be greeted by a garrulous buffoon surrounded by his servants, all decked out in seventeenth-century costumes? How deliciously fitting, come to think of it. Still, for sheer ceremony or a professional whim, the spiel was a bit too elaborate. And too forward. Instead of welcoming the visitors decorously, the odd receptionist buttonholed them, one by one, with tales of physical woe. Some, indeed, quite unappetizing. The shameless fellow seemed riddled with disease and spared no detail in describing symptoms, aches, malfunctions, examinations, therapies—the clinical lot. Of course, not all were embarrassed or bewildered by his capers. To these select, never interrupting his irrepressible torrent of complaints, he introduced himself as Monsieur Argan. Some beat him to it and addressed him as Herr Pallenberg. A few embraced him compassionately and called him Bulli—Max Pallenberg's, Reinhardt's incomparable comedian's, nickname. Soon, a sea of laughter filled the vast entrance hall and the ornate staircase as, the party by now assembled, he and his retinue joined the rear guard ascending and entering the grand ballroom where the remainder of the cast of Molière's *Malade Imaginaire* mingled with le tout Salzburg—which, in the twenties, was le tout monde—for drinks, a sumptuous banquet and the subsequent surprise performance in its very midst. But the star of the evening was not Max Pallenberg. Nor Molière. Nor even the brilliant chef de cuisine. Nor, for that matter, the instigator of the entertainment (which visibly entertained him the most). The star was Leopoldskron.

Max Reinhardt's baroque castle, former seat of the Firmian family, which had given the region several gloomy prince-archbishops, had become the symbol of his anything but gloomy life style. It was a misleading symbol: Lucullan feasts, garden galas, performances in the park à la Louis XIV, *soirées musicales* as in the days when the boy Mozart played there for his episcopal sponsor. Everything was in grand style: tea on the terrace with duchesses, poet laureates, war profiteers, excellencies from the Reichswehr, the diplomatic corps. A truer picture offered the more *gemütlich* gatherings of the inner circle that followed, from midnight to morn, in the library, a miniature replica of the magnificent library of the St. Gallen monastery, its carved shelves stacked with leather-bound tomes largely unread by the hardworking host. For ordinarily his social life was negligible. What there was of it came through professional necessity and, in his everyday life, usually took place around the theatre or in restaurants. Nor did he spend in Salzburg more than five or six weeks of the year:

summers when he was rehearsing for the Festival and winters when he managed to steal a week or two away from his crowded theatrical schedule in the big cities.

Host? Technically, yes. Reinhardt owned the castle. He *was* the castle. But he himself rarely invited anyone to it. When he did, it was, more than likely, someone he had found, on meeting, momentarily engaging and to whom, on leavetaking, he vaguely felt he owed a politeness, mumbling his customary escape formula: "You really ought to . . . uh . . . come to Leopoldskron . . . uh . . . sometime. . . ." The actual inviting—he hardly ever knew who the visitors would be, when or whether they had arrived or which one was a house guest—he left to his *maître de plaisir*, Rudolf Kommer. Leopoldskron was a remarkable crossroads: scenic, bustling with traffic and, it is safe to say, the only place of its kind in Central Europe. Many an exciting project was conceived there, many a career launched, many intrigues set brewing and many a love affair born and shattered. These goings-on diverted and stimulated my father. Undoubtedly it flattered him that he was the center of so much attraction. But he preferred not to occupy that position, rather to observe the dazzling proceedings from the periphery.

The array of guests belonged to Leopoldskron as much as the boiseries and chinoiseries he had installed to cover the crumbling walls of the shell Leopoldskron was when he acquired it in Austria's dark days of 1917; belonged as much as the exquisite period furniture, the paintings, the porcelain and silver, the statuary he had placed over the grounds and the exotic birds strutting through the park. He was one of the first and, in his time, one of the few collectors of antiquities and objets d'art on a grand scale. But he was not a collector of dead things. He was intent on giving back to a relic its original reason for being, imbuing it with *life.* The doing, however, took years of patience and devotion as well as enormous sums of money and, as he was a busy man—and far from a Croesus—this passion exacted considerable sacrifice from him.

He made it gladly. Leopoldskron was his pet production, one in which fantasy and reality overlapped and merged into one, an aim he pursued in all his productions. There were those who thought it was his most reckless and extravagant production. But as his brother Edmund was in charge of the purse strings and did not untie them lightly, funds were forthcoming only for projects and objects that my father's heart was stubbornly set on. Still, such stubbornness had first to overcome a minimum of three fraternal vetoes before Max's demands would be fulfilled. After Edmund's death the man at the brakes was replaced by the strictures of the Depression. Which meant that beauty and luxury stopped at kitchen, laundry, heating, plumbing and all the dreary necessities behind the scene. In 1932, a catastrophic year for the Reinhardt enterprises, my father telegraphed his Berlin office to scrape the bottom of a nonexisting barrel for fifty thousand Reichsmark (today the equivalent of roughly one hundred thousand dollars), to build an open-air theatre in Leopoldskron Park. His bookkeeper compared him to Marie Antoinette.

Leopoldskron was, literally, "for show." Not a show put on to make an impression or to increase the prestige of its owner or, as some of his detractors would have it, to satisfy his megalomania. He needed no palaces to impress. Achievement gave him status. When I say "show" I mean it in the sense of play. My father *played* Leopoldskron and, although megalomania was not one of his faults, he never played modestly.

Some were enchanted by the play, others—mostly the uninvited—were annoyed. Many were envious or simply begrudged a caterer-of-amusement such feudal airs. Thus Leopoldskron became the butt of widely circulated jokes and endless acrimony. When Wall Street millionaire Otto H. Kahn arrived at the castle to attend a dinner party, on seeing candlelight flickering behind the tall windows and liveried servants hurrying toward his car with flaming candelabra, he exclaimed: "What's the trouble? Short circuit at the Reinhardts'?" Duff Cooper, Lady Diana's husband, in his memoirs, *Old Men Forget*, makes a nastier point:

> Each room, admirably arranged, was too like a stage setting, and my feeling of being in the theatre was confirmed when at dinner a white-whiskered major-domo, worthy of an archbishop or an archduke, bore in a bottle wrapped in a napkin and containing, one supposed, either the best champagne or imperial Tokay, and proceeded to pour out of it some indifferent beer which was the only liquor provided with a meagre repast.

So, while the grandeur of Leopoldskron moved the German-born senior partner of Kuhn, Loeb to nothing more than an American flippancy, it impelled the politician and writer—being a proper Britisher—to condescension. That someone from the land of laundered vegetables and shivery puddings should find an Austrian dinner—especially one offered by the proverbial gourmet and spendthrift Max Reinhardt—"meagre" is self-revelatory. That he recalls only beer having been served justifies the title of his book. Beer, in Austrian houses, is served as an apéritif. And Austrian beer is good. It would seem that the consort of Reinhardt's highborn Madonna in *The Miracle* gained from his lofty vantage point the foggy view that Reinhardt sought the effect of serving champagne without wanting to serve champagne. Behind the mask of the lord of the manor he detected the parvenu and farceur. What escaped him was his own role in the play Leopoldskron: a comic bit allegorizing jealousy and snobbism. Reinhardt, when an "old man," did not "forget": on hearing that Duff Cooper in World War II was being appointed governor of Singapore, he commented: "Then Singapore is lost." In point of fact—unforeseen by Reinhardt and of course through no fault of Duff's—two weeks later it was.

Too literate for cornball quips and too vitriolic for condescension, Karl Kraus, the Viennese *arbiter literarum et elegantiarum* and Reinhardt Public Enemy Number One, wrote in his periodical *Die Fackel* (The Torch):

> Barnum & Bailey will live on in the memory of mankind as pikers, small-time peep show operators whose Florida mansion was a doghouse compared to Leopoldskron.

And written *ibidem* in the Hitler year 1935 by the Jew Kraus about the Jew Reinhardt:

> Next to the headlong plunge of the German nation into barbarism there is no more sickening example of degradation than the sycophancy surrounding Leopoldskron, than the sniveling after invitations there. Hotel concierges make the reservations. Those able to squeeze in feel they are in heaven, count themselves blessed when the magician holds court, are enchanted even when he declines to receive.

Kraus, we see, despised Leopoldskron—and its proprietor—and Nazism in equal measure. Yet it was mainly the former that drew his invective. Questioned in a letter to the *Fackel*'s editor about the reason for castigating everything under the sun except Hitler, he replied: "He leaves my thoughts at a loss." This problem he did not have with Reinhardt. To paraphrase Samuel Johnson's remark about the novels of Congreve ("I'd rather praise them than read them"), Kraus could have said of Reinhardt productions: "I'd rather condemn them than see them." For he rarely attended them. Leopoldskron, assuredly, he never saw from the inside.

One year before my father was born, Richard Wagner laid the cornerstone of his Festival House in Bayreuth. Four years later, in the completed structure, erected at great cost according to the master's painstaking specifications, he supervised the production of and conducted his *Ring des Nibelungen.* Without this first in modern theatrical history, Reinhardt's

Salzburg Festival—and its sundry offspring all over the globe—would have never happened and could not be explained. For Wagner did not only revolutionize the music of his age. His imprint on my father's generation as absolute ruler of the performing arts, toppling every one of the conventional dictatorships over them—of the almighty sponsor, the star performer, popular taste, technical and financial curbs—as blender of *all* the arts, as creator who bent every detail of execution to his will, as builder of a dominant ivory tower of strength, as theatre builder and festival founder, cannot be overemphasized. Like Wagner, Max Reinhardt craved the ideal ambience for his art and found life in the big cities too distracting from its cultivation—for producer and consumer alike. Unlike Wagner's, his product was only partially his own, making it much harder to flush out the indispensable donors and to procure the necessary means (in much harder times), to lure his consumers into the provinces and to endow his festival with an organic cohesion (saddling Salzburg with a problem of identity never entirely solved).

Following in Wagner's giant footsteps, he wanted to present in special circumstances something special; something *festive*; a Bayreuth of the speaking stage. He dreamed of a natural stage setting with local color, a local heritage, providing the essential unity and uniqueness. His goal was to revive long-lost traditions—of the medieval mysteries and the rural Dionysia of ancient Greece, the ritual wombs of the theatre as we know it (the German term *Festspiele* [festal games] connoting more vividly an origin in the *agōnes*, as adjuncts of the sportive contests).

And like Wagner, Reinhardt sought to link his professional with his private life and to house in one place not only his art, but the artist. But whereas Haus Wahnfried was a second step after Bayreuth's Festival House, Leopoldskron preceded the Salzburg legacies; preceded them, in fact, by many years. Reinhardt, too, laid a cornerstone of one (in 1922, projected by Hans Poelzig, the avant-garde architect of his Great Playhouse in Berlin), but it was never built. (The ones that eventually were lacked the Reinhardt cachet.)

The town where Mozart was born and, ill-treated, had grown up hating, had, for some time, envisioned a testimonial to its belatedly favorite son. But, except for desultory operatic and orchestral attempts, these plans never materialized. Contrary to an obstinate Salzburg myth, it was solely the fortuitous result of my father's house-hunting that made Salzburg the world's ranking festival site. It could as well have been Darmstadt, on Lake Zurich, in the alpine foothills around Munich or the Engadine—all regions that had been under serious consideration and subjects of negotiation. When the die was cast with the acquisition of Leopoldskron (from a

Berlin businessman) the "intrusive outlander" incurred fierce local resentment and opposition, both among those that favored a (music) festival and those that did not. There were citizens' demonstrations protesting that the foreign visitors to be expected would gobble up the hungry natives' bread, and the papers fumed against the threat of "tourism," oddly enough, a term of abuse in those days, in that part of the world.

My father enlisted the pen of the Austrian poet Hugo von Hofmannsthal, the pull of composer Richard Strauss (then head of the Vienna Opera), the blessing of his friend the archbishop (Rieder) and the clout of another ally, the province's farsighted governor (Rehre). Bernhard Paumgartner, conductor, music historian, latter-day president of the Salzburg Festival and early collaborator of Reinhardt's, recalls in his memoirs that, in 1919, he accompanied Reinhardt on a walk through town when, crossing Cathedral Square, Reinhardt stopped abruptly, as though a divining rod in his hands had registered, and declared out of the blue: "Here's where we must put on theatre." There exists a striking drawing by Emil Orlik of my father's back. In my mind's eye I see this back close up, with the cathedral in the distance, and hear the tuning of instruments, the nailing together of boards, orders called out by stage managers, hear verses by Hofmannsthal, choral singing, hear and see dancing steps, see the cathedral turning into a stage backdrop, see scaffolding rising before it, the podium gradually filling with players, and, in the foreground, bleachers shooting up, where a polyglot public gathers, hear again the canon "when at last the bells are tolling," hear Salzburg's bells tolling; a medieval morality play seizes the heart of the baroque city, the setting sun functions like a precise spotlight, on cue pigeons rise on their wings, the banquet forges ahead to its boisterous climax, when the fateful calls, first from afar, then closer, sound from the heights: "J-e-e-e-e-e-d-e-r-m-a-a-a-n-n!" from the church steeples, from the fortress above, and the sudden apparition of Death petrifies the assembly, his reaching out for (protagonist) Moissi's heart, the marrow-crushing scream of Paramour, flight, terror, greed, farce, faith, repentance, redemption. And dominating all of it, I see that back.

And how did he see it?

> When I founded the Salzburg Festival on the square before the Cathedral, I was thinking of a wonderful fifteenth-century Marian play, which at that time was being performed by lay actors in neighboring Hallein. It seemed to me the fulfillment for the unbelievably grandiose and, at the same time, intimate space between the façade of the church and the column of St. Mary. But it [the adaptation by Max Mell] was not ready. Therefore, I chose for the first weeks, as a provisory stopgap, Hofmannsthal's *Everyman*,

> which I had previously produced in irreverent Berlin with moderate success. *Everyman* was only to introduce the coming festivals temporarily—we played it for eighteen years to sold-out Cathedral Squares. The emergency—to speak with the voice of the [Broadway] "angels"—produced a smash hit.

By 1979, *Everyman* had a run of forty-two years. Few plays have enjoyed such durability. Is it due to the writing? The work is hardly ever performed anywhere else. Or is the deciding factor not rather the environmental conception, the genius loci and genius operandi? It would seem so, because, for the first time in theatrical history, a *direction* has been preserved (with minor ad hoc refurbishments) and passed on to future generations.

It was, then, not the "Festival Town" Salzburg that attracted Reinhardt, but Reinhardt who awakened the festival town in Salzburg. For his divining rod kept working—in the open-air Rock Riding School, which he converted into a legitimate staging area, in Fischer von Erlach's Collegiate Church, where he played Calderón-Hofmannsthal, and, above all, in Leopoldskron, where the play never ended.

The "diabolical Molnár"—as my father, in a letter to Rudolf Kommer, described his playwright friend with the charming imagination and venomous charm—knew his Reinhardt diabolically well. One summer night, in 1927, he fetched Gilbert Miller, who had presented most Molnár plays on Broadway, to drive him to a reception given in his honor at Leopoldskron. Through Otto Kahn, the guarantor, it had been arranged for Miller to manage the guest performances of Reinhardt's Deutsches Theater in New York in the fall of that year and Miller had traveled the long distance to Salzburg for preliminary talks. En route to Leopoldskron, Molnár chatted about their host. The portrait he painted was fascinating: He himself was enthralled by the man. But, he had to admit, with one or two tiny reservations. As a matter of fact, he felt it his duty to apprise the guest from abroad of certain oddities the evening held in store for him. To begin with, as the initiated knew, "all that glisters is not gold" in the Reinhardt ménage. Reinhardt did not limit his creation to the stage. Those who knew him well went along with his quirky frolics, good-humoredly pretending not to see through the masquerade of "guests" he introduced as field marshals, princes, diplomats, tycoons, cardinals and other "celebrities" born of his fantasy. The Salzburgers were long accustomed to this faiblesse, which, confidentially, he was able to indulge to his heart's content by mobilizing for his private festivities the Festival's vast reserve of extras, costumes and props. But the best part, Molnár ended with a chuckle (I heard its roguish echo when he told me the story years after), was that these bogus notables were so authentically outfitted and so expertly coached they were a hundred times more convincing than the real article.

Miller sat tight-lipped. For Molnár the evening was made. He knew in his wicked bones that, in the course of it, the notorious social climber beside him would reach an imposing peak of hurt vanity. For Miller the evening was ruined before it started: to be made ridiculous by a Central European upstart—world-famous or not—was intolerable. Not for nothing was he a distinguished Manhattan producer and, no small bonus, the son-in-law of gilt-edged stockbroker Jules Bache to boot.

By the time their car approached the festively illuminated castle and the strains of a Mozart serenade greeted their ears, Miller's indignation had reached a rolling boil, and spilled over at Molnár's announcement that "now the fun begins": Dammit, he didn't find one bit of it funny! Phony is not funny. To hell with the "enchanting park." It was phony. *Everything* was phony: the moonlight streaming over the lake, the fragrance of roses and wisteria, the pink marble, the thousand candles blinking in the crystal chandeliers of the two-storied ballroom, the gallooned footmen moving with trays of caviar and champagne among beautiful, bejeweled women and important-looking men. Who else but a pack of extras could radiate such preposterous distinction! Everywhere he turned, nothing but monocles, medals, decorations, uniforms, tiaras. And the shy, self-effacing host lingering in the background—the bloody hypocrite! Near-explosion came when, faithfully in line with Molnár's scenario, Miller was presented to His Eminence the Archbishop of Salzburg, accoutered, quite naturally, in all his prince-of-the-Church magnificence, and thereafter, in rapid succession, introduced to the Chief of Staff of the German Army, a British cabinet minister, a coal magnate from the Ruhr, a Spanish philosopher and a Nobel Prize–winning scientist.

Miller took it all like a man. But when, to top the comedy, Rudolf Kommer—that eternal Jew from Czernowitz with his sarcastic smirk and eyes bulging Jewish soulfulness—waddled toward him and had the audacity to present him to the Crown Princess of Italy, Mr. Gilbert Miller went right up the baroque wall. With a sneer he turned his back on Her Royal Highness's outstretched hand. Icicles all over the place—which slowly thawed into little incredulous whispers. Of all the monocles present there came glinting through Molnár's alone a message of approbation. Her Highness acquitted herself royally. With a serene smile she mingled with the crowd, making it delightfully easy for everyone to forget the embarrassing incident.

Everyone but my father. Miller's behavior did not shock or anger him.

It puzzled him. Kahn, he reasoned, could have sent him a jackass, but never a boor. Gilbert Miller snubbing royalty? It didn't make sense. Why, he would gladly have spent his father-in-law's entire fortune for a chance to hobnob with a Savoy! A mystery. Or was it? As the evening wore on, the suspicion began to grow in my father's mind that a marionette show—with a Molnárian plot—had just been performed under his nose. To everyone's relief, the immediate problem was eliminated by the marionette eliminating itself: Gilbert Miller fled into the night without a word of fond farewell—Kommer hot on his heels.

When, pale and perspiring, the latter returned and recounted Miller's version of the events leading up to the crime, my father's suspicions were confirmed: Mephistopheles *was* at the bottom of it all. He wished ill luck to the Reinhardt tour. He was jealous. Jealous that Miller, his ambassador to Broadway, was about to become Reinhardt's too. And jealous that his wife, Lili Darvas, leading lady in the touring company, should be going to New York with Reinhardt. My father thought this plot one of Molnár's most hilarious. The role that had been written into it for him did not offend him. Molnár could always count on him for a laugh. But what tickled him most about the whole affair was the avenging stand Miller took as a result of it all. Not only did he leave Salzburg that same night in a blazing huff, but, although Kommer made Reinhardt's innocence crystal clear, he cursed—no, not Molnár, but Max Reinhardt for his "humiliation"! He never forgave him and could never be persuaded to speak to him again. Whereas with Molnár he remained the best of friends "till death did them part."

I have always rated this one of the best Molnár anecdotes. And with their vast tapestry, that is saying much. But with the years I have come to think of it as an even more significant Reinhardt anecdote. Had Molnár's idea been concocted out of thin air and had Miller been the target of an all too obvious hoax, it would still have made an ingenious jest. Yet it would have shed no light on Reinhardt. But Molnár, in his superb malice, drew on the truth for his lie. He had, as so often, created a farce, but, like every good farce, it had a core of humanness. It was true that for Reinhardt the play did not end with the curtain dropping. It was true that Leopoldskron—as all Salzburg—served him as a splendid set and all of its inhabitants a splendid cast. The only difference between Molnár's and Reinhardt's fun was that there were those moments when Reinhardt could dispense with a Molnár, or even a Molière, when he needed no extras, costumes and props, when he put together an ensemble that provided its own wardrobe and spoke its own lines.

THE DIARY

SEPTEMBER 26, 1943
(continued)

Following dinner—poor except for the truffles lovingly prepared by Eleonora—he fetches a mink blanket, souvenir of more opulent times, and tucks her in gently on the tattered sofa. Then he does something he's never done in my presence before: he kisses her on the mouth. For a while no one speaks. At last he breaks the silence. He asks about Bergner [Elisabeth Bergner—M.R.'s St. Joan—who just opened on Broadway in The Two Mrs. Carrolls]; *wants to know whether she had a success. Eleonora goes into raptures. She's a great friend of B.'s. Papa teases her about her exaggerated loyalties and I about her penchant for exaggeration period. Papa's not displeased to hear of B.'s success although she isn't his favorite type of actress. He has never been small-minded about the good fortune of others or known envy. What occupies him isn't Bergner, but—latterly—success. Regardless of whether he enjoyed it or not in the past, it never existed for him as a problem. Not too long ago he roared with laughter when he told me how his endearingly naïve father, forever a stranger to the theatre, asked him after a flop: "Max, why don't you just put on hits?" He no longer laughs about it. He asks how* The Merry Widow [the Broadway production with Jan Kiepura and Marta Eggert] *is doing. This success does annoy him. He resents that the New Opera Company* [which produced it and also his Rosalinda and was to co-produce Helen with him] *goes in for schmaltz operettas and employs as director a former assistant of his, who shamelessly steals his ideas. In general, it irks him that he's obliged to compete with this genre. He never had to in Europe. His Deutsches Theater didn't compete with the Metropol Theater* [Berlin's popular operetta house], *his stars not with operetta divas and tenors, Shaw not with Lehár. But on Broadway all productions are shows and each is expected to do top business—whether it's Shaw or Lehár. In assessing success or failure, American show business does not differentiate between cultural and popular values or the various categories of entertainment. Papa's shows were theatre and his business was art. M.R.'s problem with Broadway—and vice versa—is a psychological one.*

Traveling Second Class

AMERICA WAS MAX REINHARDT'S love at first sight and he remained true to it through twenty years of conquest, defeat and misunderstanding. Wrapped up in the world of the theatre as he was, it is only natural that this love also encompassed the American stage. He ranked Rouben Mamoulian's original production of *Porgy* among the finest he had seen. O'Neill was to him one of the greatest dramatists of the epoch, Norman Bel Geddes one of its most imaginative scenic designers. American jazz, with its roots in the Negro spiritual and as sublimated, for instance, by George Gershwin, made, in his judgment, the most vital contribution to contemporary music. He called the American Negro a natural actor. He found the atmosphere of Broadway so electric that, disregarding the local *Kultur*-dog-pack, he commissioned a German adaptation (*Artisten*) of an effective tearjerker by Watters and Hopkins, *Burlesque*, and gave it a spirited mise en scène on the hallowed boards of his Deutsches Theater with a stellar cast buttressed by U.S.-imported Negro dancers. Concluding his second visit to the States, he wrote to Otto H. Kahn:

> I take home with me an immeasurable impression of the New York of today. What the New York of tomorrow portends surpasses the powers of my imagination.

In a platonic way, New York opened its arms with no less fervor to Max Reinhardt. Brooks Atkinson, theatre critic for *The New York Times*, provides an example:

> In America we are only just beginning to recognize the supreme importance of the director—perhaps because we are only just developing directors of commanding influence. . . .
>
> No mincing of words alters the simple fact that Dr. Reinhardt is, at the age of fifty-four, the greatest and most versatile director of the world. . . . [He] gives us all an opportunity, whether we agree with his methods or not, to expand considerably our ideas of the capacities of the modern theatre.

In the realm of ideas there reigned mutual harmony. But when it came to the actual embraces, relations could be bumpy and "the capacities of the modern theatre" in America proved limited. What is more, the romance got off on the wrong foot. Not that *Sumurûn* was a failure. But the third-hand Reinhardt importation, in no way characteristic of his output, created a first impression never to be totally eradicated. The image of the "Central European showman" would forever linger with America's press, public and professionals. Never would he lose the aura of the "outsider."

The Oriental pantomime, based on *The Arabian Nights*, which opened at the Casino on January 6, 1912, originally conceived as a tidbit to spice up the exacting literary repertoire of Berlin's exclusive Kammerspiele with stylish exuberance, reached Broadway (and Thirty-ninth Street) via England. Reinhardt's English impresario, Charles B. Cochran, had no doubt chosen it from the rich stock of available Reinhardt productions for its muteness and consequent accessibility to a London audience without translation. Expanding its showy qualities to fit the Coliseum may well have enhanced its popularity, but hardly its distinctiveness. Still, in London, Reinhardt had held the reins himself and the Berlin cast had been kept intact. In New York, a deputy was put in charge (Richard Ordynski, the "Polish Reinhardt") and of the original cast only a fraction had made the crossing.

American connoisseurs were quick to pinpoint the three genuine Reinhardt ingredients: the stunning decor by Reinhardt's house designer Ernst Stern, contrasting voluptuously colored costumes with sketchily insinuated sets, juxtaposing sensuality and fantasy; a fresh pantomimic style leaning on acting, rather than dancing; and the endeavor to merge players and spectators by use of the floral bridge borrowed from the Japanese theatre, permitting the actors to enter and exit through the audience, launching and climaxing their scenes in its center. The notices were mixed and the engagement lasted sixty-two performances. Two coincidences intensified the delusive light in which the absent and much ballyhooed "theatre magician" introduced himself to America: a pair of kitsch extravaganzas with equally Oriental themes, *Kismet* and *The Garden of Allah*, was selling out in Manhattan at the same time. Superficial analogies inevitably struck the mind.

Reinhardt's second foray into the New World in January 1924, though led by him personally, with enormous financial success and, this time, on a high artistic level almost unanimously acknowledged, was not calculated to revise the first impression. Again, the vehicle was a pantomime, again on an unprecedented scale, thus consolidating the image of the master showman and delaying America's acquaintance with his mastery of his most important and subtlest tool: the spoken word. Four years later, Brooks Atkinson would recall:

> We had a sample of Dr. Reinhardt's quality in the colossal production of *The Miracle* at the Century Theatre. . . . That was a stupendous enterprise. Under the sweeping management of Morris Gest, Norman Bel Geddes had transformed our largest theatre into a Gothic cathedral with an extravagance and a thoroughness never equaled on the stage before or since. By an imaginative use of professionals and mass effects, Dr. Reinhardt . . . summoned a medieval fable to life, up and down the aisles, across the stage, with a reverent yet hysterical emotional authority.

The Miracle too came by way of London, which was, indeed, its birthplace. But whereas the London première, except for its local entrepreneur (Cochran again) and the multitude of supernumeraries, had been a one hundred percent Berlin creation, the revival on Central Park West drew heavily on native—and English—talent. Of it, the young American designing genius (my father's words) Bel Geddes deserved the prominent place Atkinson accords him.

The local entrepreneur chosen by Mr. Kahn (who had pledged $300,000—recouped in a matter of months) bore the most publicized name in American entertainment since Barnum: Morris Gest. Like Barnum, it was he who did all the publicizing. He did, in fact, little else. Publicizing was his primary function, *his* genius, his soul. "Morris Gest presents Max Reinhardt's *Miracle*," as the posters and ads and programs screamed, was misleading. They should have screamed: "Morris Gest publicizes . . ." The wording compounded the fast-growing, basic misunderstanding. The role played by Max Reinhardt, who *welcomed* an impresario at his side—a role *he* respected, even though foreign to him—became blurred in American show business. Who but an impresario could put on such a superproduction? And why should an impresario "present" an impresario? (In the case of Stanislavski, Duse and Nijinski, all of whom Gest had brought to America, no such problem of identification arose. The delineations of the respective tasks were clear. But Gest did not bring a Reinhardt production to America. It was an American enterprise.) Gest did not help clarify matters by elbowing Reinhardt out of the limelight he spread so lavishly, particularly during the years he took the show on the road and Reinhardt was thousands of miles and headlines away, so that in many minds it was "Gest's *Miracle*" and not Reinhardt's. On the other hand, in New York, the most touted event in American theatre history was bound to deflect enough light onto Reinhardt to link him with pageantry for the rest of his American days.

What puzzled the unconcerned angered those in the know. George Jean Nathan, the most "intellectual" of American critics, wrote in the American *Mercury*:

> Preceded by that species of irrelevant and trumpery press-agency which, somewhat disconcertingly, he would seem fond of allowing to make him appear rather like German silver, Max Reinhardt, the foremost active producer in the world theatre, has come across the Atlantic to display his wares. That this virtuoso of dramatic production should permit himself publicity devices that Peaches Browning and even Otto Kahn might balk at is gagging to those of his critics who peculiarly believe that art and dignity should have something in common, and who have difficulty in determining just what connection there can be between some of the very finest dramatic presentations of the modern stage and a lot of free lunches at Salzburg, to say nothing of widely disseminated photographs showing the impresario [!] and Miss Julia Hoyt posed against the façade of Schloss Leopoldskron, eating sizeable hunks of *Wiener Lungenbäuscherl* [*sic*]. For while such stuff may be all right on the part of self-advertising vaudeville actors and pentecostal clergymen, it is hardly an admirable business for a man of Reinhardt's attainments.

I am far from suggesting that my father discouraged the hoopla which announced, accompanied and recorded his American "attainments." I know from his own lips that he believed in its utility. Certainly, the investment an undertaking as huge as *The Miracle* required would have been reckless without a generous dose of "self-advertising." And since his Maecenas, according to Nathan, was a prime perpetrator of the excess and the Maecenas-appointed manager its very exponent, why should Reinhardt, on unfamiliar territory, be expected to act holier than thou?

There was, nevertheless, a contradiction in Reinhardt's operating method that irritated his critics, sometimes baffled his admirers and was the source of additional confusion. Like Nathan, he believed that "art and dignity should have something in common." One might even say he considered his life and work a synthesis of the two. Yet he was acutely aware that quality must be *sold*; in fact, he maintained it had to be *pre*-sold. To leave its lot to chance, to the judgment of fallible arbiters or to the fatalistic hope that a worthy effort can automatically count on its just desserts was, in his eyes, ingenuous. And anti-theatre. An audience, he would say, will laugh over the true comedian before the fun even begins—on his entrance. If not, it is usually too late. Ideally, the success of a première is decided prior to its start. Laughter, success must be "in the air." He had no compunction about ensuring that they were. No salesman himself, he had no compunction about being sold. Not everyone was able or willing to go along with this fine distinction.

Whether *The Miracle* would have caught on with the mass public as it did—and had to do, failing bankruptcy—without Gest's drumbeating (which ranged from an incessant barrage of huckstering press releases that inundated New York's readers with skyrocketing statistics of building, painting, carpentering, wiring, casting, costuming, [ecclesiastical] researching, financing records, to the highbrow commissioning of Oliver Sayler to write a Reinhardt biography) would forever remain dubious to my father. He gave him full credit for the extraordinary energy he exerted in that respect. It just about compensated, in his opinion, for the appalling mistakes in organization Gest committed and the consequent waste and disarray he caused—for which Reinhardt received a good part of the blame (an opinion fully borne out by Geddes's fragmentary autobiography, *Miracle in the Evening*). My father was entertained by Gest's extrovertedly bohemian life style and total lack of *Sitzfleisch*; by the ham actor offstage who—in my father's description—"never once sat through an entire rehearsal or performance of 'his' show." And he was grateful to him for bringing him together with his leading lady, an "*echte* lady" in the Gest vocabulary, Lady Diana Manners (Cooper).

My father and Kahn saw no reason for recasting the actress who had played the Madonna in London twelve years before, Maria Carmi, then wife of Carl Vollmoeller, who was credited with the authorship of *The Miracle*. (Authors' royalties, taking into account the realities, were divided between Vollmoeller, Reinhardt and literary sidekick Arthur Kahane and, of course, the composer Engelbert Humperdinck.) The internationally famous beauty had since changed husbands. But though she had thereby nearly gained the status of an "*echte* princess" (Principessa Machabelli), Gest's promotional instincts—healthily—tended to new blood for New York all the way. Diana had made two silent films of little import in Hollywood. Gest, however, was dispassionate about talent. He looked for youthful beauty and exploitable glamour. The daughter of the Duke of Rutland had an abundance of both. She also had intelligence, sparkling wit and charm. It did not require a Gest to feel confident she would captivate Reinhardt, once dispatched to Salzburg. He was an anglophile, a pigeon for aristocratic birds of paradise, an idolizer of beauty, a consenting victim of charm and, like many actor-directors, intrigued by provocative dilettantes. Wit and intelligence—not overly dear to him in an attractive woman—she wisely reserved, when visiting Schloss Leopoldskron, for the less potent, more appreciative and linguistically superior social sidekick Kommer. The captivation proceeded according to schedule. Nevertheless, my father wrote a letter during the rehearsal period that reads: "She [Diana] is not my Madonna. Too much statue, but because of it and as such simply perfect, by no means unintriguing. A living wax figure and therefore touchingly childlike." But then, the letter was addressed to his private "Madonna," Helene Thimig.

Meanwhile, what to do about Carmi, who had a contract? A dilemma that inspired Gest to escalate it into a publicity marathon—referred to in the press as the "battle of the Virgins"—estranging the contestants with increasing acerbity. When paladin Kommer, ever handy with a Solomonic solution, proposed determining the issue of who was to play the première by going through a sham ceremony of drawing stacked lots, Diana's husband, Duff Cooper, left the disgraceful scene in gentlemanly indignation. Gest subscribed to no such code of honor. The trick provided him with a suitable climax for his sideshow in the journals. Those in on the ruse discreetly shut their eyes to it. The others bowed to a decision beyond appeal which, predictably, favored the lady over the princess. After the opening, Diana and Carmi alternated. When it was Carmi's turn—another Gest stunt sanctioned by my father, who welcomed the test of interpretative versatility—Diana doubled in the part of the Nun. Understandably, the arrangement made Carmi drop out before long, and the famous opera soprano Mary Garden took her place. Opposite Diana's Madonna, Rosamond Pinchot, another well-born amateur, played the Nun. The niece of a former governor of Pennsylvania was Reinhardt's discovery, but fitted snugly into Gest's scheme, satisfying his recently acquired taste for exalted lineage.

An American participant who deserves more recognition than he received was Ernest de Weerth, nominally Geddes's assistant in charge of costumes, but, actually, the costume designer, and a most gifted one at that. In addition, he made himself my father's English mouthpiece—and pet. His immediate boss, Geddes, was not an unalloyed boon to my father, owing to his overindulgence in spirits. On the night of the opening, my father missed his ungovernable collaborator during the curtain calls. Refusing to take another bow without him, he sent the entire backstage crew scurrying in search of him. They finally located him way up in the flies, curled up in a coil of cables, dead to a sober world. Fortunately, the world that mattered that night was not sober. It was, at any rate, sufficiently intoxicated not to stop cheering and stamping until Reinhardt reappeared with the rumpled, blinking cathedral builder and the latter assumed his rightful, if unsteady, place beside the only sober man in the house.

Of the European contingent, two great actors deserve mentioning: Rudolf Schildkraut and Werner Krauss. The first, one of Reinhardt's Berlin Shylocks, was on loan from the Yiddish Art Theatre on Second Avenue to which his ancestry and a deep affinity had drawn him. The second, familiar to American film-goers from the *Cabinet of Dr. Caligari*, is the hero-villain of another story. His affinity would draw him to the Nazis, whose luminary he became, after they robbed the director to whom he owed so much of all worldly possessions (Krauss volunteered, among other breaches of taste, to caricature no less than thirteen Jews in Goebbels' infamous film *Jud Süss*).

The Miracle, per se no artistic milestone on Max Reinhardt's path, yet one that proved decisive in his career, had a New York run of 298 performances, followed by a tour through the United States lasting five years, playing Cleveland (December 1924), Cincinnati, Boston, St. Louis, Chicago, Philadelphia, Kansas City, San Francisco, Detroit, Milwaukee, St. Paul and Dallas (January 1930), where it folded. "Dalles," in Yiddish, meaning penury, my father insisted on reading a symbolic significance into the homophone.

Three years before this closing, Kahn footed the bill (once more, never presented for payment) for the third Max Reinhardt opening in America: a limited engagement of the company of the Deutsches Theater with seven original Reinhardt productions. Again, most of them took place at the Century which, however, this time, was not turned into a house of God, neither of Christianity nor publicity, but instead, served as showcase for mortal masterpieces. But in German. Broadway speaks English. The celebrated visitor, seen for the first time in his true light, had become more of an outsider.

This trip, as well as his fourth American venture, the California *Midsummer Night's Dream* of 1934, receive their due in other chapters. The sizable credit accruing from the second was used up in the movies, a field yielding graver misunderstandings between Reinhardt and his working milieu. On the stage, it was hurriedly frittered away by an ill-managed tour of the same play, with a diluted cast, to Chicago, Milwaukee and St. Louis, which not merely floundered, but brought embarrassment.

At the root of the calamity was, once more, a misunderstanding. His. He underestimated the demands made on him in America, on his time and personal attention. He failed to see that in America it was even more difficult to coast on past achievements than in Berlin. Not even a Reinhardt—let alone one robbed of his highly effective Berlin staff—could, in one year (1934), prepare a two-million-dollar film (*A Midsummer Night's Dream,* which suffered from delegation of authority and cursory involvement), attempt the foundation of a new festival (in California; foiled by local intrigues, betrayals in his own camp and his absenteeism), tend an old festival (in Salzburg, where he made fleeting appearances during the few summers Hitler was gracious enough to let pass unmolested), watch over the creation of a Biblical music drama for Broadway (to become *The Eternal Road*), wrest a Reno divorce from a recalcitrant and resourceful wife, and, simultaneously, send a tour through the Middle West, contributing to it nothing but his name. I had the misfortune of catching up with it at the Auditorium Theatre in Chicago. My father's comment, on arriving for the dress rehearsal, was an understatement: "This is 'A Winter Night's Dream'!" It was a winter's nightmare.

Into another nightmare grew his fifth American venture, *The* (well-named) *Eternal Road,* a saga also dealt with elsewhere. Again, a mammoth production, but of unimpeachable artistry, with awesome statistics, it cemented the faulty image for good: of the profligate genius, the unintegrable stranger, the beloved untouchable.

His *Faust* production at Los Angeles' open-air Pilgrimage Theatre in 1938, his sixth on U.S. soil, permits swift disposal for the opposite reason: it had nothing to recommend it specifically and was of no general consequence whatsoever. The California Festival project was dead long before this luckless attempt at resurrection. During rehearsals, my father saw and heard with his mind's eye and ear a splendid cast, magnificently framed, performing Goethe's masterwork in its linguistic grandeur, ideally interpreted by a Max Reinhardt in top form in Salzburg five years before. A Hollywood audience saw and heard the reality and was put off by its mediocrity. Against a poor copy of the Salzburg backdrop, an undistinguished cast (led by Conrad Nagel and Margo) plowed through an awkward English text that retained nothing of the lyricism and philosophy of Goethe's dramatic poem, confining itself to communicating its plot—not the most valuable asset of *Faust.* My father's direction resembled a parody of itself, as unassimilated gestures and inflections, seemingly unmotivated surges and empty pauses added to the onlooker's puzzlement. This unnecessary confirmation of the lesson that German poetry—from Klopstock to Brecht—is all but untranslatable into English and therefore unperformable, ground my father's American career to a halt.

Barely a month later, a deceptively hopeful gust of wind hit becalmed Reinhardt from a corner as unexpected as it was logical: Loyal Thornton Wilder, being, apart from his literary gifts, equipped with an encyclopedic knowledge of the European theatre, and a student and fan of Max Rein-

The young Max Reinhardt and his wife, actress Else Heims.

Else Heims-Reinhardt with their two sons, Wolfgang (left) and Gottfried.

Max Reinhardt the actor, 1895-1903. In Maxim Gorki's *Lower Depths*, in Ibsen's *Rosmersholm* and in Ibsen's *The Pretenders*.

Left. A *Midsummer Night's Dream*, Berlin, 1905. Max Reinhardt in the wings, rehearsing Else Heims, Paul Paulsen, Eduard von Winterstein and Grete Berger.

Below. Wedekind's *Awakening of Spring*, directed by Reinhardt, Berlin, 1906. The cemetery scene: Bernhard von Jacobi, Frank Wedekind and Alexander Moissi.

A *Midsummer Night's Dream*. Photograph taken during the actual outdoor production, 1905.

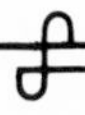

The Reinhardt company on tour, Brussels, 1910. Max Reinhardt is second from the left.

Hamlet, directed by Max Reinhardt, Berlin, 1910. Alexander Moissi as Hamlet, August Momber as Fortinbras.

Max Reinhardt's productions of *Oedipus Rex*. Berthold Held rehearsing the cast, Berlin 1910; Sir Martin Harvey as Oedipus, London, 1912.

Stage design for Reinhardt's London production of *The Miracle*, 1911.

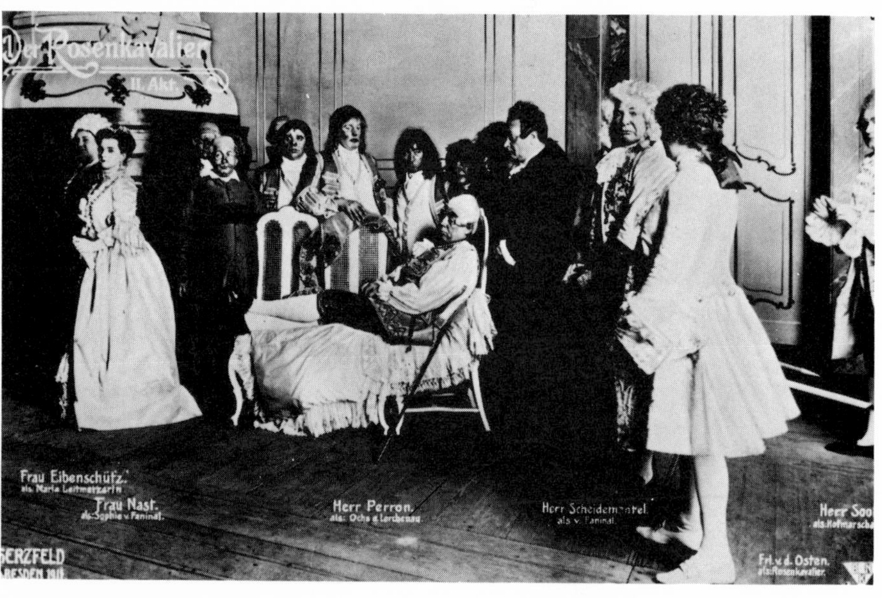

Première of Richard Strauss's *Der Rosenkavalier*, Dresden, 1911, directed by Max Reinhardt. Act II: M. Nast, C. Perron, Karl Scheidemantel, E. von den Osten, F. Soot.

fingers. This friction between aware naïveté and phony sophistication eroded the play. During the tryout in Boston, the prima donna realized how futile her little victory had been. But her belated overtures to my father, even a tearful, dramatic and possibly sincere genuflection, failed to melt the ice in his veins, which would set the temperature for the critical reception to come, resulting in thirty-nine performances.

The subsequent history of this, his seventh production in America, reads like a primer of what to do and what to avoid in order to pick up the gold lying in the Great White Way. Ruth Gordon, an actress more noteworthy for her acumen and will power (she had her legs broken surgically three times until they were made straight) than for visceral talent, recognized quickly what pearls had been wasted and before what swine. She gave her friend Wilder more expedient advice than Reinhardt did (if he ever gave him any; he was not a play-doctor, a specialty of Broadway; he either inspired a work or enriched it through interpretation). She persuaded him to rewrite the play, throwing the main emphasis on the female lead, custom-tailoring it for herself. For all its egoism, it was shrewd dramaturgical therapy that robbed the quaint, perky old-timer of much of its charm, but souped up its motor sufficiently for a considerable run. Without admiration, love, gratitude or tears, or any *je ne sais quoi* (the whole point of Broadway being *savoir quoi*), a Broadway hit was engineered to expect specifications: *The Matchmaker*. Its hum sounded irresistible to the keen antennae of the street's musical engineers. Broadway and Tin Pan Alley—eventually joined by Pico Boulevard (Twentieth Century-Fox)—combined to put on the market their sleekest, gaudiest model in many a year. All the bugs—those fascinating bugs!—were neatly eliminated. "Goodbye, Merchant!" "Stick around awhile, Matchmaker!" "*HELLO*, Dolly!"

The brief spurt over, Max Reinhardt returned to the West Coast, where he stayed marooned for four years, his only activity being school productions, some of which were tested commercially outside and proved uncommercial. Again, another chapter.

The insolvent *Merchant* opened my eyes to the psychological gulf separating Max Reinhardt and the American theatre: When, early one evening in November 1938, I stopped by the Guild Theatre (now ANTA), where my father was rehearsing the Wilder play, to fetch him for dinner—mine (his lunch). As the rehearsal was still in progress, I took a seat in one of the last rows. On stage, my father was going over a change of scenery that was intended to take place in full view of the audience, without its breaking up the play's action or mood. It was an intricate maneuver requiring a dexterity on the part of both actors and stagehands that, apparently, had not yet met with his satisfaction. When, for the umpteenth time, his unruffled "Once more, please" reverberated through the all but empty house, I settled back in my seat for a long winter's nap. But I reckoned without the arrival of Herman Shumlin, the co-producer, an experienced Broadway director in his own right. Dropping into the seat next to me, he whispered in my ear: "Why does he waste his energy on these mechanics? That's nothing for him. Any stage manager can handle them in half the time—and frankly better. I'd be delighted to take this nonsense off his hands myself." Obviously he did not consider my father a craftsman. Yet his admiration for him was genuine. So was his desire to help. Though why he admired him or why he should be the one to help him neither he nor I could answer. When the rehearsal was over, he gave me no chance to throw myself between his battering-ram solicitude and my father's distaste for it.

In the taxi cross-town, my father was pensive. "Most of my life," he said, "it has been my good fortune to afford traveling first class. Not, mind you, that when I had to travel third it made me unhappy. It's traveling second class I've always detested. And that's what I'm doing now." It was only because I wanted to cheer him up that I insisted he did not even travel in the same train with Shumlin. The end of the ride confirmed, of course, that he had.

Panning the play, George Jean Nathan omitted mentioning its director —the same director about whom he had this to say, ten years before:

> That Reinhardt is the most talented director and producer operating in the theatre in these years is certainly not news, except perhaps to a few Russians. With Craig, the greatest genius of them all, in forced retirement in Genoa, with Stanislavsky, a skillful fellow, calmly relying for eminence upon a few already ancient achievements, with Danchenko, ever thus better than a second-rater, idiotically frittering away his time out in Hollywood, and with Pitoeff going in simply for a series of exaggerated imitations and caricatures in France, Reinhardt has the field pretty well to himself. He is an extraordinary fertile and alive figure, indefatigable, imaginative and resourceful; he works like a Trojan; he has, unlike these other producers, a sense of internationalism—all drama, whatever the land of its origin, is of interest to him; he has a mind that adapts itself to a diversity of drama and a fancy that filters it with a various force and beauty onto a fluid and galvanic stage. It is Reinhardt's outstanding characteristic, indeed, and the quality that has raised him to leadership among the active producing talents of the day, that he is, in a sense, a different man in the instance of each separate production which he makes. Where the majority of producers have a very definite and unmistakable personal label that sticks betrayingly to each of

> their presentations, however essentially different the dramas themselves may be, Reinhardt changes his directing personality according to the drama he happens to be dealing with. There is not one director Reinhardt, there are a dozen director Reinhardts. But there is only one Stanislavsky, one Gémier, one Granville-Barker, one Copeau or one Sierra, be the play farce or comedy, tragedy or allegory.
>
> . . . Reinhardt, with Papa Craig peeping over his shoulder, has brought more actual life to the modern stage than any other practicing director and producer of his time. His influence has spread over all lands and seas. He has been Gordon Craig's Paul.

Whether he had or not, or whether—to adhere to the hyperbolic metaphor—Craig's role was not rather that of John the Baptist, Reinhardt's influence on the American land remained flimsy.

Two efforts—his eighth and the final one—in which the sixty-nine-year-old youngster showed a remarkable flexibility and truly bent backwards to function on Broadway's terms: merry *Rosalinda* and doleful *Sons and Soldiers* (which, indeed, broke his back) concluded the stormy affair. Each, therefore, deserves a special place, each epitomizing that long and intimate dialogue at cross-purposes.

THE DIARY

SEPTEMBER 26, 1943
(continued)

I try to distract him with a more optimistic subject: report on the breakthrough of the Allies at the Salerno bridgehead and that, thank God, the war's finally nearing a happy end. This seems to put him in a reflective mood. Why? Does he think things aren't going fast enough? Or not fast enough for him? Does he seriously believe he bit his tongue? Or does he know what happened to him and wants to keep it from me? Or is he not sure and simply afraid? Sometimes I've the feeling his eyes are posing a terribly important question which he's at a loss to answer himself. I resort to double scotches, which he, routinely, reacts to with amused disapproval. The building groans from top to bottom. Almost a parody of a Hitchcock film. I'm carried back to the dubbing rooms of MGM when the mixers rehearse the reels by themselves and the scenes practically drown in assorted sound effects until cutter, director and producer arrive and express the hope that some of the lines will eventually surface. But no cutter, director or producer has come to the rescue of our lines, which, sparse enough as they are, grow less and less audible in the steadily swelling din. But just as in a movie—after all, once they're on the screen, the actors can no longer protest—the distortion doesn't affect the three of us. We ignore our surroundings, not only the noise but also the setting into which none of us really fits. Indeed, we act as if we ignore the plot which entangles us. I can't help thinking that the thriller which holds us all captive—if it were only that, a film, soon over and forgotten!—is actually a silent picture with added sound effects. The few words we exchange have nothing to do with reality or our true thoughts.

evening,
SEPTEMBER 26, 1943

The longest day of my life. Rise early, badly hung over. But I've got to get to a pay phone while he and Eleonora are still asleep. [The beach house had no phone.]

The weather's beautiful again. Invigorating and clear. My brain refuses to admit that at one stroke his—and my—entire life should have undergone a total change. At one stroke . . . I stand in the booth where it all happened. I imagine how it happened. I remember his speaking to me and my not being aware of anything.

Don't have the proper coins for a New York call. On Sunday not a soul around to change money. So: a collect call. Darvas. I wake her up. I apologize and tell about the dogfight and how Papa was bitten. But carefully avoid mentioning the speech impairment. For there's no doubt in my mind that the slightest rumor about Papa's affliction would kill his prospects on Broadway for good. Who'd entrust a producer's or director's responsibility to an incapacitated seventy-year-old? First to shy away would be our music dragon [Yolanda Merö Irion, manager of the New Opera Company]. She and Darvas are both Hungarians and friends. But realizing that my manifest anxiety and urgent pleading that she recommend a top doctor—on Sunday—are out of all proportion to my casual account, I appeal to her friendship for utmost discretion. I stress the fact that a dogfight is always unnerving.

But I've frightened her. After all, she's a doctor's daughter. She recommends Dr. F., a Viennese by birth, who takes care of most of the Hungarian colony in New York. She promises to get in touch with him and to ring me back.

Wait an eternity. The thought that my absence will be noticed at home makes me jittery. At last Darvas calls: Dr. F. in Long Island over the weekend and can't be reached at the moment. She gives me his number, I'm to try him in a little while.

Wait another eternity. Finally get him on the line. Apologize for collect call, mentioning Darvas. Reaction not too friendly. Introduce myself, identify patient and impress on him necessity for keeping things confidential. Even more unfriendly. Report what occurred and describe symptoms. F. doesn't hesitate: "Everything points to a stroke." "But there are no other signs—his body movements are normal. . . ." F. explains aphasia: loss or impairment of speech or of the powers of perception, despite healthy speech organs or eyes and ears, due to diseased or damaged parts of the brain. The affected person may be able to think quite normally, but he cannot, or can only imperfectly, translate his thoughts into words—or translate what he hears or reads into thoughts. The most important thing now: to prevent further strokes. Bed-wetting on the subsequent night strongly indicates a second one. I'm to be on guard for any signs of paralysis. In any event it's vital I bring my father to New York immediately.

F. will interrupt his weekend and wait my call in town at 6 P.M. I implore him to be diplomatic with Papa, at least in the beginning to pay lip service to the fiction that he bit his tongue. Which annoys F. more than ever.

To the pier. Inquire about boats. There aren't any on Sundays. Charter a private one and make a deposit to ensure it will wait for us from four o'clock on. Rush back. How do I get Papa to New York without telling him the truth? If I do that I may as well give up now. I pass the chapel. Play with the thought of entering and praying. Detest my weakness: It was a doctor I wanted to talk to, not God. But halfway home, I'm not at all sure whether I've made the right choice.

A weight drops from my mind when I step inside the door. Neither Papa nor Eleonora is in sight. Not that my secret excursion escaped her. I caught a shadow scurrying away on the first gallery. I knew it was hers. A bell rings in the kitchen. Papa's signaling for breakfast. Where in God's name did he find that damn woman? Throw my inhibitions to the wind and take the tray from her. The decision to go into his room is painful for me. When we were boys our greatest fun was to watch him dress in the morning, to maneuver his shoe trees in our war games on the carpet and his empty toilet bottles in naval engagements in the bathtub, to attend his elaborate shaving ceremony—doesn't he turn every disagreeable chore into a solemn ritual? And we were always welcome visitors. But today my interest is less innocuous. I must look for possible "signs of paralysis." And what am I to do if there are any? I don't know which frightens me more: such an eventuality or that he sees through my solicitude.

My entrance surprises him. Thank heavens agreeably. I detect no physical change in him. On the contrary. He seems more relaxed. And his speech more distinct. He wants to go swimming with me. Swimming! Is he in a condition to? Shouldn't I try to prevent him? Or am I overly pessimistic? I temporize: "Isn't it too late in the year—I mean too cold?" Mocking laughter. But when I ask: "Oughtn't we to start back to New York as soon as possible? There's so much to do now!" his face darkens. And at once his speech defect is evident. Am desperate. What shall I do? I mustn't excite him, yet mustn't indulge him. As if I had offended him or suggested to him something outlandish, he flies at me: "I n-need th-these f-few d-days o-o-of rest d-des-perately!" I indulge him.

"It's difficult for me to breathe except in the true unreality of the theatre and the improbable reality of our time makes it even more difficult." This is how he once described the stagnation of his days in California. The words come to my mind as we leave the house in swimming trunks and terry-cloth robes and step onto the beach, Micky pulling the way. A radiant Eleonora stands in the doorway, waving us on. Generously she grants me these few hours alone with him as she knows full well we won't be gone long and she'll have him back again.

Rarely has reality reached such a degree of improbability as this noontime on this God- and man-forsaken island. Barefoot we stroll along the water's edge as we've done hundreds of times along the Baltic, the North Sea, the Adriatic, Atlantic and Pacific. On most of these beaches I was the child; now the roles are reversed. Now it's up to me to protect him. How can I dissuade him from swimming? It angers him when I warn him of the danger of neglected dog bites and remind him of the serious infection Wolfgang once suffered in identical circumstances. It's foolhardy, I tell him, to go in the water until he's consulted a doctor.

At last he gives in. Have I convinced him or does he perceive the reason for my anxiety? But he insists on my swimming. Unable to give him an alibi for not going, I leave him reluctantly, swim out and watch the lone figure grow smaller and smaller in the distance.

Childhood in a Pocket

THE BALTIC. HIDDENSEE. A small island off the coast of Pomerania. Summer holiday with Papa. I was two years old. Through the fog of sixty years I still see plainly the magnificent ship he and Wolfgang built out of sand and boards. It had a real sail and a helm for Captain Reinhardt to steer his vessel over the seven seas, battling wild storms and wilder pirates, with his two sturdy tars at his side.

The North Sea. Zandvoort. Holland. One year later. On short baby legs I trotted with all my might to keep up with the manly stride of my big brother and Papa. But I was now considered old enough to be initiated into their cabal of grown-up male jokers. They swung me off my feet and sat me on some sort of pole. I say "pole" now, but so far as I was concerned then it could have been Mount Everest. I wailed in terror. They sprinted away down the beach, whooping with laughter. Through tear-dimmed eyes I followed them, the two callous betrayers whose company I would have sold my soul for, until I saw them make a circuit and start back toward me—a *new* me, a me knuckling the tears from his eyes and quivering his lips into a brave grin when he was hauled down from his acrophobic perch.

And Westerland. On the North Frisian island of Sylt. I was now six years old. It was the summer our papa left our mama. That the conflict between them—a conflict that was to cloud my entire life—came to a head on the seaside during our summer holiday strikes me, in retrospect, as quite fitting. Most of the dramatic turns in my relationship with him came about in identical circumstances up to the culminating one on Fire Island which rounded out the suite with its leitmotiv of thundering surf. There, just as in Westerland, we stood in the shadow of a world war and could, with little stretch of the imagination, hear the rumble of cannon, far out beyond the horizon where the armies of our two homelands, the old and the new, were deciding our fates at this moment. In Westerland the war had ended shortly before, leaving the beaches with a blanket of spine-chilling war scars. Twenty-five years later, on Fire Island, the only visible evidence of war was the uniform I arrived in—and that did not have too martial a look. It was a dress uniform the Brooks Costume Company, a supplier of theatrical apparel, had made for me according to rather unorthodox instructions and which, after several skirmishes with civilian laundries, had treacherously switched color from army khaki to Schiaparelli pink. Although one thing to be said for it—indeed, *was* said for it by my future wife with a grin of nasty delight—no South American general's uniform could compete with it for dash and zip. Wearing it on the post was, of course, out of the question.

Sylt, on the other hand, was polka-dotted with the wreckage of naval encounters. Occasionally, with good luck, a mine was swept onto land, its gruesome bulk gingerly approached by a defusing crew. I danced with excitement and bombarded my father with blood-and-thunder questions about a mine's killing potential, about the villains who had planted it, about our revenge on them. His answers—no one knew better than he how to whet a child's imagination—were echoed in his speech "About the Actor":

> The art of acting originated in the earliest childhood of mankind. . . . In children the nature of the actor is reflected at its purest. Their susceptibility is without example. And the urge to mold and dramatize in children's play is irrepressible and truly creative. They want to discover and create the world all over again themselves. With lightning speed they transform themselves into everything they see and transport everything into what they wish it to be. Their imaginative powers are conclusive: This sofa here? A railroad!

> Obviously. And in no time at all the engine sputters and hisses, a whistle blows; through the train window strange and wonderful landscapes are seen flying by; a suspicious conductor demands a ticket; it is produced and, before you know it, the end of the journey has been reached; the first chair within grasp pulls away from the other taxis; an out-of-breath hotel porter huffs and puffs under the weight of a pillow he carries. And this footstool? An airplane floating through all the seven heavens! What is this? Theatre. Ideal theatre and exemplary acting. And all the while, the clear, ever-present awareness that it is nothing but play—played in dead earnest.

And in another passage:

> I believe in the immortality of the theatre. It is the happiest hiding place for those who have secretly put their childhood in their pocket and made off with it to play to the end of their days.

This was the marvelous playmate I lost overnight during that summer holiday on Sylt.

The Adriatic. The Lido. From my eleventh to my fourteenth year. By court order I am permitted to visit my father at prescribed periods. Both he and I overact at our limited reunions. I do not show him how badly I want him back. He shows how badly he wants me by making me an honored guest in his big world and by letting me sit next to him when he works.

> Usually he has his working scripts finished at the first rehearsal. He enjoys preparing them during the summer on the Lido, on the sand, in front of his cabana; I once watched him build all the sets for *Julius Caesar* out of wet sand. In the autumn, he returns with a completed concept. The whole play is before his eyes, the revolving stage is partitioned, every position, every gesture, every word annotated. He has done his work before he begins; and yet, it is only now that he begins. That is his secret. There are directors who have finished their work before they begin and those who only begin when work on the stage begins. He is both of these combined. Out of the two concepts, his own and that of his actors, it is his passion to beget a third, a child of the two. . . . He devours the personalities and ideas of his actors. He is a great man-eater—and those who are eaten thrive on it.

These words were written in 1909 by Hermann Bahr, Austrian playwright, essayist and herald of Max Reinhardt's new theatre. They could have been written with the same justification in all the years that followed, on all the sands of all the beaches that inspirited him. His *Helen* script, I knew, had been completed on Fire Island. According to Bahr, this would have meant another of his "beginnings." In the halcyon Lido days. In the Fire Island days would those eaten continue to thrive on it? Had he still an appetite for people?

But the Lido is not just a beach resort. It lies off Venice and, for him, Venice was more than the pretty postcard city of the canals touted by travel agencies, more than the museum mecca of culture cultists. Museums aseptically preserve and display objects of art, render them lifeless. He wanted to know them alive and he found them in churches where rare triptychs, marble saints and old-master madonnas were not merely displayed, but prayed before. He found them in crooked cobbled streets and sleepy squares brought awake by the sound of life—vegetable vendors, stray cats and dogs, bicyclists, beggars, priests and prostitutes; in old-fashioned gardens abloom; in time-patinated theatres animate with modern performances and in antique shops where nothing is more lively than the haggle between buyers and sellers. No other city conjured up its colorful past for him as vividly as the proud, mysterious Serenissima. He never wearied of putting her on the stage (in his many *Merchants of Venice*, *Othellos*, in *Tales of Hoffmann* and the revivals of Gozzi and Goldoni) or on the screen (in his second film, *Venetian Nights*).

Finally, she herself became his stage (in his outdoor production of *The Merchant of Venice* on Campo San Trovaso in 1934). In an interview for a documentary film I made for the centennial of his birth, Giorgio Strehler, one of today's most gifted directors, gives an eyewitness account:

> I remember the day—I was nine years old—when I took a walk with my mother through the streets of Venice. In an old square we came on a scene that fascinated me. I wasn't aware that it was theatre, but sensed that something dramatic was afoot. We stopped and watched. Suddenly I saw a small man spring violently away from the group of people he had been talking to—only much later would I learn it had been Max Reinhardt—and turn on a group nearby, throwing his arms wide, laughing and crying at the same time, a man possessed. I asked my mother who the man was. She said he was an excited gentleman. I asked why he was so excited. Because, she said, those other people are not doing what he tells them to do.

When I was nine years old, my impression of him was that of an enraptured spectator of the play Venice put on on her own. Together, we viewed it from luxurious box seats (the windows and balconies of the palazzi), were intoxicated by the incidental music (the calls of the gondolieri), strolled during intermission across the grandest of grand foyers (Piazza

San Marco), ate with gusto at the rich buffets (Ristorante Antico Pizzo and Taverna La Fenice) and wandered off—he to browse and I to groan through the "theatre's" fabulous storage house of props (Venice's warren of *antichità* snares). Then there were the times when he would redirect the entire play for me. Under this guidance I saw, as though it were happening under my own nose, the mighty Colleoni riding into battle, was given an audience with a formidable Doge, stole a look into the dreaded Council of Ten, witnessed Casanova's flight from the lead chambers and got an earful of the hottest news on the Rialto. Sometimes I received news—not through him, but about him—that was hotter than I dared to dwell on, its theme being some Venetian beauty he had seduced or been seduced by. It was never easy to determine to whom the honors went.

From all over the Continent, England and America the *cercle doré* of the twenties and thirties streamed toward its centripetal force, Reinhardt vacationing on the Lido: actors and actresses hoping for a part, playwrights hoping their latest oeuvre would be his next production, choreographers, set designers and musicians, all with their respective hopes for a Reinhardt connection, celebrity-collecting snobs, financiers happy to invest a bundle for the return of an uncertain invitation to Salzburg, society ladies happy to give their all unconditionally. This was the big world little Gottfried was precipitated into by parental competition. All were not complete strangers. Some, like Hugo von Hofmannsthal, I had met in our Berlin house before war was declared between my father and mother; then, I had been greeted with a handshake and suitably shipped off to play in my room. But now, as my father's "honored guest," I could stay on as long as I liked, with my eyes and ears wide open. Very soon I became expert at estimating at what depth under flattery and flirtation the bedrock of ambition lay. I also learned to know Hofmannsthal better and gained an insight into his complicated relationship with my father. More than any of the others, Hofmannsthal wanted to pin him down, to have Reinhardt direct this or that play of his, mostly *The Tower*, the play closest to his heart. (He had rewritten it after my father's suggestions and continued to re-write it for as long as my father provided helpful hints. It shattered him that, when it was finally finished, my father never produced it.) No one suffered more than he by Reinhardt's artful dodging and no one persisted more in exposing himself to it. Yet theirs was a mutual dependence. Hofmannsthal's thin dramatic blue blood needed transfusions from Reinhardt, the sanguine theatre man who had groped his way to the finer things in life, and Reinhardt needed the nourishment of the poet's unerring taste and supreme cultural authority. Ill at ease and cramped among the mock-glittering company bivouacked around Reinhardt's cabana, Hofmannsthal was forever in a dilemma. Remaining close to him was obviously what common sense demanded, yet his soul yearned for *his* poetic union with Venice. Hypernervously, he remained tangential, at the same time adapting himself to the chichi beach-pajama squad and fleeing it. I see him sitting, restless-eyed, in the motorboat crossing back and forth between the Excelsior and the Danieli, stroking his soigné mustache with slow regularity, first one side then the other, with each stroke posing and answering anew the question: to be or not to be with Reinhardt?

The Ferenc Molnár–Lili Darvas honeymoon was one of the pleasantest I ever spent. His wit was adorable, her sex appeal irresistible and the picnic-lunch atmosphere of their get-togethers on the beach in the noonday sun after the nights he chose to spend in his hotel in Mestre, the smoke-ugly industrial center on the mainland, while she, preferring sea air or the proximity of my father, chose to spend them in the Excelsior Palace, was filled with firecrackers of eccentric jealousy that sizzled dangerously, but never exploded. The honeymoon had two consequences: It clinched the separation of the newlyweds and it turned a Hungarian actress into a German star.

Naturally, I met Carl Vollmoeller (adaptor of Greek tragedies, writer of verse and plays and the first man to cross the Sahara Desert by automobile). Snickering references to him as Mr. Ubiquitous preceded his arrival and I was dying to get a look at this senior-playboy phenomenon who, according to the acid chitchat, was so adept at arriving in the right place at the right time that, one day, as he drove his car through the side of the Brandenburg Gate leading from Berlin's center to the West End for a party, he saw himself driving through the opposite side leading from the West End to his lavish apartments on Berlin's Pariser Platz for one of his exclusive after-dinner orgies. In his pied-à-terre on Paris's Place Vendôme and in his summer residence on the Canale Grande (Palazzo Vendramin, where Richard Wagner lived and died) there were always swarms of young female careerists dancing attendance on him, setting their hopes on his constant rendezvous and transactions with the powers-that-be in the theatre, films and the *haute volée*. Many climbs to fame (Marlene Dietrich's for one) gave proof that the young ladies did not dance for naught.

Among the other incandescent figures I met were Otto H. Kahn, marathon talker and mainstay of the Metropolitan Opera House, together with two of the Met's artistic buttresses (both Viennese), Artur Bodanzky, conductor of German repertoire, and scenic designer Josef Urban, who convulsed us daily with his roly-poly rendition of a ditty entitled "I'm the Best-Looking Man in Vienna."

And there was David Belasco's son-in-law, Morris Gest, with his black velour, wide-brimmed slouch hat, flowing four-in-hand tie and the most percussive chuzpah in show biz, assassinating the English, Russian and Yiddish languages, which, having done it with quick tonguework, he would desert for a lingo all his own.

Then, too, there were the old familiar faces in this new frame. For one, Francesco von Mendelssohn, Eleonora's handsome, clever, Aubrey Beardsleyish younger brother, who played the cello with the same virtuosity and self-detachment he played at life, now ensconced in lavender and vice in a *garçonnière*—unique in the world—above the big clock in Piazza San Marco's tower house, whose arch connects Venice's two historical components: its powerful grandeur (the Piazza) and its hustling mercantilism (the Merceria).

And, neither last nor least, Bukovinian world citizen Rudolf Kommer, ex-littérateur, suspected spy, half man, half coffeehouse, serving the restless, bored and lonely of high and café society.

I first fell victim to his knack for bringing mismatched personalities together in fatal union that summer when, waterlogged after hours of playing porpoise in the Adriatic, I went back to our cabana to dry out and he corraled me as I slunk past the people-clutter around my father and led me up to a blonde languishing in a deck chair interlocking my father's. Not until Kommer nudged me forward, whispering: "Pssst! She's Grace Moore, the great American diva" and, aloud: "Miss Moore, may I present this dripping-wet cavalier, our host's pride and joy," did she unfasten her smile from my father and fix it on me, cooing: "Oh, you darling boy." And Kommer was in business. "Gottfried," he said, "why don't you sing a real German tune for the beautiful American lady?" With my child's wisdom I sensed I was being had for some childish adult game, but it didn't bother me a bit, because it gave me the chance to sing—by request, at that—a song I was absolutely mad about (the German hit of the year): "Ausgerechnet Bananen." With the first bars barely out of my throat, the American diva howled. The people-clutter howled and beat the sand with their fists. Even without my theatrical blood I would have known I was a smash. What I didn't know was that my "howling" success with a "real German tune" was due to my fatherland's version of "Yes, We Have No Bananas."

The Atlantic. Hendaye. In Basque country on the French side of the Franco-Spanish border. Across it, in San Sebastián and Pamplona, my father and I watched our first bullfights and shuddered at the elegant cruelty of them. At sight of the great black animal run through by the matador's blade, sinking to the ground and, dying, raising his eyes in bewilderment to the blue heavens above, I would turn my head away and see that my father, in high excitement, was watching the frenzied audience.

I was now a jaded, seventeen-year-old big-city rake, according to my lights. According to my father's, I was a lily-white youth to whom he was in duty bound to explain the facts of life. He took a few deep breaths, cleared his throat and, staring concentratedly at a rowboat grounded on the sand, a seagull overhead, a boy wading—anything to escape looking at me—confessed boldly, the one and only intimate confidence he ever made me, that he had never touched a woman until he was twenty. Because sexual intercourse before this age was inappropriate. I wondered, purely academically, what quirk of logic had made him settle on this particular age. My momentary preoccupation lost me the link that carried him over to the subject of venereal disease, which he was now launched on. However, I assumed that whatever it was, it held the answers to why venereal disease after the age of twenty was appropriate. The sex seminar having come to an end, he could now, at last, look me in the eye and go on to the importance of keeping the body fit and healthy. Through diet. He paused, and by way of explanation, added that it must be a diet so pure and so free of excess as to make the use of toilet paper superfluous.

On Fire Island, I regretted the fantastic luck that, for seventy years, had kept him from a single day's serious illness. For had he not preserved his health so pertinaciously, had, instead, been exposed to the little illnesses usual in the course of a lifetime, the shock of suddenly discovering that his perfect body was imperfect might not have been so devastating. As it happened, the shock was more devastating to him than his illness.

Warnemünde, back to the Baltic. 1930. Another seaside holiday. But not *with*, but to *escape* Papa. At the side of my embittered mother. What she fled was Berlin's week-long jubilee celebrating Max Reinhardt's twenty-fifth year as head of the Deutsches Theater. She could not endure the ignominy of being ignored—after all, although they were separated, she still bore his name and was still very much an actress—while honors were being showered on the "Professor" in the same city where, as young actors in love, they had begun life together. Understanding her reasons for bitterness made it no less bitter for me to be deprived—because of her—of being together with my father in one of his most glorious moments. I did love my mother. I even liked her. The reason then that, instinctively, I always resisted her and felt greater warmth for my father—although I remained loyal to her to the end of her fight with him—was (heretical aside to Mr. Freud) probably due to a Jocasta complex. But this time my reaction toward her was one of uncomplex disapproval. I thought her selfish and egocentric for taking advantage of my loyalty and leaving me no alternative other than to accompany her in her self-imposed exile. I felt I was entitled to be with my father at what I sensed to be a high point in his life. Too soon afterward, it became clear to me that it had been the *highest* point.

When it had passed, bad years were to follow—for him, for Germany, indeed for the world. But in 1930, Germany could still afford to pay an entire week of homage to Max Reinhardt; the state of Prussia was lavish with decorations and scrolls; Berlin gave him the key to the city; academe (the universities of Kiel and Frankfurt) bestowed two honorary doctorates on him; the press heaped their most flattering phrases on him; the theatre—guilds, unions and management—gave him rousing testimonial banquets. Crowning all the honors was a festive performance of *Die Fledermaus* at the Deutsches Theater, which, for the occasion, had been made into a bower of flowers. I shook with pride on reading about all of this in the four-page local daily that was my only connection with the world outside my mother's suffering. My having to be absent from it made me want to absent myself from her and, daily, I swam as far away from the shore as my strength would carry me to postpone the moment of return to a family problem I had no way of coping with.

Swimming away from the shore of Fire Island, where over my shoulder I saw my father standing and waiting for my return, I looked into a troubled mirror of things past. Of what was ahead of me there was no reflection, no answer to what I wanted to know most: Had he still his childhood in his pocket?

THE DIARY

SEPTEMBER 26, 1943
(continued)

I swim back. A host of thoughts must have gone through Papa's mind too as he gazed after me out there in the surf. I don't know what they were, but one effect is apparent: The wall he built around himself shows signs of cracking. Perhaps it came to him that his self-isolation is approaching a point of no return. As if to demonstrate a new communicativeness, he rubs me dry with a beach towel. The air is now downright nippy and I start to shiver from head to toe. "R-run up-p a-and d-down a l-little!" he suggests. I do for a minute.

On the way home I talk to him earnestly. I ask him to consider my side. Surely he knows I'd do anything in my power to please him. But I'm not my own master. I'm in the Army. Tomorrow, for example, at 6 A.M., I've got to be at reveille again. And I wouldn't have a moment's peace leaving him alone here. Besides, I insist on a doctor having a look at him without delay, whether he thinks that's excessive of me or not. And how does he expect me to handle all the negotiations that are beginning now in New York without him? "If you've the slightest bit of affection for me you'll come back with me tonight!" Long pause. Heavy, heavy sighs. Capitulation.

"How was it?" Eleonora sunbeams through the door. "You two've been away forever! I hope you're hungry because I've cooked you the most beautiful dinner in the world." I hate to destroy her paradise—for his sake as well as hers. And my own. How good a place a home that, for once, is not a battleground. But it's not to be. He simply shrugs his shoulders and points to me, the villain of the piece. I refuse to be drawn into a debate: "Sorry, Eleonora, plans have changed. We're having dinner in New York."

Packing is probably the most elaborate of all his ceremonies. And the most time-consuming. A boon for Eleonora: She corners me. I explain about Dr. F. It doesn't go down well. She counters with a proposal of her own doctor; he'll come out here; he'll do anything we ask of him. Which is exactly what I fear. I've heard too much about the prescriptions he writes at her request. I decline firmly.

Darkness has set in by the time we, plus dog and carts top-heavy with suitcases, make our way to the landing pier. We walk in silence. A funeral cortège. Papa being the chief mourner—a gallant mourner burying his pain over my deception in making all the arrangements for departure behind his back. But he's resigned. There was a momentary flare-up of resistance when we left and he told the housekeeper he'd be back in a day or two. Mercifully, he turned away immediately and was spared her vulgar grin. The boatman takes our carts. Papa looks at me meaningfully, gives a derisive laugh: He's being manipulated!

The return crossing is in sad contrast to our arrival. Where there were joyous anticipation and justified hopes there are now depression and justified resignation. Even the weather has turned against us. It drizzles steadily and the dancing whitecaps have become hostile, choppy waves. Eleonora's seasick. She throws up over the side of the boat. Papa insists on holding her up. Not only that, he removes his overcoat—leaving him in nothing but a too thin suit—and wraps it about her shoulders. The drama's all mixed up: a marked man's sole concern is a lady's momentary indisposition.

In the car we remain silent. I'm dead tired and have to fight off sleep. The lights of the giant city twinkle merrily as if they want to mock me. Then dark, ominous shapes loom up on the road ahead—shapes that disappear as I approach them. But the moments come when I have to brake sharply to avoid colliding with decidedly tangible ones. Turn my head at a red light and see that both have fallen asleep. His head resting on her shoulder. His mouth open. I think: death mask. Think what would happen if I too fell asleep, at the wheel, and all three of us . . . Green. I step on the gas and speed on toward whatever fate is to be ours.

Gladstone Hotel. Can't believe it: We've made it. Late—it's ten, F.'s been waiting since six—but we've made it! Walking the gauntlet through the lobby proves less grueling than I dared hope. Without prearrangement—which would have been offensive—we three perform our respective parts deftly. I make a beeline for the desk to pick up our room keys and intercept a page with the mail. Eleonora sees to the baggage, then rejoins us. He strides straight to the elevator, looking neither right nor left, acknowledging greetings of the hotel personnel with friendly nods. Happily, no one addresses him. I'm close behind and, rude-seeming or not, ignore the boisterous "Hi's" from my army buddies in the bar who find it peculiar that I've suddenly become a teetotaler. Luckily, no one comes over to find out why.

A Feast That Cannot Be Compared

THERE WAS A LOT MORE to that bar than met the casual eye. In fact, to the entire hotel. In fact, to the entire square of sedate-seeming streets (Fifty-first to Fifty-fourth between Madison and Lexington avenues) containing those matrixes of *la vie extraordinaire*, the Hotel Ambassador and the Voisin Restaurant as well as the crummy rooming house, 59 East Fifty-third Street, my first hearth and home in America. I remember . . . I remember . . . but only with a great tug at sentimental recall. For revisited today, the face-lifted area is unrecognizable. Gone are the quaint red-brick schoolhouse and the convent serving its God serenely, while cocktail bars on either side served his abominable adversary; gone the rubescent steak joints and the delis that delivered with a smile any order over a dollar and a quarter; gone the neon signs (permanently flickered out over vital letters) spelling "Drugs ore" and "Shoe aker"; gone the little Greek florist who grandly stuck a carnation in your lapel gratis when you bought your lady a corsage. Today, unjowled of the quaint, the seedy, the colorful, funny and human and reconstructed out of glinting glass, solid bronze and marble, the area's features are nicely taut, have the confident, noncommittal look of modern technology at its most efficient. I have since taken it in carefully from all angles, from the Lever Brothers and Seagram buildings vaulting into the sky to the abstract sculptures swooning with significance on the sidewalks. And, as with most face lifts, I see both the improvement and the oncoming glacial age.

The Hotel Ambassador: On my father's first trip to America in 1923 he stayed there. It was permanent headquarters of Rudolf Kommer, his aide-de-camp and valued bridge to important New York connections that, minus the aide-de-camp's convoluted masterminding, would have been made by the famous visitor *instanter*. And it was semi-permanent headquarters for dancer-actress Tilly Losch—a Reinhardt discovery—object of Kommer's concentrated, faithful, theoretical passion. (Having taken Tilly under the lethal protection of his wing, he assisted her in pulling off two socially brilliant and disastrous marriages—the first of which he extricated her from with super-Kommer shrewdness, unleashing Mayfair's juiciest scandal about hetero- and homosexual corespondents. The second she got herself out of—Kommer having died in the interim—with a cunning no less dooming than her deceased protector's.)

It was at the Ambassador that my career in Hollywood was launched in 1933 by a half-clad, half-shaven Ernst Lubitsch opening his door to my timorous knock (by previous appointment I was presenting myself as a candidate for the job of his assistant on the picture *Design for Living*) and blurting out: "You're early. Well, come in. How's your father?" I said: "He is very well, thank you, under the circumstances." It was my first meeting with a Hollywood bigwig ruffled up by, as I was immediately told, the terrible crisis in Hollywood. I soon learned that Hollywood is always in a terrible crisis. Especially when you are applying for a job.

Voisin: One block distant from the Gladstone. The most disoriented toddler would have chosen as the obvious route between these two points the one that took him a few steps west to the corner of Park and Fifty-second and then right, straight to Voisin on the corner of Park and Fifty-third. Not so the Gladstone cognoscenti. Our custom was to duck through traffic across Fifty-second Street to the service entrance of an apartment building on the opposite side, where, through columns of overflowing garbage cans, we would descend to a subterranean labyrinth leading intricately around supporting beams to another flight of stairs which, when ascended, got us into Voisin via the kitchen—whereas the noncognoscenti had to enter through the front door. What appealed to my father about this clandestine route to his favorite New York restaurant was its similarity to the secret passageways of the Austrian emperors which led them to church, library, theatre, riding school or places of assignation in their sprawling "Burg" without the tedious need to leave its confines under the eyes of the common herd.

It was at Voisin that I first discovered how to succeed in opening a charge account at prices I could not afford. Two Austrians partnered it, tyrannized its English chef and bowed and scraped before its clientele of Park Avenue society, top show-business people and those Europeans who could afford its gilt-edged menu. On his first visit to America, Max Reinhardt could afford it easily. Nine years later, his son, on his first visit, could barely afford the adjacent Columbia Drugstore's bacon-and-tomato sandwiches on toast which were his three squares a day, except for the days he could indulge his pampered palate at Voisin as the guest of his friend Raimund, the younger son of Hugo von Hofmannsthal.

Raimund's own taste buds, whetted some years before by tantalizing glimpses of Papa Reinhardt's grand style, were being indulged by a lady who loved him above the fabulous Astor fortune (hers). Did Raimund wish for a castle at the side of an Austrian lake like Reinhardt's? It was his. Did Raimund wish for candlelit galas à la Reinhardt, with nobility waltzing through the night and a valet who traveled everywhere with him and his own chauffeur and carloads of custom-made silk shirts and bedrooms full of mistresses? Granted. Were there whims that came to him on the spur of a jaded moment? Perhaps a self-designed car with a Cadillac motor, Rolls-Royce chassis and body constructed by an old Viennese firm of carriage makers gathering dust since horse-drawn vehicles went out of fashion and reopened especially to accommodate the poet's son? His for the asking. Would it amuse him to have a table reserved week in week out at Voisin, where he would hold court? Presto! There it was. And, presto! on his arrival in New York, Max Reinhardt's nineteen-year-old son found himself beneficiary of a standing invitation from his friend Raimund to partake freely of the large-grained, gray Persian caviar, pâté de foie gras, iced Russian vodka and Krug '28—it had to be '28—that were the permanent fixtures of the von Hofmannsthal table. Raimund's courtiers, some on the distinguished fringe, most not, were all amiable enough. He did not really care. The only thing he cared about was that the conversation be diverting, the girls pretty, and that the one girl who made all this munificence possible should not disturb his table with her presence. Was it not repayment enough that he had made her his wife?

At one of my brownstone single-room-with-kitchen-privileges receptions Raimund's lazily roving eye settled on a lady. He asked me to invite her to dinner at Voisin, where, the plot ran, he would opportunely join us, I would opportunely receive a call that would, opportunely, cause me to rush off and leave the business of carrying on with the lady to Raimund. It all worked—up to the telephone call which arrived too soon and for the wrong conspirator. Raimund returned from the booth, kissed the lady's hand and flew off, a glowworm that had lit our table for a magic second—and left me stuck with the bill. One double brandy unpanicked me. Two made the bill a mere bagatelle. With the third I was a new man. Another man. I was Raimund. Better still, I was Raimund playing Papa. I asked for a large Havana cigar. The waiter lit it with slivers of cedarwood. Clearly, the ritual merited an impressive tip. Ten dollars? Make it twenty! They were added to the bill—along with my autograph, the first of an impressive collection I contributed to the cause of gastronomy.

The Gladstone: Its bellboys were hail-fellow-well-met with the guests. And all, bellboys and guests, were skunk drunk a good part of the time. Bruno, the bar's tender, spent the better part of his making book for the races at Belmont Park and Jamaica. The telephone operators, one for the day and one for the night, would alternately chirp, "Stop buzzin', hon, I got a busy board"—and ring off. Service was as could be expected. There were no complaints. Guests who registered at the Gladstone had chosen it deliberately, despite its seaminess, because it had evolved into a sort of unofficial annex to the deluxe Ambassador around the corner. What those in need of a deluxe address without the wherewithal to pay for it—the counts, marquises and princes in quest of American heiresses, the down-at-heel American socialites and the theatrical stars "temporarily between jobs"—knew was that some kind of prestige rubbed off on their hotel by way of its grand neighbor. For example, if asked where you were staying you could lightly toss off: "Oh, just around the corner from the Ambassador. At the Gladstone. Charming little place." Predictably, Raimund was drawn by its charm. Yet raffish, enchantingly unpredictable Raimund continued to live there after he had captured his American heiress, was receiving pocket money of thirty thousand dollars a year—apart from unlimited charge accounts in the swankiest shops on Fifth Avenue, Bond Street and the Rue St. Honoré—and, with her largesse, was in a position to buy the entire Hotel Ambassador. His heiress, when still Princess Obolensky, née Astor, shared a modest floor with him in the Gladstone without the slightest demur. Needless to say, Kommer's was again the Solomonic wisdom that unraveled Alice's gnarled marital strings and brought peace, prosperity and unhappiness to the parties involved: Alice, the erring wife; Serge, her injured husband; and Vincent, her half brother, outraged that a member of his socially prominent family should want to divorce a fourteen-carat Russian prince in order to marry an Austrian butterfly. Kommer's solution, unanimously accepted, was that Alice should be made free to marry Raimund, Serge should be compensated by Vincent for the loss of a fortune through some kind of suitably chic employment, and Vincent would have to soothe his snobbery through the employer-employee relationship, to—in effect, if not in fact—still keep his prince in the family. Kommer was satisfied. He had come through brilliantly for his old friends against their enemies. And for himself he had made new friends out of their enemies.

Fifty-nine East Fifty-third Street: Starting point of my daily treks to the Ambassador to receive a biting lecture from Kommer on conduct befitting an arrogant, late-rising immigrant in the land of golden opportunity and, thereafter, continuing on to the Gladstone for huddles with Raimund about his complicated love life and my uncomplicated need of an occasional loan. Kommer's stereotype prescription for my financial ills was a sensible marriage. To this end, he introduced me to the family of staunch Republican banker Eugene Meyer—during Herbert Hoover's administration chairman of the Federal Reserve Board—who purchased the then defunct Washington *Post* (presently thriving under his daughter, publisher Katherine) for the single purpose of harassing the newly elected Democratic President, Franklin Delano Roosevelt. Enjoyment of this monomania cost him a million dollars a year. Eugene Meyer had three other daughters: Florence, Elizabeth and Ruth. I grew extremely fond of Elizabeth, but, to compound Kommer's disapproval of my irresponsibility, my aversion to marriage—which her parents insisted on—was stronger. Raimund had also extended Alice's helping hand to me most generously in the past, when I needed backing for the dismal failure that sent me fleeing to America.

On my arrival, Kommer was waiting for me at the pier. I saw his eyes brighten as I came down the gangplank, a man overflowing with hearty, tumultuous welcome. Which, roughly translated, ran: "So. Here you are. I congratulate you. You did a good deed. You saved Raimund a fortune. Never again will he have the stupidity to invest money in the theatre. He's a lucky man. Very few people are fortunate enough to learn such an expensive lesson so cheaply. You must throw that hat away." (I was wearing my father's farewell present to me, my dead uncle Edmund's prized English bowler. Uncle Edmund's head was two sizes smaller than mine.)

The Gladstone, being neither first nor third class, nor even second, was the last hotel my father would have considered staying at, had I not moved in there in 1942—in flagrant disregard of army regulations. He needed only to learn of my transfer to the New York area to wire me of his imminent arrival. With valet. Without funds. The "without funds," it goes without saying, was not stated and required no confirmation through Western Union for me to know to the last absent penny what his financial straits were. His impulsive decision to abandon self-exile in theatrically arid California was as overdue as it was ill-timed. For many years, I had advocated this sensible step, years when he was younger and more resilient and when Broadway was more adult, had not yet retrogressed into the war climate's adolescent entertainment, and when that climate had not yet dried out my finances. He blithely ignored the fact that the Signal Corps Photographic Center was not Metro-Goldwyn-Mayer and that my soldier's pay was not a film maker's salary. Yet even had he given me the time to warn him before his arrival of how little he could expect of me now, I doubt that I would have had the heart to do it.

All I could do was to carry out the uneasy assignment of asking Herr Loeffler, the Gladstone's Austrian-born manager, whom I had been ducking for weeks because of my unpaid bill—to help me select a suite for Max Reinhardt and his valet. As my guests. Hastily, I arranged bank loans guaranteed by Ernst Lubitsch and Meyer Weisgal (the first, a former Reinhardt actor, the second, a former Reinhardt producer) that, for the time being, assured my father a subsistence minimum. But then, was I dealing with a man of minimums? The futility of such calculations was brought home to me the evening I returned from the post to welcome him. As I came through the revolving door, I saw the manager circling the lobby. He sidled up to me diffidently. The expression on his face was not hard to decipher. Together, we had picked out a suite which was within my "means" and the limit of Herr Loeffler's patience. Now, Herr Loeffler's excessive insistence that the Professor was extremely happy with his accommodations gave me the answer before I asked: "But not with the ones we chose?" He smiled apologetically and said: "The Professor was so decidedly not happy with the ones we chose I took it upon myself—I hope you don't mind—to move him into more . . . well, let's say, more appropriate quarters." God bless Herr Loeffler's paradoxically embarrassed soul. I was too touched to reproach him. Whereas the occupant of the more "appropriate" quarters had no qualms about extending my obligations. It was the sort of boring detail he always left to his staff. I was the staff.

That this precipitous trip, Max Reinhardt's final gamble, paid off with one of the biggest financial successes he had ever enjoyed in America—providing him with security for the balance of the months left him—can, in no small measure, be ascribed to his residence at "the last hotel he would have considered staying at" and to its bar, the powwow center of so many SCPC braves, some of whom, following in my renegade footsteps, had checked in at the hotel, and others who would drop in after retreat for a few regenerative hours before returning to the post. For all of them it was a combination recreation center, snack bar, office and the one sure place your girl friend knew where to catch up with you. It was where, at long, long last, we all could slake our parched throats on the first, fifth or fifteenth martini that had been our maddening mirage ever since reveille; it was where the last one-for-the-road left us so delivered of army gripes and so drunk that, on the morning after, we could not remember whether we had eaten dinner the night before, made love, typed out a short, short story for *The New Yorker*, begun collaboration on a play or sold a movie script. It was where my father knew he could track me down when he needed me and where in the motley company he found me came to meet—with intense curiosity and interest on his part—some of America's brightest young playwrights. Above all, it was in this sodden escape world that the first breath of life was given to Max Reinhardt's American *Fledermaus* (*Rosalinda*). In a staider environment and soberer condition, I would never have offered Sergeant John Meehan, Jr., a former Hollywood B writer, the lunatic opportunity of rewriting the entire libretto of *Rosalinda* with me in six days—a show which had already been in rehearsal under other direction for two weeks.

Ever since its première, *Die Fledermaus* (*The Bat*, as it was known in English-speaking countries) has continued to live on in concert halls and on records throughout a world forever in love with its score. In German-speaking countries its presentation in opera houses on New Year's Eve has long been a tradition. In operetta houses it is a year-round staple. As theatre, the Johann Strauss opus has hardly ever been taken seriously. With one exception: On June 8, 1928, under Max Reinhardt's direction, it took its place among what I would call his flawless productions. Confirmation that it was considered so not only by me is that, two years later, on the twenty-fifth anniversary of his management of the Deutsches Theater, it was selected over all his other directorial efforts as the jubilee production.

He, however, did not view it in so roseate a light when, most unenthusiastically, he first agreed to direct it. Apart from Offenbach, he had no love of operetta—not even the classical kind. Musical quality alone was not sufficient incentive for him to come to terms with absurd stories and characters without character. Only the exigencies of running a theatre forced him to take on this odd job. The Deutsches Theater needed a hit to fill the house during the difficult summer months. Light entertainment was the obvious answer—provided it was not too light for the prestigious house or too light to intrigue Reinhardt as director. Clearly, the solution lay somewhere in the musical field. Sensible front-office arguments persuaded my father to forgo his summertime entertainment of lying on hot, distant sands and envisioning projects unencumbered by sensible front-office arguments.

There ensued lively negotiations with thirty-one-year-old Erich Wolfgang Korngold, son of an influential Viennese music critic dreaded by every living composer other than the son he worshipped. Erich's child-prodigy compositions had attracted considerable notice. In his more mature works he showed marked dramatic talent and skill with voices, which he had begun employing more commercially and remuneratively in adaptations of Johann Strauss operettas.

Viennese-born Reinhardt had a deep aversion to the sham Vienna depicted by coy and sentimental operetta kitsch and even more to the manufactured folklore epitomized by the universally sobbed-out "Wien, Wien, nur Du allein . . ." But give him a seat at a rough wooden table in any little *Heurigen* in Grinzing and let him chuckle over a happy-macabre Viennese folk song plucked out on a melancholy zither, and he was in heaven. I remember him with broad winks and blinks and broader Viennese dialect, singing me a song—one I had never heard before, or have heard since—entitled "Gebts ma a Fuchzgerl, i hob ka kloans Goid" ("Can you spare me two bits, I'm out of small change"). For him that was an authentic Vienna. So was the satirist playwright Nestroy and the irreverent comedian Alexander Girardi (chorus girl to Girardi at rehearsal: "Hello there, partner!" Girardi back to her: "What do you mean partner? Am I a whore?") and the savage pixie Hans Moser (Reinhardt's Menelaus in his second *La Belle Hélène* and Jailer in his *Fledermaus*). On the other hand, he would not give a *Fuchzgerl* for the operetta giants, Franz Lehár, Emmerich Kálmán, Robert Stolz, and the full weight of their carefully calculated schmaltz. He would not even give the negligible time it would have taken to sit through a performance of Oscar Straus's cloying *Waltz Dream* or *Chocolate Soldier*, although he esteemed the musicianship of Straus, a friend ever since they had collaborated on their mutual cabaret debut. And he would not let wild horses drag him into a theatre to sit through the saccharine *Merry Widow* or *Madame Pompadour*, even when their star was Germany's operetta queen, Fritzi Massary, whose talent he found irresistible. Nor could his ardent admiration for her actor-husband, Max Pallenberg, move him to attend his performance in Gilbert and Sullivan's bloodlessly clever *Mikado*. Even *Der Rosenkavalier*, whose first performance he directed, made him uneasy. The elegant sophistication of its first act, the lyrical glamour of its second, followed by the broad buffoonery of its third, was a mixture too smooth for his comfort. While he considered Johann Strauss's music to be of Mozartian purity, the cute slapstick it served on the stage offended him. Even managerial considerations would not have overcome his resistance to it, had Korngold not played the score on the piano for him and shed such radiance on the familiar airs that he was bewitched by the interpreter.

Korngold, as an original composer, left him cold. As adaptor, he understood, almost anticipated, every modulation of his director's conceptual flow and translated them so sensitively into the music of the original composers it was for Reinhardt as though, through this empathic intermediary, he himself were working with a Strauss, an Offenbach, a Mendelssohn or a Rossini. So that, when lyrics and dialogue were given a fresh face, *Die Fledermaus* was ready to race across the stage.

And race it did, in every way—in the twenty-one days Reinhardt had allotted to its rehearsals with ill grace. That he pulled this off in his Deutsches Theater—one completely lacking any kind of musical apparatus, with a cast consisting, in the main, of legitimate actors who had to learn to dance and to carry a tune, at the very least to speak lines in precise and intricate rhythm and, conversely, with singers who had to adapt to a subtle comedy style totally foreign to them—was (at least then) a phenomenon.

In her book *Of Old Europe—People and Cities*, Helene von Nostitz, Hofmannsthal's friend and correspondent, writes:

> Rare and exquisite were the hours in which Max Reinhardt's spirit and skill permeated the stage completely. . . .
>
> The evening of *Clavigo* [one of Goethe's earlier plays] is clearly before my eyes. As the curtain parted, the room vibrated with the enormous, articulate silence that is summoned by the hand of a genius—like the quiet upbeat before a Beethoven symphony which must be neither too long nor too short. A tension, an indeterminate air of adventure filled the atmosphere in which Clavigo moved before us. One knew at once that he would be incapable of keeping the faith that life exacts if its last and deepest secret is to be fathomed and that he would fail when facing the crucial test. But how was it possible that this table, these chairs, this desk set communicated all this to us? It was not by accident that a book was placed where it was or a picture hung on the wall as it did. They were in tune with the waves emanating from Clavigo to them. . . . They told of his manner of meeting life, his cruel, thoughtless destructiveness, his enchanting nonchalance and grace, his infidelity to women.

And a few lines later:

> . . . in his *Merchant of Venice* a sublime song seemed to soar when the two lovers called: ". . . in such a night!" Beyond their bench between the two cypresses, under the glimmering stars, lay all the magic of a southern night with its infinite promise, its ringing air fraught with play and dance, its rays of deep blue in which the fireflies spin.

And still further on:

> . . . that is also how he broke the spell of the rather coarse comedy in [Aristophanes'] *Lysistrata* which had been the style of the evening when, suddenly, he sent hundreds of pairs of garlanded lovers streaming down the high staircase. On and on, into eternity it seemed, the long train descended

> and filled the world with love and beauty. This audacious vision which comes only to a genius lifted one to a plane where everything becomes light, effortless and where everything seems achievable and where, for a brief moment, musty curtains are flung aside.

Reinhardt's *Fledermaus,* dispatched with his left hand—though, if we hold with Helene von Nostitz, the left hand of a genius—displayed all the virtues she rhapsodized over in her memoirs: there was the same "quiet upbeat"—"neither too long nor too short"; the same "audacious vision"; "musty curtains" were "flung aside." What he had done was to remove the arbitrariness from the old shotgun marriage of sublime music and ridiculous plot, strip that plot of its triteness and the music of its anti-theatre hegemony, take the relic out of operetta's home for the aged and make a happy home for it in the living theatre.

His genius is confirmed by Yehudi Menuhin in his autobiography, *Unfinished Journey:*

> I have always adored the music of the Strausses, father and sons, of Vienna. I recall a 1929 production of *Die Fledermaus,* by Max Reinhardt in Berlin which left me walking on air for three days afterward. Like Kreisler's, the lilting melodies of the Strausses had ideal shapes in my mind; I knew exactly how I wanted them to be played, with a zest that whirled people off their feet.

Nothing connected with this project remained within the usual framework of a Reinhardt production. Not even the final dress rehearsal, which was normally just another hard-working night for everyone concerned. Except this time. This time, the public was formally invited and Frau Adele Strauss, the Waltz King's aged widow, had been imported from Vienna and been seated in the proscenium box where no eye would miss her applauding the refaceting of the most precious of her husband's crown jewels. Frau Adele was the unwitting cause for departure from established custom: Wise heads in the Deutsches Theater realized that Reinhardt's unorthodox concept of *Die Fledermaus,* with its emphasis on acting, necessitated modification of the score (melodies composed for voices had to be transferred to instruments, story changes called for musical additions from other Strauss works) and decided that, in view of a sharp-nosed press, it would be prudent to obtain the widow Strauss's public endorsement of the innovations.

There was not an empty seat in the house, with the exception of three reserved in the center of the first row directly behind the conductor's stand.

Scarcely had the house lights dimmed when the three shadowy figures of Max Reinhardt and his two sons, crouching low, slipped in. It was the first time he had sat in the audience to watch a public performance of his own. He had directed a lark and now, for once, unhaunted by opening-night bugbears, was permitting himself the luxury of laughing about it with his boys. Despite the stealthy entrance, Berliners had recognized their darling and, rising to their feet, swamped him in a tidal wave of applause. Bursting with pride, I turned to the hero. But, eyes glued to the curtain in front of him, the hero gave no sign that he was aware of his triumph. I knew better. Without immodesty, he was completely aware that he was a hero and, with a show of modesty, he was enjoying it.

Cheering and applause finally subsided, but soon were taken up again as a pasty-faced, round-shouldered, jelly-bellied young man wheezing under the weight of an old man's fat stepped up to the conductor's stand in the pit. It was Berlin's—and my—first view of Erich Wolfgang Korngold. The focus of his walleyes, I noted, as he bowed deeply, was concentrated less on the welcoming crowd than on the figure directly facing him. And I saw my father smiling encouragement back at him and applauding (taboo of all theatrical taboos before an opening!). With this boost, Korngold pinwheeled toward the proscenium box and collapsed reverently before Frau Strauss; then, without a beat, sprang up again and connected his pudgy paw to a slim baton. Extending both arms to the orchestra, he gestured that he was drowning and begging for help.

It puzzled me to see my father, to whom human ugliness was an unforgivable sin, glowing with pleasure at the sight of this flailing bulk, the more so since he had always been opposed to the spotlighted presence of a conductor distracting from the performance. That this musical seal must distract from the performance was obvious to me. Until he flapped his fins for the overture to begin and, with the first whiplash of chords and cascading strings, I and everyone else in the audience were spellbound. I had heard the piece countless times before, performed by greater virtuosos, but never before with such drama, gaiety, elegance and mischievousness. It was then that the first magic transformation of the evening took place. Before my eyes, Korngold grew beautiful. (Pablo Casals and Bronislaw Hubermann—though fatless—were the only other ugly musicians I have seen similarly transformed.)

My father adored transformations. One quick glance at him was enough for me to detect how deeply he had fallen in love. I had a sneaking suspicion—I had seen it happen before—that the object of his love would not be held down to the role of subterranean and subordinate orchestra leader.

Yet neither would he be allowed to play the star conductor overshadowing the action onstage. He was cast as a performer among performers (just as composer-pianist Mischa Spoliansky had been in Reinhardt's production of Somerset Maugham's *Too Many Husbands*).

Korngold did not conduct with his stick. That is to say, once in the grip of his sausage fingers, it was lost to sight. Nor with his wrist, which had gone the way of all his flesh. Korngold rowed. Heroically. And the stream of rhythm on which he launched his orchestra flowed freely, melodies rippled with laughter and surged with passion, while harmonies were pure and deep as an alpine lake. Not one rubato, crescendo or diminuendo was calculated or "*voulu.*" In obedience to some inner law of his, they were simply right and unassailable. (When I did *La Belle Hélène* with him on Broadway fifteen years later, Arturo Toscanini sat in the audience at least once a week, hypnotized by Korngold, his counterpole. Their only common denominator was the primary musicianship with which the cunning Viennese compensated for his slapdash compromises and the formidable Italian for his metronomic precision and inhuman integrity.)

The next transformation, the opening scene, was no less breathtaking. In it, Max Reinhardt's "spirit and skill permeated the stage" when, with nothing more than a bit of pantomime, he conjured up an enlightening preface to a score and libretto that, formerly, had always plunged an audience willy-nilly into the bewildering intrigues of a silly, low-comedy plot. The pattern followed that of all his "perfect performances" wherein a single, symbolic scene of his invention—as a rule, an introductory one (as in *Clavigo*)—opened a vista revealing a play in its entirety and quintessence: The curtain rose on a wine garden arbored by chestnut trees in bloom; dusk's lavender light outlined the solitary figure of a dandy in a flowing cape (Falke, the deus ex machina of the piece), seated at a rustic table, puffing on a cigarette in a long holder; its exaggerated length established him as a fop and his rascally smirk, as he sipped his glass of wine, established that all kinds of high jinks were in the offing; lanterns lit up, threw their light on leaves fluttering to the strains of a Viennese waltz that drifted in from nowhere and everywhere; music was in the air; Falke breathed it in with relish; and, downing the last drop in his glass, rose, tossed a coin on the table—a cavalier's tip judging by its ring—and started swaying to the beat; he glided a few steps left, a few right, then, with feet scarcely touching the ground, sailed with billowing cape in ever widening circles to the outermost reaches of the stage. . . . Who, what was this aerial figure? A rake on the town? A bat in the night? His answer, as with a whoosh he flew off scene, was that he was both. Off scene? Not really.

For the stage, infected by his devil-may-care mood, had shaken off its moorings and was revolving toward him. Only now did the play, gestated under Falke's cape—or the bat's wings—come to life as a prank in three-quarter time.

Operetta texts—*Die Fledermaus* not excepted—are synthetic fabrications. Their roles are stereotyped and their actions tend to bog down in structural impasses. This *Fledermaus*, however, was an exception. Where, in the past, the old-hat tenor (Alfred) gargled his heart out to his one true love, in this *Fledermaus* the true-to-life tenor gargled with antiseptics. His one true love was his voice. In the middle of an impassioned scene (with a lady) he soared to a high C—breathing correctly from the diaphragm—suddenly broke off, cleared his throat and, his inamorata a forgotten rag doll in his arms, tested his vocal cords with a string of self-critical *mi mi mi*'s. The other tenor (Eisenstein) shed his hackneyed philandering-husband character for that of a mercurial egotist, a libertine cuckold straight out of Molière or Goldini. Further, he was no tenor. He was an actor (Hermann Thimig). But his parlando was so racy and his cadence so meticulous that only the most humorless purist quarrelled with this amendment of the original. In a duet, Eisenstein's wife (Rosalinde) was helped to undress at bedtime by her maid (Adele). The layers of frothy petticoats peeled off one by one with undulations and wicked coloratura giggles provided erotic spice. And the part of Prince Orlowsky, a *Hosenrolle* (German theatrical term for a female in pants playing a male), was, sacrilegiously, played by a man (Oscar Karlweiss) wearing the pants.

The second act had always opened with Orlowsky's guests arriving—coyly fluttering fans and whispering stage nothings—in the papier-mâché grand ballroom of his palace and had gained momentum with the respective entrances of chorus, ballet and protagonists—singly or ensemble—singing their golden song-o, culminating in the grand-slam finale. Reinhardt made Orlowsky's guests arrive plausibly in a foyer where they divested themselves of cloaks and wraps. Instead of the usual introductory choral blah, the ladies delivered, in vitriolic, versified recitative, a rundown of the other ladies present, while the gentlemen, each in turn, scanned their opinions about the weather, the stock market and sex. Each rendition was punctuated by a biting *um ta ta, um ta ta* crash-smashed out on the spinet at Korngold's side. (Of these crash-smashing hands the greatest pianist of his time, Artur Schnabel, once said to me: "With those two fat puddings of his Erich Korngold plays the piano better than all the stiletto-fingered virtuosos I have ever heard.")

Korngold's *um ta ta* exploded into the grand waltz, and the stage, captured by the atmospheric spell, began to spin once again. The couples in the foyer danced through open doors into a Biedermeier-period ballroom come alive—alive to the last glittering crystal on its chandeliers—and were swept up into a fête in full swing. Not a fête hectically charged with ballet numbers. There were no numbers, no "big" entrances or exits. Dancers, singers, extras and principals blended into a guzzling, nuzzling, stamping, glee-squealing tapestry which, by sorcery, was whisked away from sight. The stage was suddenly daringly bare. Absent of all action save for a tryst-ing couple who quickly vanished among tables laden with food and drink that materialized out of thin air for the banqueters roistering around them. Then, with the same sleight of hand, the banqueters vanished behind a cluster of eurythmic bodies, slowly, tentatively, opening like an enormous morning glory folding back its petals at the touch of dew. Their dew was champagne. Bending backward to the ground, they drank it to the last drop. Lyricism triumphant. Until the next moment when the merrymakers, loosed once more, surged forward, galvanizing the elegiac stillness into an abandoned cancan. The curtain descended on a jubilant polyphony. Words danced. Rhythm spoke. Light sang. The stage was life. It was theatre absolute.

One could imagine Goethe journeying all the way from eighteenth-century Weimar for this occasion. For he wrote:

> There is poetry, there is painting, there is song and music. There is the art of the actors and what not. When half these arts and the attractions of youth and beauty come together in one single evening, and that on an important level, they create a feast that cannot be compared with any other.

I was present at this feast and it left me with more than a pleasurable memory. It made me better understand why my father was what he was. It is illusory to believe—as anyone will agree who has watched painters at their easels or has sat in on an orchestra rehearsal or listened to story con-ferences between writers—that peripheral observation of creativeness in action can supply the key to what it is that ignites it. The truth of the matter is that one can get no closer to talent's impetus than a spectator can to the heart of an erupting volcano. Still, in an artist's life there are mo-ments of childlike self-absorption in which, whether it is through despair or elation, he unwittingly reveals some part of his inner mechanism. This dress rehearsal of *Die Fledermaus* was one of these moments. My father's exultance in having pulled off so daring a tour de force, in having mastered his craft so brilliantly with a trivial, unwanted project, was unrestrained and—to me—completely revelatory.

No one, certainly not my father, dreamed of digging up this 1928 Berlin treasure for a 1942 New York exhibition. In Berlin, *Die Fledermaus* had been a standing-room-only record breaker. When exported, it met with rather less enthusiasm. Vienna, overpossessive of its Johann Strauss, resented the liberties Reinhardt took with him. Paris, emotionally uninvolved, was indifferent. On the tenth of November 1933, my father wrote to me in Hollywood:

> . . . I am directing the *Fledermaus* here in Paris at the Théâtre Pigalle with French actors, singers and dancers. There are few Germans with me and, anyway, most of these are Austrians, Czechs, and Jews about whom so much fuss is being made in the world today. . . . I doubt that the spoiled and totally self-absorbed Parisians (there are practically no tourists here these days) will find this dish with Austrian wine palatable and that the undercurrents working against emigrants here—as they are more or less everywhere else in the world today—will let us reach port safe and sound.

His fears were not altogether exaggerated. On "reaching port" in Paris, the reception accorded him was reserved. Whereas the reception he met in Italy (in 1934) could not have been more unreserved. Milan was the scene of a theatre scandal rare in his experience. On opening night, the storm clouds of audience antipathy, gathering since Act I, burst indignantly in Act III, when Frosch, the sozzled Imperial Jailer, kept insisting—the audience had long resigned itself to the futility of the effort—on hanging his kepi on a hook painted on a wall of the set. It is a gag that Central European audiences never fail to fall out of their seats laughing over and, the more it is repeated, the more they are convulsed. In Milan, convulsions were induced by nausea. The shouts of "*Basta!*"—augmented each time Frosch fumbled for the painted hook and his kepi fell "bafflingly" to the floor—shook the theatre to its foundation. To save it from collapse, the curtain was rung down before the third act was over.

But even had these frustrations not convinced my father that "this dish with Austrian wine" did not travel well, his awareness of its failures in America under the auspices of other producers and directors (there had been twelve of them on Broadway, running the gamut from Shubert corn to sophisticated Theatre Guild flops d'estime) would have discouraged him from wanting to revive it there in 1942—until one morning, by a quirk of the fate he so firmly believed man's fortune hangs by, he read a run-of-the-mill item in *The New York Times*'s theatrical section, announcing that the New Opera Company (founded and sponsored by culture-bent society ladies to foster young American singing talent) was going into rehearsal with *Rosalinda,* the thirteenth American adaptation of Johann Strauss's *Fledermaus,* with Erich Wolfgang Korngold as musical director, with Oscar Karlweiss in the part of Prince Orlowsky and with the directorial reins in the hands of a Felix Brentano.

It was one thing for him to reject a fusty nineteenth-century museum piece as a vehicle for his comeback on sophisticated Broadway, but quite another to be rejected by a Broadway producer putting it on with his former key collaborators. It was a message not difficult to decipher for a man approaching his seventieth year. The hardheaded manager of the New Opera Company (Hungarian-American Yolanda Merö Irion, a onetime concert pianist) had hit on a way to put on a Reinhardt production without Reinhardt or, more to the point, without his "dizzying directorial fees and royalties," his "extravagance" and the burden his exacting artistic standards would impose on this amateur company.

Felix Brentano came into the world in Austria as Felix Weissberger, a bouncing Jewish male baby. As a Jewish male adult in Nazi-threatened Europe he trembled for his life. He was able to escape to America through the grace of his employer, Max Reinhardt, who sent him on ahead to lay the groundwork for the 1934 production of *A Midsummer Night's Dream* in San Francisco, Berkeley, and Los Angeles. It was the last time Weissberger served Reinhardt as assistant. The impulse to strike out on his own had gripped him and somewhere along the line he decided to change his name. No quarrel with that. After all, his model had done the same. And nothing is more understandable than a man's desire to blot out all association with his past when starting fresh in a new country. However, Weissberger had blotted out nothing but his name. With remarkable sharpness he retained and stored away for future reference total recollection of Reinhardt at work. To bolster his extraordinary memory he had in his possession a complete prompt-book library of every Reinhardt production on which he had assisted. *Die Fledermaus* was one of them. It was a treasure trove at a bargain price for Mrs. Irion.

Had Weissberger-Brentano been pressed for a defense of his theft, poverty would have been a legitimate one. Korngold, on the other hand, who equally owed his escape from Hitler to Max Reinhardt—in the eleventh hour, Warner Brothers had sent for him, at Reinhardt's request, to do the score of his film version of *A Midsummer Night's Dream*—was affluent. The only excuse he could manufacture was that the New Opera Company was not using the copyrighted (Berlin) Reinhardt-Korngold version of *Die*

Fledermaus and that, therefore, his participation was simply that of Johann Strauss interpreter. Karlweiss did not owe his emigration to Reinhardt and so had no need to defend himself. His only need was a job.

There things stood. Until the day that Korngold arrived in New York and watched a rehearsal of *Rosalinda.* Its plagiarism of the Reinhardt-Korngold *Fledermaus* was too blatant to be tolerated. In an ultimatum to the New Opera Company he insisted that either they buy the rights to the Reinhardt-Korngold *Fledermaus,* engage Reinhardt and demote the counterfeit director or he would have nothing further to do with the project. Mrs. Irion at this point could not afford to let Korngold go. Instead, she sent him to my father with an offer that brought both balm to his wounded pride and the promise of a sizable directorial fee plus a generous percentage of the gross. But much more important, it brought the smell of the professional stage back to him. He had not breathed it in four years.

It was perhaps cruel to dissuade him from it. Yet I felt I had to. The show had been in rehearsal for a fortnight, with the opening scheduled in three weeks. What, in that skimpy interval, could Max Reinhardt do to make the show his? And even if he could make it his, was it wise? A categorical answer came from his partners (in a newly born production company), Norman Bel Geddes, Eddie Dowling and Richard Myers. It was NO. Together, they had just begun to explore a mine of bright, marvelous projects. Were the senior partner to precede their collective effort by directing an old fossil, it would seem that he wanted to look backward instead of forward. He understood their point of view full well. But that didn't alter his own. Or his needs. Of the four, he was the only one without outside income. He was in a dilemma. Should he lose his partners or *Rosalinda?* The decision was dropped in my lap. He sent me a note:

> I looked at a rehearsal this afternoon. Too bad you weren't there. Vocally it's excellent. . . . With Karlweiss, Balanchine's choreography and Korngold at the piano it could be something one needn't be ashamed of at all. . . . Of course at best it would always be an *opera performance,* never a Broadway show. . . . I would cut the text, which is very weak anyway, as much as possible and I would put the emphasis on music, dancing, singing and a light playing style. Weissberger has the phenomenal exactitude of a phonograph record. His own inventions, which are rare, are as mindless as a phonograph record that is stuck and keeps repeating itself over and over. . . . He is the most efficient and the most stupid assistant director I have ever had. . . . I agree with you of course: I cannot afford an out-and-out failure. . . . It is

important that you look at a rehearsal as soon as possible and let me know your decision. . . . It is late (in the morning). Love,

Papa

The next day I attended a rehearsal. It was a perfect demonstration of "out-and-out failure." The text was not "weak," it was weak-minded and, in my opinion, whatever the wonders my father might perform in remodeling it, they would never be sufficient to entertain audiences that had cut their eye-teeth on slick musicals. At its very best, this "opera performance" could only be offered as a limited engagement. The New Opera Company, Korngold and Balanchine could afford the luxury of one. Indeed, they were not looking for anything more. Max Reinhardt could not. Any production of his on Broadway would, automatically, be considered a Broadway show—no matter what *he* chose to call it. And a limited engagement, in his case, would be tantamount to a flop.

This, I knew, was not the verdict he wanted to hear from me. I tempered it by telling him that, if he was bent on doing *Rosalinda,* he could only do it by not alienating Bel Geddes, Dowling and Myers. One way of getting around this would be by not taking official credit as director. This would also lessen his responsibility for the show vis-à-vis the critics. (Eventually, this compromise was agreed on, the credit reading: "The entire production under the supervision of Max Reinhardt.") In addition, the libretto must be rewritten from scratch. He had brightened perceptibly at the first half of my strategy. The second left him stunned. He protested that there was no time. Besides, who would undertake to do the job? If we had no other choice, I said, I would find a collaborator at the post. We could do it in a week. There would be no problem.

But there was one: All Hungarian hell broke loose in a lava flow of *nems* (nos) when my father halfheartedly, and I aggressively, apprised Mrs. Irion of our conditions. The muscles twitching in her face were our first warning of volcanic activity. Then came the loud rumble: What? Should she suspend rehearsals for a week? Postpone the opening? Also it would not be a week! It was a craziness to believe it would be. Never would she agree to such a craziness. Never! *Nem nem nem nem nem nem* . . .

I smiled—my years of exposure to executive bluster in Hollywood had not been for naught—and said yes yes yes yes, it would be a week. And it would not be necessary to suspend rehearsals or postpone the opening. The schedule I had in mind was two days in which to rewrite and deliver the dialogue for the first act—musical scenes, unaffected by it, could be restaged during that time. Then two days more for the second act. And another two for the third.

That night, in another under-the-door communication, my father expressed his misgivings about Mrs. Irion's grudging surrender:

> Gottfried, I beg you to make sure that our six-day commitment is kept punctiliously. The time for rehearsals and learning lines is so terribly short I break out in a cold sweat just thinking about it. . . . We have taken on a formidable responsibility. At this late date it will not be easy to get these amateurs [his reference was to the singers] launched on a completely new dialogue, especially as they have to sing and dance at the same time. Every one of their movements will have to be gone over from the beginning. Next week will be a horrible ordeal—for you and your collaborator as well.

"You and your collaborator" faced the "horrible ordeal" behind a barricade of scotch and soda and, on the morning of the sixth day, they handed over the last of their booze-immortal lines. The cast drank them in like mother's milk. Only Karlweiss, whose entire store of English consisted of roughly five phrases, shrank away in distrust. The old lines which he had learned by rote had become reassuring friends in a word wilderness and the suggestion that he abandon them, struggle for new friends in a barbarous language, terrified him. Weissberger-Brentano's recalcitrance was to be expected. Having finally become a director in his own right, it had cost his pride no pain to use Reinhardt's ideas. But displaced by Reinhardt—albeit unofficially—those ideas lost their appeal for him. He struck back by sabotaging Reinhardt at every turn. Musically, this was annoying, but of no great consequence, as Korngold and Balanchine jumped into the breach whenever Brentano became too disruptive. Textually, however—English being far from Reinhardt's forte—an easier target was provided the saboteur. My father defended it by recruiting his American soldier son as his night-shift dialogue director.

At 4:30 A.M. on the day of the opening, Meehan and I were somnolently grinding out last-minute changes my father had suggested when the telephone rang. At the other end came his voice: "Herr Karlweiss is here with me. He has a few questions I think you can answer better than I. Can he come down?" "Papa," I groaned, "not now! Please!" "Please be tactful," he whispered, "he's very nervous." Then, louder: "He would like to have a few words with you." "I'm sorry, Papa, this is no time for comedians." He coughed, dropped his voice again and said: "We will have no comedian if you don't convince him. He refuses to speak the new lines. I cannot budge him." Then, again louder: "So I may tell Herr Karlweiss you're waiting for him?" Before I could remonstrate, the line went dead. I wished it had been Karlweiss.

A few ugly wishes later, Karlweiss shot into my room, flushed and panting. He did not even hear my invitation to sit down. He was too agitated to do anything but pace the floor while mumbling over and over: "Hitler I have to thank for this!" I half filled a glass of scotch and handed it to him. He drained it and handed it back to me, moaning: "Hitler I have to thank for this!" With the same refrain he drained the refill I put in his hand.

By my watch it was five-thirty. John and I had to be at the post by six. I dripped the last drop of the bottle into Karlweiss's outstretched glass and said: "Stay as long as you like, Oscar. But we've got to go now. We too've got Hitler to thank for something!" "Hitler . . ." he hiccuped. "You're goddamn right!" Meehan exploded. Then, with all his pure Irish-American hatred of kookie Continentals, he spat out, as he slammed the door behind us: "You got Hitler to thank for this and I got you to thank for Hitler!"

Whatever Hitler's iniquity to millions, to Oscar Karlweiss he came through as benefactor. Before the première had ended, he was a star. Having persisted in the old lines at the beginning and being the only performer not to get a ripple, he had switched over to the new ones in midstream. With howls of laughter greeting each delivery. Another star incubated that night was Shelley Winters. And many of the "amateurs" Reinhardt had succeeded in making into professionals. And many of the professionals he had succeeded in making less hackneyed. Helene von Nostitz would not have called *Rosalinda* a "pure" or "perfect" performance. No one did. There was only a faint echo of it all. But the echo was loud enough to make *Rosalinda* a hit. The hit my father needed. It was a triumphant paradox: the "Broadway show" he was convinced had not been in the cards turned up as his trump. Max Reinhardt, the "dreamer," had demonstrated he possessed the one quality popular opinion did not credit him with: pragmatic craftsmanship. He had rescued a show through a last-resort hypo usually applied by producers to their sick out-of-town tryouts—without ever taking it out of town. The nonprofit New Opera Company became a profit-making Broadway producer.

We listened to the first hallelujahs on the midnight radio broadcast between supper courses at "21." Final confirmation that we were in reached me at five o'clock the following morning in the kitchen of SCPC's mess hall, where I had begun KP duty (pots and pans). With hands prickled full of steel wool—the only instrument effective against the Cream of Wheat blobs clinging to the insides of our man-high kettles—I snatched up the *New York Times, Herald Tribune, Daily News, Daily Mirror* and *Brooklyn Eagle* that had been smuggled to me by a comrade. One after another, I spread them out on the draining board, turning the pages to the theatrical section, lingering over every word of the notices. How long the mess sergeant stood watching I do not know. I only became aware of him when, in mute rage, he scooped up the newspapers in his simian arms and stuffed them into the baker's oven. Inspired by this auto-da-fé, he regained whatever power of human speech was his: "Sonofabitch sonofabitch waddya think this is the public liberry? Now you get your readin' ass up there!" He shoved me forward and pointed to the copper-tin hood over the stove: "And start polishin' real shiny!" Somehow I shinnied up the sloping side. I was no acrobat. I was an author. At that, only one of the authors of an operetta and, although it ran for 521 performances, not counting the countrywide tour that followed thereafter, in no way a challenge to the glory of *Cat on a Hot Tin Roof*. But I defy anybody to deny that I was the first and last author to celebrate his reviews on a hot tin roof.

Two weeks after our run-in, for reasons I can claim no credit for, our mess sergeant hanged himself in the SCPC latrine. It was an even bigger hit than *Rosalinda* in the Gladstone bar.

There's no one in the elevator except the operator. I step out on my floor: "Be right up." Escape before he can detain me. All at once I'm infinitely grateful to Eleonora for being there; for taking him upstairs; for staying at his side and making it possible for me to do the things I have to do now. And all at once I'm convinced it's no accident that people are "accidentally" there when one needs them.

My first stop: not my own room, but Silvia's [since 1944 my wife], *two doors away from mine. The sympathy she pours out is more for me than for my father, whose age in her opinion—unlike mine—makes such a tragedy natural. Am fighting with all my being precisely this kind of fatalism. Would wish for encouragement in my rebellion against fate. But maybe she senses how hopeless this rebellion is and wants to spare me a cruel disappointment. Tries to console me. I don't want consolation. I want to weep and to gather fresh hope. She can't weep with me and my account must have left little leeway for hope. Besides, Eleonora isn't too well disposed toward her—Eleonora isn't particularly well disposed toward girl friends of her male friends—so this aspect of the drama leaves Silvia cold. Understandably. But the side issues, and I see as many closing in on me as there are women involved, don't preoccupy me at the moment.*

Go to my room to weep unashamedly, to gather fresh hope, but mostly to telephone. Dr. F. is a block of ice. Apologize profusely for tardiness of my call. Suggest with all the tact I can muster he arrive in about one hour, as, hopefully, this would give me the necessary time to prepare my father for a doctor's visit. Ice Block informs me that he puts up with such treatment only for Lili Darvas's sake.

Heavy-hearted, I go upstairs to Papa. Eleonora opens the door, a towel tied around her as an apron. She has prepared dinner for him. He sits stiffly in a wooden-backed chair, his face turned to the door, to me, a defendant waiting for the verdict. Eleonora puts on her hat and coat: "Be back in about half an hour. Just getting my things." Is she moving in? Apparently. Naturally! A glance at him shows me that he finds it as natural as she does. He offers me a cigar and takes one himself. Is he permitted to smoke? Even though these cigars are fortunately—unfortunately—no longer the expensive—and heavy—Havanas he used to smoke. We puff away, don't talk. My eyes meet his, and there it is again: that searching, almost stealthy look as if he wants to know from me what I want to know from him—whether he knows. . . .

Announce doctor's visit, trying to sound casual. He changes color, jumps up, starts walking up and down, terribly distraught. Stops in front of me. Not a trace of tenderness in his eyes. I'm his enemy. But all the implements of speech now fail him. Not a syllable comes out. His anger is strangled. A peremptory gesture cuts off any attempt to placate him. Then he about-faces, walks into his bedroom, slams the door. I'm alone, paralyzed, not knowing what to do next. How long I sit there I don't know. Suddenly he's back. Still storming. Threatening. But attempting to hold himself in check: "Wh-who i-is th-this d-doctor?" I tell him. He shakes his head. "What is it, Papa? Do you know him?" Instead of answering he demands to know where I got him. "He's Darvas's doctor. If she has him he must be good." Again he shakes his head, more emphatically. Then comes the ukase: "N-not him! Under n-n-no c-circumstances!" I try reasoning with him. But it's impossible to reach him. Now my nerves go. I'm more severe than I mean to be: "If you don't know him what in God's name have you got against him?" Amazingly, fluency returns to him. He snaps at me: "That man gossips." Then he drops into a chair and buries his face in his hands.

The phone rings. F. is in the lobby. I say I'll be right down. "Papa, I've another thought. Would you see Eleonora's doctor? I don't want to torture you, but you simply have to let some doctor take a look at you!" He looks at me imploringly, shrugs his shoulders in a gesture of hopeless submission. I suppress my feelings, promise to send Dr. F. away. It isn't an easy promise to keep. Less easy the decision to leave him alone. Anyway, it all makes no sense, for if F. is the gossip Papa claims he is, the affront which I'm about to deal him will only incite him to spread nasty rumors. And what does Papa really mean by "gossip"? About what? Not about being bitten by a dog! So he does know after all?

Doctors are in a way like conductors. A doctor of genius has his musical counterpart—although these are far fewer than is generally assumed—just as bad doctors and run-of-the-mill doctors—the last by far in the majority—have theirs. In both vocations integrity, charlatanry and primadonna-ism exist in varying degrees. Both have their humble servants as well as their exhibitionists, their job-dedicated craftsmen and their reckless take-a-chancers. Some egos demand no less nursing than an orchestra or a patient.

When a complicated operation is performed successfully or a daring diagnosis confirmed, it evokes the same glow of vanity in some doctors as a brilliantly executed crescendo, provocative tempi and ovations by the public do in the breast of some maestros. Since everything in their circumscribed worlds proceeds only at their command, they see themselves the center of a vast universe. But should they err or miss, the temptation is to place the blame elsewhere—on colleagues or assistants: "the audience flopped," the patient, the uncooperative wretch, died. Both the staff of Aesculapius and the baton seem to instill in the men who wield them an illusion of magic power. Both serve as scepters of arrogance. Papa, who venerates the fanatical integrity and merciless perseverance of a Toscanini, although these characteristics are totally alien to his own nature—both admire each other sincerely, but I doubt they could ever collaborate; why have they never done so in Salzburg?—who distrusts Bruno Walter's priest-like solemnity and serene nobility and to whom the hazy profundity of a Furtwängler is perhaps more admirable, but even more suspect, who has always disdained to play a part in life and who is even less inclined to watch others do it, has up to now, through a magnificent constitution, been spared the stellar performances of healing artists. Something tells me that this is a thing of the past and that from now on he'll be exposed to everything he abhors in his own profession.

Dr. F.'s concert is over before he has a chance to put on his big act. I size him up as a run-of-the-mill doctor compensating for his lack of innate authority and compassion with hypersensitive conceit. I try to put him off till tomorrow—when, I hope, Darvas can straighten things out—saying my father retired for the night, physically and emotionally so low that it would have been cruel to subject him to the ordeal of an examination. My arguments are roughly brushed aside. At this moment all that matters to F. is his injured ego—the one who's really injured is ignored. F. charges me with being irresponsible. How dare I deprive a man in this condition of a doctor's care! He probably guesses that I'm stalling. I remind him that it was he who warned me against exciting or fatiguing the patient. Discussion hopeless. He walks off in a huff. As a parting shot he advises me to get "some other doctor." I'm glad he's made this shabby exit. Papa never would have accepted the antics of this mediocrity.

Telephone Eleonora from lobby. I couldn't have made her a greater gift than by asking her to call her doctor. I feel her joy waves over the phone: Now she has all the reins in her hand! I barely have time to hang up before she flies in with her suitcase, kisses me on the cheek and is on her way up to Papa. I wait in the lobby for Dr. H. I don't have to wait too long. Dr. H.

is the opposite of Dr. F., an unprepossessing, humble conductor of a provincial orchestra, sure of his repertoire and upholding his solid convictions. Inspires confidence. Mine at least. Papa may be less enthusiastic about him because of his embryonic looks. Much as I want to like him—do like him—he strikes me as a not altogether finished person. Give him a rundown of the entire picture. He understands at once. I go up to Papa first.

I meet the same posture, the same attitude as when I entered last. The accused in the dock, but no longer awaiting sentence; apparently it has been pronounced. The only remaining question: when will he be led into the death cell? I tell him I've got rid of F. and that the new man is waiting outside. He stares at me as though we'd never discussed him. Again I try coaxing him. A lost cause. His only response: "T-t-tonight so l-l . . . ?" The "late," never fully articulated, hangs in mid-air, along with the big question mark. "Yes, why not? Then we'll have this silly business over with. You never go to bed at this hour anyway!" He makes a last stand: He needs a good night's rest, there's so much to do ahead—auditioning, conferences with the set designer and the costume designer and of course with Darvas and and and . . . So he doesn't know after all!

"One more reason," I persist, "to get the whole doctor thing over with!" He looks at me, weary-appealing. I can't bear to see him so submissive to my will. But neither can I afford the luxury of pity. Start for the door when a desperate "J-JUST A M-M-MOMENT!!" yanks me around. He's got up. Panic flares in his eyes: "B-but w-what sh-shall I s-say?" I don't understand. Honestly not. "W-w-well . . . h-he's b-bound to . . ." "To what?" "T-to, well, you know, to . . . n-notice . . . ?" He's trembling. I ask quietly: "What's there to notice? You can tell him everything, Papa!" And now there comes a gesture of hopelessness that topples the little self-control left me. "Th-that I . . . th-that I . . . m-my God, you know it y-y-your-self!" and he smiles awkwardly to hide a shame that can't be hidden any longer. And at last he sputters out the truth that he no longer can speak properly and that it has nothing to do with his having bitten his tongue. So he knew all the time.

Papa and H. hit it off from the start. H. goes through the motions of checking the by then barely visible wounds, doesn't linger over the introductory bars, moved adroitly in on the main theme. And that is fortunate because Papa watches him like a hawk. He is evidently fed up with pretense. I believe it is a relief to him no longer having to drag along a crushing burden all by himself. First there is trivial, almost cheerful chitchat and before we know it the dainty little man has a strong, friendly arm around Papa's shoulders and proposes, as if it were an alluring caprice, to retire *together into the next room. His diplomacy is reminiscent of M.R.'s own when he has on his hands a rattled actor gone up a dead-end street, calming him and leading him to an open road. H. is a sensitive conductor, the kind one runs into—with luck—in the smaller towns, who proves equal to any task or any guest performer of the great world.*

It's funny to watch Eleonora bustling around like a housewife. [Besides drawing room with dining alcove, balcony, bedroom, bath and kitchenette, the apartment had another small space which, since the desertion of Papa's valet, served him as a sort of storage corner. That is where she settled down now.] *This creature of disorder brings order into everything; every tedious chore becomes a delight to her. At midnight, out of nowhere, our kitchen sorceress even produces a large bowl of fruit for Papa's table. Tell her I never knew she had a domestic side. She smiles a Mona Lisa smile. My announcement that I'm going to telephone Wolfgang as soon as H. has made his diagnosis she finds only normal. I get quite another reaction when—perhaps a bit meanly—I propose the most normal of all things: calling Thimig, who'll surely fly here at once. The indignant glance I earn rebukes me for daring to utter so profane a name in this hallowed moment. But all she says is: "Yes, that's probably necessary," and fluffs out of the room.*

Since the afternoon we arrived in Fire Island, Thimig's name hasn't once come up. In pronouncing it, I've reminded myself of her existence. Poor Eleonora. Thimig's entrance will be her exit. At last Papa, looking much more composed, returns with H., who says: "I'm very pleased with him!" Clearly he knows how to handle people. It couldn't have been an easy matter to keep Papa in good temper during all the poking and prodding that must have been so repugnant to him. Without going overboard, H. expresses optimism. Quite overtly he talks about a spasm in a blood vessel of the brain, which, however, needn't have done permanent damage. Papa winks at me as if to say: "Nice kettle of fish, eh." Embarrassed, he picks up the cigar that has gone out. H. objects: "You'll have to give up smoking for a while now, Professor! You must promise me that!" Like a dutiful child, Papa discards the cigar. H. assures him that, if he cooperates, recovery is possible in from four to six weeks. Convinced or not, Papa graciously plays the game. I can't wait to take H. downstairs and hear the unadorned truth. But there's a delay: Eleonora enters looking all fallen apart. She asks H. to come into her room. Whatever he did to put her back in one piece worked: when they rejoin us she's herself again—full of life and love.

H.'s optimism was not an act. There are no discernible impairments except for the light aphasia. The three possible causes: (1) A clot in one of the blood vessels feeding the speech center. (2) The spasm already mentioned, which also would cut off the supply of blood. (3) Rupture of a blood vessel resulting in hemorrhage. The last would be the gravest, as there would occur irreparable damage to that area of the brain. Less grave would be a clot, even though, when blood has a tendency to coagulate, there is always present the threat of a new thrombosis. A spasm would cause relatively the smallest damage and with today's remedies for preventing recurrences chances for recovery would be favorable. H. honestly subscribes to the last theory, as the blood supply could only have been blocked temporarily, or else other functions would have been affected as well. In this belief he didn't hesitate to talk to my father openly; to lie would have served no purpose. Not merely because an out-and-out lie would never have convinced him, but because recovery in a case like this depends to a great extent on the help provided by the patient himself. For a patient is only able to help when he understands in principle what has happened to him and doesn't minimize it. On the other hand, he mustn't give up either. Fortunately, Papa has the heart of a young man. But his blood pressure is too high, probably due to advanced arteriosclerosis, which should and could have been recognized sooner. H. is appalled by my father's admission that he hadn't had a checkup since he can remember. Our main concern: To prevent new spasms. To this end: Lots of sleep, if need be with the help of sleeping pills; absolute quiet and rest, with the help of sedatives; no visitors, no excitement, no exertion, no stimulating conversation. And it would be better if he didn't try to write. The possible discovery that he might not be able to could bring on just the kind of shock to be avoided at all costs. So: little company but lots of fresh air—perhaps in some sanatorium out of town. Yet a sanatorium atmosphere might have a depressing effect, be more harmful to his psyche than beneficial to him physically. The therapy, which actually has already begun, will include anticoagulants—as a preventive to further strokes—antihypertonic—to lower the blood pressure—and leeches applied to his temples—to reduce tension in the brain. To my question as to how long the recovery might take: "That no one can say. If everything goes well, from six to eight weeks." "So rehearsals for Helen are . . . out?" Certainly for three to four months. But there's no reason to fear for his life? But of course there is! Every reason! There's always reason to fear the worst when a person has suffered cerebral injury. Then my stepmother ought to come at once? "Only if your father asks for her." In no case must her arrival precipitate a crisis. Ideal would be for her to invent some pretext for a trip to New York that *has nothing to do with his illness. Alternatively, she could come east, live elsewhere, keep her presence unknown, receive daily bulletins and be available in case of emergency. And how do we deal with the outside world? I elaborate: So long as there's hope for complete recovery his opportunity for work must be protected. Talk about what has happened to him would finish not only Helen but all his chances in the future. H. gets the point and proposes we stick to the story of infection caused by dog bites. Although I express my confidence in him, I say I must ask him to arrange a consultation with the best specialist obtainable. Moreover, as M.R. not only belongs to his family, but still so much to the public, it's my duty to call in a recognized authority in the field, not merely in my or his, but in public opinion. H. is far from offended. On the contrary. He feels the responsibility is too great for him alone and was about to propose consulting America's most esteemed neurologist, Dr. Foster Kennedy.*

He asks me whether Papa has fears about his next project and for this reason might be escaping into illness. He has found this to be the case with a number of refugees not as successful as they were in their own countries. Nothing ever changes! Here is this nice general practitioner, extremely empathic and competent, reverting to the most banal Freudian clichés the minute he turns his interest from the body to the soul. Try to make clear why my father, even as refugee, has never known fears regarding his work, never knew illness or escape into it. His psychological problem is quite another one: For him human defects signify human failure or divine punishment. And the perfectionist M.R. is ashamed of them. The danger is that he'll fall to brooding, grow secretive and encapsulate himself further. Our job is to help him gain a natural, uninhibited attitude toward illness and the exigencies of recovery.

Summit

IT WAS THE DAY of Arthur Kahane's funeral. He had been the kindest, most intelligent and erudite—if, in business, not the most astute—of all of Max Reinhardt's collaborators. And he had been a dearly loved family friend. I was to meet my father at the Deutsches Theater and go to the cemetery with him. However, I was late getting out of school and, when I finally arrived, learned that he had gone ahead of me with my brother. While searching the street for a taxi, I ran into my uncle Siegfried, the third-oldest Reinhardt brother and manager of the purchasing department of the Reinhardt enterprises. He was on the same quest as I and for the same reason. Much as I liked this uncle, I had exchanged very few words with him. Of the entire tight-lipped Reinhardt clan his lips were the closest sealed. Like Edmund—although lacking Edmund's sharp mental faculties—and like his sisters Irene and Adele, he had inherited the withdrawn, melancholy nature of their mother, while Max, his youngest brother Leo and sister Jenny had the good fortune of having this maternal cloud pierced by rays of their father's buoyant spirit.

Now our common destination brought us into closer quarters for a longer period than I had found myself in with him before. A most fitting companion, I thought, for the kind of journey we were making. But, surprisingly, as we turned onto the long, shadowy avenue leading to the graveyard, he became, for him, positively chatty: Suddenly raising his eyes from the floor—an innovation in itself—he looked almost directly at me and blurted out that he and Arthur Kahane had ridden to work on the same train at the same hour every single morning of their lives for a quarter of a century . . . not only on the same train which Kahane boarded three stops later, but in the same second-class smoking compartment . . . and each morning, as Kahane entered, they lifted their hats in greeting, then sat silently facing each other for the remainder of the thirty-minute ride. . . . On leaving the train, they would lift their hats formally in farewell, walk in opposite directions toward different exits and along parallel streets to the Deutsches Theater, where they had adjoining offices. At that point he turned off his words as though they were drops trickling from a faulty faucet and I was left to wonder what had caused the trickle in the first place—until, apparently reinvigorated by the sight of the tombstones we were now driving by, he opened up again: "Our long friendship is now ended. I shall miss it." On this explosion of confidence his lips clamped shut for the rest of the day.

Kahane's silence was, characteristically, a sign of sensitive respect for another's mode of being. Siegfried's was induced by the burden of a heavy heritage. In view of Max Reinhardt's full and rich public life, the extroversion inherent in his profession and in his nature as a seducer in life, one might be inclined to think that he had escaped this heritage. But that would be an erroneous conclusion. For none of these speculations is incongruent with the reticence that, indeed, was his, a reticence almost touching on the pathological. It is a hoary old tale, that of the comedian who has been blessed with the gift of brightening other lives with laughter and whose curse is to have his own darkened by deep neuroses. This is not to suggest that Max Reinhardt be labeled an unmitigated neurotic. Yet his paralyzing reaction to direct contact with people, his inability to communicate with them freely, is indicative of the dark pockets in his soul. In point of fact, not the *absence* of inhibitions, but how he brought himself to *cope* with almost insurmountable ones, provides the clue to his undisputed effectiveness. It is worth noting in this connection that even Siegfried, with his unbearable depressions and repeated suicide attempts, was able to try his hand at acting. By the time his oldest brother was establishing himself in Berlin, he had already toured extensively in America.

> In addition to everything else, there was a dreadful night last night and today a more dreadful morning. Siegfried, who returned from his tour yesterday, refused to speak a single word to anyone, lay in his clothes on the sofa the entire night long, all twisted and in absolute despair. Yesterday morning, at a quarter to seven, he left the house and was gone—missing—till today. The worry, fear and anguish my dear parents went through you simply cannot imagine. We sat around, stood still, waited and ran in the streets and every moment increased our terrible certainty that he had done harm to himself. We didn't close an eye all night.
>
> Early today we went to the police. We had given up all hope when, suddenly, shortly after noon today, he turned up in an alarming state. He said he had roamed the woods throughout the entire night and wanted to make an end of it all. Until now it has been impossible to get any other word out of him. These were hours of indescribable torture. My eyes still burn like fire. I'm completely finished. We are faced with the dark riddle of a most unfortunate nature, of a man who buries everything inside himself and who cannot bring himself to express his thoughts and feelings. Even now he is quite unable to talk to us.

Thus—marked "personal"—Max Reinhardt wrote from his Berlin apartment to the Berlin apartment of "Fräulein Else Heims" in the year 1905. The letter begins with "My own dearest, beloved treasure, my darling, my Bimbam, my little wife" and goes on—in addition to other expressions of endearment—to expressions of concern for my mother's health (a concern that was in time to curdle into derision) and complaints about the difficulties he encountered in taking over the Deutsches Theater—an event that was imminent. Theatre problems and family problems were, in equal proportion, to occupy a good part of his life; were, gradually, to become intertwined, as—to extricate the members of his family, at least the males, from their perpetual financial and emotional crises—he would give them jobs in his theatre, although the rescue proved felicitous in Edmund's case alone. But even in the otherwise ideal relationship with Edmund, the "unfortunate nature," the "inability to express their thoughts and feelings," the necessity always to have to divine what the other *really* had in mind, led to misunderstandings.

It is not difficult to imagine how the functionings of a temperament like this affect a man who has suffered a stroke and who must live with its consequences and possible recurrences, particularly when the consequences are not perceptible to the eye, when the threat of recurrence hangs over him like a rain cloud ready to burst and when verbal expression, a block he succeeded in removing only by having trained himself to be its consummate master, had deserted him; and when, at the same time, his thoughts race, furious as a storm wind, through a mysteriously damaged brain and have somehow to be contained, to be "buried inside himself" even more deeply.

I realize that in the thirty years since father and son found themselves so unexpectedly confronted with this problem the layman has become much more enlightened about it. Therefore, my father's unsophistication about things physiological and psychological—unusual even in those days—and our mutual reluctance to call what had happened to him by its proper name may surprise some readers of today. Only a few years back, I read two books dealing with the subject that are cases in point: *Stroke: A Diary of Recovery* by the afflicted author, Douglas Ernest Ritchie, which describes dispassionately, in scrupulous detail, each phase of his illness, and Lord Moran's almost tactlessly candid memoirs of his famous patient, Winston Churchill. Both reflect the tendency in medicine to inform the layman about his condition without any punches pulled. Secret horrors are brushed away like the flimsiest of cobwebs and the patient is rid of the morbid notion that disability is humiliating. Frank understanding of his symptoms and matter-of-fact acceptance of biological reality, it is assumed, will dispel both mistaken optimism and premature resignation. Alas, not the slightest whiff of this fresh wind drifted over Fire Island or through the Hotel Gladstone. There, unaired fear imposed on the Reinhardts an even more stringent etiquette of privacy than was their normal custom to extend to each other.

When I think about the contrasting candor with which Churchill—a welcome guest at Leopoldskron—toward the end of his prime ministership discussed the ups and downs of his physical and mental capacities with his doctors, his intimates and, not less constrainedly, with bare acquaintances, even going so far as to correspond about them with the head of another state, I am still amazed. For I watched my father facing the same hurdles, if on a lonelier, more tortuous and, unhappily, more precipitous course.

Clearly, the child Max Reinhardt lacked Churchill's aggressive, though no less childlike, directness in every respect. To reach his ends he needed twisted detours and his *gêne* was not merely a beneficial, if inadvertent, brake: it lent support to his productivity. It was, in a way, a lubricant for the intricate Reinhardt machinery. It was part of the Reinhardt charm with which he conquered. It shielded him against unrecognized dangers and enemies that continuously threaten a child's life. And it produced the abundance of gentle tact which opened to this pathfinder so many forbidden doors. But it also closed doors to him that are open to others more outgoing and through which, when in need, they may reach sustenance.

Children, as a rule, are bad patients. In his way, the willful boy Churchill was no exception. My father, being untaught, full of dark forebodings and equally willful, was, by any standard, the worst. The feat of "putting one's childhood in one's pocket and running off with it to play to the end of one's days" can only be accomplished at the expense of adult circumspection, patience and experience. Max Reinhardt was a precocious, hypersensitive, fantasy-possessed, play-mad, cruel-tender child to whom tenderness from others was as necessary as food and drink. His mind grasped everything and his heart felt all the things he wanted to grasp and feel. But in the plentiful storehouse of his thoughts and emotions there were gaps that never ceased to puzzle those close to him. The truth of the matter is that he simply had never stopped to take notice of many of life's cliffs and shallows, but, beyond that, was assisted in circumnavigating them by an immensely favorable wind blowing his way. It is no wonder then that, later, when the wind subsided, every obstruction, great or small, stunned him all the harder and sudden exposure to the ugliness of adult life left him defenseless. Which accounts largely for the paradoxical mixture that made the man: part canny judge of people, part their victim through wishful thinking; and it accounts for the constant hazard of his being outwitted as easily as . . . well, a child, and for the saving grace of his being able to hold his own in the most difficult situations like a . . . man, and a most astute man at that. He was Nestor and Parsifal, an enthusiast and a skeptic, courageous and quickly intimidated, a gambler and an evader of decision, at one time trusting providence, at another taking refuge in procrastination, immune to fatal catastrophe, but an easy prey to the most banal mishap—depending on whether his reaction was that of a burnt or spoiled child.

For this healthy autodidact medicine was terra incognita with all its primitive taboos and medicine-man mysteries. He, therefore, could not possibly take in stride his own disintegration in the bluff and hearty Churchillian manner, nor could he encapsulate it in the narrow retort of merciless self-analysis as Ritchie did. My father was headed for a dramatic reversal of dammed-up circumstances. Churchill's attacked brain automatically became a theatre of war where all the obstacles either angered or fascinated him, were met with counterattack or, failing that possibility, were laid siege to. In any case, he saw to it that their historic significance, as on all his battlefields, was promptly brought to the attention of the world. Ritchie's brain turned into a classroom and a laboratory where the pernicious problems were defused by painstaking research. Max Reinhardt's brain had all at once changed into a sinister labyrinth where he saw only riddles and the finger of God and where his own stammered words made him shiver.

Antithesis often supplies the most direct elucidation of a thesis. And the Churchill-Reinhardt facet of this supposition extends even to their offspring: In 1931, my brother and I visited my father in London, where he was producing an (anticlimactic) revival of *The Miracle*. One night, after rehearsal, we had late supper at the Savoy Grill with Churchill's son Randolph. We were, of course, well aware of the grand old man's passionate, much ridiculed prophecies about the German menace and the danger of our homeland's relapse into nationalism and militarism. But, on this evening, to find his son stubbornly reducing the Cassandra oratory to a feverish preoccupation with National Socialism struck us as excessive. Hitler, manifestly, was an ogre to him and he kept firing questions at us: What was the Nazis' actual number? How firm a foothold had they gained in the country? Who financed them? Why was there so little opposition? When, in our opinion, would they take over? After a few perfunctory replies and polite attempts to change what we thought a dull subject we finally assured him—to my father's distinct satisfaction—that the Führer, a comedy figure only taken seriously abroad, presented no crucial problem in the Weimar Republic. Randolph sneered. Then, with a scathing observation about suicidal ostriches, he rose, bid us a cool good-night and left the table. We lingered on for coffee and a few observations of our own: how tragic it was that that gallant dinosaur had produced such a puerile ass of an heir. My father beamed at his fair-haired progeny, little realizing how soon the "puerile ass" together with *his* father would, lingering over brandy, whiskey and other alcoholic beverages, have good reason to dwell on the puerility of the Max Reinhardt heirs.

Nor is it only the dying Winston that sheds light on the dying Max.

There is a story told that the first time he stayed at the White House during World War II, Roosevelt, impatient to discuss an urgent bulletin from the front, had himself rolled unannounced into the apartment of his late-rising ally, just as the latter, naked, pink and steaming, stepped out of a hot tub. With profuse apologies Roosevelt ordered an immediate retreat. Which his guest swiftly countermanded. Head held high, he declared: "The first minister of His Britannic Majesty has nothing to hide from the President of the United States!" Significantly different was the historic meeting between two leaders in the realm of the arts: August Strindberg and Max Reinhardt. They too had little to hide from each other, but, due to their respective natures, every compulsion to do so. Though they had never met personally, they too were allies of a sort. With his plays Strindberg had pumped fresh blood into Reinhardt's reformation of the theatre. And Reinhardt, the Strindberg pioneer, had been a decisive factor in putting the controversial depictor of the war between the sexes on the bourgeois map. Their counselors considered personal contact between them as essential to the future of the theatre as the meeting between the two great statesmen was considered by *their* counselors to be for the future of world affairs. And the questions of protocol in preparation for this "summit" were as delicate, if not more so, as the Anglo-American. Who was to pay the first call on the other? Where was the appointed rendezvous to take place? And on what date? The answers by the principals would have been unequivocal: "neither"; "nowhere"; "never." For neither dramatist nor interpreter had the slightest inclination to mar the harmonious alliance by an uneasy tête-à-tête.

Without doubt, their wishes would have prevailed, had not one of the Scandinavian tours of the Deutsches Theater brought the issue to a head. Obviously, it would have been an affront to Reinhardt had Strindberg steered clear of every Reinhardt performance, just as it would have been unthinkable for Reinhardt not to pay a formal visit to the author in the city in which he lived. Intricate negotiations—needless to say, against the considered judgments of the two most concerned—finally produced results that eased them out of their corners: Strindberg would "drop in" on a Reinhardt performance incognito—thereby eliminating the necessity of a visit backstage—and Reinhardt would return the compliment by "dropping in" some Sunday for an informal call at Strindberg's apartment. Agreement on the date was, by mutual consent, set far enough in advance to offer each victim the hope that some fortuitous snag might, after all, prevent their encounter.

Vain hope. Strindberg had sidled into the theatre, huddled in a back-row seat and been duly ignored. And now the dreaded afternoon was upon my father, who, attired in funeral black and with suitable mien, climbed the ill-lit stairs of the middle-class Swedish apartment house redolent with kitchen smells. Each door he passed gave forth its own variety of odor which, through some time-honored alchemy, merged with the others to produce that single, identifying smell of buildings of this sort the world over: that dismal blend of onions frying in rancid oil and rooty vegetables simmering with greasy meat in an eternal stew, the smell repugnant to him ever since his days as a young bank clerk when, tired, hungry and dispirited with the seven-to-six monotony of his life, he would return to his parents' small, overcrowded flat in Vienna's Mariahilferstrasse, trudging up five flights of loathsome smell to get there and losing his appetite in the process. He was to escape this smell deliberately and successfully the rest of his life. He was to exchange hunger for culinary pleasure, grayness for all the colors of the rainbow, drab flats for luxury hotels and castles, boredom for enchantment and spiritual uplift. But not for himself alone. He would invite an entire world to share his enjoyment. But on this Sunday afternoon he was back in Mariahilferstrasse.

On the top landing he stopped, frozen by the sight of a polished brass name plate on one of the doors, inscribed: "August Strindberg." For a long moment he stood praying for time, praying for an eleventh-hour miracle that in his heart he knew would not arrive. Instead, a dutiful impulse forced his hand eventually to the bell. Its thin tinkle had no visible or audible response. He waited another ten seconds . . . twenty . . . forty . . . by his watch a full minute and a half . . . and still silence. Two minutes. The situation was getting under his skin. Having mustered his courage to this point, he was determined to go through with the blasted meeting. He rang again. Louder. Protestingly. Still no reaction from within. He began to fume. But with nothing to vent his steam on, he decided to take to his heels—when a tiny, almost nonexistent *sqa-weak* stopped him. He listened. There it was again: close, but exceedingly cautious as though two feet were shifting on ancient floorboards. Holding his breath, he peered down and, in a ray of light glinting from under the old, warped door, saw the telltale shadow of two shoe tips. Suddenly, one of them moved and the movement was accompanied by the same incriminating *sqa-weak*. Intrigued, my father leaned closer and now was sure that he could hear the sound of breathing—constrained and so little audible as to be perceived only by an understanding soul. The insubstantial barrier separating him from his theoretical host of the afternoon might protect, but could not conceal, the panic, the possum-like guile and quivering neurasthenia that penetrated the door like X rays. My father's anger melted. In its place rose an exhilarating sense of having the upper hand, a feeling which impelled him to pull the bell once again and to enjoy sadistically the sound of stifled breathing it produced. But that was all it produced. Content, savoring every second, he turned and tiptoed down the stairs, stopping every now and then to look back to assure himself that the status quo had not changed.

He had barely reached the landing below when the balance of power was abruptly upset. The creak of a door opening stopped him in his tracks and, as he reeled about, caught him exposed in a shaft of light from above. He heard shuffling footsteps and, blinking up, was now able to make out a pair of eyes focused on him from over the top of the banister. No movement or sign of recognition was forthcoming on either side, nothing but the noncommittal clash of eyes. Thus Sweden's great national playwright and the world's foremost director mutely took each other's measure until, his curiosity apparently satisfied, the former terminated the meeting by an abrupt retreat. The shaft of light vanished, as the door slammed behind him. Only after my father heard the sound of a chain being dropped into place did he resume his descent, with steps that had regained their self-assurance now that the miracle, as so often in his life, even when despaired of, had taken place after all.

As he came through the doorway, his ever-present retinue waiting dutifully on the sidewalk surged forward in anticipation of juicy details of the momentous, if oddly brief, encounter. However, he held his peace. And if he met their curiosity with the same unholy smile I saw on his lips when, very shortly before his death, he described the eventful non-event to me, I rather think they considered it wise not to press him. It took him almost thirty years, he admitted to me, to overcome the ache of embarrassment enough to "speak freely" about his first—and last—meeting with August Strindberg.

SEPTEMBER 26, 1943
(continued)

The morning, the day, the evening, the night have no end. Call Wolfgang in Santa Monica. Give him the entire grim picture. Can almost hear his mute distress. Promise to write at length. Meanwhile, ask him to let Thimig know everything immediately—including H.'s comments and recommendations. In any event, to let me know when she's arriving.

And now the twenty-sixth of September has come to an end after all—several hours ago judging from my watch. I feel both full to the brim and drained. I know I've done for him whatever is humanly possible and yet nothing. I'm afraid what is humanly possible isn't enough.

MONDAY,
SEPTEMBER 27, 1943

Playing hooky. Went to bed too late and was simply too exhausted to get up. Called "Greenie" [Technical Sergeant Harold Greenspan], *asked him to "combine"* [which meant that he'd mobilize some other GI to answer "here" for me at reveille. Later, when Greenie phoned me that my absence had gone unnoticed, I would slip into the building and sit virtuously at my desk].

Caught another hour of sleep, but then more than just another day began. Another life began. It's marked by the prospect of his death. For the first time I look at it without blinking. The last days were too blinding. Whatever the outcome of Papa's fight with the enemy inside him, it can at best have been the first engagement and the most we can hope for is a truce. Peace is gone forever. This produces an entirely new situation. To lose one's "begetter," or to face the possibility that at any moment he may go, is surely a monstrous experience for everyone. It tears at one's own roots, the life "begotten." I imagine this applies equally to those who may hate their father, even to those who desire, subconsciously or consciously, his death. For them ineluctable guilt feelings can only double the monstrous-

ness. In my case it doubles for quite another reason: In my sky this father was a fixed star outshining everything around me. No longer. He has suddenly come much, much nearer and at the same time lost much of his radiance. From now on I must live with the thought that the light may go out altogether. Despite all laws of nature, I cannot grasp it. I cannot accept it.

Before leaving the hotel, I take a peek in upstairs. Eleonora reassures me: Papa's sleeping peacefully, breathing regularly. H. is expected early in the afternoon.

Report to Colonel Cohn [commanding officer of our post, five foot four, former producer of Mae West films and vice-president in charge of production at Paramount when I got my first Hollywood job there. Dorothy Parker called him "a pony's ass." When he was fired from his executive position, that other irrepressible wit, albeit mostly verbal, Herman Mankiewicz, wired him: "Your loss is the industry's gain." So much for the wits. As for Manny Cohn, his wits were about him at all times. But Hollywood's organizing brains and creative brains pursued different goals and were at odds with each other. The organizers found the creators not creative enough—on company money. And the creators found their employers boors and blockheads. Both were, according to their lights, a hundred percent right. Except the organizers ran the show. Making them, when the need arose, two hundred percent right. As exemplified by another Cohn, Harry, president of Columbia Pictures, who had a problem getting his words out and, when annoyed by writer-producer Sidney Buchman's supplementing his halting utterances with promptings of the mots justes, put him in his place: "Okay, Sid, you got the words, but I got the studio!" Max Reinhardt was one of the few creators in Hollywood who found "having a studio" no more ignominious than "having the words"]. Manny Cohn is not ashamed of his civilian record and he doesn't—unlike many of his fellow officers—feel the need for revenge on his present underlings. Have no problem whatsoever getting him to okay my request for a two-week furlough—I intimate the seriousness of Papa's condition. But that gets me off the hook only so far as army film making is concerned. Meaning I still have to get permission from the real Army, i.e., my company commander. Here I meet with less understanding. Holds forth at length on what would happen to Allied chances for victory if every American soldier with an ailing father were granted a two-week furlough. Admittedly, an unassailable point of view. But am tempted to point out that neither I nor the entire SCPC combined can shorten the war by a single hour. I don't. Am turned down anyway—and completely dashed.

The Beverly Hills Commandos

"Never in the field of human conflict were there so many who did so little and got so tired" (with apologies to Winston *Churchill).*

Believe me, I understand completely how much your time is taken up by military duties and it worries me that your nights have so little rest. . . . That you sacrifice so much of your limited time to help our plans along is not only terribly touching, but it is well nigh crucial to their success.

Enclosed are the documents you simply must sign, dear Gottfried. They have been awaiting your attention for days.

Geddes complains that he has no reaction from you about the Saroyan play. It seems Dowling has made cogent suggestions. Without knowing them I am convinced that yours are better [A possible explanation for Dowling's break with the partnership shortly thereafter] . . .

A pity that we cannot reach Greta Garbo. Having to perform almost exclusively in pantomime, she would be perfect as the Madonna [In Maeterlinck's *Sister Beatrice*, a play about the *Miracle* legend] . . .

Please return the enclosed dinner list with any suggestions that may occur to you . . .

In addition to Saroyan we now definitely have the new Molnár and *Six Characters*, in which I firmly believe—as well as *La Belle Hélène, Orpheus* and *Tales of Hoffmann.* Now, with God's help, we have enough good material for several seasons.

I know it is impossible, but could you somehow manage to get a seat for the Toscanini concert for Madame de Renaudes [The donor of Micky II] . . . ?

By all means have a look at the Noël Coward film [*In Which We Serve*]. Its underacted style is precisely the way *The Russian People* should be played. Apart from anything else, it is the most powerful propaganda film I have ever seen.

Please talk to our lawyer about the tax business. He complains that he hasn't been able to get through to you.

Today *The New York Times* called again. I didn't want to commit myself until I talked to you . . .

THESE EXCERPTS ARE MINIMAL EXAMPLES of the encyclopedic afterthoughts my father would write me—after we had talked the night into day about these subjects—and slip under my door before he was ready, at last, to go to bed. To ensure that I would not ignore them in my sleep-blinded haste to make reveille on the dot, they would blaze up at me in capital letters in the familiar purple ink: "IMPORTANT!," "URGENT!!" or, in severest stress, *"READ AT ONCE!!!"*

That his bundle-in-one son, secretary, interpreter, agent, business manager, banker, assistant and collaborator need scramble for reveille, step lively to the "hut-two-three-four" barks of a drill sergeant and perform KP, latrine and other unaccustomed chores, my father would ordinarily have taken for granted as normal in any soldier's line of duty. (His respect for enforcement of official rules was religious.) What was incomprehensible to him was how a lowly buck sergeant managed to get away with the freedom of movement I did at the SCPC. He himself had never done any soldiering. If anything, in the war years of 1914 to 1918, he had been something of an anti-military participant. For it took no more than the signature of the Direktor of the Deutsches Theater to obtain instant deferment from war service for any artist or stage technician declared necessary to the furtherance of Max Reinhardt's theatre. Had this been possible in my case, everything would have been understandable to him. Indeed, on my imminent induction, he proceeded as though it were. And he could not fathom why his straight-to-the-top demarches (the last an eloquent letter to his friend and frequent Leopoldskron guest Sara Delano Roosevelt, the President's mother) should fail—even meet with gentle reproof—when he had made it so clear that, deprived of his son's supporting presence, the Reinhardt Workshop would collapse. (That the theatrical life of a nation must not be stifled even when it is fighting for its survival was one of his firm convictions. He would quote innumerable precedents for it, from the Greeks during the Persian wars to the Russians in their present struggle against a surely no less barbaric invader.) Of course, he was immensely grateful for the laxity that let me be—both for my sake and his. But he suspected it was too good to be true and feared that the sword which, his influential connections had admonished him, should be in my hand would descend on my—and his—head any day. Why this did not come to pass may need a bit of clarifying.

The SCPC was in no way a unanimous body of slackers. Among us there were brave, red-blooded guys—Irwin Shaw is one of the striking examples—itching to bust out of claustrophobic safety, hammering at every bureaucratic door that stood between them and where the fighting was going on. For a long time, Irwin (his history tainted him as a moderate left-winger) achieved nothing but raised eyebrows from Army Intelligence. Even his public withdrawal of probably his best play, *Bury the Dead*—a pitch for pacifism—did not get him into the firing line. Then, one morning, in the mimeographed orders distributed for all to read, came the news that Private Irwin Shaw had been transferred (where to remained, of course, a military secret; but the implication was clear). Loud cheers for Irwin: "The eager beaver finally made it over the water!" Alas, the body of water intended for him to cross turned out to be not the torpedo-infested Atlantic, but the garbage-turgescent East River separating Astoria from Manhattan, where, at the Capitol Hotel on Eighth Avenue, a former commercial hostelry taken over by the Army to house married officers and NCO's, the chafing warrior was harnessed to a night clerk's desk. Nevertheless, in time, Irwin's odyssey did end overseas. To my father's dismay, his departure came at a time when he needed him most: when the final rehearsal weeks of *Sons and Soldiers*, the Shaw-authored, Reinhardt-directed play, were approaching.

William Saroyan was another SCPC militant whose indefatigable crusading eventually got him across the ocean. But it was not abhorrence of Fascism that actuated his belligerence, instead, his abhorrence of our top sergeant's grammar, which he was vigilant in correcting every time a command blasted from that megaphonic mouth. Saroyan and my father had met in the Gladstone bar and, from the first moment on, were *en rapport*. Bill Saroyan was not the kind of playwright who sat long hours over his typewriter, waiting to hear the beat of inspirational drums. He could whack out a full-length play in a single week. A man admirably fitting my father's present needs. But our top sergeant's revenge put an instant crimp in their fulfillment. For months we had seen the danger ahead and had warned Bill of what the consequences would be if he persisted in educating the oaf. Many of his higher superiors enjoyed—in moderation—the GI monkeyshines of a Pulitzer Prize winner. It did not worry Bill that our sergeant did not know or give a hoot about the difference between a Pulitzer Prize winner and a prize heifer. Soldier Saroyan maintained the same irreverence as civilian Saroyan had when he declined the coveted literary honor. Our company commander, another Regular Army man, agreed with his sidekick that "that pain in the ass wise guy should get shipped to the front pronto."

Saroyan's front was London; his bivouac, Claridge's, the world's most exclusive, luxurious hotel; his duties, the writing of anti-Axis propaganda for Herbert Agar (a former Kansas City newspaper editor), head of the Office of War Information in Britain. No deadline was imposed on him nor the need to wear a uniform. In repayment for this largesse, he wrote a stirring treatise, expounding the logic of the enemy cause. Agar read a copy —the original being safely in the hands of the author's New York publishers—and promptly had a heart attack.

I was another restive SCPC-er. Producing films for rookie cynics who guffawed or, at best, dozed quietly through them was not my idea of a fruitful contribution to the common cause. As a matter of fact, long before America entered the war—on the day it was declared in Europe—I sprang to with a letter to the French Minister of Information, playwright Jean Giraudoux. I hoped that my name—through his acquaintance with my father—would be a recommendation when I wrote that I wished to offer my services to France in any capacity in which I might be of help. My background, I indicated, made me an obvious supporter of a country fighting Nazi Germany. Adding some of the qualifications I believed should make me a natural candidate for a useful job. They were: mastery of the German, French and English languages, personal experience and academic knowledge of Europe's historical, ideological, political and geographical scene, economics and philosophy as well as an inside-out knowledge of the truckling supermen now serving Hitler—having sat on the same school bench with so many of them (Wernher von Braun for one, who left the Collège Français, having flunked mathematics). My letter in the mailbox, I saw myself welcomed with open arms. My view was not shared by the French Minister of Information. Nor was it by his American counterpart when I went through the same song and dance after Pearl Harbor.

Unbeknownst to the world, on the morning of December 7 in 1941 another crisis affecting Christendom was reaching its climax on the mainland of the United States in the southern part of California. Its precise location was a dubbing room at the Metro-Goldwyn-Mayer plant in Culver City.

I had produced a featherbrained comedy written by S. N. Behrman, starring Greta Garbo and Melvyn Douglas under the direction of George Cukor. Its plot hung precariously on the credibility of a New York smoothy's having a vacation fling on snowy mountain slopes with a skiing instructress, a simplehearted, upright girl, until he, surfeited with her spiritual and physical health, drops her on her pristine slopes and takes off for New York. However, when she follows him to the big city, masquerading as her nonexistent, high-living, low-moraled twin sister, he falls madly in love with her.

In those days, cinematized sexual intercourse was—well, it just wasn't. The edicts of the Breen Office, the industry's self-elected censor, were complied with so rigidly that no major studio would consider shooting a script without its seal of approval. The script of *Two-Faced Woman* was turned down by the Breen Office on the grounds that it conveyed implications of a premarital carnal relationship. What, I proposed as an alternative, if the lovers were not illicit lovers? What if the cad *marries* the girl of high principles and then abandons her? And what if she, through her masquerade stratagem, wins him back? The Breen Office liked that. So the offending scenes were rewritten and the picture was shot. The result satisfied everyone but the Legion of Decency, the cinematic watchdog of the Catholic Church. It protested vehemently that it was adulterous for a man to have love relations with his sister-in-law. My counter-argument that his sister-in-law was, in truth, his wife they dismissed as Hollywood sophistry and enlisted no less an authority than Francis Joseph Cardinal Spellman, Archbishop of New York, to support their contention. He, even more incensed than his minions, took time off from shepherding X-million souls to wage a one-man crusade—in a world torn by strife, with his own country on the brink of it—against my sinful *Two-Faced Woman*. He whispered his caveat into the ear of his proselyte, Louis B. Mayer, and Mayer thundered into mine to "flush the filth down the drain where it belongs."

That is how it came about that, on the morning of December 7, 1941, I sat in a dubbing room at MGM, mixing sound tracks into a composite that Heaven's deputy would, hopefully, reward with his blessing. Between reels, I listened, as I did every Sunday morning, to the weekly New York Philharmonic's broadcast. When soloist Arthur Rubinstein struck up the second Brahms piano concerto I thought, to hell with Heaven's deputy, here is Heaven itself! Short-lived bliss: the concert was abruptly cut off by an emotion-choked voice announcing that Japanese planes had just bombed Pearl Harbor and destroyed three-quarters of the United States fleet. Every last one of us in the room, as everyone in America listening to the radio, realized instinctually that life and its pursuits had been radically changed. Everyone save New York's Prince of the Church, who, undeflected by earthly cataclysm, fought on to redeem the soul of MGM's evil daughter.

Up until the very day of Los Angeles's first air-raid alarm, when he flew in and asked for a viewing of the expurgated version. I ran it for him and gained the sanction my employers set such store by. (The public chose to withhold it.)

At the first opportunity, I traveled east for my second try at meaningful assignment in the war effort. Before an appointment could be arranged in Washington with playwright Robert Sherwood (Roosevelt speech writer and later biographer), who, as Coordinator of War Information, was in charge of propaganda aimed at enemy populations via radio, bombardments of leaflets and every other means of infiltration, open and clandestine, I received a summons from my draft board. Promptly renouncing my efflorescent hopes, I booked a seat on a plane leaving for Los Angeles the next day and packed my bags—when a call from Sherwood's office came, advising me I was expected the following morning. Just as promptly, I postponed my departure, canceling the flight. It was a flight that made headlines: "L.A.-bound Plane Crashes, No Survivors"; "Wife of Clark Gable Killed in Crash"; "Carole Lombard Dead." I owe it to Robert Sherwood that I did not become an early war casualty, even before I was recruited.

But that is all I owe him. The German desk—the only spot he thought suitable for me—had already been promised to Thomas Mann's daughter, Erika. She had benefited by the intercession of the Nobelist's ardent admirer Agnes Meyer, wife of the *Washington Post* publisher (who, in the emergency, had made his peace with the Administration), with the President himself. We were old friends, Erika and I. What is more, I admired her enormously for her zealous stand against Fascism—taken so many years before her father saw his way clear to follow her example—and for finally overcoming his diffidence in speaking out. Nevertheless, this did not alter my opinion—for reasons that lay in the apolitical past, in a Berlin so deftly captured by Christopher Isherwood's "Camera"—that she was the worst possible choice for the task. For Germany had once been scandalized by the asocial capers of Erika Mann, her brother Klaus and their partners in a hell-bent-for-exhibitionism quartet: Pamela Wedekind, elder daughter of poet Frank Wedekind, and actor-director Gustav Gründgens (later to make an elegant switch from his freewheeling pre-Hitler decadence to life with Göring, as exotic house pet who was rewarded for his tricks with jurisdiction over the swastikaed Prussian State Theatre). That the Hitler trauma and emigration to America had provided a catharsis for Erika and Klaus—he would find his final one in suicide—no one then living in Germany could possibly know. Clearly, employing Erika to appeal, over the airwaves, to the good conscience of Germans for resistance to the malevolent characters ruining their country was as sensible as inviting Messalina to exhort the citizens of Rome to join her in a public morals campaign. But could I say this to Bob Sherwood? Naïveté about the Nazi syndrome and misconception of the facts of German life were not confined to American lowbrows. I remembered a conversation I had back in the thirties with Clifford Odets, another liberal American playwright: I had stuck a cinder in his pinko eye with my gloomy prophecy of the democracies' inevitable conflict with Nazi Germany and he had put me in my bourgeois place with the party-line homily: Hitler will never dare to hand arms to his own people, because they will inevitably use them against him.

Back in Los Angeles and classified 1A, I was put on a conveyor belt of unclad draft-age bodies that rolled me past army medics checking teeth, eyes, ears, nose, throat, chest, heart, prostate, urine, blood, blood pressure, nerve reflexes and, at bare-assed journey's end, delivered me and my psyche to an army shrink who blitz-read the identification card I handed him. With a quick smile, he invited me ceremoniously to take a seat opposite him, then, settling comfortably behind his desk, engaged my naked person in an hour-long, ever more denuding conversation about my famous father.

My famous father. I was now on the point of leaving him stranded without a penny to his name and no prospect of future support from me. I had tried and failed to avert this bad dream when, on the strength of my unfulfilled three-year contract with MGM—suspended for the duration of my military service—I asked, felt justified in asking, for a modest advance that might contribute in a small measure at least to sustain him in my absence. Negotiations for it involved my obeisant approach to the Holy Trinity: Nicholas M. Schenck, head of Loew's Incorporated, MGM's New York–based parent company, providentially visiting the Coast at the moment, Louis B. Mayer, head of production, and Edward J. Mannix, studio manager. Tough digressive sledding it was. Schenck fixed his glacial eyes on me (They never failed to make me think of the rich old man who, solicited by a beggar, replies that alms will be forthcoming on condition that he tell him which of his eyes is made of glass. The rich old man takes great pride in its perfection and is abashed when the correct answer came without hesitation. "What," he demands gruffly, "makes you so sure?" Once again, the beggar replies quickly—perhaps with hope of approbation: "I see some pity in it.") and expounded on the desperate economic crisis our great country was struggling through. As conclusive evidence, he described his inability to afford any longer the servants necessary to keep up his Long Island estate.

Without pause, like a relay runner, Mayer rushed in, exhorting me not to pamper my father. For his own good. He cited his own regrettable weakness in indulging his family. "Mr. Mayer," I said, "all I ask is what you've led me to believe I'm entitled to. Six months ago you promised me a raise. Which I never received. Now then, in view of the fact that you have been underpaying me all these months don't you think it only fair that I be compensated under the circumstances?" He sat forward, nodding gravely and said: "You're right, Gottfried. I cannot deny you're being underpaid. But you're wrong in wanting to change that situation. Put yourself in my position. Just think how much dead weight a big studio like ours has to carry. Have you any idea how much talent we have to *overpay*? Of course you have. You're a bright feller. And you know as well as I do that if we didn't have bargains around to counterbalance the overpaid, the studio would go broke." I understood his point, but not why I had to be its goat. When I said so, he walked over to me and curled a fatherly arm about my shoulder. "I'll tell you exactly why," he purred. "When I get into my car to go home at night there's a long hard day in back of me. I'm tired. Frank starts driving. I lean back. And I think. Like a picture in front of my eyes I see all the people working for the company, the overpaid and the underpaid. And each time I come to Gottfried Reinhardt I smile. I say to myself, I like that Reinhardt. He's underpaid." His grip on my shoulder tightened lovingly. "Keep it that way, Gottfried!" he said.

I was no match for this iridescent brush-off. But three weeks later, on the day before my induction, realizing that I would not be able to keep up the payments on my life insurance policies, I put pride into my empty pocket and, with a modified request, approached Mayer a second time: Would the studio, I asked him, at least take care of my insurance premiums while I was in the Army? He blinked at me through calluses forming over his eyes. "In other words," he said, "you're asking for credit." "No," I answered, "I'm asking you to help me keep my policies from being canceled. My father is my beneficiary. If I die he has no other protection. But naturally I'll sign over to the studio first claim on my policies to recoup the premiums." On these words, his eyes moistened over: "Sure sure sure," he choked out, "nine years of faithful service . . . a man deserves . . . it's the least he can expect . . . no question about it." Yet there was a question, a tiny one according to Mayer's definition: "We've got to have—just as a formality—the General's approval." (All the insiders referred to Schenck as the General.) The General was by now back at his post in the Loew Building, 1450 Broadway, New York City, three thousand miles away, too far for the immediate okay I needed. I asked Mayer if he did not agree that the amount in question was too negligible to bother the General about. His answer was a stern, involved lecture on corporate ethics and the duty of company officers toward their stockholders. His mind then put at rest, he stood up and shook hands with me. I stared at him. At his back. He was hurrying toward the door, en route to his racing stables, blessing me over his shoulder for being the devoted son to my father that I was, regretting that he had no son of his own, vowing that he would telephone the General at noon and, before striding out of sight, advising me to check with Nicky Nayfack later in the day for the without-a-doubt-positive answer.

I checked with Nicky Nayfack telephonically at half past two that afternoon and was told he would "get right back" to me. I waited five hours until he "got right back" to me and asked me to his office. What made him so vague about the passage of time? Nicky Nayfack was a simple cactus of the non-flowering variety (genus: *Nepotismus;* species: *motio pictus*) thriving on Culver City soil; he was Nicholas Schenck's nephew and had all the time in the world to keep me on tenterhooks before turning me down. Angry and tired though I was, I was still clear-minded enough to tell him that the lousy advance I asked of MGM would be more than covered by the collateral. Even in the case of my death. He raised his eyes for the first time since I entered his office from the sheaf of papers he had been riffling through broodingly and said: "But what if you're maimed, Gottfried? Permanently? Where does the company stand then?"

Early the next morning, at a pickup street corner in West Los Angeles, I was herded onto a bus transporting me and my fellow passengers to an assembly point downtown, whence, regrouped, we were sent south to Fort MacArthur, our induction center. To leave everything of accustomed life behind was clearly—judging from the gripes and consolations exchanged on all sides—a wrench for everyone on that bus. No, not everyone. There was an undersized little twerp with an oversized head who did not open his mouth once during the entire ride—except to show his white teeth in a bright happy smile of confidence. Though he was vaguely familiar to me, I would not have given him a second thought, had not his smile—for what reason I wondered—widened with each depressing phase of our trip. At Fort MacArthur, he trotted up to me and said: "Hi. Don't we know each other? My name's Laemmle, Carl Laemmle, Jr. You're . . . ?"

I was my father's son. The undersized little twerp with the oversized head was the son and heir of the many-million-dollared Hollywood pioneer, Carl Laemmle, and there was no more spoiled, cushioned scion of the nouveaux riches than Carl Laemmle, Jr. He became my puppy, stringing along with me for the rest of the day (and years), with indestructible good cheer. I was delighted that, here, at my side, was proof I was not the *most* implausible soldier in the American Army. There was no more reassuring news I could give my father, who, I knew, would be sitting at the telephone, waiting for the promised evening call from my destination. In addition, I would be able to perk him up with a description of how I had resisted temptation that afternoon. Neither Junior nor I, I could tell him, had succumbed to the seductive siren song of "better pay, better rations and more prestige" offered us. Nor even to its almost irresistible coda: "Last chance to join the Parachute Division! Raise your hands, guys!"

I looked at Junior. His arms were nailed to his sides and I could not help taunting: "Grab it. It's now or never." He was sweating, but his voice was cool as he whispered out of the corner of his mouth: "It's not for me." "Why not?" I prodded sotto voce. "I'm too light," he elucidated.

My father was soothed to hear I had met my first brush with military danger so wisely. And he was happy for me that I had "run into and made friends with a pleasant young man who is, at the same time, a colleague with mutual interests." As usual, my father translated mutual interests (theatrical) into practical terms: Would it not be a good idea to discuss his planned productions with my charming new friend, Mr. Junior Laemmle? As a potential investor? I did not think so. But with limited coins, on a long-distance call from an army-post pay station, I could not begin to explain why, as a potential backer of shows, Mr. Junior Laemmle would prove even lighter than he had as a potential parachutist. Anyway, he had more pressing concerns at the moment: Not a single item of GI wearing apparel thrust at him in the supply room was small enough to fit him. As a last resort, he was tried for size in leftovers from World War I. It has often been said that generals always prepare for the last war, not the one at hand. Now here was a private to give living proof of this hypothesis.

Camp Crowder, Missouri, a basic-training installation, was our next stop. It was twelve miles distant from the town of Neosho, the geographical center of the continental United States. In no other way, however, was there anything central about it. In fact, it was so peripheral it was out of this world. It was on the moon.

On my twenty-ninth birthday, I received a letter from my father, in which he wrote, among other things:

> May the Almighty bless you and fulfill all your wishes and my prayers for you. Up to now the world has never looked so desolate on any of your birthdays as it does today. Despite the fact that spring, traditionally a time of new

hope, begins on the day after your birth. But what does that mean today? News in the papers that turns the stomach and, for me, strangling taxes and headaches in trying to pay them.

"Da Fira" [a reference to Hitler spelled mockingly in Austrian dialect] has apparently restrained his blitzing heart once again and postponed annihilating the Reds. . . . There are still a few borders left that this son of a border patrolman has not yet crossed. But with "holy right" on his side, he will succeed in crossing them too. Then, one fine day, he will go home and ask his own grandmother who begot him. In the interim his cloven-hoofed public relations man is limping to and fro, preparing a welcome for him—down below.

That it was mutilated Austria's lot to have so monstrous a voice sound from one of her most insignificant corners is only compensated by the immortal Austrian voices of Gluck, Haydn, Mozart, Beethoven, Schubert, Brahms, Bruckner, Mahler, Lanner and the three Strausses. They conquered the world before he did and they will be victorious after him. . . .

By separate post we are sending you a small part of our "daily bread," a little cheese, salami and some cake and chocolate. Soon we may have to part with these ourselves. . . .

Try to win as many friends as you can and the good will of your superiors. All of them are important, even the most inconsequential. . . .

Getting through life is not an easy matter for anyone. . . . It is basically composed of two elements: struggle and love. There will never be a life without struggle, whatever pacifists may dream. Even love is struggle.

As you probably have heard, Stefan Zweig committed suicide in Brazil. He was so disinclined to struggle that, as early as 1934 (sensing what was to come), he left Salzburg and moved to Paris. Very soon after (it was still before the war), anticipating Hitler, he fled to London and became a British citizen. When war broke out in Europe, he escaped to the United States, forever escaping war, forever the first to escape. Long before war began to approach here, he fled again, to Brazil, and he was happy until the danger of war threatened even there. Then he fled the world.

Hofmannsthal, who could not endure him, always said that he had an infallible instinct for doing the right thing, even in the most difficult situations. I prefer to think that he or Hofmannsthal erred.

There is no way to avoid struggle. I beg you to be of good cheer and to feel yourself embraced and kissed with all my love.

Papa

My father's recommendation that I gain the good will of my superiors was not always easy to follow. One night at Crowder, I was shaken awake from deep sleep by the noncom on duty and told that there was a long-distance call for me. "Pick it up at Office Barrack II," he snapped, "fast!" Office

Barrack II was just a short distance down the road. But the night was paralyzingly cold. And my pajamas were designed for southern California's subtropical climate (I had not yet accustomed myself to the common practice of flopping into bed in the day's underwear). By the time I groped in the darkness for my army greatcoat and boots, found them and mushed through the snow-covered road to Barrack II, long minutes had ticked by. My entrance into the large room lined with filing cabinets and desks at which a number of officers were still at work was apparently awaited. A lieutenant pointed distastefully to the unhooked receiver lying like an uncoiled snake among his papers. I picked it up and heard my father's voice at the other end of the wire, asking why I had not written him in so long. Was I in good health? When I replied that I was fine, just fine, he was only partially relieved. Any army troubles? he asked. I assured him, omitting mention of the chain reaction of astonishment developing around me, that there were none. With his worries thus dissolved, there came to his mind the most natural question in the world for him: "Is it beautiful there where you are?" The cold, ugly looks fixed on me inside the room restrained me from laughing and the cold, ugly landscape outside restrained me from answering truthfully. To keep him happy—it took very little invention—I said that where I was, although not scenically beautiful, was rather unusual, completely different from any place I had ever visited. Then, after promising to write soon, I hung up, carefully thanking the lieutenant whose telephone I had held up so long for his kindness. "So you know how to speak English, too!" he exploded with a glare that started at my sleep-rumpled hair, coursed like flaming napalm down along my unbuttoned coat, the baby-blue, orange and white striped silk pajamas peeking out from under its hemline, my muddied boots and trailing laces. "Private!" he roared. "You're out of uniform! Plus you're out of your mind! You think we're running a freak show here?" With lily-livered hypocrisy I saluted, reciting all the mea culpas expected of me, about-faced and made for the door, where a second lieutenant tapped me on the shoulder. "Hey, soldier," he said with a snotty grin, "who was the last President you voted for?" "Hindenburg, sir," I answered. The man, no student of history, squinted at me suspiciously: "Are you kiddin'? What are you, Pennsylvania Dutch?" "No, sir," I replied, "I'm an enemy alien," and took advantage of the stunned hiatus to escape.

Basic training over, those of us with motion-picture experience were informed that we would be transferred to the Training Film Production Laboratory at Fort Monmouth, New Jersey. It was news welcomed by everyone except Junior. He died a thousand deaths thinking about all the officers awaiting him there who had been his employees—or unemployed—when he was head of production at Universal Studios. Our train had hardly pulled out of the station when his hypochondria flared into a psychosomatic bronchitis which took on momentum with each turn of the wheels. I was tremendously impressed by his expert appraisal of the specimens of sputum he collected in Kleenex. At the first stop, he insisted he must ring up his doctor in Beverly Hills. I begged him not to make a spectacle of himself. Junior lashed back indignantly: "Spectacle! I'm half dead. I need medical help." Me: "At this distance? How can your doctor even tell what's wrong with you?" Junior: "I'll cough over the telephone."

To distract him, I tried, against my better judgment, to sound him out about investing in my father's projects. Junior, my affectionate puppy, whose mind could not take in the contents of any reading matter save the racing form, answered that he would have to read the plays first. But he warned me not to count on him too much, as all the cash presently at his disposal was about to be tied up. He explained that, once in Monmouth, he would use his first pass to head for New York to meet an old pal he was importing from Hollywood; together, they were going to form an elaborate betting syndicate based on Junior's authority on horse racing, which would cover all the tracks in the area.

I was amazed, then, when, on the weekend this was supposed to take place, I found him in the barracks where I had said goodbye to him that morning, still in army fatigues, pacing up and down frenziedly. "Junior," I asked, "how come you're still here?" "I'm trapped," he squeaked. "The guy who opens my wall locker for me didn't show!"

Junior's locker adjutant finally did show and Junior took off in his dress uniform in the black seven-passenger Cadillac limousine he had hired. When he returned, it was, for me, not a minute too soon. That afternoon, during the antediluvian drill exercises that were a major part of our daily routine, I had, in weather nothing short of diluvian, picked up a chill and fever. Nevertheless, I had kept on "marching up and down again," not, let there be no mistake about it, through Kiplingesque heroism, but through not wanting to tangle with my top sergeant. In his opinion, if you went on sick call—you could be in the terminal stage of cancer—you were just plain malingering and deserved to have the bejesus kicked out of whatever life was left in your miserable body. In view of his idiosyncrasy, every time a felt a sneeze coming on, I tightened my facial muscles until it was squeezed away. Not one twitch deceived his hawk eye. "Private," he roared at me, "wipe that dumb grin off your face!"

When Junior found me lying on my cot, face flushed beet-red and teeth chattering, he was in his element. Before he even plunged a thermometer under my tongue, he diagnosed pneumonia. And when he read the 104-degree fever it registered, his satisfaction knew no bounds. He summoned the top sergeant to come to my cot and, brandishing the thermometer under his nose like a Crusader's sword at an infidel, demanded an ambulance to transport me to the infirmary. Though livid at Junior's high-handedness and suspicious of my low state, he called for the vehicle. But, as I was carried out, yelled: "If that temprachure ain't the same at the infurmery I'll eat your ass out! Both of youse!"

It was during my convalescence from a three-week bout with pneumonia that I received a twelve-page letter from my father (by actual count, twenty-four pages, as two of his handwritten lines, meticulous as copperplate engraving, were compressed between each single ruled line of the legal pad he used), dated April 17, 1942:

> I hear from Mrs. Viertel [Salka Viertel, wife of director Berthold Viertel, actress and screen writer, and close friend over many years] that you have been very ill. I'm terribly saddened by this news and hope fervently that you are over the worst by now. Perhaps it is of small comfort to you, but I may tell you that things that don't destroy one make one stronger in the end. . . .
>
> As for myself, time is running away at such a terrifying speed that to catch up with it and to find a hold somewhere I have to run after it head over heels. But then, downhill is, after all, the fastest route. . . .
>
> With this thought in mind, I would have preferred to be briefer, but that would take me more time than I have.

There followed a detailed account of his demoralizing daily life: His gem of a housemaid had left and the laundry she had done so exquisitely was now piling up, necessitating the expense (for which there were no funds) of giving it out to be done; Paul, his valet, was being difficult about his unpaid salary and could only be placated with chattel mortgages on various objets d'art; the Reinhardt Workshop faced bankruptcy. In short, on all sides, everything was a shambles. BUT (the word was underscored three times), he went on, he saw a ray of hope. Namely, that he had run into Stella Adler (actress–drama teacher) and her friend Harold Clurman (director-critic) at a dinner party. Although temporarily employed by major studios, their talents were given no outlet and they felt just as restive and out of place in Hollywood, professionally, as he. They had commiserated with each other, put their heads together and, as he expressed it, come up with an idea for a Continental-style program that could revolutionize the American theatre.

An example of their program:

> . . . So you can see why I am so excited. In other words, a *permanent* theatre (we'll try it first for one season). Five plays, new ones and old ones of enduring quality in a house not situated on Broadway. Without ballyhoo. Our accomplishments must advertise us! Based on subscription which, to begin with, will certainly not be wide, but which will gradually grow. . . . The unions will welcome and support a theatre of this kind. As a start, a few good names will be needed as an attraction. . . . A season of *forty weeks.* Each of the five plays would run an average of eight weeks. If a play proves to be very successful—and, as always, there is sure to be one out of several that does—it will be moved to another house, *on* Broadway, and, thereafter, may find its way to the road, perhaps even to films.
>
> Beyond that, we feel a studio theater ought to be formed in which young talent has a chance to appear in more *experimental* plays. They [Clurman and Adler] set great store by a children's theatre (which, for instance, is one of the biggest attractions in Moscow). . . .
>
> The price of tickets is to be correspondingly cheaper than Broadway's. The house is to have a thousand seats. . . .
>
> We agreed that for an entire season a hundred thousand dollars must be at our disposal in order for us to work in peace. That is surely not too much for *five plays*!

Now came an exhaustive list of contemporary authors whose as yet unwritten works would comprise part of the repertoire, the balance to be supplied by revivals of classics and "important plays which have been produced *inadequately* in the past." The list extended from Shakespeare to Odets and included Dostoevski and Thomas Wolfe (some of whose novels he thought should be dramatized). Then:

> I am not worried about the repertoire.
>
> I am not worried about the actors.
>
> I am least worried about the ensemble and the quality of the performances.
>
> Even success isn't my concern so long as everything isn't bet on one card—which unfortunately is the custom here. That is only attractive to gamblers.
>
> Finally, I believe that the psychological moment favors the project.
>
> The only thing I'm not sure about is whether the necessary money can be raised. . . . I really should go to New York immediately. It is already very late in the day. However, there is *still* time left. But for my trip and

> stay in New York and for small advances to authors and adaptors we need funds at once. *Therein lies the whole problem.* The so-called initial money is always the most difficult to obtain.

Without question, it was a splendid plan. Theoretically, it was even a healthy one. In every way, it was remarkably prophetic. But for him, at this stage it was unrealistic. I certainly could not raise a hundred thousand dollars for him. I could not even raise a hundred thousand cents for him at this moment.

The letter continued:

> I find both, Miss Adler and Mr. Clurman, most sympathetic. They are intelligent Jews with an inner drive toward better things, toward art. Both were in Europe, know the Russian, the French and the German theatre. . . . I have never seen her act. Though that never made much difference to me when I was casting. What is important is that she looks good, is of theatre blood, has a strong temperament, pronounced humor and a sharply critical brain; above all, she is a personality, which, in the theatre, is always the most important thing.
>
> I believe ours will be an excellent combination, one bound to make sense to anyone who *understands* the theatre.

It did not. Not to anyone at all, as things developed. The psychological moment was not favorable; "Off-Broadway" to backers of shows sounded as wacky as "off to see the Wizard"; unions, their members no longer orphans of the storm years, had shed their New Deal idealism in wartime prosperity; plays that did not exist did not find financing—not even five of them; revivals were box-office anathema; "good names" could afford to pick and choose and what they chose was not a program advancing the general weal of the theatre, but specific vehicles that would enhance their good names; "twenty thousand dollars for a play" was an anachronistic estimate. In a nutshell, riding-high New York show people were of no mind to welcome the overthrow of their contented way of life by a European myth and his fellow travelers: a high-charged Stanislavskian actress and a gifted founder of the suspiciously intellectual Group Theatre (which, despite its distinguished accomplishments, had been forced to close shop). After this swell of optimism I was shaken when my father subsided abruptly with: "I can't go on any more. Love, Papa."

Stella Adler and Harold Clurman had returned to New York City, tried and failed to raise "the initial money" or even a microscopic part of it. This did not dampen my father's—obviously regained—determination. Where there's a son, there's a way. When the Signal Corps acquired the old Paramount Studio in Astoria (christening place of our unit and inspiration of its motto), the Training Film Production Laboratory transferred there and became the SCPC. My father delayed his departure only for as long as it took to raise the money for his fare by selling some of his furniture to Warner Brothers Studio. As much as his spirit blazed, there was no doubt in my mind that this New York round was to be his last. His last round anywhere. His only chance to win it, so far as I could see, was for him to integrate into the *existing* American theatre. And he must be in a position to give orders, not take them, must be a producer on his own as he had been abroad. As a start, I rustled up the most interesting playwrights I knew, made luncheon, cocktail or dinner dates with them, introduced them to him and sat back while he captivated every one of them.

A new day began for Max Reinhardt. Once again, he received plays to read, to edit, to develop, and, potentially, to cast. His hope flowed, sometimes ebbed, but, most important for his morale, he was again afloat on a lively artistic tide. And yet, it needed support. I found it in Norman Bel Geddes, to whom, twenty years before, my father had given his first big chance. Geddes was happy to work with Reinhardt again. Not through a sense of past obligation, but because, as he said to me: "Your father's genius is timeless." In the years intervening, Geddes had successfully put on shows on his own. After my approach, he got together a producing partnership he thought would be effective: director-producer, Max Reinhardt; actor-producer, Eddie Dowling; manager-producer, Richard Myers; and designer-producer, himself. They eventually opened with Shaw's *Sons and Soldiers.*

To achieve this end, I stretched to the breaking point the liberty afforded me by army regulations. They permitted all GI's to use their free time as they chose, provided there was no collision with the subject of their military duties. I was on safe ground in that respect. Nevertheless, a few days after the press reports of my connection with *Rosalinda,* I woke up one morning to find myself on the transfer list to V-mail (the microfilm agency of the military postal service). Smelling professional envy I confronted my immediate superior (Major Robert Lord, a former Warner Brothers producer who had just sold a script to his old studio) with my suspicions. This raised a thin sneer: "Could be, Gottfried," he said, "playwriting didn't do you any good." Rather than engaging him in a debate about the propriety of an officer's writing over an enlisted man's, I went over his fatuous head to another motion-picture major, stationed in Washington, who had no playwriting ax to grind, and presented my argument. With no rebuttal, I won it on the spot.

Had I appealed to the head of the entire Signal Corps, Major General Dawson Olmstead, he would not have been aware that my proposed transfer involved any change of duty at all. Shortly after I had disentangled myself from the threat of playing an army post-office clerk, he paid an official visit to our unit. It was, apparently, intended as one of those man-to-man contacts with which warlords manifest oneness with their troops. We, above five hundred officers and men, were lined up in the yard standing at attention when he took up his position on a platform erected for the occasion. His address, although long on patriotic clichés, was mercifully brief. "Gentlemen," he concluded, "you take care of the V-mail and I'll take care of the female." Our icy silence froze his wide smile to a bewildered smirk. The day was saved when, suddenly, from one corner a roar of laughter blasted and spread like wildfire. It came from the corner where Junior had snickered: "Tough audience, what?"

Though the SCPC's function was as much of a blank to my father as it was to our commanding general, my father at least took the pains to inform himself about it:

M.R.: How did it go today at your . . . uh . . . Signal Corps?
G.R.: It went. Like all the other days.
M.R.: You sound bitter, Gottfried.
G.R.: I'm just tired.
M.R.: You look tired. I've been meaning to talk to you about this. Forgive me—it may seem odd but I'm not quite clear—what exactly are you working on out there?
G.R.: Shit.
M.R.: Gottfried, I am not against your drinking as much as you are lately. Although I am against it. I suppose it is the company your army life obliges you to keep. But must you use such language?
G.R.: Papa, it's not "language." I'm answering what you asked me. I'm working on shit.
M.R.: Very well, Gottfried, if this is your new style . . .
G.R.: Papa, I'm just trying to tell you what the film I'm producing for the Army is about. It's called *The Disposal of Human Waste.*

"Tired-looking" as the reluctant effort I put into the making of this film may have left me, it did wonders for my prestige with the honorable mention I received for it from the Medical Center at Carlisle Barracks, Pennsylvania. Whereas with my next, *K Rations and How to Chew Them,* a film I gave my all to, I fell flat on my face. K rations, rich in dextrose, the emergency sustenance provided fighting men who find themselves stranded without nourishment, may not, NOT be gulped down. K rations, the hero of the piece, must be chewed slowly and deliberately. Here the plot thickens: Hasty consumption, the villain of the piece, causes nausea and dizziness. I fell so in love with this drama I could not bear the thought of anybody else's directing it. I held the lowest rank in my crew. Both my star and cameraman were commissioned officers. I was even outranked by my head electrician, a staff sergeant. This posed problems. Not that mine were unique. For example, Private Cukor (formerly top Hollywood director George Cukor) was ordered out of the room by a major, his former assistant at MGM, during the socializing that preceded and followed the Cukor-photographed interview with Undersecretary of War Robert P. Patterson in Washington. And I, in the middle of directing *K Rations,* had to leave my entire crew immobilized for a number of hours to report for short-arm inspection and had to stand in line for the flesh-mortifying ceremony that commissioned personnel were, of course, exempt from.

K Rations and How to Chew Them faded in on Lieutenant Dan Dailey, Jr. (playing a dumb GI), squatting in a seared battlefield, chomping recklessly away. He seems very happy. Little does he know that he is abandoning his tender innards to the terrible clutch of Hasty Consumption. Thus, he opens his mouth—on the screen it looks like a shark's moving in for the kill—to take another hefty plug of K rations, but, in the nick of time, is stayed by a kindly sergeant, an old hand who gently, but colorfully, warns him of the danger of his rashness and demonstrates exactly how K rations must be masticated. Fascinated—perhaps a little bit wiser?—the private follows the sergeant's example and starts rotating his jaws slowly *slowly* around the K rations he has now taken a teentsy cautious nibble of. He salivates. He smiles. He takes an even teentsier nibble and grinds his molars around it in jaw-defying circles again and again and again until we fear his head must split asunder. The film fades out on the private's ecstatic rubber face chawing, cheek to cheek, in unison with the kindly sergeant's leathery one.

In the projection room at Carlisle Barracks, the trial run was a wow. Well, that is, if the hyena laughs of the enlisted part of my audience counted for anything. Official reaction I never did get to find out. The picture was never shown again.

It was high time for me to make a change. Useful as my being in the SCPC undoubtedly was to my father's ends, it was of no use whatever to anything else that was of importance to me. Without telling him—I didn't dare to—I applied for Officer Candidate School at Fort Myer, Maryland, the Army Intelligence Training Center. On my first furlough I followed it up with a personal visit. I was surprised at the smile of welcome given me by the major in charge. He assured me he would see to it that my application was processed as speedily as possible—with his endorsement. "What, by the way," he asked me quietly as I stood up and thanked him, "makes you think that your application will be favorably reviewed?" I was stunned to hear this eroding question after our constructive hour together. "Because," I said, "it makes sense." He shrugged. "Since when," he said, walking me to the door, "does the military make sense?" I reflected, but did not answer. He patted my shoulder, ventured a confidence: "Young man, there are three kinds of intelligence—human, animal and military. In that order. Never forget it. Good luck to you." Shortly after my return to the SCPC, I received word that my application had been rejected.

So, back once and for all to grinding out *How to Slice Army Bread, How to Understand Ohm's Law, How to Camouflage Convoys, How to Handle the M1 Rifle, How to Storm a Pillbox,* more how-tos than you could shake yourself awake from; back to viewing, assorting and assembling the rushes of film shot by overseas field units; back to envying friends and former colleagues, the John Hustons, Willy Wylers and John Fords, high-ranking officers given the latitude to shoot exciting war films like *The Battle of San Pietro, The Memphis Belle, The Battle of Midway*; back to after-reveille marching in the streets of Long Island City or later, when the SCPC branched out to an office building between Lexington and Third avenues on East Thirty-second Street, along a route that led us past Bellevue Hospital, where, from behind its barred windows, a faithful audience of mental patients awaited us matinally with thumbed noses, catcalls and floods of obscenity. I always wished there had been a way to let them know that we were brothers under the skin, that departure from rational behavior had put them behind bars and us in front of them as a ludicrous traffic nuisance.

Unexpectedly, Army Intelligence suddenly took an interest in me after all. Though not in the direction I had aspired to. What brought it on was an eavesdropper's report of a conversation I had, in German, with an old friend in the Gladstone bar. The language, apparently, was suspicion number one. Suspicion number two was my comment that big battleships were obsolete, that their gigantic construction costs, the delicate problem of concealing them from air reconnaissance while in the shipyard and the inevitable torpedo or bomb that smashed them to smithereens the minute they put out to sea made clear to everyone except admirals that they were very expensive dinosaurs. This seemingly was sufficient evidence to stamp me as a Nazi sympathizer. Much later, it was indicated to me on the QT that I was a grave security risk. Tangled is the way the Army lets you know it considers you a grave security risk, without telling you why or giving you an opportunity to disprove it. Colonel Manny Cohn was as faithful as steel to army regulations. Yet he chose to temper it with a touch of human kindness. He summoned me to his office and said: "Reinhardt, don't ask any questions. You're in trouble. There are charges against you. I'm not saying what they are. I'll take care of you. Keep your nose clean and sit tight." Keeping my nose clean and sitting tight meant twiddling my thumbs because I was no longer allowed to touch classified material. And, for some obscure reason, everything processed by the SCPC was classified "top secret."

Sons and Soldiers started with a bang on all sides. Financing came gushing in with MGM's offer of complete subsidy on a pre-production-deal basis; the Morosco Theatre was secured and a cast of talent and name value—among others, Geraldine Fitzgerald, Millard Mitchell, Karl Malden and Stella Adler—assembled with ease. The only exception to this impressive company was a young actor around town. My father found him so promising he cast him for the leading role. This choice caused the only controversy between writer and director: "Professor," Private Shaw warned, "I have nothing against this—what's his name—Peck, Gregory Peck? He's terrific-looking. Maybe he can even play the part. Okay. But where does that get us? Hollywood will grab him up and my play will be a flop." My father found this reasoning irrational. Shaw, though wise to Broadway, had never really been a winner there. My father, though having been a winner there at times, as we know, never really understood it. Beyond that, what he envisioned, as always, was a production, *his* production of a play. Whereas Shaw envisioned a play, *his* play, produced. Experience had taught him that what faced critical fire was the play, not the production. My father had never feared critical attack. His experience was that he had more weight with audiences than the critics had. And even glamour boys under his wings were taken seriously by the public (and by the critics in the end). That there could be *no* public without good reviews was something Max Reinhardt had yet to learn the hardest way.

Irwin did not carry his point or pursue it for long, as he was soon in Europe and too absorbed in his activities there as a freshly appointed warrant officer to give further thought to the dubious contribution an obscure actor might make to his play. Rehearsals, with the obscure actor included, went ahead swimmingly. Even the dress rehearsal, true to theatre superstition, was a shambles. This cheering intelligence was, as usual, slipped under my door:

. . . chaotic is the only way I can describe it. Geddes has again partially achieved beautiful effects and again was dangerously drunk and irritable. I was quiet but inwardly gravely troubled. Love,

Papa

On opening night, audience response exceeded our wildest expectations, while the connoisseurs—I remember particularly an effusive Moss Hart—crowded backstage to congratulate my father and the actors. The consensus was that they would run forever. After this exciting appraisal, we celebrated until dawn. I, with no KP on the day's agenda, stayed up for the morning papers. (For once my father went to bed before I did.)

The reviews were crushing. Again, to a point where one of New York's most influential critics was so outraged that his valuable time should be abused by having to write about this drivel he forgot to mention the director. While the actors, including the young unknown (who was promptly snapped up by Hollywood scouts), as though extraneous to the play and to the direction that had inspired them, were lauded to the skies for brilliant interpretation of their roles. It was a Saturday morning, which meant that, after reporting to the post for neatness inspection, I would be dismissed at noon for a free weekend. To do what? I could not face my father after the catastrophic press. I could only delude myself that the afternoon papers might be kinder and that, if I put off going to him until they were out, I would meet his smile and not—my foreboding—his despair.

Late in the afternoon, I knocked on his door. There was no answer. I waited and then walked in. He was sitting stony-still on a chair in the middle of the room, hands crossed in his lap. On the floor all around him were scattered the newspapers we both had read. "They're too silly, Papa," I said. "Yes," he answered, "it's all too silly. I waited a long time for you. It's late. I have to change now or I won't get to the theatre on time." I did not believe my ears. Was it possible that of all the plays he had done he would choose *this* one to attend a second performance of? In a house that would be empty, haunted? I begged him not to expose himself to such self-torment. He cut me short angrily. I could not let him walk this via dolorosa alone.

To my surprise, when we arrived at the Morosco an hour before curtain time, the entire company was waiting onstage. He had not told me that, contrary to the custom of a lifetime, he had called a rehearsal *after* an opening to give his critique. The actors listened to it raptly and, as though it meant the show's chance for survival, each, in turn, toiled painstakingly over the slightest nuance in word, movement or breath he suggested. From the front row I watched him expertly, lovingly, tirelessly trying to breathe life into a corpse. Didn't he know, no matter how admirable his efforts, that death cannot be denied? There was no way of telling what was in his mind. When he stepped down from the stage, his face was impassive as he walked—with me at his side—to the box office and waited, vainly, for the arrival of ticket buyers.

We strolled along Forty-fifth Street and we could see—down Shubert Alley—to the 44th Street Theatre, where people were jostling and pushing to get into *Rosalinda.* The sight gave my father no pleasure. Success "over there" left him indifferent. Dominant in his mind was the failure "here." He shook his head, unable to grasp that in a city of so many millions there wasn't even a handful curious enough to want to see a play directed by Max Reinhardt, whatever its negative reviews. He turned to me with a tired smile: "I'm going in now. You . . . I suppose . . . are not?" I could not, because I had guard duty with the Beverly Hills Commandos that night, but, had I been given a choice, I could not. I simply could not. My father went in, watched the performance and, after the curtain dropped, polished it lovingly as he did every night of the twelve nights before the play closed.

Phone Eleonora: H. has already been there. Electrocardiogram encouraging. Call Darvas, make a date with her after six. The hours drag on. Six o'clock at last! Dismissed. No, still another headache: I'm told to report to Major Litvak immediately. Irritating. Whatever is burdening his soul can damned well wait till tomorrow. I know what he's working on: a propaganda picture, Know Your Enemy Germany. *Have been familiar with the project for a long time, ever since the Army first assigned it to civilian film makers* [my friends Ernst Lubitsch and the German writer Bruno Frank]. *My two civilian friends proved too militant for the military. The Army took the project away from them and went about making it itself. I'd love to work on it. But not as Litvak's office boy.*

[Curiously enough, via many detours, in the end I inherited the picture after all, and, last in the long parade of its producers, it was I who finally finished it—after the capitulation of the Third Reich. Proof that it's more difficult to make films than war—in any event, that it takes longer.]

What a relief that Litvak's designs, however unintentional, turn out to be a blessing! He asks whether I know Albert Einstein and George Grosz. Say yes to the former, but doubt he still remembers me from our casual acquaintance in Berlin. And Grosz I've never met at all. "But surely both of them know your father?" They do. Would I take on the job of getting them to make a contribution to Know Your Enemy? *Would I ever! It's my furlough solution! No company commander, not even General Eisenhower, can dictate to me how I'm to go about recruiting these distinguished gentlemen or limit the length of time I'll need to do it in. See no purpose in mentioning that Grosz has given up the satanic satire that Litvak has in mind for idyllic landscape painting and that I've absolutely no confidence in the Einstein ploy. First, don't even know how or whether I can get through to him. Second, his unique coiffure and costume would make him an unlikely candidate for the role—envisioned by the foxy major—of inflamer of the hearts of our GI's, hearts as unintellectual as they are susceptible to humor, with or without a rousing philippic against the Furor Teutonicus in the pidgin English as spoken by Herr Professor Einstein. I congratulate Litvak on his inspiration, but insist I must be allowed to do things my own way. No interference or any control of my movements. "Goes without saying, Reinhardt!" The surname is a compromise. The natural "Gottfried" has fallen victim to military protocol. For "Sergeant," Tola Litvak is too intelligent.*

Meeting with Darvas not the most auspicious. To begin with, she's irked that I'm late. Situation not improved by my evasions re Papa. She doesn't believe a word about the "accident." Difficult to say to a good friend that trust in her friendship cannot be risked, yet her help is needed. Ask her to straighten out Dr. F. mess. Say Papa flatly refused to see a doctor who would klatsch to every refugee in New York. "And who's treating him now? Someone from the moon?" Lili can be very snippish. I lie: "An American dermatologist." "Not Eleonora's doctor?" Mumble out a lot of jabber-wabber about vaccinations, inoculations, scratch and/or patch tests Papa is receiving. Haven't the vaguest clue what I'm talking about. And she knows I haven't. Ask her to go to Irion with some alibi for postponing rehearsals. She refuses. Not unkindly, but because she honestly doesn't believe that on her own she can present my point of view convincingly. We agree to go as a united front tomorrow.

Papa has settled down into a prescribed daily schedule. There's a single minor mutiny: "B-but I m-must g-get out of h-here!" Eleonora understands this language easily by now and translates: "Papa and I want to go for a walk now and again." He keeps nodding in confirmation. I accede with every reason to object: Am nervous about the elevator, the lobby, the streets, the inevitable encounters.

TUESDAY,
SEPTEMBER 28, 1943

A day off from school. What a glorious feeling! Not even having to "combine." If only the cause for my elation weren't this nightmare! Too depressing the use I have to put my newly won "freedom" to:

1 *Long, detailed letters to Wolfgang, Mama and Salka.*

2 *Call Korngold in Hollywood. He's miffed by "still another delay." Complains bitterly that in view of everything he had every right to expect Helen contract months ago. "In view of everything" I would have to be Talleyrand to make credible why, after months of pleading with him to hold on till we raised financing, now that nothing stands in the way, we still hedge. Am no Talleyrand. Quandary: If I make light of*

Papa's illness K. won't swallow it. If I so much as hint at partial truth his sharp mind will ferret it out altogether. But to admit it would only produce one of his Götterdämmerung moods. Am relieved he thinks Papa and I are just procrastinating again. Anyway, manage to keep him on the hook. For how long is something else. He threatens to drop out and accept a film just offered if he doesn't know by the end of the week.

3 *Call Kohner* [Paul Kohner, friend and agent, specializing in refugee talent], *exhaust every brand of sweet talk to get him to hold on to our Menelaus. Reaction same as the other K.'s: Either we sign contract within a week or Bressart no longer available.* [Felix Bressart, that marvelously silly, sad and sly comedian of Berlin stage and screen, not only had the gift but was one of the few émigrés who had been given the chance to make American film audiences laugh and cry—Ninotchka, The Shop Around the Corner, Comrade X. Comedians, especially those with a hammer-heavy German accent, sooner or later make laughter curdle into yawns. With Bressart it was later. When it happened, he made a sly, sad and abstruse move: He became an osteopath. His clientele was a mere handful of well-wishers from the past. When it gradually shrank to nothing he died, anything but comically, by his own hand.]

4 *Most disagreeable meeting with the Music Dragon. Snorting more Magyar fire than usual. Darvas lends valiant support, but Irion distrusts me. Doesn't believe in the twenty thousand from Paley. Promise written confirmation.*

5 *More agreeable: Meeting with Corbett.* [Leonora Corbett, our Helen, English actress, of music-hall origin, who blitzed Broadway in Noël Coward's Blithe Spirit. Married—but not working seriously at it—to John Royal, one of the heads of NBC.] *Need no support here. She trusts me. Believes I mean what I mean because I'm the errant Paris—in woolly government issue—who's stealing her away from her Royal Menelaus. But being a lady of varied commitments, she agrees to postponement of our Trojan War only with reservation.*

WEDNESDAY,
SEPTEMBER 29, 1943

Enter the maestro to end all maestros, Dr. Foster Kennedy, the incomparable. In his super-presence the incidental presence of Dr. H. is tolerated. But nothing more. From the way he talks, walks, deigns to sit among us, breathes the rarefied air he carries with him, it is evident that he's the greatest. The patient is only there to give his sunburst personality something to shine down upon. This prima donna outpeacocks all the prima donnas Papa has loathed his whole life long. If the name Max Reinhardt means anything to this haughty Scotchman, he keeps it well concealed. All in a medical day's work. Stay in the room this time. I want to know exactly what's what. "What" is everything. Papa's life. Or death. The examination is brutal, deliberately so in my opinion. For Papa a trauma. He's frighteningly docile. What a torture it must be to have every inch of one's body probed by a stranger's fingers and to have one's infirmities callously pointed out. Reflexes are measured, it is determined whether and where muscular deterioration has set in, an old man is abruptly given orders to do knee bends, to lie down, to get up again, to walk a straight line, to stand still and rigid. His arms and legs are gone over, his eyesight, hearing, equilibrium, sense of smell, powers of speech and perception, his blood pressure and heart are tested—heart and soul, inside out. Self-respect is not a measurable function, much less a palpable organ.

Foster Kennedy confirms H.'s diagnosis. Complete rehabilitation possible within six weeks. Recommends—nonsense: commands speech lessons. Halfway to the door he remembers: The fee for his visit will be two hundred and fifty dollars. A deterrent? It would seem so, as he makes a point of "little purpose in a second consultation unless there's a radical change." We're told we are "in very good hands." But the tone in which we're told it implies that the hands are just good enough for us and vice versa. That subtlety is the better part of healing never occurs to this autocrat.

Follow him outside for a few words alone. Am brushed off: Everything to be said has been said. "Never beat around the bush in front of a patient." But speech lessons? Max Reinhardt must learn to speak all over again. Like a child. But as he can't do it on his own, he'll need a coach. In essence, hitherto "mute" brain cells, cells never used for this purpose, must now be educated to take over the work of the damaged or destroyed ones. The teacher he'll send tomorrow is tops in his line.

Call Wolfgang again. Is greatly relieved. Ask when Thimig's arriving. Learn she isn't coming east for time being, decides to await developments. Supposedly has chance for job in anti-Nazi picture at Columbia. Hitler's mother or something.

Am summoned upstairs by Eleonora. Very important, she says.

Papa looks at me with an I-won't-be-said-no-to look. As usual Eleonora interprets: Tomorrow is Rosh Hashana and he insists on going to a synagogue. Wonder would he have had the same urge if he were well? Am *convinced he knows why I'm against it: On these high holidays seats have to be reserved in advance. Cannot risk making reservations in his name. He cannot possibly handle a fuss made over him. Even using another name would be of little help. He's sure to be recognized. But cannot dissuade him. His mind is set. I promise to make arrangements.*

Unfortunately, Meyer Weisgal, our technical adviser and liaison officer with the Jewish world, cannot help me this time. It would mystify him—not knowing about Papa—that I'm looking for a hideaway synagogue and that he hasn't been invited to join the party. Fall back on Franz Horch [former director of the play department in the Reinhardt theatres], *a man with a resourceful, New York–based brother. Bless gullible Horch for not questioning my cooked-up story. Resourceful brother comes up with a suitable synagogue and reserves two places in fictitious name. Eleonora will go along.*

THURSDAY,
SEPTEMBER 30, 1943

Everything went smooth as silk. Eleonora guarded him like a lioness, no one took notice of him and he returned home happy. He tells me about his mother, about her piety and solemnness, and about his father's serene, trusting nature [I always felt it a sign of special affection for me that he gave me as middle name his beloved father's first name: Wilhelm] *and how important it is never to let family bonds be split and never to lose sight of one's heritage. My own mama and a favorite story of hers come to mind; how every Sunday lunch, for years, she served her "solemn," kosher mother-in-law—of whom she was extremely fond, albeit nerve-racked by her unbroken silences—roast pork palmed off as veal, without ever being discovered.*

Eleonora is floating: Papa is recovering! She swears by it. Not that I have to be sold. His speech more fluent, he's no longer resentful of a regime, all around he's much more relaxed. The days fall into a fixed pattern. With less embarrassment Eleonora and I fill in the words that escape him; the medicine prescribed is taken unprotestingly; he submits to whatever is on the therapeutic agenda—part skeptically, part curiously, part doer, part observer. Eleonora prepares his breakfast, lunch, dinner, waits at the table, cleans away. Eleonora is the perfect petty-bourgeois homemaker. Almost. What she is, is her own version of the story by Grünfeld [Heinrich Grünfeld, cello virtuoso and Berlin wit of the twenties: A man's ideal wife would *be a lady in the drawing room, a cook in the kitchen, a cocotte in the bedroom. What most men get is a lady in the kitchen, a cook in the bedroom and a cocotte in the drawing room]. Playing "lady in the drawing room" comes naturally to Eleonora—it's no play. Playing "cook in the kitchen" is tougher labor. Playing "cocotte" is her most ambitious effort. [Being Eleonora, she went about it in the most quixotic way when she set her cap for Rudolf Forster, the Dauphin in Reinhardt's* Saint Joan, *Antonio in his* Merchant of Venice. *Tracking down the most libidinous of all her racy friends, she induced him to make a connection for her with the fanciest streetwalker available on Vienna's Kärntnerstrasse—a street known for excellence in that trade—and to set up a course of lessons in the art of seduction. Apparently she graduated with honors, for Forster followed her to America and married her there.]*

Lull at dinner. Lash about in my mind for something to divert Papa with. Clear up mystery of Forster's sudden flight from Eleonora. [The counterfeit was no enduring substitute for the real thing and Kärntnerstrasse eventually triumphed over Hollywood Boulevard.] He notices that I'm only pretending to eat. "I s-see you've already had your d-dinner!" His old implicit reproach comes to me with the same sad, gentle smile. And my answer, stereotyped over the years, leaves me with the same bad conscience it always has: True, I've eaten before dinner—a frequent offense of mine—have gorged myself on Corbett's hors d'oeuvres. If Papa's reproof tonight had been followed by the question whether I had been with Mama, together with cutting remarks about her "opportune gall-bladder colics," we'd have come full circle. But, as it is, my reaction—the traditional one of dutifully gulping down under his watchful eye what's put in front of me—that resolves the issue momentarily.

Double Portions

I SUPPOSE MY BROTHER had known for quite a while that something was brewing. But to a six-year-old, the sudden, inexplicable disappearance of his father came as a startling surprise. Aside from my yearning to be with him, I was left with a feeling of intangible uneasiness. No question, a severe blow had been dealt my mother, one that she seemed able to take with less and less equanimity as the orphaned family continued to play out the summer holiday, pretending nothing had happened. But there were all of a sudden conversational taboos.

My mother was, of course, not the type of person to give up the only man she had ever loved—and would ever love—without a struggle. Nor was she only a strong-willed, emotional, sensual woman. She was also an actress. And he was Max Reinhardt. She had determined to remain "Frau Professor," in the theatre, in society, in her heart, if not in his. She felt she had earned that distinction. She had been the first great passion in his life. Every word of his ardent love letters remained imprinted on her keen one-track mind:

> My sweet, madly beloved Else-Baby, my dear, dear darling! I am sitting home lonely. Downstairs they are singing melancholy songs and in my heart burns a deep, fervid longing for you. It is indescribable. This morning I had you, this evening I saw you, tomorrow morning, tomorrow afternoon and tomorrow night I will see you and yet, I am dying of a passionate, unquenchable desire for you. Ah, what did I not want to create and make once I had furnished my own apartment! And now that everything is here, more beautiful than I had thought, I am simply incapable of doing anything. My thoughts are with you continuously. A painful, tormenting restlessness fills me and a deep inexplicable anguish is rending my breast. It is utterly terrifying. Else, don't believe I am saying this just with the usual exaggeration of someone in love. Unfortunately, it is all too literally true. Bless you! Good night! A thousand hot, sizzling kisses. Your Max.

Thus, in 1902, five years after they had met, in a note from house to house in Berlin. And, ten years later, in a wire from Baden, near Vienna:

> BELOVED, MY FERVENT THANKS. YOUR DEAR WORDS AWOKE ME IN MY BIRTHPLACE. ALWAYS, ALWAYS, EVEN IN SORROW AND ANGER MY DEEP LOVE FOR YOU GLOWS UNDIMINISHED. NEVER FORGET THAT. AM IN MIDDLE OF WORK, EMBRACING YOU LOVINGLY PIRSCH [PET NAME] . . . ALWAYS YOUR MAX.

He had made love to her the very night before his unannounced departure from the island of Sylt and nothing had indicated an abatement of his desire for her body. She did not understand the abruptness of the break and refused to believe in its finality. She had shared his beginnings, good times and bad, false starts and risky gambles. She had not attached herself to success. She had, as she herself often proudly and truthfully repeated, detected genius before most others did and lent invaluable support to its burgeoning. A recognized beauty, talented in her own right, intelligent, a good judge of people, Gentile, a native of the merciless city the young, starry-eyed stranger from a milder climate was attempting to make his steep way in, she gave him professional comradeship, filled his strong physical needs and partook of his soaring dreams of great accomplishments, at the crucial moment bringing him back to earth with her common sense. For both worked together in the same company, looked back on similar humble upbringings, plotted common rebellion and common enterprises and were to one another a much-needed source of strength in their formative years.

But there had also been a more down-to-earth aspect to the union: it opened to the ambitious, visionary, shy, insecure Jewish boy from middle-class Vienna doors in Berlin that might have remained closed to him, at least for some precious time. She was just as ambitious, her sights, of course, set a little less high, but not insecure, and a dreamer only to the extent of her unshakable belief in him. This sober belief had a contagious effect on the sober North German environment.

Her build, somewhat on the Junoesque side, a symbol of auxiliary power during his first steps into uncharted territory—and later, once ensconced there, becoming more and more overpowering to him—was tall for an ingenue, whether playing solemn heroines or young ladies with a twinkle in her vivacious gray-green eyes. His eyes were a radiant blue, apt to express deep astonishment and, when amused, devilishly mischievous, when angry, burning with biblical scorn. My mother eventually became convinced quite literally that he was Satan. But in those early days, she saw in him a superior being that could do no wrong, even when he obviously did—like steadfastly refusing to marry her, like being notoriously unfaithful to her and, at the same time, so jealous that he could not bear her kissing her partners on the stage—an oddly unprofessional attitude for such a master of his craft, which cost her many choice parts, and inevitably created ever more rivals for her on the stage and ever more unfaithfulness off.

> . . . SHOCKED THAT AFTER ALL WE DISCUSSED, SAID, WROTE AND YOU FINALLY PROMISED, YOU AGAIN REQUEST LEAVE OF ABSENCE. AM NOT IRRITATED OR STUBBORN, JUST DEEPLY SAD AND FULL OF LONGING. . . . I REPEAT QUITE CALMLY AND IRREVOCABLY: NEVER, AT NO TIME, WILL I RESIGN MYSELF TO THAT. YOUR MAX.

A typical reaction to one of her requests for permission to go on tour away from his theatres, angrily expressed as late as 1912 in a telegram from Paris.

This domineering lover and boss was smallish for a man who fought stoutness all his life. The character roles in which he used to be cast in his early acting years—mostly old men with bad postures—allowed him to hide his immature awkwardness behind heavy makeup and long beards. After the performance, when it was time to take them off, he drew himself up at her side to the erect figure he purposefully developed. Forbidden to wear high heels, she joined him on that brisk walk which would take him to all the dreamt-of places, from many of which she—and her no longer welcome common sense—would be excluded. This prospect she found repugnant and was determined to shut out at all costs, costs too high for her, as it turned out.

Whether she saw herself, for the first time, facing an opponent as single-minded as she was herself and of the same youthful innocence that had once so excited him in her (my father never relished maturity in women, either of body or of soul) or whether she felt her marriage was anyway drifting toward the breaking point, she chose, for the first time, not to ignore a vexing infatuation, and became obsessed by the necessity of destroying an all-consuming passion. Had her tactics been less unyielding, this latest amour, as the true friends of both agreed, might well have ended like all the others and remained one in a life rich in episodes and thinly spread with leading parts. Putting up so fierce and unexpected a resistance, she only solidified Helene Thimig's spell over him and cemented their attachment beyond any he had previously formed (and unfailingly severed). Moreover, seeing Helene Thimig continuously challenged, foiled and humiliated filled him with a guilty conscience, a sense of obligation, a protective instinct normally alien to his nature. Surely, my mother had never benefited from any of them. Thus, it was she who actually forced the dominating role on her rival. But she committed an even graver error. By her uncompromising stance, she played directly into the hands of her main adversary: her string-pulling brother-in-law.

It was not her first error on that score. Edmund had never been her friend, although, ironically, it was her advice that had prompted my father to make him his partner. My father adored his family, but the record of its members instilled him with little confidence in their capabilities. My mother sensed that this brother, every bit as ambitious as Max—*for* Max—even shyer and more insecure, the very opposite of a visionary, in fact a confirmed realist to whom even Max's most daring flights of imagination were utmost reality—that this brother, whom she did not particularly care for, was different and interesting, despite a history of professional and personal failure.

Her premonition proved as beneficial to my father's business fortunes as it was disastrous for her home life. Edmund became his brother's slave and master. He sacrificed his own existence and ran the other's brilliantly. Ever grateful that (in his own words) being in the habit of leaving his toys about when through playing, he had found someone else to perform the thankless task of tidying up after him, Max Reinhardt henceforward made no decision without Edmund. And every penny to Max or to anybody else was doled out by Edmund. Soon, Max had no inkling any more how much he took in, how much was laid aside, how much he owed. No accounts were ever kept between the brothers. It was a perfect partnership based on complete trust. It was, in many ways, a mystic partnership, one which, in any event, left little room for a female companion, let alone the possessive wife Fräulein Heims had all the earmarks of becoming. If Max, because he cherished his freedom, resisted marriage, children, an orderly household—ideals my mother heartily embraced and her family vociferously expected her to live up to—they were downright anathema to the eternal bachelor Edmund, who had other ideas about his brother's freedom. And should Max give signs of weakening under the by no means negligible pressure of Fräulein Heims, he could always draw on the strength of ". . . er . . . my brother . . ."—soon to become household words of procrastination in Berlin's theatrical world, for they meant that, no matter how enthusiastically the Professor had reacted to an idea, before it could materialize, this toughest of fraternal hurdles had to be cleared first.

There arose a further hurdle in my mother's early path, in the person of a colleague, the most "modern" German actress of the period, the mouthpiece of Maeterlinck, Strindberg, Wilde, Wedekind and Hofmannsthal, Gertrud Eysoldt, of whom the critic and theatre historian Julius Bab wrote:

> . . . [she] has the sexless, gaunt, pointedly moving body of a boy, the thin, cracked voice of a child, the volatile, grimacing mien of a cat. . . . Eysoldt produces art so long as her cunning brain directs her weak physique to transform into heroines of weakness those demons that modern authors create through passionately exaggerated stylization: seductive in impotence, driven by lack of will power, naïvely dangerous: Salome, Selysette, Lulu . . .

Though physically and mentally the antithesis of Else Heims, she had two driving impulses in common with her: the craving for Max Reinhardt the director and Max Reinhardt the male. While able to satisfy the first, she failed in the second. And like several others who suffered that frustration, she compensated for it by settling for and succeeding with the brother. It was, after all, the next-best thing: he lived in the same house, their offices were in the same building, their voices, their charm, their reticence were deceptively alike, their interests intimately intertwined. It seems to have been possible as well as tempting to obtain the benefit of the utopian by way of the feasible. At the same time, one could exert power over the man of one's choice through another, a scheme for which Eysoldt's style was ideally suited. My father's ever wide-open ears were especially attuned to this insidious voice because its owner was not only an arresting personality on the stage but the inamorata of his beloved brother. Not only did she bombard him with vicious epistolary diatribes against his would-be bride (all promptly read and collected and carefully filed by the target so that later they could serve as material for readings to her sons) but many more subtle ways of warning Max and poisoning his mind were open to her by distilling her venom through Edmund's fraternal solicitude.

That in the face of this camarilla (there were many other ill-wishers who detested their idol and sponsor's being monopolized by someone in their midst) my mother got as far as she did testifies to an extraordinary degree of stamina and resolve. Of course, Edmund looked just as warily on other love affairs and, since there was a never-ending string of them, there might have been a way for my mother, once established, to arrive at some modus vivendi with him—as later Helene Thimig succeeded in doing—based on their shared threat from new and younger interlopers. To her subsequent regret, she did not find it. On the contrary, she fought Edmund openly and made a deadly enemy of him. At one of her few triumphs in this doomed campaign, when, in 1908, she bore my father their first child, he consoled his devastated brother by making a trip to Paris with him. He was neither present nor married when the baby arrived. Deeply wounded, she swore never again to have a child with my father. By her own admission, four and a half years later, I was due more to carelessness than perjury.

Edmund never overlooked anything and kept his vows. He never forgave her. And when she finally brought off the marriage in 1910, legalizing a bond that had, by then, lost much of its tensile strength, significantly the anticlimax took place in England, out of Edmund's reach. But it was no victory over him. It merely hardened his hostility and made it more difficult for the now lawful wife to collect household money, any money, to obtain the roles she felt entitled to or the raises and lucrative leaves of absence her colleagues were able to wheedle out of him. For it was that simple: Whoever wanted something from Max had to get it from Edmund.

Helene Thimig—or "Madame," as she was referred to in the presence of my mother; the name, as though the individual behind it were thereby erased, was the strictest conversational taboo of all—was no exception. She gained Edmund's conditional good will and many of her wishes, unlike my mother's, were granted because of it. But for the position she desired most, to become officially First Lady of the Reinhardt Theatre, the official hostess of Leopoldskron (enabling her, for instance, to escort the Archbishop of Salzburg to the front door and bid him goodbye, instead of having to pretend that she too was leaving like every other guest and to sneak back when the coast was clear), to share formally at his side, as the new "Frau Professor," the honors heaped on him, she had to wait until long after Edmund's death, until a time when there was no more Reinhardt theatre, no Leopoldskron, few honors, and the title of "Professor," once awarded by the Duke of Coburg, had given way to the more up-to-date and suitably American "Doctor." What took my mother twelve years to achieve took her successor sixteen and was even less of an achievement. Like my mother, she simply could not get past the brotherly guardian of the status quo—nor, for a further five years, past his ghost.

True, she and Edmund, with the help of Auguste Adler, her school chum whom she had strategically placed at my father's side as his ever-present amanuensis, and, if anything, more sharp-witted than she herself, conspired at a hundred schemes to wrest a divorce from my mother. Max Reinhardt sued her from Riga (Latvia) to Reno (Nevada) with way stations in Berlin, Vienna, Prague and Pressburg. He changed his legal residence and nationality at will according to the current venue. He had her shadowed by private eyes (fun to pick them out under the windows of our house). No likely or unlikely candidate in Berlin's society was spared being dragged through the courts and newspapers as a correspondent. Every economic squeeze play was employed. Funds were cut off (after all, she was a self-supporting actress!). She was blacklisted by the first theatres in Berlin and Vienna (no manager wished to earn Max Reinhardt's disfavor). Then, after enough sticks, a carrot was held out: a part, a bonus, a promissory rendezvous of reconciliation. All for naught. No stratagem worked—legally, economically, psychologically.

Why? Was my mother invincible? Almost. As this fight became a cause gradually filling her entire life, she concentrated on it at the expense of everything else, whereas her opponents, by necessity, had other preoccupations as well. On the other hand, the power, the money, the best brains were on his side. And Edmund had long since gained the reputation for getting his—Max's—way more often than not. So what was wrong? Perhaps Edmund got his—Max's—way in this case too; at least according to Edmund's interpretation of his brother's wishes. And who is to say that his interpretation was wrong? Max was freed of all connubial tyranny. Yet he remained a married man, protected against acquisitive designs by other aspirants—including Thimig. The emotional inflammability of the situation and its tactical complexities—Max had to be largely kept out of them if he was expected to do some work besides—ensured that Edmund held not merely the purse strings, but all the reins.

That the weights were thus distributed I found confirmed each time an opportunity presented itself to settle the conflict amicably. For there did arrive those rare moments when friends who never grew tired of mediating or we—very tired—children unexpectedly caught my mother in a reasonable, my father in a generous mood. (Normally, he could not see why he ought to pay for something he no longer wanted and she refused to admit that she had lost what she was fighting for.) But whenever anyone succeeded in effecting an expedient rapprochement and divorce and property settlement seemed in sight, there invariably came that eleventh hour when my uncle stepped in and turned back the clock. Alimony and security, as if by sleight of hand, dwindled all over again to vague, insulting offers, followed by a vertiginous climb of demands on her part in direct proportion. Almost to the relief of the belligerents, the continuation of a war that the majority of neutrals found embarrassing and totally unrewarding for either side was each time assured anew.

As in most world wars, the true aims were kept carefully camouflaged. As official reason, the welfare of the children was invoked. Their fate in a broken marriage, their peace of mind, their support, their education, their custody, their financial security and inheritance, rights of visitation and vacation were to be wrung from the opponent or fixed by the courts. But more properly, the children were a weapon; used, in fact, quite unscrupulously. My father and mother would be horrified to read this accusation today—and *were* when I challenged them both with it prior to forcing them, at last, to bury the hatchet (in Shoshone hunting grounds), or rather forcing them, at last, to come to realistic terms with the world by taking that hatchet away from them. Nevertheless, their shock was perfectly genuine. For I could not convey a more erroneous impression than that the sons of these parents were not very much loved. My father spent every free minute allowed him with us and, once my mother had lost him and, to a large extent, the outlet for her talent, she lived exclusively for us. Yet this love, real as it was, never moved either of them to give a thought to what this war from which we were to benefit so much cost *us*. They closed their eyes to the headlines greeting us on our way to school, reporting ever new legal maneuvers, degrading judgments, scandalous allegations promptly reflected by the grins of our classmates and the turned-up noses of our teachers.

Two actors of their caliber might have remembered that there are scenes of deliberate rawness which may be playable, but painful for a captive audience to witness. Even more painful were the mawkish peace feelers. (On the stage such acting would have been condemned by both of them.) And for children never to be able to count on whether they would be allowed to join their glamorous father next time or whether he would allow the object of their filial loyalty the means of keeping her latest promise to them did little for their welfare. Nor was it served by the unrelenting strain of having to cut their father's recognized mistress in his own theatre, to snub his personal secretary or to turn their backs on the powerful uncle living in the same house, let alone having to return to him lavish and much-appreciated presents. Completely carefree periods were all but nonexistent in our youth. Unthinkingly, in drawing yet another weapon against each other, our parents had placed a sword of Damocles forever dangling above our heads.

For my brother this uneasy state did not date merely from that day on Sylt. He was chosen as the spearhead for my mother's strategy even before he was born. When the news of his impending arrival failed to produce the hoped-for marital response from my father, and even the—ignored—challenge to a duel by my mother's oldest brother seemed unable to bring about the intended result, she packed her things in short order, moved out of her mother's flat and, without any ceremony, became a squatter in my father's house, there, in his absence, to be ceremoniously delivered of her firstborn by Berlin's most eminent gynecologist, Professor Bumm, who had brought all the Hohenzollern princes into the world. The welcome my brother was accorded—the publicity, the round of distinguished visits, the presents, the flowers—was indeed princely. And no wedding could have established so firmly Else Heims's legitimate tenure at Palais Wesendonck, once the home of Richard Wagner's poet–lady friend and now the first in Max Reinhardt's row of fine town houses, royal apartments and castles. (Edmund was careful never to take flight again.) She would leave her new home only to exchange it with her *husband* for the much more beautiful, Prussian rococo palais on Kupfergraben, where, in due course, I happened and grew up. In those days, however, she was taking no chances: the second name she gave to the "prince" (I often heard her describe him thus herself when she looked at the abundance of authorized photographs presenting mother and son following the spectacular confinement) was Reinhard. As a middle name, even without the final *t* of the paternal surname, it proved to be a redundancy. But in the meantime, it assured her son Wolfgang at least of the *sound* of that surname whose legality would remain in abeyance for some while to come.

Ten years later, after the open rupture, the tactics obviously had to be different, but the aims and the strategy remained the same. So did the weapons. Her unwavering idea was to effect a reunion. The children were the enticement. It turned out that my father had left the beach resort for Salzburg to prepare the inauguration of the Festival in the coming year (1920) and to supervise the restoration of Leopoldskron, both undertakings from which my mother was barred to make room for Helene Thimig. He asked for permission to take my brother along. This was, of course, indignantly refused. But soon prudence won out over indignation. Prudence, however, recommended granting only a modification of the request. Why send the son who is old enough to have begun enjoying a real rapport with his father? Having disrupted the family, let him miss this wonderful boy's company a little! Rather send the six-year-old, with the housemaid. Papa is sufficiently fond of him not to break the last family link heedlessly. On the other hand, the little one, without his mother, as yet without appreciable interest in his father's activities, and in a strange place, will pose a problem. The continuous watchful presence of the maid will pose a problem. Disrupting a family, alas, always invites problems. Are they worth shouldering? In the end, Mama will come to the rescue with the longed-for boy, remove the problem and unobtrusively slide back into her rightful place.

It was a plan meticulously adhered to and repeated in multiple variations over and over again. It never succeeded. Because the problems my mother thought up were inevitably dwarfed in his mind by the hopeless problem of returning to the fold, of taking her back in irreparably changed circumstances.

The day before I was packed off to Salzburg with irascible Luise—poor Luise, to become increasingly caught up in the cross-fire between her two employers did nothing to mollify her humors—we had a sumptuous farewell meal at the Kurhaus, featuring lobster and soufflé Rothschild. Even though enjoying it enormously, I recall, I was puzzled. Not that my mother ever disdained good cooking or good-sized portions, quite the contrary. But a middle-class trait which she never lost and, in contrast to my father, who had deliberately outgrown his parental milieu, never intended to lose, coupled with an innate parsimony overruled only now and then by a debonair mood, limited her gourmandising to special occasions, preferably in what she thought was the legitimacy of the home. Of course, I could not know that my mother wanted me to take along a particularly pleasurable gastronomic memory of "home," thus perhaps forestalling my abject surrender to the gastronomic bait awaiting me. But I felt somehow that the send-off was not in character and this stuck in my mind so lastingly that today I can pinpoint the first lesson of my *éducation alimentaire* to my last day on the Frisian island.

Indeed, the time I spent with my father the rest of that summer was in the main restricted to extraordinarily good meals, thus initiating a general pattern we were faithfully to maintain ever since. The reason for this was simple: Once he had made an open break with the family, the only hours of leisure he could devote to his sons were, except on vacations, the luncheon and dinners hours. As a consequence, in Salzburg, where he worked hard, I learned to appreciate the Austrian cuisine, above all its desserts. Being a born Austrian, my father was an excellent mentor on the subject. The result of this very agreeable instruction added visibly to my mother's distress, when she and my brother, according to plan, pounced on us in Salzburg unannounced. Though we boys were spared the terrible scenes that, as we heard later, recurred every night in the castle and were to be the cause for our eventual banishment from it, my father now spiced his tutoring with devastating ridicule of North German culinary barbarism. Our susceptibility to food and fun appeared to my mother as a possible chink in the armor of our fidelity. In this, she was wrong. We were seducible eaters, but not traitors. Still, her suspicion had a welcome result: Before returning home, she engaged an Austrian cook for Berlin. Meals in our household from then on gained steadily in refinement and importance.

To no other war have the words attributed to Napoleon (that all armies march on their stomachs) applied more aptly than to the one between my parents. At the outset, the logistical problems posed thereby still remained within reasonable bounds, for both sides were still provisioned by the same source of supply. My father did not move out of our house till 1921 and, though direct communication had stopped and the upper story occupied by the family had been aseptically divided into two separate entities never trespassed upon by the other party, the children and, of course, the servants still shuttled back and forth and the trays, while served in different dining quarters, stemmed from the same kitchen. My mother had laid down that my brother and I were to take our meals in her wing exclusively and that it was up to my father to take his seat at the family table or not. As he preferred not to, we were allowed to attend his breakfasts and dinners merely as onlookers.

That we did not stick to this passive role is not surprising: he wanted us to taste the delicacies put before him and the butler delighted in smuggling us illicit china and silver. As my father kept highly unorthodox hours—working on his prompt books into the early hours of morning, he rose late and, rehearsing till late in the afternoon, he usually had his midday meal at the end of the day—these clandestine snacks raised hell with our digestion. For they usually occurred either directly preceding our official lunch or were precariously wedged in between *Jause* (the Austrian version of high tea) and supper. Yet, if we declined an offered tidbit, my father was hurt to the quick. To show no appetite on the other front constituted an even graver offense. We had the choice between gastritis through nervous tension while eating or gluttony. My brother opted for the first, I for the latter.

That Salzburg was so soon inaccessible to us seemed cruel to me. I had loved roaming with my brother and cousins through the vast halls of Leopoldskron, sliding down the marble banister of the staircase, hiding in the medieval armor, playing with the rabbits and a goat my father had given me one Christmas, which I was allowed to keep in a stable of my own, learning chess and shoe polishing from my father's valet, a former footman of the Hapsburgs (to be precise, of the transvestite Archduke Ludwig Victor, exiled by Franz Joseph to the confines of Klessheim Park), learning to swim in Lake Leopoldskron, boating in their free time with the masons who were repairing the terraces and stucco walls and watching the yearly *Fischerstechen*, a local custom which demanded that the colorfully costumed young men of the region stand erect in rowboats and push each other into the water with long sticks. I remember how I cried when I was spotted on our lake in the midst of this merriment and told that I must forgo it. It was the year the Salzburg Festival first opened and my father wished me to attend. I had seen several rehearsals, crawled over the bleachers and under the stage platform, ridden the various traps and I had watched the for me otherwise dull proceedings from the heights of nearby Mönchsberg, sipping *Kracherl*, a cheap, colored soda pop indigenous to Austria, that I had grown extremely fond of, although it was not part of the paternal curriculum. I thought, all in all, that I had paid enough attention to this Jedermann and was entitled instead to enjoy the other open-air show which I found so much more vital. I was wrong on both counts. My father insisted on my presence—for which I am more grateful to him now than I was then—and the tradition of the *Fischerstechen* died before long, while that of *Jedermann* endured.

Forty years later, I staged the same play in the same place myself, following my father's conception. It was a stimulating *Wiedersehen*. Especially so, since, soon after those first summers in Salzburg, I had become a complete stranger to the Festival, to the castle, the lake, even the *Kracherl.* As my taste for this beverage ebbed and my interest in my father's work grew, I began to resent bitterly the exclusion from so important a center of his life. But there was nothing to be done about it. My mother permitted us to go to Salzburg only in her company, and since Mrs. Thimig reigned there as unofficial châtelaine and, along with her family, dominated the professional scene, this was out of the question. My brother and I never saw a single other Max Reinhardt Festival performance and we never attended a single one of the legendary galas at Leopoldskron. Shortly before I left for the United States, when I was almost twenty, personal business took me through Salzburg. I met my father—where else?—in a restaurant. The magnificence of the castle was shown to me on the sly and described by Rudolf Kommer, who confirmed once again his acumen for intercession.

On Kupfergraben, holidays caused the greatest complications. One Christmas Eve brought the tension to the breaking point. In previous years, we had been given our presents from Papa at 6 P.M. in his study and from Mama in the "white dining room" an hour and a half later. Papa no longer took part in the common Christmas festivities. Perhaps because his presents were, in their isolation, considered too lavish or it was felt that the follow-up necessarily became an anticlimax, the arrangement would no longer do for Mama. Papa was notified that presents would be given out under the Christmas tree at 7 P.M., either in toto or not at all, and neither before nor after would the children be available for separate bestowals. My brother's and my traditionally feverish stage of anticipation was thus brought to a unique pitch. And as on this night we could traditionally stay up as long as we liked, we were ordered to bed for a few calming hours in the late afternoon. It goes without saying that we did not sleep a wink and were anything but awakened by the commotion outside our bedroom door. "But, Herr Professor . . . this is impossible!" we heard Luise exclaim sternly over and over again, interspersed with my father's equally stern and repeated "Let me in!" His voice in this part of the house was a sensation. His imminent visit made our heartbeats drown out the scuffle in the corridor. Then Luise apparently gave in and our hearts stood still: wearing a derby and heavy overcoat, holding an umbrella in one hand, packages in the other, he entered the room. "Your mother won't let you come to me, so I've brought you your presents. Unfortunately I couldn't wait for her generosity. I'm in a hurry, I have to catch a train." He kissed us each on the forehead and left a package on each bed.

"To catch a train with that woman!" This was my mother's voice, icy, deliberate, sharpened to kill. "She has the bad taste to wait in front of my house on Christmas Eve! A father, leaving his family on Christmas Eve! Splendid *father!*" She was standing in the door, dressed for the evening, frozen in anger; her aim could not miss. But that was not enough. She wanted to make sure that there was no chance of resurrection. "Splendid *father!* Splendid *father!*" she repeated at regular intervals without surcease. The performance was perhaps a little too studied, but otherwise excellent. His was neither. To anybody but two thoroughly frightened boys and an exasperated servant it would have been ludicrous. After a few moments of paralysis, he let out a curse (the exact wording has escaped me) and raised his umbrella menacingly. I have no way of knowing whether he would have actually brought it down on Mama or whether she was reckoning with that. But she did not bat an eyelash and broke the monotony of her two well-measured words not for an instant. In any event, whatever my "splendid *father*" had intended was nipped in the bud by a very angry Luise. She stormed in and wrested the weapon from his hands. "Splendid *father!*" must still have rung in his ears as he hurried down the wide curve of the rococo staircase, fled across the airy vestibule, through the high entrance door and down the graceful front steps onto the street where Helene Thimig was waiting, in all probability, with a shy smile which, also in all probability, remained unreturned this once.

Several months later, the moving vans stood in front of Kupfergraben 7 and I looked on as every movable object from my father's rooms was carried out, loaded and carted off. The agony lasted two days. Thenceforth, our kitchen supplied only single portions, but, in those two days, I scorned even them. When everything was over, I prowled through the empty quarters so familiar to me and yet so unreal, so bare that even the scent of lavender and good cigars that I loved so much was gone. The apartment remained under lock and key until, one morning, the Hungarian Institute of Berlin University took possession. Up to then, it created a gaping vacuum in a house otherwise filled with life, relatives, staff and conflict.

There was, to begin with, Edmund's suite of rooms on the ground floor, in the charge of Fräulein Grete and two police dogs—dangerous adversaries of my pinscher—off limits to us nephews, except for the kitchen in the cellar, a door from which led into the garden. Through it, we could watch my uncle's lady friends flitting in and out. For a while, it was the spouse of imperial Germany's pre–World War I ambassador to the Court of St. James's, the noble figure of Mechtilde Lichnowsky, poetess and onetime liaison of my father. She too eventually chose the brother, not, like Eysoldt, because of total frustration, but because of the estrangement that inevitably followed fulfillment. However, this step could not shield her from my mother's revenge: "Famous Princess Charged with 'Love Piracy.' Unexpected Accusations by Wife of Stage Sorcerer Max Reinhardt" read the banner line of an article filling an entire page, based on an interview Else Heims-Reinhardt had given Hearst's New York *American* and which greeted my father when he arrived in 1923 to prepare *The Miracle.*

Across from Edmund, directly below us, Jenny Rosenberg, my father's favorite sister, lived with her husband, Hermann, and her three children, Eva, Hans and Gretl, our playmates. My father's mother, the only one of my grandparents I ever knew, and his sister Irene shared the apartment with them until their deaths, along with his younger sister, Adele, before her marriage to a penniless man much younger than she and disapproved of by everyone, most especially Edmund, who deplored this additional burden to the family budget.

Uncle Rosenberg, who managed the bookstalls in the Reinhardt theatres, was more gregarious and more accessible than the blood relations, but—except for Max and Edmund—equally incompetent. The only bone of contention between us children and him was his predilection for holding his siesta—until a fateful date his entire life could have been called a siesta—under one of the mulberry trees in our garden. Like the others, this specimen was a relic from Frederick the Great's efforts to foster Prussian silk production and a center of our cops-and-robbers and Wild West games. I do, though, recall one incident when Hermann Rosenberg proved to be most effective, revealing an otherwise undetected talent for the stage. We were on the crest of the 1918 revolution and a group of Spartacists spoiling for a fight threatened to break in our front door, unless we let them in at once and provided them with sleeping quarters. Suddenly, Uncle Rosenberg appeared in a window in field-gray uniform—I suspect it was the only time he ever wore it—to inform the leaders in his best Prussian military manner that a company of soldiers was already billeted on the premises. The Spartacists beat a hasty retreat.

Alas, Hermann and Jenny Rosenberg were not always to run into Germans so credulous and harmless. The two dear people deserved a more benign fate than was in store for them. Thanks to his inherited Polish citizenship, they were allowed to remain unmolested in Hitler's Germany till shortly before the outbreak of hostilities. This reprieve turned out to be a Greek gift: Early one morning, both were dragged from bed and counseled that they might by all means take plenty of razor blades along on their unplanned trip to Poland—where the deportees were neither at home nor welcome. They had hardly installed themselves provisorily in Lvov when the German juggernaut flattened that part of Poland (leaving the other part to the then friendly Russia) and the victorious warriors were given a free hand for three days to deal with the Jewish population as they pleased. By that hand, the Rosenbergs perished. Knowing this hideous end of two lives of purest innocence cast a dark shadow over the comparatively sheltered existence of my father in exile.

Since our house was only a stone's throw from the Lustgarten (public gardens where all of Berlin's open-air mass meetings took place; terminal of every demonstration and starting point of most riots), the confrontation with the Spartacists was not our only contact with the revolution. We were, for instance, pinned in the direct line of fire during the last exchange of shots between the Imperial Loyalists (on the roof of the Archaeological Museum up the river from us) and the Socialists (barricaded in a girls' school a few blocks to our rear) when, at lunchtime, in the midst of stamping boots and hundreds of throats bellowing the Communist anthem, an unmistakable voice reached our ears through the carefully closed windows and drawn curtains: "Professor! Come on down and join us! *Here's* where you're needed now! *Here* is where the real theatre is happening these days!" The voice belonged to none other than Alexander Moissi, the brightest star of the Deutsches Theater, who had enthusiastically mingled with the demonstrators, swinging a clenched fist, a red band around his right arm.

The Professor, after cautiously reconnoitering the lay of the land through a slit in the portiere, for once decided against an open-air spectacle, preferring to await developments until that scene too was played to the end. Like many actors, Moissi misjudged his master's passion for playing and ingenuously assumed that Reinhardt too believed life was acting, whereas he believed the very opposite: that acting was the truest form of life, that the true actor does not dissemble, but unveils. (This ingenuousness brought both of them into serious fixes, such as when Moissi had himself invited by a gynecologist friend to witness incognito a Caesarean performed on a Salzburg lady. Moissi was so moved by the "performance" that he elicited the name of the young mother and, the following day, sent her a fan letter along with two dozen roses. The gallant gesture did not have the intended effect. The lady raised such hell that Salzburg's pet actor was from then on persona non grata, forcing my father to replace him in the title role of *Jedermann.*)

The cellar of the Knobelsdorff structure—the same architect built Frederick's Sans Souci—was a wondrous, labyrinthine setting for further "cops and robbers" and similar plays and also the home of the Schuhmachers, the caretaker couple whose male component doubled in the part of usher at the Kammerspiele Theater in the evening. Through such ramifications the theatre permeated our daily life everywhere. I hardly knew a Berlin craftsman or repairman who did not have a job in the extensive workshops of the Deutsches Theater. The front office handled all our travel reservations and larger purchases and we received, of course, all cash—provided it was approved—from the cashier. Frau Schuhmacher sympathized secretly with my mother, but her husband never failed to show his unconditional devotion to the brothers Reinhardt. Edmund rewarded him by granting him a tyrannical regimen over house and garden.

The garden was a sizable green zone, a unique private oasis in the metropolis, a feudal living privilege and an ideal playground for children. Encircled by ugly bare walls of factories, a high enclosure above which nineteenth-century modest apartment houses loomed, an arm of the river Spree with the Museum Island on the other side and a wooden fence separating it from a busy street lined with government buildings, the area formed one of the few really beautiful, secluded corners of Old Berlin. Two right-angled wings dominated it with their vine-covered façades. The grapes which we harvested from high ladders tasted exquisite. But they were not our only yearly harvest. We had walnuts, hazelnuts, cherries, gooseberries, red currants and Uncle Rosenberg's mulberries. In spring, the garden was aflame with lilac, jasmine, acacia and chestnut blossom. A venerable old coach house offered additional opportunities for romping. But Herr Schuhmacher, since my father's departure, encroached on all of them: The coach house served him as workshop and tool shed, the garden was gradually swallowed up by his proliferating crops of vegetables and flowers and the cellar vaults he considered his personal domain anyway. One place which he could not spoil for us was the spacious balcony overlooking the grounds. From this vantage point, I succeeded, one fine day, in taking my revenge on him: as he was honing his scythe directly below me, I peed on his bald pate. This did not ameliorate our relations and, after his livid complaint, my family, interpreting my action differently, punished me severely for what I thought was a justifiable act of self-defense. The caretaker treated the wife and children of his master like squatters. And we in turn treated the brother and general manager of our breadwinner like a leper.

Ungreeted by us, averting his eyes stealthily, Edmund crept out of the house every morning and back into it at night. There came the moment when he had had enough and he moved out too—making more room for the expansive Hungarians. But his spirit continued to haunt the house for a long time afterward. I shall never forget when, one midday, I returned from school and discovered that the entire furnishings of the entrance hall, the staircase and upper landing—all valuable antiques—had disappeared. My mother was on tour in Switzerland and learned of the outrage only after her return. Her impotent rage knew no bounds. Edmund had clearly maneuvered her into outmaneuvering herself. A judgment in one of the many suits for alimony she had brought against my father had given her the right to attach his property. The bailiff had gone to the theatre and seen Edmund, who directed him straight to Kupfergraben, where he removed the objects—with the help of an obliging caretaker—which, according to the letter of the law, belonged to my father, but had long been used exclusively by us.

The last time I visited the house—now in East Berlin—a bronze plaque hung in the entrance hall which had resisted the changes of time and regimes unscathed. Dedicated to a more dignified aspect of Max Reinhardt's life, it pointed to his having lived and worked there and quoted a letter by Maxim Gorki congratulating him on the German-speaking première of his *The Lower Depths*. Whether, with that tribute, concord returned to the embattled building, I cannot judge: It housed the Society of German-Soviet Friendship.

Eventually, court decisions established my father's financial obligations toward the family as well as the time my brother and I were allowed to spend with him within the year. In summer, he was allotted half of our six-week school vacation and, when in Berlin, he had the right to take us out on Sundays. Sunday, for him, was a workday like any other, but, luckily for us, not for everyone else. So, out of consideration for the actors, the crew and, not least, his own pocket—or, rather, Edmund's pocket, where all problems accumulated that "childhood" had little use for, such as overtime—he condescended to an end of rehearsals at 3 P.M., and usually broke off around five.

Consequently, his Stutz or Cadillac would drive up to No. 7 Kupfergraben at a quarter to three to fetch us to the theatre. At this hour, we would normally be finishing our Sunday "dinner." For Sunday meant anything but a workday to my mother. Like all holidays, it was sacred to her and the main repast represented a particularly sacred ritual. As a rule, it started off with a potent broth, so hot that our tongues remained insensitive for the rest of the day (which may have been the subconscious motive for the unreasonable temperature). This was followed by a rich roast with a rich sauce and ample garnishings, in preparation for a dessert as delicious as it was difficult to digest. The prospect of our having to consume, a few hours hence, another comparable meal was not merely ignored, but considered heresy. Though secular law permitted the duplication, my mother could not have made it clearer that damnation was its inevitable result. Every glance at one's watch or out of the window to ascertain whether the chauffeur had arrived was condemned as roundly as the deadly sin of refusing a second helping, let alone skipping a course. Whoever made himself guilty of such an offense was bound to hear a sermon culminating in the rhetorical questions: "Could it be that you are saving your appetite for Horcher's?" "Your mother's table, I take it, isn't good enough any more for you, eh?" Or "Let's face it, you simply can't wait to make pigs of yourselves at Horcher's!"

Among Berlin's good restaurants—and there were many—Horcher's was the one my father liked best. It was my favorite. No doubt, it was the best restaurant I had ever been to (up to then, and even now). It was the first that presented cognac in snifters, where saddles of venison and hare were carved with a spoon, where mashed potatoes were made with whipped cream and caviar was served with baked potatoes (Idaho style) and where *every* dish was prepared at the table, from the opening of oysters to duck à la presse, consommé Rana to crêpe Hélène. The old Horcher (long deceased) —whose son (recently deceased), in the last year of the war, was flown together with chefs, headwaiters, silver and recipes by Göring to Spain as a gift to Franco and who, there, became an "old Horcher" in his own right —was proud of being able to satisfy every whim of his customers and to bring to the table on order the most esoteric culinary creations for the mere price of a small fortune. It could be the whims of UFA Films, the Deutsche Bank, the Ullstein newspapers or IG-Farben (chemical), the Kaiser Wilhelm Gesellschaft (institute for natural sciences), the Deutsches Theater or the Six-Day Bicycle Race; the orders might come from a Hjalmar Schacht (Weimar's and Hitler's financial wizard), an Ernst Udet (the flying ace), a Carl Zuckmayer (the playwright), an Emil Jannings (the Reinhardt actor), an Albert Einstein, Marlene Dietrich or Gustav Stresemann (Minister of Foreign Affairs), a Hugo Stinnes (the tycoon), a Gerhart Hauptmann, Richard Strauss, Hermann Göring—or Max Reinhardt and his sons. For my mother, Horcher was something like the antichrist. When, in 1954, I visited the Madrid offshoot and found myself in the company of an American three-star general, the war criminal and Mussolini abductor Skorzeny, Ava Gardner and the Jewish architect Ernst Mendelsohn, who had made the Berlin of the twenties a modern city, I was not so sure she had been mistaken.

The Sunday ride of the Reinhardt boys in the back of the limousine through the north of Berlin, their bloated bellies tucked into a cozy fur rug, used to arouse split emotions in me. There was the happy anticipation of seeing our father again, watching him at work, followed by a few precious hours with him. And there was, of course, the unmitigated pleasure of smelling greasepaint. But, alas, we were the invariable heralds of some maternal message which, we knew, would upset him. And we feared his anger. I enjoyed the comfort of the opulent vehicle and what we, today, would call the "status" conferred thereby, but I was only too conscious of the contrasting misery around us. One of the most distinguished play-houses of the world, along with the surrounding real estate which formed the basis of my father's fortune, lay in an impoverished sector of Berlin. Theatres are often relics of bygone urban prosperity. Those who run them tend to hesitate to follow the drift toward more affluent and fashionable, usually more western parts of the city. The more venerable the tradition of the house, the more conspicuous its contrast with the necrotic district it stands in.

When we stepped out of the car, a liveried chauffeur holding open the door for us, we were at once surrounded by screaming, begging street urchins and, as we entered the theatre, the blank stares of the loitering unemployed followed us dully. This disparity colored my entire youth. My brother and I would sneak into one of the last rows and try to attract as little attention as possible. But, in that, we almost never succeeded. There was invariably a lot of waving and handshaking. The actors on stage resented commotions in the audience, as they cared very little for the social byplay of a Reinhardt rehearsal. So long as my father presided over the proceedings, they did not dare to demur. Manners loosened, however, when, before his arrival, his assistants were in charge. Then this or that ensemble member was apt to vent his anger with full force, as happened when Rudolf Forster caught a baronial friend of my father, a well-known social lion in the insurance business, whispering in the orchestra. Forster interrupted the scene and asked the intruder to leave: "I don't watch you insuring, either, Herr Baron!"

Not long after we had taken our seats, my father, whether at his desk on the stage or in the front rows, would signal his pleasure at our presence. He either indicated by sign language that he would be with us soon or, if the rehearsal was going to take longer, for us to sit closer to him. In the latter event, he would not be averse to leaning back ostentatiously and asking me, by no means sotto voce: "Are you dying of hunger?" And following it up with the burning question of where I'd prefer to go that afternoon. If he was able to wheedle out of me the name Horcher, he broke into triumphant peals of ironic laughter, which the actors, when they were rehearsing a comedy, acknowledged gratefully, but, in the case of tragedy, registered with consternation.

To go to a restaurant with my father was a festivity. Not only because it promised superb food, expertly ordered and expertly prepared, but because he had a very personal relationship with the restaurants he liked. Whether it was Sacher in Vienna, Horcher, Pelzer or the Neva Grill in Berlin, Walterspiel or Schwarz (a Jewish place no longer in existence) in Munich, La Fenice in Venice, Voisin or LaRue in Paris, the Savoy Grill in London, Voisin or "21" in New York, the Trocadero or Chasen's in Hollywood—my father was always received, from owner to busboy, with special cordiality and respect. Other prominent guests were automatically relegated to the background as he was deferentially escorted to his table. There were few who did not recognize him right away. At most tables, conversation temporarily ceased while eyes followed the red-carpet entrance —an astonishing fact in days that knew no television, when news photos and illustrated magazines were not so prevalent as today and when the subject was a man who worked *behind* the scenes. His popularity was without example.

His popularity with the culinary profession was all the more peculiar as he did not believe in over-liberal tips and rarely ordered a drink. Nor was he a big eater. As customers went, he was, therefore, not exactly a bonanza. Nor could the reason be his fame. The profession is quite blasé in that respect. I believe it was his complete lack of affectation. Most guests treat restaurateurs and waiters either condescendingly or submissively, arrogantly or self-consciously. He treated them like colleagues who had mastered their craft as he had his. No shenanigans of the connoisseur. He never went into the kitchen to give the dishes an impressive preview, never conferred with the chef, never sent anything back, never made a fuss, never checked his bills, simply commented, if asked, on what he had found good and what he had not. Consequently, the personnel vied with each other to serve him and, though practically none of them had ever seen a Max Reinhardt production, felt a certain kinship with his artistry. This may sound hyperbolic, but one of gastronomy's greats once put it thus himself: During a celebration after a Reinhardt opening at the restaurant Walterspiel in Munich, the proprietor, to everyone's surprise, took the floor and, in an impromptu speech, elaborated on the essential characteristic the theatre and haute cuisine have in common: The product both bring to the customer requires long, careful, patient preparations and is consumed by him with great—and equal—dispatch. Most artists present were indignant about what seemed to them a presumptuous analogy. My father was not merely amused, but convinced of its validity.

His credit with the restaurant trade benefited him, however, in a much more vital way. To it he owed nothing less than his international emancipation. In 1910, the English impresario C. B. Cochran, on his yearly Continental circuit, stayed for a few days, as always, at the Hotel Bristol in Berlin. Freely pouring out his heart to his old friend the bartender, after several double whiskeys he complained bitterly of the poor choice of Berlin theatre offerings. Nothing to bring to London. Herr Pelzer—the name of the mixer who, soon, would open a first-class restaurant of the same name on Wilhelmstrasse—asked him if he had been to the Circus Busch. Ordering another whiskey, Cochran reprimanded him for his bad memory. Had he forgotten that circuses were not among his preferences? Pelzer assured him that he was not recommending an ordinary circus entertainment but *Oedipus Rex*, Max Reinhardt's newest, sensational hit. Whereupon Cochran indulgently explained that the only kind of entertainment he cared for even less than circus was Greek tragedy. The idea of combining the two was producing an acute nausea in him which proved remediable only after further double whiskeys. The chronicle leaves it open whether Circus Busch owed Mr. Cochran's visit that night to the many drinks Mr. Pelzer served or to his powers of persuasion. It was probably the combination of the two that did the trick. One fact is undisputed: In the very same year, Cochran brought *Oedipus Rex* to London, followed in 1911, and equally under his aegis, by Reinhardt's *Miracle* and *Sumurûn*.

Delicious and unforgettable as the meals with our father were, they were just as taxing to our systems. Our spirit was oh so willing, but the flesh simply could not keep up with it. Yet should I in his opinion order too little or leave food on the plate, the culinary tug-of-war started all over again. At once, all his sarcasm vented itself on us. He took our lack of appetite as a personal slight: "You've already eaten with your mother, of course!" Or: "I suppose it would be asking too much of two boys to wait so that they can eat with their busy father whom they see once in a blue moon!" These and similar rebukes came showering down, as though we had committed a capital crime. There was nothing left for us to do but to deny the misdeed and fatalistically settle for hopelessly spoiled stomachs during the remainder of the week.

Travels with Papa were the high spots of our youth, and not only because we were permitted to come to his table with a healthy appetite. More important emotional appetites were marvelously stilled. But even these blissful respites did not remain unmarred by the parental war. My father's valet would appear, chalk-white, at the breakfast table and mysteriously ask my brother to join him in the anteroom; soon after, my brother, chalk-white, would return and ask my father into his bedroom; then my brother would reappear and take me into our room. I knew what was up and still, each time, it struck me like a thunderbolt when my mother made her entrance, both bold and wary, in this chalk-white lion's den. The result was always the same, always contrary to her careful calculations: no reconciliation, no welcome to the family idyll, but, at best, all-around unease and, now and then, a financial concession to put an end to the unease as quickly as possible.

Change of scenery: I am in America. A year and a half now. Employed by Metro-Goldwyn-Mayer as assistant to the producer Bernie Hyman. I owe my steady job largely to his good will toward and interest in me. But I am under the impression that my name has something to do with it as well. That this is an error, that, in fact, the very opposite is the case, I learn only when my father arrives in California a little less than two years later. I am proud to be able to fetch him from the train in San Francisco as an independent, self-supporting son. He is no less proud. In the New World I am, all of a sudden, weary of the farce of not greeting Mrs. Thimig and, for the first time in my life, to my father's infinite gratification, I shake hands with her. In a letter, I report the new policy of détente to my mother in London, where she and my brother have put up their first migratory tents.

The Los Angeles Chamber of Commerce, with the strong participation of the motion-picture industry, gives my father a glittering welcoming banquet in the grand ballroom of the Biltmore Hotel, Sam Goldwyn presiding. I see the chance to show my appreciation to Bernie Hyman for everything he has done for me and offer him a prominent seat at the speaker's table. He stuns me by declining: he will not only have to forgo the speaker's table, but the whole dinner. When I catch my breath and ask why, he explains reluctantly: "I never really wanted to tell you, Gottfried. But it's you I like, not your father." "But you don't even know him!" I protest. "That's the point," he replies, and proceeds telling me how he chased him all over Europe and never caught up with him. His aim was to sign the actress Nora Gregor (the subsequent mistress and wife of the Austrian Fascist leader Prince Starhemberg) to a long-term contract with MGM. Hyman learns that she is contractually bound to Reinhardt and that only he, personally, can release her (probably one of Edmund's ruses). For weeks, Hyman haunts the Reinhardt antechambers in Berlin, Vienna, Salzburg, Paris and London. Daily, he is told the Professor happens to be very busy at the moment, but will see him the next day. On more than one of these "next days," he hears that his quarry, alas, was called away unexpectedly on business. Eventually, he gives up and returns home with a holy wrath toward the phantom that has spoiled the career of the lady—and his private happiness.

The story comes as a revelation to me: I realize that I am standing on my own feet. And I perceive that my father—he, of course, never knew of Mr. Hyman's existence—by his stalling, by letting people wait and slipping away, has made enemies that count, enemies he cannot afford in his present situation. And knowing something about Hollywood by now, I foresee a dose of his own medicine.

I am glad to have my father in America, but our relations have changed: I am not only independent of him financially, I am also more at home there than he is. I have acclimatized quickly, made good progress in English, am forty years younger and more adaptable. It is only natural that he begins to lean on me in many respects—in respect to film, the New York theatre, even food: It is the son who takes his father out now. I am excluded from only one domain: his finances. Papa fears my loyalty to Mama and keeps his monetary problems away from my scrutiny to his appalling disadvantage (as it turns out). My relations with Thimig have, at least externally, been normalized to a degree where one can say peace has broken out.

It is a deceptive peace. One morning I read in the Los Angeles *Times* that Max Reinhardt has started divorce proceedings against Else Reinhardt in Reno. I can't believe my eyes. They are, however, by this time, focused on the "most beautiful beach in the world," outside of Riga, where he once rented a villa for three months to establish residence. At that time (1930), an American lawyer dangled in front of his eager eyes a legal divorce without consent of the wife, which, allegedly, was valid throughout the world. This proved a costly error, and my father could marry Helene Thimig after the Latvian decision in neither Vienna, Berlin, nor anyplace else without risking charges of bigamy. I recall the despair of his Berlin and Vienna managers bemoaning his prolonged absence. He, however, ignored them, especially as the municipal theatre of Riga acquainted him with the genius of Michael Chekhov, a nephew of the writer, whom he considered the only contemporary actor capable of doing justice to Hamlet. Besides, he greatly enjoyed a vivacious ballet company there which, along with Chekhov, he promptly sent to Berlin.

His theatres in Berlin could live without the Latvian State Ballet, even without Chekhov. Hollywood *can* live without Reinhardt, but he, at the moment, cannot live without Hollywood. Yet a California lawyer has now been obliging enough to sell him the identical scheme with the identical reasoning—and the identical result. All my arguments and appeals are for naught. Residence in Reno is being established according to a well-tried formula, and a unilateral divorce secured that lacks validity in any state but Nevada, Arkansas and another one whose name has escaped me. In the meantime, my mother performed the unique trick of procuring an immigration visa to the United States within the space of one morning. The London *Times* had informed her about my father's latest gambit and, by afternoon, she was well on her way aboard a transatlantic liner.

The resumption of the anachronistic struggle in my new homeland, again carried out in the public eye, I cannot tolerate. No longer am I a weapon in the hands of my parents. I have become an autonomous weapon that turns on both of them. After long-winded negotiations, I am finally able to persuade them to call it quits "amicably." Except that my mother categorically refuses to abide by the recent Reno decision. It rested on incompatibility. My mother insists on adultery or, as a last concession, malicious desertion in order to stamp him once and for all as the guilty party. Which is why the divorce has to be pronounced a second time, again, in Reno, by the same court. It is, to my knowledge, the only time in the history of jurisprudence that one and the same judge legally divorced one and the same couple twice, based on—as it developed—identical legal grounds.

Before this happens, one obstacle has to be overcome: According to law, property settlements between spouses may not be contingent on a divorce. My father must unconditionally commit himself to a compensation and an annuity negotiated by me—that is, without having any guarantee that my mother will go through with the divorce. My word of honor must replace legal security, but, understandably, does not remove my father's skepsis. The anxiety increases as both parties, independently of each other, embark for Reno, Papa and Helene Thimig by train and with the usual coterie including lawyer, secretary, valet, friends and current negotiating partners; I in a car with Mama, who feels she is being led to slaughter. We leave in the late afternoon to avoid the heat of the desert. Halfway, a stopover in Bishop, at the foot of Mount Whitney, is planned for the night. At eleven the following morning, we are expected in the Reno court. A few hours after that, my father's departure by train to New York is scheduled so he can arrive just in time for a fund-raising reception at the Waldorf-Astoria, on which the fate of his forthcoming New York production, *The Eternal Road,* depends.

Arriving in Bishop, my mother, to my relief, seems to have resigned herself to the program. We spend a pleasant evening and retire early in order to start for Reno at seven in the morning. The next thing I remember is being shaken awake by a stranger—it is still dark outside—who reveals himself as a physician. The night porter, he explains, called him out of bed at the behest of my mother. He found her in the grip of a severe gall-bladder colic and gave her a strong hypodermic. She is asleep now and must under no circumstances be roused before the afternoon. It is, of course, futile to try to enlighten the good doctor about the, I will not say simulated, but, no doubt, emotionally-induced attack. Nor would it make much sense, as the injection has put my mother out of action.

If ever I felt sorry for myself, it was on that day. In my despair, I drive into the mountains at dawn, but even the most beautiful Sierra glow cannot wipe from my mind the fiasco my father prophesied and which has now occurred. In addition, my Oldsmobile starts to overheat. Precariously returning to the hotel, I learn that my father has already called from Reno twice. Calling him back proves to be a most distressing experience. His sarcasm is as acid as ever, but, for once, covers no playfulness. It is fed by nothing but fury. At last, he challenges me to admit what a vile person we are dealing with. That the straw to break the camel's back should, of all miserable subterfuges, be once again the gall bladder is only fitting. As for me, I am simply a guileless mama's boy who has been manipulated in the most transparent way and who, without wishing it has swindled his father. This is not my only telephone conversation of the day. The assembled "court" in Reno harries me, and I receive as many calls from intercessors for my father in Los Angeles. And they don't just telephone. There are also visitors. Bishop becomes the most frequented interstate way station for male and female mediators, pouncing on me and trying to get a firsthand impression of my mother's true condition.

At 3 P.M., my mother and I arrive in Reno. Having made many films, I am aware that it is unfair and unskillful to propel an audience with a "once out of the snakepit" jump from a state of utter hopelessness to a happy ending. But I have, honestly, forgotten how I made my mother wake up, listen to me, get dressed, step into my car and keep her promise. My desperation must have lent me unexpected powers. And it seems that I did not spare the tears, for I remember one of my mother's remarks whose sharpness was in conspicuous contrast to her weakened physical state: "A man doesn't cry!" I, most likely, had enough retorts at my fingertips as to what is equally unsuitable for a woman. The fact remains that, to the utter amazement of all parties concerned, my car drives up to Reno's Hotel Riverside just in time to go through the postponed court procedures that afternoon.

Still, many farcical things will take place before peace can be ratified after sixteen years of combat: My father's lawyer, whom I have advised of our delayed arrival and who, understandably incredulous, is standing guard in front of the hotel, passes out at the sight of us. A doctor must be called to bring him to. My mother is all solicitude. In court, I act both as witness and as sworn interpreter. I commit perjury. I translate "incompatibility" as "malicious desertion" to my mother. My mother is satisfied in German, the others in English. Meyer Weisgal, producer of *The Eternal Road*, pesters my father to fly to New York to rescue the meeting at the Waldorf. (The train has been missed.) Since Max Pallenberg's fatal crash, my father has vowed never to board a plane. His nerves are worn out: It is Weisgal alone who does the flying. For the first time in his life, my father throws a person out of his house.

The divorce is hardly decreed when Max Reinhardt, in another chamber, remarries. Directly thereafter, the bride rushes to a phone and calls Vienna to assure her parents that she has been made an honest woman, after all. In the meantime, coming out of court, my mother and I run into the totally shattered Weisgal in the hotel lobby. He is not only ruined, he also looks it. Having my doubts that my mother, finally having made her break with the past, is in the mood to hobnob with the producer of her ex's forthcoming show, I try to steer her clear of him, but cannot prevent the collision. To my surprise, my mother is attracted to this picture of misery and, right there on the spot, amidst the hustle and bustle, plunges into a lesson of how best to manipulate Reinhardt to get him to do something he does not want to do. According to her, the trick is to implant in his head the idea that it is *he* who wanted to do it in the first place. The detailed instructions are so persuasive that Weisgal, following them verbatim, brings my father around to taking the plane at least to Chicago—his first and last flight—from where the overnight train will get him to New York in time.

My mother is euphoric and urges me to order up champagne and caviar to our rooms. We empty three bottles of Pommery and eat two pounds of beluga—when the phone rings. It is someone from my father's entourage who hands the receiver to him. In the background I hear music, laughter, the clinking of glasses, high spirits. "Where are you?" he wishes to know. I answer superfluously: "In my room." "Well, it's time for you to leave it! Come down! Right away! We're all in the lobby!" I use evasions, pretend to be tired, claim I am already undressed—all in vain.

My mother first does not want to let me go, but at last grants me a short leave of absence, and I join the happy circle around the newlyweds. The excitement of the last days has affected my stomach. They are serving

—champagne and caviar. My father's hawk eye spots immediately that I am taking only token mouthfuls. He frowns and chides me in the familiar manner: "I see you've already eaten with your mother!" But then he laughs uproariously and embraces me. All my independence is knocked into a cocked hat. I am a child again and eat and drink and eat and eat. Hours later, I go upstairs—and maintain the tradition.

THE DIARY

FRIDAY,
OCTOBER 1, 1943

Ask dear old Bruno [Bruno Eisner, Viennese pianist] to arrange a meeting for me with his close friend Einstein. Know that Einstein can best be lured through musical channels. Participating in chamber music with professional artists is his favorite pastime and the best of them are happy to give him this pleasure at the expense of their own. Bruno is astonished by my request. Photograph Einstein for an army film? Quotes me G. B. Shaw's observation: Einstein's the only violinist who looks like a violinist. How apt! Jascha Heifetz looks like a banker. Bruno promises to do his best.

Dig up George Grosz's address and call him. We agree to meet the coming Tuesday in front of New York Academy of Arts, where he's teaching.

Sudden crisis: Papa balks at speech teacher. Says this asininity is too much. I cajole, wheedle, stand on my head, but he can't be budged. No more speech teacher! Don't really blame him. It's beyond the bounds of reason to expect Max Reinhardt to take lessons in how to enunciate properly at the age of seventy! Anyway, either his powers of speech return to him naturally or not at all. Forcing his will is to cripple his will. Another block is that the language is English. Eleonora takes me to one side, describes the last session: The man kept prodding Papa like a backward child to pay strict attention and to repeat each word after him carefully. There were many errors and many, many severe corrections. At first Papa was cooperative, but when the rigmarole became too offensive he got up and left the room. At this point the man flounced out with a few words he did not expect his pupil to repeat after him. I see to it that his flounce-out remains permanent.

SATURDAY,
OCTOBER 2, 1943

Something disturbing: Eleonora tells me that on their way to their daily walk they ran into Ernst Lothar and wife, Adrienne Gessner, in the elevator. [He, novelist and theatrical producer, the last manager of Vienna's

Theater in der Josefstadt during Reinhardt's regime; she, brilliant comedienne and one of the few emigré's who made it on the American stage.] Supposedly Papa carried the day, charmingly smiled away their attempts to engage him in conversation. Am uneasy, nevertheless. Lothar's a busybody and Gessner, a gossipmonger; and they live in our hotel.

Eleonora's not surprised that Thimig isn't coming. I am: "But when the husband you love so dearly has had a stroke what can possibly stop you from taking the next plane out?" Eleonora grins: "Anything can when you're Thimig. You still don't understand her. She does only what fits into her scheme of things." "That's absurd! You can't really mean she doesn't want to come!" "I mean at this moment she wants to make the picture." Female backbiting. "Come, come, Eleonora, you know they need the money!" Eleonora goes on biting: "Is it money your father needs now?"

SUNDAY,
OCTOBER 3, 1943

Terrific news: Einstein ready to see me. I'm to come to Princeton *[where he was a member of the Institute for Advanced Study]*.

Today is Mama's birthday. Send flowers and put through long-distance call. Amazing woman. She was prepared to hear worse news about Papa and, interestingly, not unlike Silvia, neither shares nor particularly encourages my optimism. Can it be that in her heart she hopes for a drama that will create his need of her again? She did offer to fly and take charge when I told her "Madame" wasn't coming. Well, drama or not, the windfall came to someone else. It wouldn't be Mama if she didn't promptly come up with: "Aha! So Eleonora's finally made it after all these years!"

MONDAY,
OCTOBER 4, 1943

H. arrives with Dr. Groedl. Another refugee. Viennese. Eminent heart specialist according to H. My first impression: pure artist rather than virtuoso, one in the best Austrian tradition—medical or musical; tragic that men like this are lost to Europe. The rationale? Same as in Poe's short story in which guards exchange places with lunatic inmates. Groedl's opinion as cheering as his personality and its effect on Papa. We're going forward. Steadily.

But the way is tangled: Eleonora calls. Terribly exercised. Whispers into phone: "Come up! Right away! You've got to help . . ." I tear upstairs. And there he is, bent over his desk, sorting out a pile of unanswered correspondence—mostly, I note, congratulatory messages for his seventieth birthday. Eleonora, dear Eleonora—her laughter peals out falsely: "What do you say to your father? He insists on answering letters! This minute! Here I've been waiting all my life for him to answer me, the whole world's waited, but just because the doctor says 'Don't write' he decides he has to!" In one respect she's right. There's never been a more unwilling and remiss correspondent than Papa. Except when he's driven by some burning desire or the need to compensate for a frustration. Then come yard-long treatises which consume more time and energy than his most taxing directorial efforts. An answer to birthday wishes exactly one year ago comes to my mind.

Ambassadors

BESIDES MAX REINHARDT'S ANNOTATIONS in his prompt books and besides his diaries (which he kept only in his very early years), his letters and recorded speeches (carefully prepared and read from the manuscript) are the only firsthand evidence of how his mind worked. First*hand*, surely. But do they really reflect the spontaneous working of his mind?

Ipso facto, when he put his thoughts on paper, he expressed what was on his mind. But being an "unwilling and remiss correspondent," not given to report everyday impressions or to react lightly to the impressions of others, his "treatises" almost always served a purpose. His pen never chatted or mused. In formulating his preoccupations, the words became means of persuasion. In his youth, he wrote to impress the addressees with his personality. He tried to be convincing per se—as lover, artist or generative force in society. In the prime of his life, most of his messages—to the annoyance of many letter writers (especially writers)—were limited to telegrams or entrusted to auxiliary pens. When he went to the trouble himself, it was invariably because a statement in writing seemed the only effective one—and then his aim was either to win others over for specific ideas or to defend his own point of view. In his last years, having time on his hands, he spent more and more of it elaborating in ink what he could not produce in his own medium. His letters to me and to other helpmates, actual and potential, with their polished questions, balanced proposals and tactful exhortations, usually composed before he retired for bed at six or seven in the morning, made his sleep easier. Getting things off to a start was sometimes enough to lull him into the illusion that answers had been received, desired goals achieved and loose ends tied up. For the first time in his life, the *need* to write was primary, the content secondary.

And for the first time in his life, he filled page upon page with complaints—about his fate and about those he thought were responsible for some of its injustices. But even then, his sentences were never unpremeditated. They reflect less and, at the same time, more than the working of a mind. They show a mind constantly working for some improvement. Not being a literary man, he was awed by literary expression. In his own autodidactic way, he became a master of it. But it was never natural to him.

That is why, I believe, he refused to write his memoirs, although several publishers had made him attractive offers. At a time when in his natural medium one door after the other was locked to him, this could have been a gratifying, lucrative and legitimate outlet for his unused energies. His own reason for declining the offers (also of lecture tours): "I want to make theatre, not talk about it." Although he talked—and wrote—about it almost as well as he made it, he clung to the Goethean maxim: "Bilde, Künstler! Rede nicht!" ("Sculpt, artist! Don't speak!"). The reply to a congratulatory message on his sixty-ninth birthday gives a foretaste of what his memoirs could have been:

> Since our exodus from the Old World we have wandered through a desert of terrors, quite unencumbered by earthly possessions. The end is not yet in sight. That, in the scramble of our time, you remembered my birthday, which, in my years, one almost prefers to forget, has moved me deeply. The outer happiness that we were able to plant and to harvest in Europe has difficulties in growing on foreign soil. Perhaps it must fall like manna from heaven. The real, always boundless, happiness is a gift that was given us on our very first birthday. It is important never to forget it, not to leave it lying around someplace, let alone sell it. Some lose it in their diapers. Others, however—I have talked to them myself—succeeded in being happy even in the concentration camp! They survived it. No *Anstreicher* [reference to Hitler's stint as a house painter], no Streicher [the notorious Jew-baiting publisher of *Der Stürmer*] could pale the innate color of their joy to live.
>
> Not quite so resistant, I have temporarily fled hellishly hot New York [to

Atlantic Beach, Long Island] in order to spend said birthday and that of the New Year (5703) more coolly and calmly. . . .

But I shall soon return and, like my ancestor Jacob, resume wrestling with the "angels." (That is how, amusingly, the backers of shows are called here.) So far they have not blessed me. Their heavenly realm is too much of this earth. At the mention of the word "art" even the unbaptized cross themselves. And if you talk about more than one play, they think they have caught you unawares: "So you don't believe in a success yourself! Or you wouldn't plan several plays all at once." The theatre happens to belong officially to the entertainment industry and the angels who are fighting for its poor soul have fallen very low indeed.

That the theatre is the eternal playground of the human creature . . . , that it has been consecrated by the greatest minds of all ages, never ceasing to struggle for its perfect form, that it has prepared revolutions in France and Russia, which are still continuing today, that even the Catholic Church, in the period of its sublime wisdom, reenacted the Passion of the Savior through the medium of the theatre—all that means little to them.

They remain true to their tenet: Theatre is no art. It is a business. It is not a surefire business. But they itch to gamble. If one places his chips on the right number, on the right name, on the right star (and one must have a good nose for this), it is possible to make millions. That is the chant of the angels. And the stars join the chorus. Who can oppose such powers?

And yet: the art of the theatre encompasses all arts, the arts for which across the entire country museums, galleries, concert halls, libraries, academies, universities are built and millions are spent. Why should a permanent institution (which doesn't exist here) not gather the best artists in all fields? Luck—on which every, even the purely commercial theatre depends—might have it that a contemporary Shakespeare will write the play (if one insists on excluding his immortal works as "revivals"), a young Goethe will put it on (as he did in Weimar), that a still unknown Beethoven or Mozart will compose the music for it, that Toscanini will conduct it, that a Palladio of today will build the sets (Geddes would certainly not do a worse job), a modern Titian will design the costumes, a Leonardo will arrange the groups (is there a dramatically more exciting group than his Last Supper in the Certosa?) and that a still undiscovered Rembrandt will add to the whole the magic of light and shadow, so decisive for the theatre.

Have not the greatest composers, conductors, painters, actors, dancers of our time worked with me, given me their counsel? Their ranks are by no means broken off. I have found a continuance in the astonishing wealth of talent in American youth. Must people die first, before they are recognized as artists? Of course, the theatre (as by the way, every art) can be prostituted at the lowest level. It poses no preconditions, it is accessible to all, understandable to most and, therefore, the most influential, most powerful and most popular of all the arts. It is the most alive, the truly democratic art. It is created by talents that rise from the bowels of the nation and it is created anew every evening through the collision between the prepared performance and the unprepared public.

The ancient Greeks knew it and spent as much money for it as for their wars of liberation against the Persians. The medieval Church and the German princes sheltered it—and the Russians of today are sending their actors to the front, not to fight, but to play. Their troops are victorious.

Only the angels on Broadway don't know it as yet. Their motto remains: "Business as usual."

Enough. I only wanted to thank you. I only wanted, in your honor, to ride down my inborn aversion to writing letters. But my unaccustomed pen, once dipped into ink, overflows with all my heart is full of.

I am not deluding myself. I know: the theatre I am thinking of does not exist [in New York]. But its birthday is near, whoever will come and sire it. New York, today, is the capital of the world. It will have its theatre. It surely will look different from the way I imagine it. Our reality is the fantasy of a higher being with other time measures. If we were able to grasp our reality in its entirety, instead of being chained, physically and psychically, to the moment, we would probably understand the grandeur of its simple conception. In it, even Adolf the Great is but a minute insect. Like the fly in Aesop's fable, he sits on the carriage wheel of time and has no inkling of the driver. Proudly he hums: Look how much dust I am whipping up!

I hope to see you again soon and am, meanwhile, sending you my most cordial regards. Please give my regards also to your dear wife. Her enchanting nature expresses itself in the uniquely clear musicality of her language [German]. It delights the ear of an old theatre man and awakens—despite everything, despite everything—in a racially alien Jew, not rooted, of course, in that soil, the longing for his ardently loved mother tongue.

Yours,
Max Reinhardt

The fewer the opportunities for expressing himself professionally in English, the more eager he was to express himself in his "ardently loved mother tongue." Nor did utilitarian considerations deter him. The above letter is addressed to someone who had no connections with the American theatre and, even if he had, would have been powerless to do anything about my father's laments. We have come across his name before: José Chapiro. My father met him through their mutual friend, Gerhart Hauptmann, and he took an immediate liking to him, making him his ambassador to France and Spain. A writer of sorts in his own right (his works include a biography of Erasmus), and something of a Jewish scholar, Chapiro was a typical example of my father's increasing inclination to entrust business dealings to would-be intellectuals dabbling in would-be business. Max Reinhardt's representation in France and Spain, accordingly, resulted in very little business. But it did result in other conveniences, as the following cable he received from Chapiro documents:

> AMBASSADOR [the German in Paris] WISHES YOU TO STAY AT EMBASSY BUT DRAWS YOUR ATTENTION TO MADRID AMBASSADOR'S AND WIFE'S SIMULTANEOUS ARRIVAL. SINCE PLANS FOR THEIR VISIT PREDATE YOURS HERR VON HOESCH MUST GIVE BATHROOM TO THE FORMER. OTHERWISE YOU WOULD RECEIVE BEST APARTMENT IN PALAIS HORTENSE. BUT AMBASSADOR WILLING TO PUT HIS OWN BATHROOM AT YOUR DISPOSAL WHICH YOU MUST SHARE WITH HIM HOWEVER.

One of the longest letters my father ever wrote (the typewritten copy—I have quoted from it elsewhere—numbers fifty-six single-spaced pages) was addressed to another bizarre ambassador, Rudolf Kommer, who was no mean letter writer himself. Again, my father's outpouring of words was a reply. But not to a congratulatory message. The letter he took issue with had been half philippic, half apologia, enumerating, in Kommer's opinion, every error my father had ever committed and complaining about my father's ingratitude for his services. My father found these services wanting. As to the errors, he was willing to plead guilty to some, but he did not agree with his pitiless critic that his entire life had been misspent. The exchange was as fruitless as it was bitter; an ex post facto settling of accounts between two former friends and associates who had nothing more to say to each other, but insisted on saying everything. Among a wealth of topics, my father's missive includes a portrait of the recipient. That he felt moved to paint it for him personally makes the author as interesting as the subject.

> . . . To the unforgettably colorful, alas by then already somewhat fading human landscape which the sunset of European culture still shone upon belonged among others [and now follows an exhaustive list of guests at Leopoldskron, of which I name only a selection] Otto H. Kahn . . . Morris Gest . . . Grace Moore . . . Belasco . . . Geddes . . . Stanislavski . . . Diana . . . Rosamond Pinchot . . . Iris [Tree] . . . Claudel . . . [General von] Seeckt . . . Toscanini . . . Tristan Bernard . . . McCormick . . . Hearst . . . Werner Krauss . . . the angelic Archbishop Rieder . . . the satanic Molnár . . . Moissi . . . Tilly Losch . . . Noël Coward . . . Hugo von Hofmannsthal . . . [Lillian] Gish . . . Lady Oxford . . . Mr. Morgenthau . . . Mrs. Sara Delano Roosevelt with grand- and great-grandchildren . . . Winston

Churchill . . . Castiglioni . . . Werfel . . . Weill . . . Hedy Lamarr . . . L. B. Mayer . . . Anton Kuh [the sharpest German-speaking wit of his time] . . . and many more whose names escape me at the moment and sundry dramatis personae who have no names but played small and essential parts, plus guests, waiters, servants, etc., etc.

The most heterogeneous elements were cast together in a troupe which I would never have been able to coordinate on any stage. They belonged to the most varied strata, spoke different languages, had different faiths and even different ABC's. Some had written the glories of their era and others could not even write. There were duchesses and anarchists, drunkards and aesthetes, princes of the Church and atheists, dreamily dressed fairies [*sic*] who arrived with their beaux and undistinguished fairies who just brought a secretary, Jews, Nazis, film producers and poets, generals and malingerers, musicians and those uninspired by any Muse. At first, they stood frozen, staring at one another. But soon they were all staring in surprise at a person who happened to be in their midst as if by accident and who chatted nonchalantly and without ever stopping. He chatted with the virtuoso brilliance of a pianist, eliciting complicated cadences from the keys without seeming to touch them. He would turn from one to the other, called most by their first names and acted with such ease that one would think this centrifugal mass of people, alien and feeling alienated, were the oldest acquaintances and had simply run into one another again, and that he was continuing a conversation long since begun. His speech squeezed gently past the cigarette forever burning between his lips. It trickled along with the steadily dropping ashes over the as yet icy silence of the others. And gradually this silence thawed.

First one replied with a word, then another injected a question which was caught on the fly, a third found himself drawn into the chitchat, a fourth tried to hold on to his half-superior, half-embarrassed smile, but, just in case, cleared his throat in anticipation of his moment, a fifth burst into laughter, a sixth, by now bathed in pleasure, slapped the belly of a seventh. And finally everyone was talking and screaming topsy-turvy as if around the tower of Babel.

The man himself hailed from much-embattled Czernowitz. Like his home town, he let himself be conquered now by this, now by that nation, now used his mother tongue, in the next breath another one, without changing his tempo or his native intonation. Czernowitz was being constantly occupied and vanquished, and could not even retain its name. R.K. [Käthchen] K. was also always occupied, but never vanquished, and he remained *R.K.K. a. Cz.* [from Czernowitz, Bukovina]. He appeared in tails, patent leather and opera hat or in dinner jacket and, on demand, coyly décolletéed in lederhosen or swimming trunks. There was no spoilsport who did not start to grin at the sight of him. He was the heart of the whole company and pumped blood even into its stiffest and most congealed members. He entertained and found entertainment in everybody. He formed friendship upon friendship and quarreled with some to the point of physical violence, without, however, extinguishing his cigarette or his wit. He spiced the fat life of the rich with sharp truths, gave away boxes of candy, flowers and books, lunched, dined, supped (sometimes in repetition with first and second understudies), he debated, talked politics, criticized without surcease and, when he failed to incur enough contradictions, he started contradicting himself. He arranged divorces for excitable men, married off women, played with their children, concluded agreements between producers, poets, directors, musicians, slipped the schnorrer an amount he had just won at bridge from the millionaire, conversed with a bishop about a madonna from a house of ill repute in Vienna's Singerstrasse, and drew lots from a hat, deciding the fate of other madonnas.

At night, in the bar, he could make Jews yodel, Nazis *jüdeln* [talk with a Jewish inflection], and the German general sing prophetically, "O, thou, my Austria!" Thus, between his morning coffee and nightly liverwurst, he in his own way solved all political, economic and social problems about which, before and after, whole nations slaughtered one another. The entire show was accompanied by an irresistible, dry humor whose facets reflected a mirthful self-irony.

But the stories and the events I am really thinking of didn't happen on the spectacular surface, but in the hush of privacy: not with the protagonists of the elite, but with those other, nameless supernumeraries. In this realm, the Czernowitzian developed a unique, gracious dexterity with which he handled difficult, often awkward situations. He treated indifferent, sometimes altogether undesirable and unattractive people with a noble tact, revealing a tender consideration otherwise foreign to him. Without the slightest condescension, he could make every servant his friend and disarm every enemy with the perfect gallantry of a born aristocrat. The less close people were to his heart, the more he let it speak in his gruff kindness. These seemingly insignificant impromptus to which I was only an uninvolved witness are for me established facts. They make up for all the services you failed to render me. They were simply poems. But they weren't written, they were simply true. Nothing in them rhymed with money. They seemed to have no rhyme or reason. And they did not even have a punch line. Their core was—well, Kommer.

Surely, a piquant portrait of a man. Sharp-edged, humorous, affectionate, and, at the end, a bit rueful. One of Reinhardt's declarations of love? Of love unrequited? Ruptured? The beginning of the letter:

I have, invariably, listened to you attentively, mostly with pleasurable gaiety, always fascinated by the charm of your dialectic, often inwardly convinced,

> often with indomitable opposition—and at times in the sad recognition that something in which I believed was being buried thereby.
>
> . . . When words are crossed, they become, like all weapons, most cutting and dangerous. I hope that the aim of these honed words in your letter is clear to you. Because it is not to me. Do you want me to laugh, rage or cry? You lay about you blindly, but you are very wide of the mark, Mr. Kommer. Where you are aiming is not where I am.

My father concludes:

> . . . Let there be no further mention of what you have written. Let us keep things the way it reads in *Julius Caesar*: If we do meet again, why, we shall smile. That is all.

The letter is an adieu to a friend by whom my father felt abandoned, to an associate who had left him in the lurch; an attempt to come to terms with a cuckoo's egg in his nest. How had it got there in the first place?

In 1923, with *The Miracle* in the offing on Broadway, my father was on the lookout for a go-between to serve him in America. During the summer holiday which he spent with his sons at Garmisch, he discussed the problem with actor Pallenberg and his wife, Fritzi Massary. Stimulating as the interlocution undoubtedly was, it must have been just as uninformed, since neither of the advisers had ever been to the States. But they had a friend, Alfred Polgar (Viennese critic, essayist and master of the literary tidbit), who had introduced them to a man who had fallen on hard times. He needed help. In their eyes, even more than Max Reinhardt. Their Greek gift in a scintillating wrapping was Rudolf Kommer.

His advertised qualifications were that he had once been on the London staff of the *Frankfurter Zeitung* (then Germany's foremost quality newspaper, for which he wrote a highly critical review of Reinhardt's first *Miracle*), had escaped to America at the beginning of World War I, was interned as an enemy alien and subsequently deported to Austria, where he was inducted into the secret service. After demobilization, he barely eked out a living by translating English conversation pieces and, in summer, was a regular, welcome, entertaining and always-ready-to-help member of the small Garmisch circle. His motives were mainly nutritive, but also, though less easily satisfied, erotic: he was hopelessly smitten with Fritzi's daughter Liesl, nineteen, smart, attractive and sex-oriented, and most kindly disposed toward the new friend of the house, but not quite so kindly as he dared to hope. When she ran away with the promising—if not necessarily marriage-promising—novelist and playwright Bruno Frank, the unlucky suitor consoled the worried mother and excited stepfather with the assurance that, should the bounder jilt an unwed Liesl in any—including the family—way, he would be on hand at all times and willing to save the honor of the poor duped girl. To everyone's relief, this help, in the event, was not required. Liesl did become a very happy Mrs. Frank, and Kommer received a fundamental lesson: to my knowledge, he never again exposed this particular weak spot in his makeup.

The allegation of his sponsors that he possessed the best connections in New York, was at home in the theatre, had a winning personality and spoke perfect English mirrored reality only in the last two instances. The internment camp had hardly been the place for establishing American connections and neither his journalistic stint nor that in Intelligence for the Austrian embassy in Bern in the last year of the war could have been conducive to expertise in the theatre. To his credit it must be mentioned, however (and there were always two sides, credit and debit, to the Kommer question mark), that his connections as foreign agent did enable him to save the life of Austrian Signal Corps private Franz Werfel. Werfel had been court-martialed for failing to pass on vital information on the Galician front. Poetizing in the trenches, he ignored the ring of a field telephone in his charge. Kommer succeeded in getting the death sentence commuted. According to one of his beguiling stories, Kommer owed his civilian position less to his linguistic and globe-trotting aptitude than to the fact that—similar to Laemmle's case—no soldier's cap in the Austro-Hungarian Army fitted his pate. But now, those times were *tempi passati* for him. Now, this plump Bukovinian with the bulbous, almost hairless head, deep-set wise eyes and mocking lips, was standing hat in hand one night, by appointment, at the gate of Schloss Leopoldskron.

Ignorant of the fine points of his visitor's biography, Max Reinhardt had prepared a royal solo reception for him. Not until Kommer had been duly regaled with food and drink, charmed and (hopefully) impressed, did my father, with the Turkish coffee, reveal to him his American plans. Kommer needed no preamble: "Herr Professor," he said, "with all my respect for you, I find the idea, from the American point of view, feebleminded." My father was perplexed. Only closer acquaintance would teach him that Kommer divided the human race into two categories: impostors and the feebleminded. He put himself, with more than intended justification, into the former. Me too, for that matter. My father's personality, according to this theory, was split: his gifts, which Kommer admired, while mostly disapproving of their exploitation, the spell to which he succumbed, especially in the fat years, stamped him as a master impostor; with regard to leading an everyday existence, he considered him a prize example of feeble-mindedness.

It was a unique, though refreshing, experience for my father, as he told me. He decided on the spot to draw this pixieish spirit of contradiction—as a counterpole, as it were—to his side. But he had no easy time carrying out the decision. Kommer predicted a "guaranteed debacle" for *The Miracle* on Broadway. On the other hand, he admitted that it would be feeble-minded to rebuff the wishes of a millionaire (Kahn). The two men wrestled till dawn. Only then did the courted petitioner give in to the eager benefactor and agree to represent him.

With a letter of introduction from Max Reinhardt to Otto H. Kahn, the oddity from Czernowitz took off for New York. The introduction was to open an all-important portal to the envoy—one he bolted shut behind him the moment he had entered it. By the time my father followed him to America, he gained an audience with Kahn only on Kommer's intercession. Kommer had become Kahn's bridge and backgammon partner, procurer of attractive femininity, entertainer and jack of all (diverting) trades. Instead of a go-between, Reinhardt had secured a barrier. But the letter did not unlock only that portal. It turned out to be a magical *passe-partout*: Kommer was on his way to becoming a desired member of New York's elite, equally at home among the upper Jewish ten thousand and the upper anti-Semitic ten thousand (who were enchanted by this "token Jew"). My father remained largely unaware of the differences in altitude on this dizzying climb, nor did he see himself as its immediate cause, since, in a few months, Kommer had accomplished no more and no less than assuming the stature of which his three Garmisch inventors had already sung their praises.

It would, however, be a gross underestimation of Kommer's abilities to give my father exclusive credit for causing the lightning promotion. Once he had been given the entree, few other than this social artist could have maneuvered so agilely on so slippery a floor. Initially, his close relation with Max Reinhardt (its commercial aspects wisely played down) gave him the identity indispensable in America's society race: no first-, second- or third-generation upstart could look upon him as an upstart. But beyond that, he never decked himself with his lord and master's plumes. On the contrary: as soon as he felt accepted, he sought to plant his existence squarely on his own two feet and to blur as much as possible his traces as Reinhardt's manager. Subtly encouraged by himself, it did not take long before a general and never-wholly-to-subside guessing game started as to the sources of his livelihood. For no one ever saw him at work, no one ever saw any results of it, and he appeared to have an infinite amount of leisure time. Alexander Woollcott devoted an entire piece in *The New Yorker* to this seeming phenomenon. It was not unusual to imagine him Max Reinhardt's patron rather than his employee. And yet, a single item would have been sufficient to solve the riddle: Kommer received ten percent of all Reinhardt's income in all English-speaking countries.

Until the mid-thirties, one could live quite agreeably on that. And the newspaperman who never again wrote another article, the translator who rapidly discontinued those activities, the disappointed author who, henceforth, limited the scope of his pen to extensive correspondence, made modest demands in terms of creature comforts. Till the end of his days, he lived in a single room with one bed, albeit always in the best hotel. This, not for the sake of good living, but for the address. In Leopoldskron too, his (permanent) quarters were modest. For lunch, every day at precisely 1:15, he would be host to a sprinkling of those aspiring to success or to the ladies' favors. For this purpose, he kept a reserved table at the most elegant restaurants in town, from which, however, he excluded all married couples. For that was one of his iron rules: to feed either the husband or the wife, otherwise unmarried individuals, and to mix them according to his gusto. The clientele thus gathered by him was so welcome to the innkeepers that they accorded him a generous cut rate. At the Colony, in Manhattan, during his absence, his photograph over his table would remind trespassers of their temporary privilege.

This eccentric life style was to Kommer's liking. He defied classification—which is something snobs, social as well as intellectual, must practice. Without it, they cannot exclude or include, cannot limit or allot proper places. None of this was possible in the case of Kommer. He cracked every hierarchy. As he achieved nothing, no one could criticize his achievements. As he seemed always engaged in some—intangible—effort, no one could call him an idler. As he knew how to lend to every service the semblance of a favor, he earned a great deal of gratitude, hardly ever a reprimand. As he never wanted anything for himself—except to be admitted—the rich trusted him. As he never wanted anything from women, at least never demanded anything of them, was, however, always at their beck and call, they became his strongest confederates.

Thus he played confidant, counselor, caretaker, father confessor, procurer, arbiter, entertainer to the international upper crust. No male needed to be jealous of him, no female fear his advances. For this eroticist, except in his giant head, was a neuter; asexual and continuously in love. It drove him to staying close to his dulcineas without ever coming too close to them. Accordingly, he founded a harem which no sultan could have afforded, with himself as eunuch. Swarmed around, pampered, used, respected, but otherwise a zero, he waited on his odalisques hand and foot and read the wishes in their eyes. He consoled them in their sorrows, conjured up enjoyments for them and stood guard while they enjoyed. He whiled away their time in a hundred delectable ways until . . . he must surrender them for what was always threatening. Then he assumed tactical leadership, chaperoned, composed, if desired, love letters, steered by remote control and fretted until . . . they came back for confession. They liked to come, for in this confessional they were never jolted out of their romance. For him, the essential thing was that they came—from wherever: disappointments, scandals, lawsuits, their reputations soiled, their souls injured. Then he played the psychiatrist, the diplomat, the accountant, the lawyer, the press agent. In gratitude, the beauties gave him that implausible middle name (in German, meaning "little Catherine"). Out of tenderness? A little malice? No matter, R.K. became R.K.K.

The mysterious aura surrounding him veiled his origins and his goal. His *accoucheur*, Max Reinhardt, recognized them and the resulting perils for himself only when it was too late. Until then, he savored the character part with which he thought he had enriched his *comédie humaine*. In any case, it was for him a thousand times more intriguing than the yield of a mere business connection. In a letter to me, he expressed it thus: "I always respected him more for being himself than for his accomplishments. . . ."

In the literal sense, Kommer's origins, to be sure, were anything but mysterious. After all, it was he who incessantly rubbed everybody's nose, Jewish or Gentile—before it could be turned up—into them. The "a. Cz." not only accompanied his name on his calling card, was not only emblazoned on his most valued furniture (his luggage, so familiar to the personnel of the Ambassador in New York, the Ritz in London, the Adlon in Berlin, the Imperial in Vienna and the first class on Atlantic steamers), it was also continuously on his lips. When at a dinner in Leopoldskron, he could not resist enlightening his neighbor at table, General von Seeckt (the military genius behind Germany's rearmament after World War I in nonviolation of the Treaty of Versailles), about his un-Prussian birthplace and generously volunteered that His Excellency, of course, would hardly have heard of this godforsaken hole, His Excellency replied: "Czernowitz? Oh, yes, my good man, a great deal as a matter of fact! I took it three times in the last war." (Kuh about Kommer: "Behind the mask of a Jew bastard hides the Jew bastard that he is.")

The New York *Miracle* laid the foundation of Kommer's house of cards. Through Reinhardt, Gest and Geddes, he forged his link with show business. Through Kahn the doors of high finance opened to him. Through Rosamond Pinchot he entered America's blue-bloodstream. Through Diana Cooper—dulcinea number one—he put out his feelers to British high aristocracy, through her husband to British politics. A cordial relation with Edmund secured an inside view into Max's European theatre web. Café society, the columnists, the puppets and the string-pullers did the rest. *The Miracle* that season was the center of attention. And Kommer was at the center's center. All roads led to him, passed by him. For my father the adventure remained a gratifying foreign interlude from which he returned to undesired "normalcy," with no discernible follow-up. Why? Why was the bridgehead not expanded? One of the reasons was that the agent he left in charge became, himself, a commuter between the Old and the New Worlds. But more important, he had quite other interests. For him the adventure had been a personal springboard.

The matchmaker—between money and art, pedigree and career—had put out his ubiquitous shingle. His schedule dovetailed with my father's needs only by fortuitous coincidence, seldom by design: six winter months in New York, spring in London, six weeks in summer as majordomo at Leopoldskron, with side trips to Berlin, Vienna, Venice (Garmisch was no longer on the itinerary). The man without property, dependent on the whims of the rich and gifted, lived a life of independence and affluence. His independence he proved by unsparingly telling anyone who cared to listen—and those who didn't—the disagreeable truth, which, according to my father, was inaccessible to him. His "affluence" took the form of charity: he took from his rich friends to give to his poor friends. He prided himself especially on helping his writer friends of yore (among them Hofmannsthal and Polgar) to whom he once looked up in awe. He gained, thereby, a certain equality of rank with the benefactors (who admired his selflessness) and with the beneficiaries (who in straight competition would have been beyond his reach). He did a great deal of good in this manner during the Depression and emigration. If my father, in his time of want, had asked him for handouts, Kommer would probably have arranged a small subsidy for him and their friendship would have endured. But to entreat him to tap a few drops from the beehive of nabobs he attended as a solicitous apiarist was a lost cause.

He liked caring for children of famous people, lending his ear to their woes when the parents denied them theirs, understanding them when they felt misunderstood by the parents, and interceding for them with the parents who would rather listen to him than to their children. We did not always reciprocate with the same tenderness. His blind adoration of reason and unconditional condemnation of all emotional imbroglios once prompted me to break up one of his sacred afternoon siestas by teasing him quite disrespectfully. I charged him with cowardice, with always preferring the easy way out rather than ever taking a chance. I immediately regretted my forwardness, for every trace of the legendary Kommerian countenance was suddenly, frighteningly, gone. He shot up from his pillows with such vehemence that I feared for his health—not without cause, as I discovered before long. "You fool!" he chided me. "Don't you realize that I haven't the vaguest idea at this very moment where to get the money for tomorrow's rent?" I looked into flickering gambler's eyes. Yes, that he was, above all else: a gambler. Not just at cards and dice, which took up a good portion of his hours. His entire existence was a game of chance.

By 1933, Kommer's position in America was sufficiently consolidated as to make the loss of Germany relatively painless. The loss of Reinhardt, of course, did affect him. Not so much financially. He had been able to do Alice Astor-Hofmannsthal one of his favors by installing himself as her business manager. That guaranteed him a more secure ten percent. But the glamour of the Reinhardt association was ebbing—his king had been driven from his major realm. Worse, the king expected more and more services from his vassal, services the vassal was neither willing nor able to perform. Had actually never performed. Finally, the king had to abdicate altogether. A king in exile was barely tolerable for the vassal. But a king looking for a job? It was fortunate for both that the king's place of exile was mainly California. The accumulating venom spent itself in letters. But my father's eleventh-hour return to New York in 1942 made the estrangement awkward. They tried not to meet. But it was inevitable that they did. And—why, they smiled. That was all.

At eight o'clock in the morning on Sunday, March 28, 1943, Tilly Losch woke me with a call for help from the Hotel Ambassador, sobbing that Käthchen had been found dead in his room. I was to come over quickly, as she could not bring herself to enter it alone. Twenty minutes later, Tilly, the hotel manager and I stepped over the remains of Rudolf K. Kommer a. Cz., and for the first time in my memory this affected circumlocution described its prosaic subject factually and graphically: He lay on his side, twisted, in the entrance hall, one arm, looking strangely reduced, stretched out helplessly, as though the heart seizure had pulled down its victim on the way to the bell. The great sphere of his head seemed shrunken to half its size, the torso, well-padded only the day before, a limp bundle of misery. It lay there until six in the evening. In these nine and a half hours, half the emigration, half of New York's society, its literary and art world, stepped across the corpse that seemed futilely intent on barring access to a cherished, bygone privacy. How the narrow space managed to accommodate the milling multitude is still an enigma to me. But there it was, ebbing and flowing, in the neat coziness of the bright bed-sitting room, with the row of shining apples on the windowsill, the gay watercolors, the rack with hundreds of records of Viennese folk songs and the orderly bookshelves covering an entire wall. The agglomeration was not in keeping with the departed's wishes. Only the final elimination of his will power permitted the different cliques of his wide acquaintanceship which he had neatly separated from each other to mix so indiscriminately.

The body was not allowed to be moved until the coroner had completed his inquest. He, however, could not be located till that Sunday evening. The haphazard contact between the components of Kommer's magnetic field—millionaires and beggars, ravishing beauties and ancient hags had arrived from every corner of the city and from as far away as Washington and the far side of Long Island—proved (Kommer would have predicted it) a failure. There was a total lack of communication. In this human whirlpool only one person was missing: the one who had unleashed it. Max Reinhardt.

Tilly, the first to be notified, and I did our best to gather the most rudimentary information about our friend. For we woke up to the fact that we were in the dark about practically everything concerning him. We had not even been aware that the chain smoker had suffered from angina pectoris and undergone medical treatment for many years. We knew nothing about his family, who his doctors and lawyers were, what his bank and insurance connections were. I had met his personal valet who used to press his Austrian peasant linen shirts, but I did not know his name or where to get hold of him over the weekend. And I had met the broker who was ghost-managing Alice Astor's business affairs for her manager. But, again, I had no clue of how to contact him. Nor was anyone present better informed. All we were able to unearth was that his famous multivolumed set of pedantically kept, leather-bound, handwritten address books, one for each city (every New Year's Eve, in strict seclusion, he used to perform the ritual of crossing out the deceased of the year just past), had vanished along with all other personal documents.

Only days later, we learned that we had not been the first callers that morning after all. G-men had stepped over their quarry even before us. Rudolf Kommer was under strong suspicion of espionage for the Axis powers. This was no secret to me, as I had been interviewed several times by the FBI, who had been quite frank with me. Other friends of Kommer and myself, among them the writer Ben Hecht, had had the same experience. Thinking back over everything I knew and had heard about him, it seems to me quite probable that he should have wished—and perhaps offered to use his political connections in England and with the Nazis (some of whom, like Hitler pal Putzi Hanfstaengl, who had been with him in the internment camp, kept cropping up in his inner sanctum)—to work toward a negotiated peace. This, in his mind, would not have been treason. It would have fitted perfectly into his philosophy and his ideas about the Kommer mission in life: to be the eternal mediator and to worship at the altar of objectivity.

One more time, the disparate congregation of Kommer adherents gathered in one room: at one of New York's posh funeral parlors, Campbell's, on upper Madison Avenue, courtesy of William S. Paley. The sage of Czernowitz had come a long way in fifty-four years. It was a ghost-like crowd of which each single member was of flesh and blood but had barely heard of any second member, never seen any third, and could communicate neither linguistically nor conceptually with any fourth. Here and there, a familiar face or kindred soul acknowledged the common bond. But it was an illusory acknowledgment. That common bond was broken. The congregation's elusive center, its farfetched raison d'être, had ceased to be. Already, it seemed as remote as Czernowitz.

I was in charge of the mise en scène, with the best directorial idea, however, stemming from Tilly: sturdy Viennese folk tunes sounded ethereally on the organ. It had not been easy to procure the necessary organ parts—necessary because Campbell's organist neither knew this type of musical sprinkling nor was in favor of it. A thorough search of New York's music stores proved fruitless. An indulgent habit of mine came in handy: one of my haunts was the Champagne Room of the nightclub El Morocco. There, an Austrian pianist and a Hungarian violinist supplied the entertainment. Together, after closing time at 4 A.M. (I would not budge until the last guest had left), they concocted a comprehensive medley under my watchful, if tired, eye. The pianist was the first to fold. A close second was GI Gottfried. But not before he had dragged the violinist to his hotel, installed him in his sitting room and equipped him with score sheets and pencils. Getting up an hour and a half later, he found the arranger gone, but the transcription ready. Ready for reveille, and, after premature interruption of Signal Corps duties, for the obsequies.

The effect of the musical background was stunning. Those who knew the airs were moved to tears. Above all, my father. He cried unashamedly throughout the ceremony. He was saying goodbye to much more than a former friend, to his favorite tormentor and destructive aide. He was saying goodbye to an "unforgettably colorful landscape which the sunset of European culture still shone upon. . . ."

One incident threatened to disturb the tenuous peace between the Waspish and Jewish, American and European elements: a German poet, Kommer beneficiary Hermann Borchard, who in a concentration camp had suffered several maimed fingers and crushed eardrums, insisted on placing a white rose inside the coffin, on the chest of his benefactor. Since the coffin was closed, this provoked acute protocol difficulties with the mortuary personnel. Neither they nor Paley was able to deter the worshipper. He could not hear and he did not want to hear. Finally, by sign language—or perhaps it was my uniform that did it—a compromise was reached: Borchard was allowed to place the rose on top of the casket. In its forlornness, it was more impressive than the sumptuous floral arrangements drowning it. Frank Crowninshield of *Vogue* and *Vanity Fair* spoke a dignified, articulate eulogy in English. Erika Mann spoke brilliantly, touchingly, about Kommer's qualities and faults in German, a language, she said in an English preamble, that was an essential and beloved part of him. The two portraits had little in common, but they supplemented each other perfectly in sentiment and content. Another symbolic aspect of the event's incongruity was supplied by the accouterments of the assembled ladies: each one, to the bafflement of the others, wore the identical costume jewelry. Kommer had helped a refugee couple specializing in the manufacture of these articles by arranging the financing of a store for them. The goods did not sell well. So the investor doubled as the emporium's chief customer, presenting every one of his lady friends with a sample of the stock he bought. So long as he lived, there was no danger of the bearers' finding out about the unoriginality of their attire. They never met. Death had now torn down the fences.

Dear Mr. Paley,

Our much beloved Rudolf Kommer died terribly unexpectedly, terribly early and terribly alone. . . . He left behind a warmth which will glow after him a long time. . . . As one of the oldest of this community I feel it is not only my duty, it is also my most sincere desire to thank you for the memorial service with which you honored our mutual friend. I was especially gratified to hear the time-honored Kaddish prayer and that Kommer's religion was not passed over in silence. . . . He who proudly used to add to his signature the name of his native Czernowitz would surely have wished that his descendance from a 5,000-year-old race be stressed, a race that wrote the Book of Books and composed the immortal Psalms. In his unshakable logic, he was surely no less proud of this than many European aristocrats whose ancestors were robber barons only a few centuries ago or many Americans stemming from early immigrants. . . .

I thank you.

Max Reinhardt

THE DIARY

OCTOBER 4, 1943
(continued)

Papa will not be deterred from answering his mail and he must not! How do I prevent him? By distracting him with the first thing that comes into my head. Luckily I have a new Schweik story: I ran into Junior Laemmle getting out of a taxi in front of the Plaza—he'd just made it back from the swamps of Alabama—and with some puzzlement I watched the doorman and a whole regiment of bellboys tug his larger-than-life-size bags up the red-carpeted stairs. Why, I asked, the sudden switch in allegiance from the plush Hotel Pierre across the street to here? His jubilant reply: He was complying with his superior officer's suggestion that a protracted stay in New York might depend on his choice of more modest quarters. [Result of the shrewd step, duly reported in the gossip columns: Junior Laemmle shipped to Desert Training Center in sizzling Indio, California.] *My reason for the recitation doesn't detract from Papa's glee. He deliberately leads me on, asks Eleonora whether she's ever heard my story of "Mr. and Mrs. William Tell." She lies that she hasn't and I'm prevailed upon to relate—to Papa for the umpteenth time—the story of how the Hungarian playwright Géza Herzek* [Wunderbar] *was seized by the idea of selling to my executive producer at MGM a film version of Schiller's Wilhelm Tell à la Andy Hardy with a sprinkling of Jesse James.* [In the twisted depths of his Hungarian mind Herzek had figured out that the transaction would be particularly logical, as he had collaborated on a treatment for Warner Brothers' Academy Award–winning film The Life of Emile Zola, which, in his own words, "dealed vit trut." And since Tell "dealed vit freedumm," the question "Vat iss trut vidout freedumm?" was squarely put to the MGM official. No answer forthcoming, it was triumphantly supplied by Herzek himself: "Notting!" The corollary being that the studio move in fast and capitalize on the axiom. Canny as Herzek's calculations were, he failed to determine that my boss knew neither the plot nor the characters of the German classic, nor had he ever heard of its author. To add to the general confusion, he went about his business of "selling"—Magyar-mangling en route the Swiss names of Mr. and Mrs. Stauffacher, Mr. and Mrs. Melchthal and Mr. and Mrs. Attinghausen—by trying to reincarnate the eighteenth-century poet-dramatist as a twentieth-century spinner of yarns. What killed the sale in the end was neither the subject nor the unconventional rendition. The fatal blow was dealt by Schiller himself: When Herzek confidently reached the climax and quoted "Mr." Tell's prophecy that the tyrant Gessler—which he pronounced "Gesslair" and, to keep it topical, kept comparing to "Heetlair"—must come through a specific narrow pass—"Durch diese hohle Gasse muss er kommen," a quotation every German schoolchild is as familiar with as his own name—my executive suddenly balked at a plot turn so arbitrary: "Why? Why must what's his name go through that goddamned pass?" Exultantly Herzek recited the explanation, i.e., his translation of the second of these immortal lines: "Beecuss dere iss no udder vay to Kuessnacht!"—"Es führt kein anderer Weg nach Küssnacht." It was not a satisfactory explanation. And the German drama about the liberation of Switzerland as reconstructed by a Hollywood screenwriter from Budapest, half interpreted by a Hollywood producer from Berlin to a Hollywood bigwig from Virginia, never saw the light of day as Mr. and Mrs. William Tell—or anybody else.] The stillborn brainchild, conceived in a crazy, mixed-up era, did, however, serve a purpose in life: For the umpteenth time Max Reinhardt breaks up. He's had a full evening, is tired and ready for bed. Have no need to worry about his writing letters tonight.

To receive is not enough for Eleonora. She wants to give as well. Has worked out a way to get Wolfgang reinstated in his job by using influence of Elsa Maxwell [the benign gossip columnist and party giver] on Jack Warner, thus giving Papa a further boost.

TUESDAY,
OCTOBER 5, 1943

Corbett doesn't understand why I have so little time for her lately. Can't tell her about Papa, so pretend have not been well myself. Which produces new snags for Helen. Mystifyingly, my "return to health" causes no hurrahs, earns me a very cold shoulder. Takes a lot of time and devotion to warm up same. [Only months hence was I to discover that she had sent a pound jar of caviar and a bouquet of tulips to my "sickbed," for which I, ignorant of them, never thanked her. The caviar, I learned, ended up in Silvia's sly stomach, the tulips, shredded petal by petal, stalk by stalk, in her john.]

Meet Grosz. A mellowed soul, giving no evidence of his former artistic acidity, his political and moral engagement. Lives in retirement on Long Island, paints pastoral subjects and is fondly preoccupied with the new *generation. As foreseen, he refuses to participate in film. Unforeseen: has no feeling of hatred for Germans. Hope Einstein less forgiving.*

Buy phonograph. Papa needs other company. Toscanini and Horowitz are with us nightly. Papa is a grateful host—and improving nightly.

WEDNESDAY,
OCTOBER 6, 1943

A lovely day: Papa much better! Speech defect almost gone. Joyously report to Wolfgang, who'll relay good news to Thimig, Mama and Salka.

Meet with Darvas and work with her on Helen *casting. Very cool wind blowing. She has heard—as predicted, the good Dr. F. "let it drop"—that I'm concealing something important and she's offended by my lack of confidence. Put her off with assurance that she can visit Papa next week. With her brand of innuendo she lets me know Irion suspects that Papa had a stroke. Ridicule the thought, quickly go on to other things. We're joined by Chaney* [Stuart Chaney, scenic designer] *and Czettel* [Ladislas Czettel, who also did the costumes for Berlin Helen]. *Although the guiding spirit is absent, our little circle is inspired by him to conjure up a Reinhardt Offenbach.*

It Is a Dream

THE LIGHTS DIM. The conductor raises his stick. Overture. The familiar strains introducing *La Belle Hélène*. It is the "orchestral overture" to the opéra bouffe and, therefore, long. Why, then, does the curtain part after a few bars? Because the orchestral overture this time serves also as *scenic* overture. The depth of the stage is as yet blocked off. By a second curtain. Between it and the orchestra pit, in the center, looms a large crate. Suspiciously light-footed stagehands hammer and pry it open. A bust of Homer is deftly fished out, followed by the evening's props and lifeless, statue-like members of the cast. The music awakens them to choreographed life. An hors d'oeuvre dansé.

From the rear of the audience, encircling it on either side, masked figures gain the stage over ramps. The second curtain parts and we find ourselves in a temple. The masked figures take up their lateral honor-guard positions. A Greek operetta chorus. Behind its solemn Spartan disguise the loose Berlin tongue of the "Athenians-upon-Spree," as befits their city, works overtime.

We are, indeed, in Berlin. It is June 1931. The trees on Kurfürstendamm are at their greenest. The cafés are crowded. The city is full of expectations. Maybe this year will dispel the specters that have been haunting it lately. Anyway, here on Kurfürstendamm, virulent poverty so far has not made a dent and manipulated violence not left a scar. I too am full of expectations, eighteen and just having passed my *baccalauréat*. I have enrolled in the Friedrich Wilhelm University—practically my last visit to it. I am shuttling between my own seminar at Café Wien—one of its chess tables—and my father's at the Theater am Kurfürstendamm, where he is rehearsing the *Schöne Helena.* I cannot make up my mind which queen I favor. It is a delicious dilemma, especially as the shuttle is so short, involving not much more than crossing the avenue.

I know *Helena* will not be one of his "perfect" productions and am, in a measure, glad of it. It fits my, my friends', Berlin's—perhaps his?—state of mind. Some of my friends are, as they insist on warning me, ideologically anti-Reinhardt, whatever that means. They are trying to drive an ideological wedge between "progressive" me and my "conservative" father. Still, they are magnetized by his nimbus. I am as sadistic in exposing them to it as they are in their acceptance of me on probation, as it were. It tickles me to take them to rehearsals and to watch their hairsplitting opprobrium melt into simple enjoyment. What is more, who cares? In the spring of 1931, in Berlin, only the wrong people cared. Unfortunately.

What transpires in the Theater am Kurfürstendamm is, by the way, not all that escapist. Paris, the tenor and Trojan antihero, is as overbearing and blinded as an SS man. His racist prejudices—toward the Greeks—lurk everywhere behind his snappy deportment. His infatuation with Helen comes close to *Rassenschande* (race shame). Helen is beautiful, frivolous, idolatrous, languidly provocative—an eager prey for the predestined rapist. Her cuckold husband, gaga King Menelaus, offers no protection whatsoever. Neither do his exalted kin and royal colleagues gathered at the palace for a summit meeting. Threatening aggression is the topic. Their decadence and cynicism, their love of pleasure and abhorrence of any kind of decision, actually invite it. It is only the inexperience, the ineptness of the wolf man in shepherd's clothing that delays the inevitable war. In the meantime, there is ample opportunity for waltzing and can-

canning on the good old European volcano. In keeping with Offenbach's and his librettists' amiably satirical spirit, fed by and directed against France's Second Empire, Reinhardt's executor of the composer's will, Erich Wolfgang Korngold, and Reinhardt's librettists, Egon Friedell and Hans Sassmann, are paying regard to the same volcano in the same coin seventy years later. (Friedell, the author of a learnedly entertaining, frankly idiosyncratic history of European culture, which he dedicated to my father, was the most genial and the wisest of that—mostly converted—Jewish tribe of—not always grateful—Heine legatees—satirists, critics, versifiers, essayists, publicists, traveloguers—which provided practically all the sting and all the wit in contemporary German literature and whose other best-known leaders were Karl Kraus, Alfred Kerr, Anton Kuh, Alfred Polgar, and Kurt Tucholsky.)

In a polyphonic tableau vivant, the judgment of Paris is rendered—evoe!—on the strength of a striptease by Aphrodite, on whom he bestows the apple, preferring her looks and promise to him of the world's most beautiful woman to the awards of wisdom or virtue, staunchly proffered in song by Athena and Hera, respectively. A spicy relish. (Gorgeous LaJana, an Aphrodite born from the foam of the Berlin gutter, must have lured Herr Doktor Goebbels with similar bait. She was to switch from Greek paganism to the German variety with ease and to link up suitably with the limping Hephaestus in the propaganda ministry.) But Paris is too dumb to reap his recompense on his own. The war party among the Greeks conspires to help him produce a convincing *casus belli* and succeeds, with the assistance of the corrupt clergy, in sending main appeaser Menelaus packing on a trumped-up pilgrimage. His sailing gives rise to a political, vocal and terpsichorean feast, a rousing Offenbacchanal.

The show—it *is* a show—is studded with delicacies, but it does not jell into a balanced meal. Deviating from his custom, Max Reinhardt hosts a theatrical buffet dinner, lavish but a bit random. The high priest, Kalchas, taking into account the siring circumstances of Leda's daughter, calls it a *Schwanerei* (*Schwan* being the German word for swan, but the typifying term for the bird's behavior sounding much more like that of another animal species, the swine or *Schwein*). *Schöne Helena* lacks the blissful unity *Die Fledermaus* had. The sets overpower with Doric severity, the costumes woo in voluptuous Attic baroque. In Korngold's paprikaed broth the Offenbach tunes bubble a little too hectically. The Gallic cool is missing. My father wavers between the Dionysian and the Apollonian and does not achieve a merger. The course of events, in themselves exciting, remains episodic. If it is true that Max Reinhardt was never subservient to a fixed style, but instead always endeavored to find the appropriate style for each subject, it must be said that, in this case, the quest was left unfulfilled. *Schöne Helena* encompasses a multitude of styles. We are continuously tossed from one mood into another, savoring, in unexpected turns, wit and tomfoolery, lyricism and sex. At least, it is our *hope* that Berlin will savor the concoction and not mind being tossed too jarringly.

The second act tosses us smack into Sparta's kingly, king-sized bed. In the master's absence, the interloper fills the carefully arranged vacuum. Having been surprised, as she claims, in her sleep, the queen insists on pursuing her dream to the end. Paris accepts the rationale by joining her in the melodious love duet "It Is a Dream." A rich dessert. Following the last line: "Since we are meeeeerely dreaming, let nature take its course!" a blackout obscures the caesura between dream and reality. But even a Homeric bedroom farce will not renounce the in-flagrante effect and an inebriated Menelaus returns prematurely.

In the self-tailored role of Hermes, the "god of merchants and thieves," Friedell turned actor does his best to interfere with the course of mythology. The unashamed advertisement of his *History of Culture* (the third and final volume having just appeared in the bookstores), however, fails to restrain the peace-loving monarch from staggering into the matrimonial sanctum. The intermezzo is a hilarious coffeehouse klatsch. A monarchic witness, Crown Prince Emeritus Wilhelm of Prussia, is so smitten with it that he requests an introduction to the librettist-performer. Backstage, the Hohenzollern gushes: "I hear your History is finished. How far does it carry us?" Friedell: "Up to you, Imperial Highness." His Highness was lucky not to have asked him the question a Viennese heckler once put to him at a party: "Isn't your history about everything that doesn't interest me?" "Oh, no," was Friedell's reply, "it isn't as comprehensive as all that."

Wine-happy Menelaus is relaxing in his pillows when, pulling up the cover, he detects six feet sticking out. The count sobers him a bit. He gets out of bed to examine the phenomenon more closely. The result reassures him. Just as he thought: four, as becomes a married couple. It was a dream. No grounds for war. Still not? Not all Greeks are content with the convenient miscalculation, sidesplittingly milked by actor Hans Moser. They bet on number six. They begin a war dance that spills from the front of the house through the aisles, onto the stage, and does not stop at the royal bed. A complicated spring mechanism catapults every hawk jumping on the mattress into mid-air. Not quite aware of what is going on, the royal dove joins in the fun. Cancannic rejoicings all around: The *casus belli* has finally been supplied by a coitus interruptus. In the ensuing melee, the incommoded pair flees. On shore, the Greeks vow revenge, as Paris and Helen recede in their cozy galley.

So far, so good. Most of the time even extraordinarily good. And much can still be eliminated or smoothed out before the opening (eighteen hours hence). That, in any event, is the consensus during intermission of the dress rehearsal, occurring at 2 A.M. The inner circle gathers at Café Reimann across the street. Friedell improvises the chastisement the show can count on from his friend Karl Kraus. It is more Krausian in style, better argued and packed with more vitriol. It does not merely annihilate Reinhardt, but Kraus along with him. In one Friedellian swoop. But our fun with satirizing satire is short-lived. Information reaches us that the third act has started.

Visually, it is the most spectacular. The irrepressibly gay Greeks are camping at the foot of the great wall of Troy. A gigantic, colorfully caparisoned wooden horse is wheeled in. But it is not the only wooden item on the long agenda and the vivacious cast is not alone in being dwarfed by the formidable battlements. The agenda itself has turned to wood. The action is dwarfed. Even the music has lost its spark. Offenbach, Meilhac and Halévy (the original librettists), Friedell and Sassmann, Korngold and Reinhardt have suffered a temporary blackout.

At 5 A.M. Max Reinhardt, for one, comes out of it. Nobody else, as yet, sees the light of day. But there it is: undeniably daylight. In the wings, in the dressing rooms, in the backyard, in the corridors and foyer, on the sidewalks of Kurfürstendamm, again, a consensus forms: Some drastic step is required. But which? That is the one question on everyone's lips. What is one to do? "Cut it," sounds the clear verdict. Cut it? Cut what? "The third act. It's no good." No, it isn't—granted. But it took the greatest pains to write, the longest to rehearse, the most money to mount. Simply cut it now? Besides, how to bring the show to a close? Is the present second-act finale a satisfying end? Is it not a promise of things to come, rather than an organic termination of what has happened previously? Are we to anticipate Jean Giraudoux: *The Trojan War Will Not Take Place*? It looks that way. At any rate, it will not take place on the stage of the Theater am Kurfürstendamm. That much is plain by now. And what *will* take place in its stead? "An epilogue. In front of the curtain. An intimate dialogue with the audience. Offenbach must have pieces like that. You must find one for Schuster," my father says casually to Korngold. Is he serious? His eyes don't blink. Yet, a twinkle seems to hover in them. Anyway, he has spoken the magic word: "Schuster."

Youthful, sexy, saucy Friedel Schuster, never before on a Berlin stage, sings and dances the small part of Orestes with a bell-like soprano and legs as long as they are irresistible. In this brief hermaphroditic existence, she manages, at each run-through, to outshine the Most Beautiful Woman in the World and to be more seductive than the Goddess of Love. She has the style the show is vainly looking for. Max Reinhardt knows a secret weapon when he is handed one. But Korngold is not far behind. Only—how? And when? In less than fourteen hours the curtain is scheduled to rise! The charwomen are impatient to take over. "*And,*" the Greek chorus of management ominously warns *unisono,* "another postponement is out of the question!" "And suppose I 'find' the right tune, where are the lyrics?" Korngold wishes to know. My father looks at Friedell, who is yawning, seeing but one way out: his collaborator, Sassmann, must be got out of bed. With that, he bids all and sundry goodbye and hastens to his own.

These exigencies recurred so frequently in my father's career that one is bound to speculate: they attracted him and he attracted them. In such situations, it was as though he thrived on the despair and suspense around him, as though he—all the more calmly—floated in his very element when faced with life-or-death decisions. At times, I actually suspected him of deliberately postponing unavoidable decisions until they *became* life-or-death. That alternative is, of course, part of every theatre man's experience, if not in a like number and the same tightrope stance. Third-act trouble, especially, may be called endemic. But most authors and directors prefer attempting to cure it on paper, where the necessary changes can be effected less cumbersomely (and less expensively). Running an unsubsidized theatre, my father too had to be conscious of this advantage and *was.* But so firmly did he believe in the ideal evolution of a play while being *played* that he could not resist playing at it for as long as possible. By such tentative practice he helped many authors realize dreams they had written only sketchily or not at all. In other instances, somewhat late and hazardously, the ax came down without mercy. Which is what happened at the dress rehearsal of *La Belle Hélène.* (The same would happen again at the dress rehearsal of Gerhart Hauptmann's *Before Sunset.* Then, in the small hours of the day of the opening, crisis-spurred Max Reinhardt roped in love-hating protagonist Werner Krauss and hereditary, if mellowed, enemy Alfred Kerr to persuade Olympian friend Gerhart Hauptmann, at the Hotel Adlon, to drop anticlimactic Act IV in toto—fourth acts being even more prone to trouble than third. Result: After a long drought, a genuine—last—hit for Hauptmann with a super-performance by Krauss, for once, enthusiastically reviewed by Kerr.)

Hauptmann was obviously worth taking every risk over, as were Shakespeare, Shaw and Molière. Was Offenbach? Broadway and London's West End would say no. (The latter said yes and no to Reinhardt's *Helen of Troy* with Evelyn Laye and George Robie and sets by Adonian Oliver Messel at the Adelphi in 1931.) So would—commercial—Berlin, if asked. (My father did not ask.) Offenbach enjoyed no particular popularity in Germany, except on the programs of hotel and open-air bands. He rested on neither the pedestal of a classic nor the podium of an entertainer. What made Reinhardt so determined an Offenbach zealot?

A poor, gifted cello-playing boy from the Jewish community of Cologne is taken by his father to study in what will soon be the Paris of Napoleon III, where he metamorphoses into not only a Parisian but *the* Parisian; where he runs theatres, inspires writers, develops stars, is the rage of the boulevard and—beyond his craft and talent proper—makes his name a symbol of his era. The analogy is conspicuous: a poor, gifted fledgling actor from the Jewish immigrant community of Vienna makes it to the Berlin of Wilhelm II, where he becomes not only a thoroughly assimilated German but one of the most representative upholders of German *Kultur*; where he runs theatres, inspires writers, develops stars and—beyond his craft and talent proper—makes his name a symbol of his era. Letters written by my father show that he was familiar with Offenbach's biography. The analogy, in all likelihood, had struck him too. Was it a dominating factor? Yes, I would say. On the other hand, he must have been aware of the profound differences between them. Homely Jacques's emancipation from his ethnic and social origins was limited entirely to his art. In his private life, he remained to the end the close-knit-family man, the hapless lover, the nervous gambler and, as a citizen, suspect to the authorities. Handsome Max quickly overcame all these strictures. He was pampered by the environment he endowed with his gifts. Jacques's struggles with problems of sex, finance and official status never ended. He forswore his religion to alleviate them, without any pangs of conscience. Max never did. Never had to. Never yearned to. But even from the point of view of artistry, there was no kinship. There was nothing "Gallic" in Max's makeup; nothing frivolous; nothing modish; nothing caricatural. Despite his pioneering in opera direction and his historical contribution to it, he made it without enthusiasm, under pressure, and he shunned that field consistently. Jacques's special métier, operetta, as we know, was not Max's dish at all. Yet he never lost his craving for it when prepared by Jacques. Why? His own explanation (in that all-embracing letter to Kommer), that in *Orphée aux Enfers* and *La Belle Hélène* the incentive lay in "Homeric laughter set to music," is not wholly satisfactory, for it does not apply to his pet project, *La Vie Parisienne,* which he never realized (because of the libretto's weakness), or to *Tales of Hoffmann,* one of his best efforts. Nor am I at all sure whether Offenbach accomplished or even intended that feat. Yet the fact remains that, after Shakespeare, Goethe, Schiller, Hauptmann, Molière, Strindberg, in that order, Offenbach ranked foremost among the authors he interpreted himself.

Add to this list the next in line, Goldoni, and the question soon loses its statistical tedium, casting a light not merely on Reinhardt's flirtation with Offenbach, but on what made him flirt generally. The enumerated dramatists, incompatible as they are, have one trait in common: They all knew the stage, worked for the stage, were dedicated to the stage. I believe that this kinship steered my father into an arena where he could treat his idols on an equal footing and continue, as it were, where they left off.

"Cut it! Yes, the entire act. [I'll] find an epilogue. Substitute something. A song. For a star. No, no, not for Novotna [Jarmila Novotna, who played Helen in Berlin]. A star already in our midst, but yet to be born." Such words, in a comparable emergency, could have been spoken by Offenbach. My father was not drawn to the tunesmith, the parodist, the *homme du monde.* He was drawn to the *homme de théâtre.* He felt the ad hoc quality of Offenbach's work, a quality it shared with his. That was their bond. It told him that every note Offenbach had written or rewritten or had left for others to fill in, every breath he had taken, every company he had sought, every trip he had made, every penny he had counted or failed to count, every liaison he had joined or failed to join, every quarrel he had engaged in or any humiliation he had tolerated, had one purpose and one justification only: the footlights. When Reinhardt put on Offenbach, he was no reverent interpreter, no high priest. He rolled up his sleeves and felt gloriously free to go on building, inventing, patching where Offenbach and his writers had left things fragmentary, either because of the trade's everyday vicissitudes or, as in the case of *Hoffmann,* because death interrupted his work. (I find it ironically symbolic that my father left unfinished his last Offenbach production for the same reason.)

And so, even before having secured a firm foothold as producer in Berlin, he staked his sixth directorial venture on *Orpheus in the Underworld,* boldly competing with Berlin's three venerable opera houses and all its competently managed, permanent operetta companies. The dourest of that great triad of German orchestra leaders in my youth—Furtwängler, Walter, Klemperer—stumbled onto the steppingstone of his distinguished career in the company of Reinhardt and Offenbach. Otto Klemperer, twenty-year-old assistant conductor at the Stern Conservatory (where my father had intermittently taught acting), took over the baton from his senior, Oscar Fried, and, thus, for the first time, was allowed to practice the art that would make him world-famous. I had the good fortune of seeing the grand old man once more, six months before his death. His partial facial paralysis made him look even more forbidding than ever. I teased him by submitting that he had picked something of a trifle as debut for his impressive pursuits. He knit his magnificent brow into the stormiest of Klemperer frowns and avowed that, that one time, he did not mind music and lyrics—over whose integrity he was to watch with his eagle eye for close to seventy years—taking second place to histrionics, for "I sensed all the while that at the center of that glitter and frivolity reigned the incorruptible energy of your father. Like everyone else, I was swept along by it." It was astonishing how, after so many decades, he was able to recall every member of the cast, most of whom he had coached musically. "An indescribable freedom on the stage," he said, "was bridled by an indefinable authority." High praise from a man who, soon after this youthful stint, went his own austere, militantly modernist and puritanically classical way; a man whom I once took to a Hollywood movie palace where, preceding the film he had expressed the wish to see, an orchestra (it was the custom in those days) intoned the overture to *Pagliacci* and who rose to his full (towering) height amid the hushed audience, to proclaim sonorously: "No film will make me sit through Leoncavallo!" I had no choice but meekly to follow him outside.

The dominant role of Jupiter in the 1905 production lay in the tried hands of the ensemble's dominant comedian, Victor Arnold. My information about him is all secondhand (necessarily so, as he committed suicide in the year of my birth, demonstrating once again the mysterious relation between *vis comica* and melancholia). My sources include Klemperer, my father himself, my mother, who shared the stage with Arnold countless times, and his only pupil, Ernst Lubitsch—a connoisseur of nature's comedic element in his own right and master at bringing it to the (cinematic) fore. Arnold joined Reinhardt in the latter's cabaret days. He, the mischievous commentator, was placed in the proscenium box with Serenissimus, a take-off on German-provincial princely dotage, where the one's inane questions and the other's pungent retorts interrupting the playlets enacted before them supplied the popular mainstay of the program.

Arnold was, I gather, a trenchant character actor who mined his comedy from the deep shafts connecting his own tragic soul to the eternal one of humanity. Tripping over the banana peel will always be an incentive to laughter. But the great comedian not only trips, but suffers thereby to make us laugh. Not in the banal sense of Pagliacci. He does not make merry in spite of his sorrow, but because of it.

There are Arnolds in every decade and in every country. The man who played Jupiter in Reinhardt's revival of *Orpheus* on New Year's Eve 1921, Max Pallenberg, belonged to a species that appears only once in a generation, if that, and is spread over the globe much more thinly. Pallenberg was not a great character actor, he was a great acting character. He did not deliver his roles, he gave them Caesarean birth. He too tripped over the banana peel, but was never its victim. He put it there in the first place to show up the futility of all dignity. He never lost false dignity—a main element of comedy. He unmasked every dignity as false. You never pitied him, pitiless as he was—with himself, his partners, his audience, his authors, with the text they put in his mouth. Language was his prime target. With lightning intuition he diagnosed all symptoms of verbal sham and murderously exposed it wherever it metastasized. He turned sentences, words, syllables, letters, punctuation upside down, inside out. According to my father, Pallenberg was the only actor he had ever known truly to improvise; not only lines, but entire scenes. On such occasions, I recall, the dialogue of his tormented or convulsed co-players did not seem to matter. Every cue, whatever its original purpose, whether audible or not, seemed to feed his hair-raising logorrhea. You did not laugh with him at human frailty or helplessness, but at the madness of a human race. The missile that armed this Jupiter, tyrannizing nightly a cast of hundreds and three thousand spectators at the Grosses Schauspielhaus was, indeed, the thunderbolt.

Pallenberg, like Vienna's beloved Girardi before him and the gigantically pixieish Moser after him (he jauntily *kicked* the banana peel out of the way, thereby losing his balance), stemmed from the Viennese folk theatre, its musical variety, a relative of the English music hall and American burlesque. But unlike them (a bit like Groucho Marx), he effortlessly broke through that category, as he did every category. With the other Max he maintained, on the personal level—as did almost no other actor—a mutually affectionate and respectful and, professionally, immensely fruitful, if now and then turbulent, relationship lasting a lifetime. That lifetime ended not in morbid self-destruction, but by a vicious accident so easily avoidable as to make it almost laughable in the true Pallenberg manner. When I said goodbye to him before sailing for America, he inquired about the boat I had booked on. Such was his notorious physical cowardice that, on hearing it was the 24,000-ton *New York*, he—unsuccessfully—used every connection at his disposal to transfer my reservations to the much larger *Bremen*, the only vessel, apart from its sister ship, the *Europa*, he considered "safe." Once in America I learned that, after missing a flight from Carlsbad to Vienna to attend a Reinhardt rehearsal in Salzburg, he let himself be persuaded by a rich acquaintance to accompany him in his private crate. The crate crashed on takeoff. My reader knows that I arrived safely in Manhattan on the S.S. *New York*.

Pallenberg's breakthrough from "low" comedy to his rarefied art of self-portrait acting came when the other Max entrusted him with the part of Menelaus in his first production of *La Belle Hélène* during the Munich summer festival of 1911. The novelist Lion Feuchtwanger, then Munich contributor to the Berlin weekly *Die Weltbühne*, wrote:

> The center . . . is Pallenberg's Menelaus. He attacks the figure where it is at its most ambiguous. He acts a touching moron who has the task of being king of Sparta and husband of the most beautiful woman in the world and who knows that he is a moron and to whom it is a riddle why he, of all people, was given these tasks . . .

He called him a "Hamlet distorted to the point of ridicule," a "Don Quixote," "very human and, when the comedy is at its highest, a little sad." In tune with the already cited Helene von Nostitz, Feuchtwanger put his finger on the *one* moment so characteristic of Reinhardt that contains the essence of the production—this time, coming at the finish—and lets us guess how it actually was:

> And when, at the happy, happy end, after the motive of the crime is grasped, on top of it all, the colossal statue of Venus begins to dance, it is more than a good joke. It is an idea that, with symbolic, graphic urgency, summarizes the gay sense of the work.

The praise was as usual by no means unanimous. Feuchtwanger's editor in chief, Siegfried Jacobsohn, detested the caper. "Reinhardt," he commented, "obviously deemed the Offenbach operetta an old shoe sole which, without lavish, manifold, juicy and piquant garnishing, was inedible." And Old Faithful, Karl Kraus, spewed:

> Eight or sixteen English girls participated in Reinhardt's *Schöne Helena*. The principals traversed the stalls on their way to the stage. The public refused to go along. The music is stolen from Offenbach.

It was a good haul. The accomplice in charge of tactics was a musician highly regarded for his taste and integrity: conductor, composer, teacher Alexander von Zemlinsky, bosom friend of Kraus hero Arnold Schönberg. An accessory to the crime was Maria Jeritza, who sang the leading part and for whom it became the springboard for a great operatic career. Kraus considered himself the administrator of Offenbach's estate. (Perhaps he thought the music was stolen from *him.*) For Offenbach, one of the few Jews Kraus liked, the critic even turned performer—in his own mind, *the* definitive Offenbach performer. He gave brilliant solo recitals in which he half-sang, half-spoke complete text and score of the stage works with high musicality and razor-edged diction, accompanied by a single piano.

His interpretation of things closer at hand was less accurate. It was true that the public did not join the entrants on Reinhardt's coveted floral bridge (a thorn in many a critic's side: Jacobsohn called it "superfluous" and "an attempt by the comedians to ingratiate themselves with the spectators"). But if Kraus meant that the public remained cool to the proceedings, the Truth Fanatic was lying. *Helen* was, in fact, so popular that it did not end, as scheduled, with the Munich engagement, but instead was repeated across half of Europe, by request.

As usual at Reinhardt festivals, the festive atmosphere did not remain limited to what went on inside the theatre. It spread outside. Of the fringe benefits, that summer in Munich, two seem worth recording: The newly discovered acting genius, Pallenberg, was able to patent his own discovery, a young, pert soubrette in one of the festival's flops, whom he married. Her totally unfamiliar name was Fritzi Massary. It soon became the most familiar name of all female performers in Germany. (Noël Coward thought so much of her that, when the widowed Hitler émigrée stopped over in England on her escape to America, he wrote a musical for her, calling it *Operette*, starring her in London.)

At the *Helena* rehearsals in Munich, the repeated presence of a fourteen-year-old boy attracted attention. A pupil of the conductor, people whispered. Whenever addressed in this connection, Zemlinsky would throw up his arms in mock despair, avowing that there was simply nothing anyone could teach that boy! If there was anyone in need of learning, it was he himself—from young Erich at that! Then and there, Erich Wolfgang

Korngold made the acquaintance of Jeritza and the impression was so strong that, not long thereafter, he wrote his first opera for her and, in his twenty-third year, his and her world success, *The Dead City*.

A "dead city" is what Erik Charell, the Berlin Ziegfeld and money-coining lessee of the Grosses Schauspielhaus—an unknown quantity when Edmund entrusted it to the young dancer in *The Miracle* and minor ballet entrepreneur—called, not Bruges, but Berlin in 1932. Dead for *him*, in any event. He did not renew the lease. My father, the lessor, for whom the deprivation meant a loss of secure income, could not understand. After all, he knew the money Charell had been amassing with his monster operettas, reviews and folk musicals (such as *White Horse Inn*). Did not the Reinhardts' share of them, to some extent, support the theatres they operated themselves? And what about *Congress Dances*, the film Charell had just made, was it not breaking box-office records? "My swan song," replied Charell, who had been summoned to Leopoldskron in a last-ditch effort to effect a change of heart. The prospect of having to remount the white elephant my father had abandoned more than ten years before, to reenter the—yes—arena of his sole major defeat, was too horrid for him to contemplate. Yet it had to be contemplated instantly, for Charell meant business. He never meant anything else. This had been a most welcome quality in the past, but now he was thinking only of his own business. No, that is not quite fair. Over the traditional Turkish coffee in the—according to the visitor—not so sheltered library of the castle, he urged: "What's more, dear Professor, you shouldn't linger either. It's over. Let's both get out of here before it's too late." "Here?" My father was utterly confused. What was wrong with Austria in 1932? "Yes, here too. Believe me. Very soon it'll be too late! Everywhere in Europe."

With most of their money in Switzerland, Charell left the continent of Europe, taking along valuable art treasures. My father disposed of no funds in Switzerland and few movable art treasures to speak of. What he owned was Berlin real estate mortgaged to the hilt. And unprofitable, unless, through backbreaking exertion, he made it so. Its prize item: the Grosses Schauspielhaus. I watched the specter of the cavernous structure whose deserted dimensions were beginning to frighten its own builder staring him in the face. I watched him fill it. With Offenbach.

I was fortunate to be able to follow in closest proximity the genesis of *Tales of Hoffmann* from the moment my father listened to the piano score in a private room of the Hotel Vier Jahreszeiten in Munich to the night of its première on Schiffbauerdamm in Berlin. More grand opera than opéra bouffe, it was, as I mentioned before, left unfinished by Offenbach. Others completed it, complemented it, posthumously. Its most famous air, the "Barcarolle," had been intended for a different purpose. Actually, the romantic Berlino-Venetian fantasy was *never* finished. Whoever tackled it in the course of time had gaps to fill, ends to tie up. The same was true of my father, conductor and musical adaptor Leo Blech (my father found him a bit "metallic," not surprising since his name in German meant "brass"), and the two literary adaptors, Friedell and Sassmann. Its innate evanescence tends to liquefy the contours. The plot meanders. The measures of the Grosses Schauspielhaus expanded action and score even further. But my father's eye was equipped with a zoom lens. He could play intimate scenes at an extreme distance without loss of privacy, judging accurately their impact on the far-removed spectator, and let mass spectacle flare close up, without overwhelming those nearby. In between, with the help of master designer Oscar Strnad, he had a world to play in. *Hoffmann* did not run away from him—or with him.

The stellar cast, vocally and dramatically, had every opportunity to shine. The costumes—by the graphic artist Paul Scheurig (my father nicknamed him "Kalte Zigarre," from his distaste for the ever-unlit butts in his mustachioed mouth)—conjured up authentic E. T. A. Hoffmann. The sets were exemplary in the science of controlling space: Alternatingly, a warm wine cellar, Antonia's boudoir (with pictures in whose frames live ghosts haunted her), the Canale Grande, Olympia's grand ballroom for Hoffmann's puppet love, the mirror in front of which Hermann Thimig's Nicolaus wrestled with his (live) double and, shockingly, lost his reflection, and the stage of the old Berlin Opera House with its horseshoe of crowded boxes and dress circles in the background, as seen by the Schauspielhaus audience over the backs of the players, afforded not only grandiose and subtle images, but genuinely Hoffmannesque hallucinations and mirages. To the duet of the "Barcarolle," Serenissima's palazzi spun in rippling three-quarter time on the giant revolving stage, past Giulietta and Hoffmann's gondola smoothly gliding under footbridges, carried in precarious balance by invisible stagehands. Opening night, alas, the gondola's beak collided with a teetering bridge, broke off and plunged, not into gentle water, but onto the harsh wooden floor of the stage. The hearts of all insiders stood still. Not for long, though, and not only for physiological reasons: Our fears turned out to be groundless. The anticipated disillusionment caused by the thud did not take place. The overall illusion was too powerful: thirty-five hundred people remained unaware of the mishap (the manège had been turned into orchestra seats).

Berlin took *Tales of Hoffmann* to its heart. Even Reichspräsident von

Hindenburg expressed the wish to see it. I was present when State Secretary Meissner with several members of the President's staff inspected the route to be negotiated from the official limousine to the selected loge and came to the conclusion that the presidential legs would no longer be able to negotiate it. The argument of Herr Bukowsky, caretaker of the theatre, that the old gentleman might be transported piggyback was ruled out by protocol. It is a pity that the decrepitude of the aged field marshal prevented no more than forays into the theatre. In politics, he *was* carried piggyback. The rest is history—at its ugliest.

Someone has said: "Genius is an infinite capacity for taking pains." Perhaps. But talent is not necessarily the same. Talent is sometimes very lazy. Hans Sassmann is so lazy that he is home, sound asleep, when the crisis comes to a head after the *Helena* dress rehearsal at the Theater am Kurfürstendamm. His partner, Egon Friedell, in the face of the crisis, does not face it and calls it an—admittedly long—day. Erich Wolfgang Korngold takes a leaf from predecessor—genius? talent?—Gioacchino Rossini. Rossini is supposed to have been so lazy that, when reclining after one of his lavish self-cooked meals, he would not get up or even reach for notepaper, already half filled, that had slipped through his fingers and dropped to the floor. He would, rather, take the next sheet close at hand and write something new. It was less strenuous.

Korngold, that dawn, does not rifle his Offenbach library for the suitable piece to conclude the unexpectedly truncated *Helena*. He sits down and composes his own Offenbach. It is easier. Sassmann takes his time to respond to the incessant ringing of his telephone, rising wearily to versify the new Korngold-Offenbach. Whether Friedel Schuster waits with bated breath for the grace notes and lyrics to arrive is not on record. Chances are she is too pooped. But then they do and she has two hours to learn them. Max Reinhardt is the penultimate riser of the lot. He must rehearse the epilogue he ordered—one hour before curtain time. Friedell is the ultimate. He must dress and make up to enact the god of merchants and thieves. He is patient. From behind the final curtain, he listens to the birth of a star and the salvation of his play.

This side of the curtain, *I* am watching it, watching Berlin lie at Friedel Schuster's enchanting feet, myself included. The wit of the lyrics, the lilt of the song, the verve of the rendition blot out the inconsistencies preceding them, bridge the abyss of open-endedness. *Die Schöne Helena* is an unqualified hit.

An anecdote titillates Berlin. Max Reinhardt knocks on the door of a dressing room. Would Fräulein Schuster have supper with him? Fräulein Schuster is desolate. A previous engagement. Would he pay her the honor to ask her again—soon? At the stage door Wolfgang Reinhardt intercepts her. Same offer, same answer. Friedel Schuster disappears into a waiting car. At the wheel is Gottfried Reinhardt. They roar off together. The story happens to be apocryphal. But it *was* a dream . . .

THE DIARY

OCTOBER 6, 1943
(continued)

Biggest thrill of my life: I meet Einstein! Was invited to Princeton to call at his house. He extremely friendly, though cold to Know Your Enemy proposal. It doesn't disturb me. The moment is too big. All I can think of is that I am sitting opposite the Galileo of our time. I look into the eyes of a wise, humorous lamb. Is he aware of his own magnitude? No question about it. He makes no bones about it. That's part of what makes this experience so extraordinary. All the other "greats" I've met—the Toscaninis, Thomas Manns, Hauptmanns, Chaplins, Churchills, Hofmannsthals, Schönbergs, Richard Strausses, Stravinskys, Pavlovas, Brechts—although above the trivia of everyday life, were, nevertheless, dependent in their artistic egoism on the stimulus of public recognition. Not so Einstein. He is dependent on no one for certitude. As he explains to me in the front parlor of his modest frame house, all he needs is a sheet of paper and a pencil; no disciple, no collaborator, no fan or critic, no applause. Once his equations are solved—down in black and white—they are conclusive. Indisputable. And anyone in the know—he put it that simply—wouldn't dream of questioning them. Scientific fact is not a matter of taste or preference or of being spellbound. It is provable or not. Twice in his life he was able to prove something, the special theory of relativity [1905] *and the general theory of relativity* [1916]. *For the past twenty-eight years he's been working on expanding his principle into the electromagnetic field. So far without success. Which he ascribes to his age, asserting that for originality in mathematics or natural science, just as in music, youth is indispensable.*

He talks about Mozart. And himself. In one breath. There is no question of immodesty. It's a matter of knowledge, security. As Mozart at the age of six grasped the forgotten laws of Gregorian music on first hearing, so he, Einstein, when given a book of algebra by his uncle at the age of twelve, went through it like a mystery novel from cover to cover, solving every equation in his head although he had up to that moment never received any relevant instruction. I wonder what the schooldays of a boy like this were. How did his teachers react to his precocity? In his witty sad way he answers that no one in school ventured to ask him any questions from the sixth grade on—which did not increase his popularity with his professors or schoolmates.

Fear my questions might annoy him. Needn't have worried. What's more, when it comes to questions he can throw a few curved ones himself. On the subject of writers: wants to know which of the two my father considers the greater, Gerhart Hauptmann or Thomas Mann. Corrects himself: Which of the two is a poet. Unhesitatingly, I say Hauptmann. Mann too ploddingly cerebral for Papa's taste. Einstein agrees enthusiastically. The "giant brain" doesn't admire cerebration, believes that cerebral output is labored love while love's labor is God-given. If at times there is nonsense in the God-given, let there be nonsense! Without the slightest embarrassment he gives as example the errors he was known to have made when, as a teacher, he demonstrated his mathematical formulae on classroom blackboards. I grow bolder, tell him I'm abysmally ignorant about his famous theory but would love to know how he came to it. Nothing could please him more than to tell me: When he was a boy of fifteen, he took a walk one night under a clear, starlit sky and, singling out a particular star, asked himself whether he would be able to see it if he approached it with the speed of light. Six years later his theory of relativity answered the question. Am awed. Cannot think of any comment. He can: Scientific fame is proportionate to the importance the layman ascribes to the questions the scientist puts to himself. Today there are a number of scientists accomplishing work equivalent in merit to his but most of them have the bad luck—so far as réclame goes—to pose themselves problems the solutions of which are not of general interest. That's how it has always been in the history of natural science. With a twinkle: Renown does not necessarily reflect excellence. And, by the way, blind alleys are as difficult to pursue as lucky finds.

Blind Alleys

BROADWAY IS FAMILIAR with them. One might say, it has almost made a fine art of them. The enervating chase after the surefire recipe, be it a pipe dream or the pinnacle of know-how, seems to ennoble the decision to drop a play after extensive hesitation or, even more heroic, to close it out of town. The savvy Broadwayite is ever ready to cut his anticipated losses. And he is chic about it too, should the abandoned property turn out to be a bonanza in a competitor's hands. My father was not that chic.

Alleys may lead nowhere. But, like his friend Einstein, once embarked on them, he would not stop before finding out for better or for worse. To be deprived of this challenge—something he learned to face only in America—was, to a man who wrote through writers, acted through actors, painted through painters, composed through composers, like forbidding a writer to write, an actor to act, a painter to paint, a composer to compose. It was death. He was not an engineer. He was a discoverer. But, unlike Einstein, he needed a lab.

Two such nonhappenings in Max Reinhardt's life are of special interest. One, because I believe that, had things run differently, his life might have been prolonged. With *Jacobowsky and the Colonel* he might have landed the rejuvenating smash he needed at that juncture. (He would have been a better director for *that* play than Kazan; and it would have been a better play.) The other, *The Russian People,* was almost certainly doomed in any event. But the doom he ran into, its Siberian chill and monolithic humorlessness, had larger implications than success versus failure on Broadway. It demonstrated not merely what spirit controlled "The Russian People," the play, but the Russian people without quotation marks, and at the expense of both.

All his life, my father felt a deep attachment to Russia and Russians. Since he was by temperament and volition apolitical, this attachment bypassed Communism, which appeared to him utopian and unpleasant and not particularly Russian to boot. But this remained a private opinion (as did all his political opinions) and it related exclusively to a system, in no respect to people, their opinions, let alone their work. He had been a friend of Bolshevik author and Czarist exile Anatoly Vasilievich Lunacharsky, and maintained good relations with him throughout the latter's tenure as People's Commissar for Public Instruction (1917–29). He made his mark as producer with the play of another Bolshevik, Maxim Gorki. The most resounding hit of his German tour in New York was a play by Tolstoi, *The Living Corpse*. Nowhere in the world did his perhaps most daring exploit, Sophocles' *Oedipus Rex,* make a more enduring imprint than in Russia. Nowhere in theatrical and academic circles is his name, even today, more revered than in the Soviet Union. (A recent exhibition of Reinhardt memorabilia in Moscow and Leningrad enjoyed the popularity of a championship chess match.) Despite the (well-intentioned) faux pas of presenting Stanislavski, on a visit to Germany in the twenties, with a handsome motorcar, which the recipient was not permitted to drive in Russia, Reinhardt's feelings toward his eminent colleague were truly fraternal. And they were heartily reciprocated. In a congratulatory message on the occasion of a Reinhardt jubilee, Stanislavski praised him, beyond his achievements on the stage itself, for one that was even more important in his judgment: creating new audiences for the theatre everywhere in the world.

Of all contemporaries who enriched the stage, Diaghilev fascinated my father most, striving to attain Wagner's ideal of the *Gesamtkunstwerk* (synthesis of the arts) as he did himself. Stravinsky was, in his estimation, the greatest living composer, Nijinsky and Chaliapin among the greatest performers of his day, Massine and Balanchine the best choreographers he had ever worked with. After signing with Warner Brothers, he chose as the subject for his second film (never shot) Dostoevski's *The Gambler*. Two weeks before he was incapacitated, he met, in Meyer Weisgal's apartment, the Russian-Jewish actor Michoels, who invited him to his country. Two weeks before his death, his eyes gleamed in eager anticipation as he talked to me about the trip.

It was not politics that made my father wish to enlist his craft in the anti-Nazi cause. It was a matter of course. For a good Jew, a good European, a good German, a good American—and he considered himself to be all of these—there was no life imaginable with Hitler and Hitlerism alive. The Russians were allies in this fight for existence. He did not care about why, since when or for how long. He was grateful for their help and wished, modestly, to the best of his ability, to return the favor by bringing to Broadway a play that, he had been told, was at present the rage of Moscow.

But how do you go about acquiring the American performing rights to a Soviet play, if you are Max Reinhardt? He did not have the answer, but foresaw few difficulties. They became mine. I knew that Communists are rigorously, capitalistically, conformist when it comes to selling goods, cultural or otherwise. (I was, among other things, a student of Brecht, not just of his work, but also his life.) So it did not surprise me to learn that there was an agent to represent Russian literary properties in the States. Her name was Black. Being, by temperament and volition, more politically inclined than my father, it also did not surprise me that Miss Black lacked final authority to make a deal. I *was*, however, taken aback when, sympathizing with my predicament, she advised me not to pursue the matter any further. My indignant protests, at length, elicited a murmur about the consulate.

The U.S.S.R. Consulate General in New York kept its gates hermetically closed to me. Fortunately, in 1942, the Zionists were on the best of terms with the Soviet Union, so that my Zionist friend, Meyer Weisgal, was able to introduce me to the appropriate liaison man from the Jewish

Agency. He agreed, on a commission basis (a percentage of my father's earnings), to arrange an appointment with the consul general for me. The consulate was then located on Sixty-first Street across from the Hotel Pierre. At the bar of the Pierre, where we met so he could escort me into the Bear's den, he asked me not to mention our monetary agreement. I answered that this was an entirely private affair, but inquired—sheer curiosity—whether there was anything improper about it. "No. Not at all," he replied, "only . . . ethically I would not feel right if they knew." After meeting the tight-lipped, dapper official, I had the impression he was aware of everything. The only subject he seemed ignorant of was the suitable procedure for my securing the rights to *The Russian People*. My emotional plea for a cultural as well as military solidarity between our two countries, demonstratively underscored by my uniform, and my reference to American citizen Max Reinhardt, victim of our common enemy, manifestly disconcerted him. It was up to the ambassador, he muttered. Although I was slowly becoming leery of these concluding sotto voces, this one was good news. The ambassador was a famous man, with a pro-Western reputation, and my father had met him. He wrote to Washington:

> Dear Mr. Ambassador:
>
> Forgive my daring to claim a few minutes of your time which is burdened with heavy duties. . . .
>
> I would like to open [a theatre in New York] with a Russian work of the present time, as I opened my career decades ago . . . with the *Lower Depths* by Gorki. . . .
>
> Today, it concerns Simenow's much-talked-about play, *The Russian People*. Unfortunately, my manifold efforts to acquire the script have remained so far in vain. An exhaustive cable to Nemirovich-Danchenko [Stanislavski's erstwhile partner] doesn't seem to have reached him. Certain traffic problems [!] have also foiled the efforts of Miss Black, the official representative of Russian authors. . . .
>
> Since the season is practically upon us, I see no other way out but to address myself to you, Sir, as a court of last resort. Perhaps it is possible for you to help us in this emergency. . . .
>
> Should you be in the position to effect something positive, you would enable me, too, to do my humble share in the common cause and you would be assured of my warmest gratitude. . . .

Maksim Litvinov's answer was long in coming. With good reason. Other worries were preoccupying the former foreign minister for the moment. His ambassadorship, having been a sop to the Western Allies after the humiliating collapse of the Molotov-Ribbentrop pact, had outlived its usefulness. Russian need for American materiel was as vital as ever, but it could by now be demanded from a position of rapidly gaining strength. The hard-pressed beggar had turned into the disagreeable partner in war who soon would make way for the dangerous adversary in peace. Comrade Litvinov was on his way out.

At last, on my repeated urging, the embassy in Washington informed me that a Mr. Basikin would receive me in the New York consulate. This time, my ingress was ethically beyond rebuke. I was ushered into a magnificent, richly carpeted, oak-paneled room with Lenin and Stalin frowning on me, life-size, from either side, in oil. A Capehart played Shostakovich. In the center, on a beautifully laid-out table, iced caviar and vodka were mitigating the painted disapprovals. I sensed I was being observed. Diplomatic tact and plain gluttony united to make me treat myself to both caviar and vodka. I was permitted to enjoy a generous portion of both, before chargé d'affaires Basikin, a road-company Vladimir Ilyich, entered. He was most affable. And most unyielding. Had I been after a project of my own, I would have left without another word, diplomacy and gluttony notwithstanding. But it irked me to have to explain to my father that a play he had set his heart on was being refused him because of some microcosmic conspiracy, however symbolic for the macrocosm. I lost my temper. I said to Mr. Basikin that I was cognizant of his country's disdain of the Western fetish for publicity. But I warned him that this paltry treatment of Max Reinhardt would have repercussions in the international press; that I would see to it. The outburst could not ruffle my host's equanimity. He took no offense, and stuck to his Stalin rocket guns. Then, another pianissimo: why did I not talk to the William Morris office?

Global politics had catapulted me back into the heart of show biz. It so happened that my father's producing partner, Geddes, lived on the west side of Park Avenue between Fifty-second and Fifty-third streets, one floor below Mrs. William Morris's apartment. He never elucidated why this neighborhood entitled him to accuse the millionairess of being a Communist. But he emphatically did and insisted that at least *he* now knew for sure that my father was barking up a rotten tree.

The William Morris office recommended I contact Miss Black. Miss Black was sincerely sorry to see me again. My account of what had happened since we parted evoked a measure of dialectical-materialist pity in her—for a hopeless bourgeois fool who would not take *nyet* for an answer. With a last breath that afternoon she gave me a—death?—ray of hope and suggested I see one Mr. Recht.

My father's assistant in those days was, as may be remembered, Stella Adler. She, therefore, knew all there was to know about his wishes and my efforts to fulfill them. What puzzled me, then, was that whenever I broached this particular subject, her always enchanting smile seemed to acquire a knowing noncommital quality. But when I mentioned to her the name Recht, she showed irritation: "Gottfried," she emoted, "give it up! Your beloved father will never direct *The Russian People*!" Stella worshipped my father and was very fond of me. I gathered that she must be involved in some passionate conflict of interest. (Passion, conflict and interest being Stella's spark plugs, the combustion generating her histrionic and erotic talents.) Her flamboyance often makes people underestimate her realism. I underestimated it and went to see Mr. *Rrrecktt*, a Czech living in comfortable quarters on a side street off Washington Square. Since "*Recht*" in German, the language we naturally fell into, means "right," I was tempted to call him "Herr Unrecht." It was a temptation I resisted. His tongue had a sharp Bohemian edge. My admittedly primitive gambit was to appeal to him on the grounds of my father's and my former Czechoslovakian nationality. Herr Recht, whose sourly amiable grin contrasted with his clipped speech, shamed me by the assurance that he knew all about Max Reinhardt and even about me. He nodded for almost an hour. He saw all my points. But, inevitably, *he* made the last. With a startling shake of his craggily chiseled mule head, he broke off my monologue: "Of course your father is the right man to direct this play. But he won't." He put an arm around my shoulder and escorted me to the door. I do not know how long he survived our meeting. I hope not long enough to learn that even Czech party liners shoot off their mouths at their peril.

It was Stella's then husband, Harold Clurman, who ultimately did direct the failure my father was spared—in my opinion. My father differed. He continued to believe in the play, if not in its performance. But he was not resentful. It had finally dawned on him that, even had Clurman stepped aside, he would never have been the Soviet choice. Communist prejudice is not easier to overcome than capitalist.

Blind—for him—was also the alley traveled by one Pan Jakobuwicz and a certain colonel. Franz Werfel had met the former on his attempt to flee "from Marseille to Marseille," as he put it at the Reinhardt dinner table in Pacific Palisades. Werfel was the greatest story-teller I ever listened to. He was also very good at writing them down, as he demonstrated with the second story to emanate from that hazardous exercise in futility, *The Song of Bernadette*. He wrote it to fulfill a vow made on the way to Lourdes, should he ever come out of his odyssey alive. He showed me his original manuscript, and I could see with my own eyes that not a single handwritten word or letter had been marred by a correction. "I did not write this," he explained to me, "I was just an instrument transmitting divine dictation." In a more worldly sphere, he was, of course, also a dramatist of note. And his early poetry is on a par with Rilke's. But as raconteur he had no match.

All of us present that evening were surfeited with stirring and frightening accounts of persecution and narrow escapes. Each week we welcomed a new arrival in our midst (not that all of those hopefully expected were lucky enough to arrive), many of whom were literary or theatrical figures, with a gift for dramatizing their adventures. Werfel alone imbued his with devastating humor. He literally made us laugh tears. The shotgun camaraderie between a twentieth-century Polish wandering Jew and a timeless, dyed-in-the-wool Polish anti-Semite, as filtered through Werfel's imaginative memory, produced a hilarious saga against the somberest background, in the best tradition of a Cervantes, Grimmelshausen or de Coster. Ever on the lookout for a vehicle with which my father might return to Broadway, I saw at once the golden opportunity: an entry with a new play. Not by Werfel, but by S. N. Behrman—based on Werfel. Behrman, another dinner guest, agreed with me. So did Werfel ("Not up my alley," he said, as behooves a German author who knows what respect he owes to his respectable Muse). But more important, his wife Alma (formerly Mahler), the mater of matres, agreed, willing to settle for forty percent of the royalties from a joke that was all right at a party in a Jewish house, but had no place in the oeuvre of the man whom she had destined for sainthood. And my father agreed, whole-heartedly. It was determined then and there that Werfel and I put together a skeleton which Behrman and I were, thereafter, to fill out with flesh. We had worked together on a number of screenplays, and it had been an old dream of ours to extend a felicitous collaboration to the legitimate stage. My leave from MGM and my army assignment in the East finally made it possible. Contracts between such old friends were considered superfluous.

The first phase of the working plan was speedily completed. On the basis of Werfel's and my spadework, Behrman and I embarked on the second phase and began to fashion what we thought would be the final text. My father and his co-producers announced the new Behrman-Werfel play, under his direction, as the debut of their newly formed partnership. But Alma had a change of heart. Whether the outline and what by then existed of the English dialogue smelled to her like a success of which forty percent seemed too meager even for a saint, or whether she thought the slant the project was taking too flippant, unbeknownst to any of us, she ordered Franzl to closet himself in a shack on Malibu Beach and forbade him to leave it except with the finished play. In these disagreeable circumstances, he managed the chore in six weeks.

The play (in German) reached Behrman and me just after our completion of act two, along with the demand that not a single line be tampered with, that no adaptation, only a translation, was permissible. My own rights in the matter were ignored. So was a clear obligation to Max Reinhardt, who faced the breakup of his producing firm because of ostensible misrepresentation. Werfel remained deaf to his or my entreaties. Behrman withdrew from the venture in disgust. I could not afford that. When I learned that my friend Werfel had sold the play to a wealthy amateur for a considerable sum, I reminded him of little me. He chose amnesia. I threatened suit—and collected. My father could collect nothing even if he had wanted to, as the play, in its ramshackle translation, proved unproduceable on Broadway. Werfel had robbed it of most of its comedy, substituting it with mysticism. My father, by far the most damaged party, made a generous attempt to console *me*. In one of his nocturnal inter-hotel-room communications he wrote:

> . . . this activity [contributing to an author's work] with all the pleasure it may give, is, *as you know yourself today*, basically a thankless business.
>
> At first, it is always welcome, but afterward it is as little recognized as anything an actor receives. Borrowers are never and nowhere grateful. Girardi [Vienna's most popular comedian around the turn of the century, whom Reinhardt called a "latter-day Nestroy"] used to say when asked for a loan: "Let's rather be enemies in the first place!"
>
> *That is the core of the Werfel tragedy.*
>
> Even Hofmannsthal did not have a reliable memory in this regard.

The "tragedy"—it was one—had a postlude, for Werfel's version eventually emerged produceable after all. After having been adapted by none other than S. N. Behrman!—a condition imposed by Elia Kazan, who, unaware of its history, had agreed to direct the play for the Theatre Guild. In these circumstances, Werfel granted to the Guild what he had denied Max Reinhardt. I learned of the new twist one week before *Jacobowsky and the Colonel* opened on Broadway through an article Sam had written for the Sunday edition of the *Times*. I knocked gently on his conscience, but elicited only the information that "unfortunately" it had not been possible to include any of my contributions in this particular version. The opening taught me differently. I pressed gently, then not so gently, finally threatened suit—and collected.

Once more, my father could not collect anything. This time, because he was dead. The real losers, however, were probably the writers themselves. By going through haphazard contortions to circumvent our common effort, they contented themselves with half-measures, coming up with a workable play, but no masterpiece. In any event, no Max Reinhardt masterpiece. Unlike Einstein, he made the discovery that, in this neck of the woods, lucky finds and blind alleys may coincide.

THE DIARY

OCTOBER 6, 1943
(continued)

Einstein talks about Copernicus, Galileo, Kepler, Newton and himself. And of how they, respectively, altered man's concept of the cosmos. And of how each was celebrated therefore: "People made a god of me." Which didn't make a scientist's life easy. Adulation reached such a pitch that to maintain a working schedule he was compelled when he turned sixty—that was four years ago—to become a recluse. From one day to the next he had to deny himself all social life, every hobby, even his beloved music. He no longer teaches, no longer travels and almost never sees anyone but his sister who runs the house. "You're pretty lucky you got through to me, but I have to disappoint you all the same."

I don't give up, argue that I'm pleading for something terribly important politically, a cause he can't possibly be indifferent to. He says his retirement includes political and humanitarian involvement. Especially so, as a point had been reached where he was so swamped with petitions for his signature for "worthy" causes that the major part of his time was consumed in signing them. As a matter of fact, very recently—for the last time!—he let himself be talked into helping the "worthy" cause of the American war effort—thereby depriving his work of time never to be retrieved. [Later I discovered the nature of that particular involvement: The top atomic scientists of the country prevailed upon him to go to Roosevelt and to warn him of the—as it turned out, fictitious—nuclear danger threatening from Germany and to put his weight behind American atomic armament. His reply was that he didn't feel he was the right man for the assignment, as Roosevelt didn't know him. They persuaded him that the President must have heard of him.]

I make a last appeal—from a half-Jew to a full one. I ring a tribal bell: If the Jews themselves cannot be mobilized against Hitler how can others be expected to fight? As I suspected, despite his protestations, he is far from detached about the international situation. My ace in the hole: Confess I've committed myself to "bringing him back alive." To the studio. To my superior officers. And if I don't, I'll be a dead sergeant. He laughs: "Sergeant Reinhardt, I would not want to have that on my conscience!" His "no" becomes a "well, perhaps." He promises to think things

Max Reinhardt. A sketch by Oscar Kokoschka, 1919.

Max Reinhardt, Gerhart Hauptmann, Rainer Maria Rilke, Frau Hauptmann.
A sketch by Emil Orlik during rehearsals for Hauptmann's *Winterballade*, 1918.

Am Kupfergraben 7, Max Reinhardt's house in Berlin, where Gottfried was born and spent his early childhood.

The library at Schloss Leopoldskron, Salzburg.

Schloss Leopoldskron.

Rudolf Kommer, Lady Diana Cooper, Iris Tree, at breakfast at Leopoldskron.

Everyman, directed by Max Reinhardt at the Salzburg Festival, 1920. On the steps of the cathedral: (foreground) Werner Krauss, Helene Thimig, Hedwig Bleibtrau.

Max Reinhardt with Lady Diana Cooper and Duff Cooper in the park, Leopoldskron.

The Komödie, Berlin. The auditorium and private boxes.

Left and right. Exterior and interior of the Grosses Schauspielhaus, Berlin.

Above. Edmund Reinhardt, Max Reinhardt's brother and manager of his theatres. Photo taken in 1914.
Left. Caricature by Olaf Gulbransson. A hypothetical interview between the Pope, Max Reinhardt as producer of *The Miracle* and Karl Vollmoeller, its author.

The Neue Freie Volks-
bühne, Berlin.

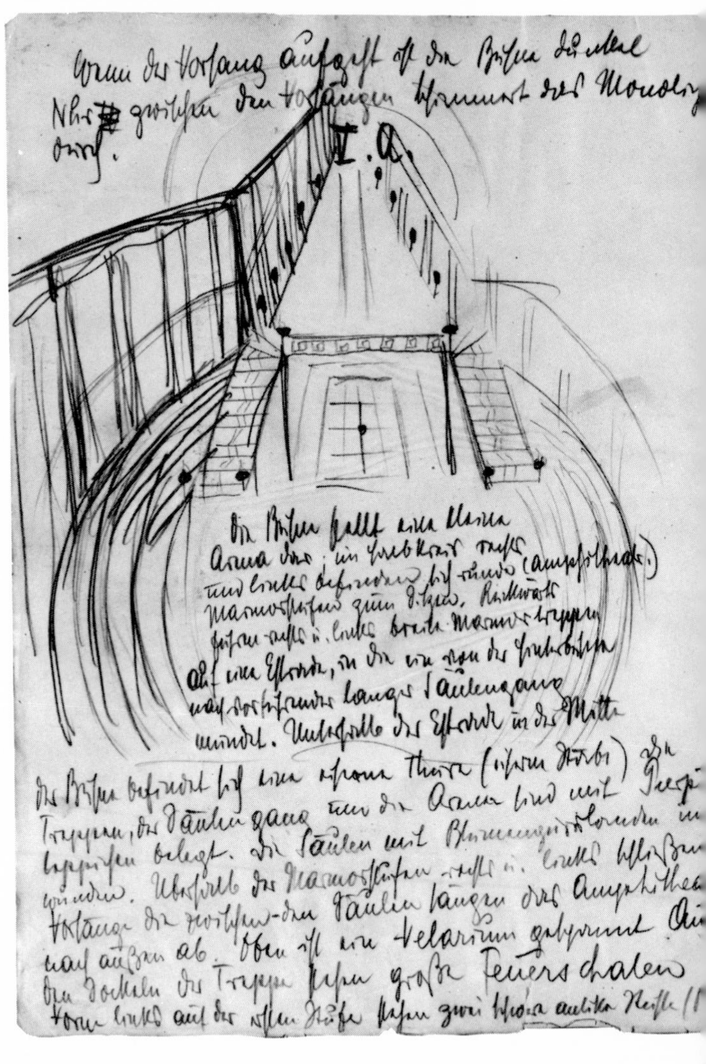

The Deutsches Theater, Berlin.

Ein Sommernachtstraum. V. 1. 55

(Zettel kommt.)

Zettel. Wo sind die Buben? Wo sind die Herzensjungen?

Squenz. Zettel! — O allertrefflichster Tag! gebenedeiete Stunde!

Zettel. Meisters, ich muß Wunderdinge reden, aber fragt mich nicht, was; denn wenn ich's euch sage, bin ich kein ehrlicher Athener. Ich will euch alles sagen, just wie es sich zutrug.

Squenz. Laß uns hören, lieber Zettel.

Zettel. Nicht eine Silbe. Nur so viel will ich euch sagen: der Herzog haben zu Mittage gespeist. Kriegt eure Gerätschaften herbei! Gute Schnüre an eure Bärte! Neue Bänder an eure Schuh. Kommt gleich beim Palaste zusammen; laßt jeden seine Rolle überlesen; denn das Kurze und das Lange von der Sache ist: unser Spiel geht vor sich. Auf allen Fall laßt Thisbe reine Wäsche anziehen, und laßt den, der den Löwen macht, seine Nägel nicht verschneiden; denn sie sollen heraushängen, als des Löwen Klauen. Und, allerliebste Acteurs! eßt keine Zwiebeln, keinen Knoblauch; denn wir sollen süßen Odem von uns geben, und ich zweifle nicht, sie werden sagen: Es ist eine sehr süße Komödie. Keine Worte weiter! Fort! marsch, fort! (alle ab)

Fünfter Aufzug.

Erste Szene.

Ein Zimmer im Palaste des Theseus.

(Theseus, Hippolyta, Philostrat, Herren vom Hofe und Gefolge treten auf.)

Hippolyta. Was diese Liebenden erzählen, mein Gemahl,
Ist wundervoll.

Theseus. Mehr wundervoll, wie wahr.
Ich glaubte nie an diese Feenpossen
Und Fabelei'n. Verliebte und Verrückte
Sind beide von so brausendem Gehirn,
So bildungsreicher Phantasie, die wahrnimmt,
Was nie die kühlere Vernunft begreift.
Wahnwitzige, Poeten und Verliebte
Bestehn aus Einbildung. Der eine sieht

Max Reinhardt's promptbook for *A Midsummernight's Dream*, annotated by him for the 1904 production.

Max Reinhardt in rehearsal.

Max Reinhardt on the Lido, Venice: *Above.* With his wife, Else Heims, and son Gottfried, 1916. *Below.* With sons Wolfgang and Gottfried in the early twenties.

The Miracle, New York, 1923. *Above*. Rosamond Pinchot and Lady Diana Cooper. *Right*. Lady Diana Cooper.

Erich Wolfgang Korngold conducting.

Max Reinhardt with Morris Gest and Ernst Lubitsch, Hollywood, 1923.

The cover of *Time Magazine*, August 22, 1927.

The celebration of Reinhardt's twenty-fifth anniversary as director of the Deutsches Theater, 1930—the occasion of his famous speech "About the Actor."

With Constantin Stanislavski, Berlin, 1928.

over and suggests my calling him day after tomorrow. Gives me his phone number on condition it remains secret with me. I swear it by all the Jewish prophets. Sees me to the door and sends his warmest wishes to Papa. Thus ends the richest day of my life.

THURSDAY,
OCTOBER 7, 1943

Recovery progressing fast, so fast my worry's no longer Papa's giving in, but how to keep him from charging forward too soon. We go over Helen script. He's as alert, as quick to put his finger on what is good or bad or superficial as he's ever been.

My description of Einstein sets him thinking. He asks for every last detail. Is intrigued by the man's total independence of mundane concerns. Does he perhaps secretly wish a pencil and paper were all he'd need to express himself? Does he perhaps wish he too could afford to keep aloof from the scramble for recognition? Surely, he has known fame too long not to realize its hollowness and ephemerality. Yet, in the theatre recognition does not merely flatter the vanity of the performer. The audience is not merely a reactive agent, it provides essential stimulus. It is, in fact, a prerequisite of life on the stage. Without it, all dramatic flow dries up. [Today's theatre gurus choose to ignore this. For them performance is a one-way street: Players are there to give, audiences to receive. They do theorize about "audience participation," but more often than not play against the audience, only succeeding in the end in playing without one. Max Reinhardt was the true apostle of audience participation. He not only played to the audience, in the midst of the audience, he needed it. The actors and "reactors" were of almost equal importance to him:

> It is to the actor and no one else that the theatre belongs. This does not mean, of course, the professional actor alone, but the actor as poet, as director, stage-manager, musician, scene-designer, painter, and, certainly not least of all, the actor as spectator, for the contribution of the spectators is almost as important as that of the cast. The audience must take its part in the play if we are ever to see arise a true art of the theatre.
>
> M.R. in his lecture at Columbia University, 1928]

Without recognition the theatre man is sterile.

Papa suspects that the "performer" Einstein has weaknesses of his own. Particularly after I tell him how catty he'd been when I pumped him about

Madame Curie, just as catty as any big-time actress or virtuoso musician about a competitor: "She discovered something several other people discovered before her." My contention that Einstein has every human foible and eccentricity but, like the Greek gods when at their most human, always remains Olympian doesn't convince Papa. His skepticism, I suspect, doesn't grow out of a difference of opinion, but of temperament. Nor is it a question of art versus science. Einstein's life and work bear out that there's no conflict between the two. One can be an artist in thought and a scientist in action. But, by temperament, the thinking man is the opposite of the man of action. Man of action! That's *what Papa is! And that, not vanity, jealousy or hunger for applause, is what sets him apart from the thinker. Einstein is a monument of patience. Time is on his side. Papa's proverbial patience is only with others. Never with himself. He knows time is against him. Papa must do. And now he can't wait to begin.*

Not "l'Art pour l'Art," But "l'Art pour l'Action"

THUS, THE HEADING of an article in 1963 by the German playwright Fritz von Unruh in the Berlin newspaper *Der Tagesspiegel*, written for the twentieth anniversary of Max Reinhardt's death. In it, he claims that Reinhardt made this pronunciamento—as a motto for his directorial conception—at the start of rehearsals for Unruh's play *Bonaparte* in 1926. I doubt the alleged authorship. The sentence is probably the child of the poet's imagination, rather than his memory, for Max Reinhardt was no friend of mottoes; neither did he label or announce his conceptions. Moreover, his knowledge of the French language was minimal and he would have thought twice before trying to sparkle in it with a play on words. Besides, as far as I know, he did not direct the play himself. Still, it seems to me that Unruh did hit on a felicitous formulation of the governing principle of Max Reinhardt's nature and work. And the picture so close a collaborator as Unruh had formed of him is more significant than what he did or did not remember. In the same article we read:

> As his marshals did for Napoleon, so the greatest actors of the period fought [Reinhardt's] stage battles for him. With a gigantic knowledge of the

> resources of the theatre, he was able to use public relations to his own advantage to make his stage the center of Germany's contemporary cultural life.

My father's nature was certainly not Napoleonic. For that he was plagued by much too many inhibitions, lured by much too many pleasures, had much too much humor and was much too playful. In addition, he did not enjoy power for the sake of power. And yet, Unruh was by no means the only one of Reinhardt's contemporaries who thought they detected Napoleonic features in him. In his 1957 memoirs, writer-editor Willi Haas called him "a legendary stage-Napoleon." Frank Wedekind wrote in a 1906 issue of *Schauspielkunst* (Stagecraft): "The founding of the Reinhardt theatre is beginning, alongside the artistic, to assume a political importance as well." Although there has never been a less political theatre than Reinhardt's, Wedekind doubtless chose his words with care. The accumulation of such manifold talents, the sureness of the single hand that led them and the triumphal quality of so many startling coups must have had an effect on eyewitnesses that went beyond artistic considerations and conveyed the impression of a concentration of power filled with a mission. The ex-soldier Unruh expresses it in military terms. The "*épateur de la bourgeoisie*" Wedekind sees a political force. Thomas Mann (in a letter of 1909 to Walter Opitz) remains in the cultural sphere:

> I was often in the Reinhardt theatre in Munich; it was a momentous experience for me and decisively stimulated my thinking. My personal acquaintance with Reinhardt excited me as all personal contact with people with a mission inevitably excites my bumble-head.

A man "with a mission" (though with other gifts and to an infinitely higher degree) Napoleon was, of course, too—an affinity too remote for so subtle an observer as Thomas Mann to make so superficial a comparison. But that he did not, as so many of his fellow observers did, speak of ecstasy and magic, rather of thought stimulation and mission, is noteworthy. Likewise Hofmannsthal, the most sensitive in Reinhardt's circle, the best authority on the subject of Reinhardt's nature and art—and someone to whom the man of action and power was basically foreign—wrote in the American magazine *The Dial*:

> Reinhardt's strength lies at the center of that complexity we call "Theatre." To the *forces* engulfing the theatre man—poetic, histrionic, rhythmic, mechanical, administrative—he opposes his own *force* and makes himself a conqueror of the theatrical whole, the like of which is rare in a century.

The italics of the word "force" are Hofmannsthal's and the word "conqueror" in the realm of the Muses seems to me quite extraordinary, coming from his pen. That he considered Reinhardt, indeed, not a "*l'art pour l'art*" artist, but a "*l'art pour l'action*" artist, is confirmed by this sentence in the same article: "In the twenty years since he became manager of one or more theatres, Reinhardt has not for a moment ceased to dictate his taste to the public." A dictator, then, a conqueror engulfed by forces to which he opposes his own force, a man of mission who also has political importance, a stage-Napoleon with marshals.

Nor can it be denied that the careers of both the martial and the theatrical commander show conspicuous analogies. Both launched themselves with meteoric swiftness outside the land of their birth. From the beginning, both found patrons within the order they—along with their patrons—were destined to topple. At a crucial moment, both were helped by a devoted favorite brother. Both were born in an era of transition, both swung themselves onto the wheel of revolution and brought it to victory. After the victory, both turned conservative. Some even claim that they betrayed the revolution. Unquestionably they craved a legitimacy of caste their origins had failed to give them. The ladyloves who accompanied them on their way up, once arrived at the top, were sent packing. Both married for the second time into dynasties, after overcoming the resistance of their respective fathers-in-law *in spe*—in both cases in Vienna. Both were small and tended toward an embonpoint. They appointed relatives to the most important posts in their empire—seldom to their own benefit. Sleep came to each almost on command. The same command was at times given also to women. When love was involved, it was, as Napoleon complained, "a disease," which neither was ever able fully to cure himself of. It was difficult to withstand the immediate spell of their personalities. Neither of the two knew vacations, relaxing hobbies or games other than their one big game. They had time for nothing else. And yet, they seemed to have time for everything. When something interested them, no detail was unworthy of their attention. Caulaincourt writes about his chief:

> He always applied all his means, all his capabilities, all his concentration to whatever was going on or being discussed at the moment. He permeated everything with passion.

Without doubt, this also characterizes Reinhardt. Whoever confronted him always met an ego fully engaged. Max Goldmann and Napoleone Buonaparte came into the world equally curious, equally covetous, equally thirsty for knowledge and deeds. Subsequently, they approached every problem ad hoc. They were snobs, but totally without prejudice, and opponents of all theories, as a result of which they continually confused and irritated the theoreticians and dogmatists. Their detractors were—and are—found mainly among littérateurs. They were understood and appreciated to the full by the truly creative spirits of their time. And by the crowd. Their regimes had an autocratic and plebiscitary stamp. They would react to criticism with impatience, usually disregarding it. Their most effective weapons were surprise and thorough preparation. They both died in exile and their homelands hesitated a long time before according them a dignified burial. The historians do not agree: were they innovators or were they simply superlative practitioners of the ideas of others?

> His genius was not creative. He was able to take over the theatrical apparatus that he found in existence, to improve it and to manipulate it with incredible skill—but he could not invent a new one.

Could that have been written also about Napoleon? It *was* written about Napoleon: in his book *A History of Warfare*, Field Marshal Montgomery used these words to criticize him. I have simply substituted "theatrical apparatus" for "military machine." The same has been said innumerable times about Max Reinhardt:

> Max Reinhardt is a dazzling talent. He is no pioneer, only a pathfinder. He did not look for new ways. He simply discovered existing ones.

This is Max Epstein's opinion, expounded in his book *Max Reinhardt*. I don't share it. Originality is, in any case, a relative notion. Everyone takes from everyone else. Important is what each makes of what he has taken. That Shakespeare plagiarized Plutarch, and Molière his Italian precursors, in no way minimizes the genius of the two men—or their "originality." It was to the detriment of neither that Le Petit Caporal absorbed and copied the tactics of Frederick the Great, or that in the work of the "Great Magician" all the currents of his era converged. War lords and stage lords share a common problem: the battles they fight, even the victorious ones, even a continuous series of victorious ones, seldom result in enduring consequences. What remains of Napoleon are not his conquests, all of which he had to give up again; what remains of Reinhardt are not his performances, over which, with one exception, the lights have gone out.

When my father took me to Paris with him for the first time, he asked the taxi driver to stop on the way from the station to our hotel at the Dôme des Invalides. There, he led me to Napoleon's tomb. I was fifteen years old and overwhelmed by the sight of the porphyry sarcophagus in the wide, circular hollow under the imposing cupola. But what made the scene unforgettable to me was my father's role in it. For a long while, he not only absorbed it in silence, he actually partook of it. It was as though he were having a private dialogue with the man who rested there below in such ceremony. Only after we resumed our ride did he find words again. I remember his calling the site the most dramatic grave in the Occident. It testified, he said, to the dramatic genius of the French, who turn *everything* into drama: their theatrically laid-out towns, even in those days illuminated in the evening like stage sets, their exalted rhetoric in the most precise of languages, which nearly every Frenchman speaks with the artistry of a Comédie Française actor, their suspenseful history whose "Napoleon" act was certainly one of the high points of the national drama. He then showed me the Théâtre Français, the Odéon and the other "scenes" of Paris, among them—from afar and close up—"the most superb set," the Arc de Triomphe, and bought me at one of the bookstalls on the Quai Voltaire a paperbound copy of L. Henry Lecomte's *Napoléon et le Monde Dramatique*, an informative work confirming the strong attraction the theatre had for the general.

There is another Napoleonic facet of my father's life. It occurred to me in the evening of it and concerns the living conditions of his years in exile. It needed no rampant imagination to be reminded of St. Helena. California is, of course, no island—although, in a way, it is even *that*—but Reinhardt's existence there was, assuredly, insular. To visit his own deserted "island" was to be captured by the protocol of bygone days, with the wide windows of the anachronistically beautiful living quarters offering a splendid view through subtropical vegetation down the steep coastline toward the ocean. The illusion was perfect. But it was more than an illusion:

As so often, I am late in coming home from the studio and about to change for dinner at my father's when the telephone rings. It is my father, uncommonly agitated. A few of his guests have already arrived, he says, but so far, of course, no trace of me! My standard excuses, for once, are not heard with equanimity to the end, but are interrupted by the bitter complaint that the Innsbruck family Rauch (butler, cook, housemaid; brought over from Austria) is refusing to serve. Cocktails are overdue. My responsibility for my father's support at once makes it clear to me that the monies put at his disposal have been spent on necessities other than the wages for his trusted retainers. The threatening danger, my father says, loomed on Paul's brow as early as this afternoon. Unfortunately, he was not able to reach me at the office. He implores me not to lose a second and to bring along enough cash.

I don't have enough cash with me and the banks have long closed. My offer of a check is declined at the other end of the line after lengthy negotiations. I have to ask my father to let me talk to the Tyrolean mule myself—which is no easy task for him to accomplish. It requires all my powers of persuasion to secure acceptance of my promised check by Herr Rauch and his concession to serve the canapés and drinks on spec in the interim. In that way, another evening can be salvaged and the "evening," after all, is for a theatre man more crucial than for other mortals. The fare and the service are exquisite, appearances are upheld. It would occur to nobody that he is being entertained not by an emperor, albeit a banished one, but by a beggar, whose motto, alas, for a long time now has read: "Not art for art's sake, but art for the sake of *inaction.*"

OCTOBER 7, 1943
(continued)

"Wouldn't you like Frau Thimig to come?" I finally dare to ask him. The sky falls in: "Certainly not!" He's tired of being watched over, mothered, pampered and pitied. It's time he's active again. . . . Action!

FRIDAY,
OCTOBER 8, 1943

Today Papa's eyes shine. He's no longer willing to be told what to do or when to do it. He has made the decision to take life in his own hands again. I go along with him, but at a slower pace: "Papa, on Monday we're going to start our old"—cheery correction: "new—life. Everything's gone better than we had a right to expect. But we'll take it a little easy, won't we? You've got a strenuous schedule ahead." He agrees amiably, but knows of course I'd never talk to him this way if everything were as rosy as, obviously, I'm failing to make it. Double failure: I tell him that I want Foster Kennedy to see him again. "We need," I say, "a verdict from the Supreme Court before we . . ." Don't have to finish my sentence. His expression makes two things clear: Kennedy's visit is the last thing in the world he wants, but he won't object.

SATURDAY,
OCTOBER 9, 1943

Sailing with the happy tide of events, I pick up threads of my paramilitary life for a few hours: Lunch at Colony with Corbett. Two hours at Manhattan Chess Club. Meet Silvia in "21" for drinks and lots of teary speculation—hers—about our future. Return to hotel to have dinner with Papa. Wild of eye, Eleonora cyclones toward me in lobby: Papa has disappeared! He's been gone for five whole hours! They were walking together and, all of a sudden, in the middle of Lexington Avenue, three blocks away from the hotel, he wasn't there! She begins to cry. Loudly. All other *sounds in the lobby cease. I try to calm her: "Now look, he didn't go up in smoke—where can he have gone?" I sit her down in the bar, order her a brandy, then rush into the street. Have no idea which direction to take. Give up search after half an hour. Rejoin her. Try to think sensibly. Don't dare to telephone around inquiring after him—anyway, whom would I call? It's not his style to drop in casually on someone. But then, if there's no place for him to go, where can he be? Something must have happened to him! No. Nothing's happened, because if it had—or was going to—why would he deliberately escape from Eleonora? Am now frantic myself. Turn on her: "Did you quarrel with Papa?" A pool of tears: "When did I ever quarrel with your father?"*

She grabs my arm and points to the lobby: He's strolling in from the street. She jumps up and rushes toward him hysterically: "Max! Where in the world were you?" I'm at her side and, more quietly, repeat the question. He doesn't understand what the excitement is all about. Eleonora screams: "But you were right next to me! We were talking—we were laughing—and then—then you were gone!" Papa sees nothing extraordinary in his unannounced departure. Today is Yom Kippur. There's a synagogue at the corner of Lexington Avenue and Fifty-fifth Street, so he went in. Eleonora, reproachfully: "Why didn't you tell me that's what you wanted to do? I'd gladly have gone with you." Papa reasons: "There are . . . things in life one must do alone." The subject is closed for him. And us. We're much too happy to have him back with us to pursue it further.

SUNDAY,
OCTOBER 10, 1943

Eleonora calls me to announce that it's such a beautiful day we simply must take a drive. Too much urgency in her voice for the "beauty of the day." Another crisis?

There is, I discover a few minutes later. The same one: Papa is irritated because Eleonora is trying anew—"without great subtlety," he complains—to distract him from answering letters long overdue. He's fed up. Either he's being lied to and his health isn't improving as quickly as we've been telling him or, if it is, he wants no more chaperoning and nagging. Forbidding him to write at this stage is absurd when next week working on Helen will be so much more arduous. Again I dare not tell him the reason for the taboo and again he doesn't dare ask. Apropos "absurd," I say, the height of absurdity is to disobey one's doctor's orders. "Is my doctor going to explain to people kind enough to remember my birthday why I haven't had the good manners to thank them?" "He doesn't have to explain anything. And neither do you. The worst thing that can happen is that people will think you're too busy to answer your mail." He gets up and, without another word, retreats into the bedroom, closing the door after him. Eleonora sighs with relief: Another battle won. But, I wonder, am I losing the war?

Wait a few minutes, then tap on his door. "Herrrrrein!" ["Come in."] His famous r's roll out five times as emphatically as any other German's. I enter, make an overture: "Papa, it is a beautiful day. How about a drive? I'll put the top down. We can all use a little fresh air, don't you think?" "As you like."

An hour later, with Eleonora and Papa bundled up in heavy coats and blankets next to me in my convertible, I start my dollar-and-a-half tour of the island of Manhattan: up the East River Drive, skirting the Triborough Bridge, along the Harlem River, Polo Grounds, Yankee Stadium, over to the George Washington Bridge, then down the West Side Highway, hugging the Hudson, past the piers where in peacetime the transatlantic liners used to dock and where now only the hull of the burnt-out Normandie testifies to a world of unsurpassed luxury, then down to the Battery. We see scuttling across the water, like a clumsy, fat bug, the Staten Island ferry and, in the distance, the Statue of Liberty, mother figure to millions of hopeful immigrants and, close by, Ellis Island, the official rock on which many of these hopes were wrecked. We breathe in the pure, fresh air of New York Harbor. The contours of the skyscrapers are chiseled against the steel-blue sky. We cruise the cold, deserted canyons of high finance, past the awesome peaks of City Service and National City, the challenging rock faces of Chase and Bankers Trust and the solid domes of J. P. Morgan and Kuhn, Loeb, from where, in other times, Otto H. Kahn underwrote issues of stocks and international bonds, the Opera's repertoire and the importation of Reinhardt. We turn onto Fifth Avenue, look up for a thrilling moment at the [then] tallest building in the world, then with a quick glance westward down Thirty-fourth Street toward the—less thrilling—site of the Manhattan Opera House, where Papa's Eternal Road had somewhat less than an eternal run. We turn right and complete the triangle on the East River. Stimulated by the mass of towering stone and swarming humanity, within a stretch no more than twelve miles long and, in the center, about two miles wide, we're in a mood to say yes to life.

I fell in love with this city the moment I saw its skyline from the rail of the Hamburg-American liner that brought me to the States and I'm as much at home in it as I was in Berlin. Eleonora is nowhere and everywhere at home. So far as she's concerned we might as well have traveled to Mars or through hell. To her it's not where she goes, but with whom, that's important. And today's company was all she wished for. For Papa the drive was a revelation. The geography of this island with its million-windowed walls has never been quite clear to him. For the first time he saw not only piers, carpeted railroad platforms, hotels, restaurants, luxury shops, stages and producers' offices, but slums, suburbs, waterways, bridges, freight yards, railway tracks, the arteries that feed the city. Of a sudden he comprehends the structure of Manhattan. Back again in his apartment, he can't take his eyes from the wonder on the other side of his window. Without pathos, as incisively as he has ever spoken, he says: "It must be marvelous to have this city in one's hands."

"Ich Bin ein Berliner"

JOHN F. KENNEDY WAS NOT. But it was a charming, politic statement to make at the time. The unbounded enthusiasm which greeted it made West Berlin, at least temporarily, forget one of the cancerous legacies of the charming, politic Kennedy administration: the Berlin Wall.

Max Reinhardt, technically, was no Berliner either. And though he too could be charming and politic, it would never have occurred to him to claim that he was one. And yet, he was. He had this city firmly in his hand and so long as Berlin held its protective hand over him, he was safe.

Nevertheless, a hold on New York had not always been the mirage it seemed to him in 1943. In 1911, after *The Miracle* in London, a stranger from the New World came backstage to congratulate the victor on his foreign conquest. Introducing himself as Otto H. Kahn, he said bluntly: "Max Reinhardt, come over to us! I'm inviting you. Everything you need will be at your disposal. You've given Europe enough and Europe has nothing more to give you. America needs and has everything to give you."

It is not idle to speculate what direction the American theatre might have taken if Reinhardt had accepted. He might have revitalized it and brought it into line with the European trends of the period, a process that was delayed by America's isolation during World War I and by the boom years of commercialism and self-satisfaction that followed. (It took the Depression to open up and give the American theatre a life of its own.) With Kahn's financial and moral support, the thirty-nine-year-old, without the language and energy problems of a sexagenarian, might have formed ensembles, replaced *shows* by *theatre*, by planned repertoires and companies operating throughout the season, might have founded schools, generated a Shakespeare renaissance, turned classics into long-running hits, stimulated playwrights and composers and perhaps erected modern playhouses like his Berlin Kammerspiele or Grosses Schauspielhaus (with less opposition from the intelligentsia and under more favorable economic conditions), thus introducing the studio stage and the thrust stage and the theatre in the round long before they became the fashion of the American day. But then, had he followed Kahn's siren call, this book would most probably not have been written, since the circumstances to which I owe my life would most likely have changed sufficiently to jeopardize my coming into the world in 1913.

My father later bitterly regretted his incredulous "no" to Kahn. Few people, he used to say to me, are given the opportunity to find themselves at such a crucial crossroads more than once in a lifetime, if ever. He was aware of having made the wrong decision. And he tried, again and again, to correct what he considered his gravest mistake. But time was getting shorter and shorter. One day, when it was *too* late, the move was no longer a matter of choice and by then he had aged considerably and America had grown much younger, was shedding its theatrical immaturity and conventionality on its own.

But in 1911, go to America? Whatever for? Was he a criminal, a bankrupt or hankering to go slumming for a few extra dollars?

The Berliners have a sort of municipal anthem which, roughly translated, goes like this:

> As long as Unter'n Linden [Unter den Linden,
> the name of Berlin's grand avenue]
> The linden trees are green
> There's nothing that can faze us,
> Berlin remains Berlin.
>
> *(Solange Unter'n Linden*
> *Die alten Bäume blüh'n*
> *Kann nichts uns überwinden,*
> *Berlin bleibt doch Berlin.)*

This wide, tree-lined street that leads from Brandenburg Gate to where the baroque castle of the Hohenzollerns used to be (since razed by the Communists and left vacant to form a vast parade ground, the Marx-Engels Platz) is located today in East Berlin and looks deserted. In my father's time and on through my childhood, it was the main artery of the sprawling, motleyed metropolis and one of its few handsome spots. On it were the major embassies, ministries and museums, the finest hotels, mansions and stores, the university and national library, the grands cafés and arcades and one small theatre, the Kleines Theater, Max Reinhardt's first. That alone established him as a Berliner.

A mall between the two roadways of the concourse was the scene of Prussian goosestepping and it was there that the defeated German Army, in 1918, made its triumphal entry into the capital of the new republic, led, on his charger, by Field Marshal Paul Ludwig Hans Anton von Beneckendorff und von Hindenburg—a brilliantly paradoxical (and ominous) event I witnessed from our tailor's balcony at the age of five. Fourteen years later, one block down, I witnessed another portentous event on Unter den Linden, one that organically, inevitably, grew out of the first one: On Chancellor Franz von Papen's order, with Reichspräsident von Hindenburg's approval, one officer and two enlisted men of the Reichswehr (the Republic's army) entered Prussia's Ministry of the Interior and arrested the Social Democratic minister Carl Severing and his aides, leading them out of the building like so many criminals and annulling thereby the Republic's constitution. The way for Hitler—paved by the villains behind Hindenburg and by his puppet intriguer Papen—was free.

Around the corner from Unter den Linden, on German officialdom's main thoroughfare, Wilhelmstrasse, were the quarters of the Empire's most representative club: Deutsche Gesellschaft (German Society) 1914. Max Reinhardt was on the board of directors, a committee of politicians, academicians, eminent jurists, mine owners, industrialists, bankers and all sorts of aristocratic letterheads. What was he doing in this company? He had never been a joiner. And even the most industrious theatre historian will have difficulty finding other boards of directors to which he belonged. But he undeniably occupied his rightful place on the second tier of this organization. The first, the presidium, was peopled with such celebrities as the Hamburg-American Line's Jewish president and friend of the Kaiser, Albert Ballin (who would commit suicide over the Empire's demise), the poet Gerhart Hauptmann (who would become a quickly disappointed Nazi collaborator), the Jewish industrialist, writer and statesman

Walther Rathenau (to be murdered in nine years), the industrialist and inventor Werner von Siemens, the industrial magnate Fritz Thyssen (whose heir would be one of Hitler's foremost financial backers), the classical philologist Professor Ulrich Baron von Wilamowitz-Moellendorff and several high and high-titled government officials.

No doubt, this was an association meant to unite Germany's elite at the beginning of World War I and to make it appear united abroad. (My father's official identification with national causes—he also signed the "Manifesto of the Ninety-three German Intellectuals, 1915," denying the alleged German atrocities in Belgium—French public opinion did not forgive until the thirties. Reinhardt was undesirable in France between Versailles and the Hitler emigration. And even thereafter it took a Rothschild to invite him. The United States and Britain proved much more conciliatory in that respect.)

In the tightrope walk Bismarck undertook when forging an arbitrary section of Germany into a nation-state in 1871, he was assisted in good measure by the German Jews. Their patriotic membership in the German Society 1914 underscores another commonplace which their Gentile compatriots later found expedient to drown in lies: that the German Jews felt German and acted like Germans. Max Reinhardt is a perfect example. They were *betrayed*—not by fanatics, but by cynics. (In the First World War, ninety thousand nonbaptized Jews, most of them volunteers, enlisted. There were over ten thousand Jewish casualties. Thirty-five thousand were decorated. Twenty-three thousand were promoted, two thousand of them to the rank of officer.) It has already been said that Max Reinhardt's theatre, during the war, functioned as one of the Empire's most efficient propaganda instruments among the neutrals.

These facts were not a secret to the "fanatics." In 1916, Houston Stewart Chamberlain, prophet of racism, mentor of Hitler and son-in-law of Richard Wagner, wrote: "Swept away they are in this gigantic uprising; no longer identifiable as Jews, for they do their duty as Germans, facing the enemy or on the home front." Hitler, Goebbels, Rosenberg, who knew every word of Chamberlain by heart and conveniently appropriated only those of his utterances that predated the "gigantic uprising" in 1914, were not filled with any holy wrath against the Jews. They exploited "normal" world-wide anti-Semitism opportunistically: they lied deliberately, unemotionally, histrionically—and effectively. This cynicism was not perceived by the average German or his neighbors (is not even now) because it was dressed up as messianism. It is to the Berliner's honor that, of all the Germans, he resisted this systematic infusion of poison longest. Hitler was never comfortable in his capital. In the final years he avoided it altogether.

So long as Germany's military power was second to none, so long as capital did not feel threatened by the unions or open revolt and the burgher felt secure in his ethics and in his pocketbook, there was no need for a scapegoat, and Jewish achievement was an integral and welcome part of the national scene. In his booklet *The Berliners and Their Theatre,* Florian Kienzel, a writer from Graz and connoisseur of the milieu, speaks of the admiration in which the great directors were held in Berlin. But one of them was truly loved: Max Reinhardt. His name was magic. Kienzel quotes the words of a contemporary diplomat according to whom Max Reinhardt was "the most popular personality next to the Kaiser and Count Zeppelin." How could so strong a bond have tied an immigrant actor and producer to a nation's populace and elite, had there existed in this nation, acutely or latently, the virus or irreconcilable hatred for everything this man radiated and stood for?

> Out of the dreamy dusk of adolescence I came to Berlin, into the clear, sharp, sleepless, dreamless air of this city—summoned by my great, quiet predecessor in this house, by my teacher, Otto Brahm.
>
> If I brought along the magic baton of the theatre marshal in my knapsack, I was not conscious of it. I arrived with the most peaceful intentions. I wanted to *play*. I wanted to continue my childhood playing. But the wide stream of work that flows through the middle of this city, the stormy wind that blows here and changes every minute, grabbed hold of me and pulled me, together with my urge to play, into a truly dramatic atmosphere.
>
> In abrupt alternation I learned to live with assent and opposition. There was always struggle about me. Thank God.

These words my father said in 1926, in a public address. They were no declaration of love. But then, they were said after his rupture with Berlin in 1921, a rupture that had never healed. It was merely puttied over in 1924. Yet even before then it would be wrong to think that he was ever enamored of Berlin. Nevertheless, Berlin supplied the impetus to his upswing and a solid foundation for it—the "dramatic atmosphere." He calls the cradle of his career "clear," "sharp," "sleepless," "dreamless," although this last epithet is unjust. His own life is best proof that it was, indeed, eminently possible to dream in Berlin and that Berlin was eminently susceptible to dreams—certainly his.

There is a theory that the "typically Viennese," "southern," "baroque" Reinhardt did nothing but make his own luscious dreams come true in gray, sober Berlin and "Austriasized" it thereby. The writers Julius Bab and Willy Handl, in their *Vienna and Berlin: Comparative Comments on the Cultural History of Central Europe's Two Capitals,* maintain:

> The overthrow of naturalism engendered by Max Reinhardt was the victory of histrionic sensuality over the literary program . . . a Viennese victory in Berlin; the warmth and the flexibility of the old Burgtheater style, transplanted into a brisker weather . . .

Reinhardt came to Berlin when he was twenty. With the exception of what he had, in his own words, assimilated "on the fourth balcony of the Burgtheater"—a theater by then largely resting on its wilted laurels—and of the imprint Vienna's architecture may have had on his roving eyes (Mariahilferstrasse, where he lived, offered few attractions in that regard, no more than the business streets that led him to his mercantile jobs or to the suburban scenes of his acting debuts), he carried in his scant luggage little knowledge, little differentiated taste, few incisive impressions, no personal or professional experience to speak of and rather amorphous concepts of his future. All these acquisitions were made in Berlin. The spiritual nourishment furnished by elementary school must have been sparing and what he profited as apprentice in factory and bank could not have yielded much more. His parental environment was full of love and care, but bereft of stimulus. The "dreamy dusk of adolescence" in all likelihood reflected a tender illusion rather than Viennese reality. To me he never painted his childhood in such gentle hues. His circle in Austria had been centered on the impoverished family, the traders who tried to train him and the strolling players or provincial colleagues who almost spoiled his enthusiasm for the theatre. A few parades in Schönbrunn Castle, the singsong of the lavender and chestnut vendors, gypsy music and Strauss waltzes listened to with his nose pressed against snow-covered windows or narrow escapes from adolescent Jew-baiters hardly turned the boy into a "baroque-committed southerner" and a "spectacle-thirsty exponent of Austrian sensuality."

Vienna's grand Burgtheater tradition, allegedly the source of Reinhardt's sensuality and love of iridescence, was founded by the important writer-producer Heinrich Laube, who deliberately turned his back on all decorative byplay and histrionic excess. He and his school emphasized the spoken word. It is true that his successor, Franz von Dingelstedt, another striking figure of nineteenth-century theatre, fostered the decorative arts and strove for spectacular effects. But long before Reinhardt climbed to the Burgtheater's upper balcony, a reaction and return to Laube's ascetic tenets had taken place. To characterize these as "warm" and "flexible" is not very meaningful. My father recalled the adolescent impression he had gained at the Burgtheater:

> . . . strongest [acting] personalities fused into an incomparable harmony. Richness in modulation, suggestive power. These actors dominated Vienna . . . without the help of sets. In the end, they acquired a ghost-like quality. In addition, there was Vienna's audience, part of the excellent ensemble! Myself, I have never done anything in this theatre. I was only an insignificant member of the audience, a far-removed actor, who was never allowed to sit down. I never occupied a seat in this house. My place was the balcony, standing room. The actors were miles away. We heard their adored voices, their intonations, but the words only if we knew them by heart, like arias. The words often came twice—once helpfully suggested by the prompter and then echoed by the actors. The stage was large, but kept in Spartan simplicity. The players performed in front of plain, painted drops, amid the barest, indispensable pieces of furniture . . .

Does this describe the "Reinhardt style" which took Berlin by storm?

It was from his native Germany that Dingelstedt had brought his lavish style to Vienna. He had been one of the first to draw on the talents of painters, architects and composers. But, unlike Reinhardt, he did not integrate their contribution into the play, did not make them servants of the theatre. Rather, he turned the theatre over to them as a playground. His true heir was not Max Reinhardt, who never knew his work, but—insofar as the mounting of his operas was concerned—Richard Wagner. Dingelstedt's opposite number in England, Charles Kean, did have an indirect effect on Reinhardt. His panoramic Shakespeare productions not only enjoyed success in their day but left their mark on Henry Irving and Beerbohm-Tree, who, in turn, influenced Reinhardt's conception of the classics (though not in the liberties they took with the text, targets of Shaw's scathing critiques).

In the 1870s, however, the modern theatre of the Western world received its strongest impulses from the ducal company of George II of Saxe-Weimar, whose provincial court was in the Thuringian town of Meiningen. This is not to say that what Shaw called the "Ibsen revolution" would not have forced Europe's and America's theatres to change their playing style sooner or later. But the "Meiningers" saw to it that it was sooner than later. They abolished the star system. An actor playing the lead today was given a walk-on tomorrow. Thus, ensemble play was founded. They did away with static scenes acted in front of changing backgrounds on rollers and reverted to the stationary set framing a choreography in motion. They developed the "play with a fourth wall," the invisible partition separating actor from audience. Actors, henceforth, no longer addressed the audience head on. The audience was ostensibly ignored by them. The characters, for the first time, spoke *to one another*, even turned their backs on the spectator when required. The Duke insisted on a style-determining concept for each production. Cast and set—another novelty—had to be dressed in suitably historic costume. The Meiningers' maxim: utmost authenticity down to the minutest detail.

The tenets of realism—ever since Zola (a parent of Ibsen) changed the literary and Meiningen changed the performing credo of the age—demanded either opulence (when the canvas was historical) or drabness (when the play called for intimacy). Here lay the roots of the theatre to come, the theatre Reinhardt and Gordon Craig grew up in and rebelled against—not by abolishing it or returning to the artificiality of speech, gesture and decor it had replaced, but by imbuing it with psychology and symbolism.

The impact of the Meiningers cannot be overestimated. In 2,591 engagements throughout Europe and America, from 1873 to 1890, under their director, Ludwig Chronegk, they decisively influenced such disparate innovators of the theatre as Sarah Bernhardt and André Antoine in France, Stanislavski and Meyerhold in Russia, David Belasco in the United States and Reinhardt's predecessor, Otto Brahm, in Berlin. To look for the source of Reinhardt's susceptibility to color, light and shade, his Craigian dedication to organizing space, to the three-dimensional, his affinity for mood, his emphasis on dynamic movement and sound, his open-mindedness to *all* performing styles, his ambivalence between a quest for chastity and inclination to voluptuousness, in the ambience of his youth is a biographer's cliché that, in this case, contains no grain of truth.

Reinhardt was a late developer. The ambience that molded him was Berlin. Berlin is where he first could afford to buy books, where he read and digested them. In Berlin he formed his first friendships, had his first love affairs, found his ethical, intellectual, artistic and economic tutors. In Berlin he attended his first concerts and expanded his youthful penchant for gypsy airs to a liberal understanding of music. The man he worked for in Berlin, Otto Brahm, his Berlin colleagues, Berlin critics and the Berlin public were the first to challenge his resources in depth. In Berlin he developed the handwriting that became clearer, sharper, more etched every hard-working day. In Berlin he learned to improve himself, to treat himself harshly, to be dissatisfied with himself. In the fourth balcony of the Burgtheater he had discovered his love for the theatre. But his love *life* he pursued relentlessly and shaped with self-discipline in Berlin.

In Berlin the spirit of Nietzsche and Bismarck wafted about him. In Berlin he set his sights on the Wagnerian *Gesamtkunstwerk,* which he transposed to the legitimate stage. And Berlin taught him, even when infatuated, always to keep a certain distance, to value matter-of-factness, to shun sentimentality, to distrust mannerism, to put his trust in the printed page. The lessons are clearly reflected in his early diaries. An excerpt from the year 1895:

> I am afraid of dissipating my strength, as my frequent abandonment of ideas, resolutions and work worries me anyway. These sporadic enthusiasms for an endless variety of things can surely not produce anything great. I still lack intensity, particularly since being in Berlin. But then, so much rushes in on one here that it either takes great boneheadedness or iron energy to withstand temptations in the long run. . . .
>
> Noa [an early Berlin friend in the theatre] draws my attention to my bad posture.
>
> I decide after much hesitation to go and see Brahm about my position here. I had almost given up the idea. Papa [his father, who had visited him in Berlin] advised me to do it. At the last minute, I pulled myself together with great effort and hurried to the theatre. Why can't I always turn my thoughts into action so promptly! I would fare so much better! But I inherited this weakness. My papa is the same. Both of us have muffed a great deal as a result. It is a mixture of laziness and shyness. So every action of mine necessitates a prior struggle with myself. . . .
>
> The old fault of timid reticence in which I recognize the roots of all my failures so far. I must overcome it. From it all shortcomings and all disappointments stem. This, strangely, became a real problem only here in Berlin.

He found it strange because only in Berlin had he begun to fight his immaturity. Although in Vienna too, as everywhere else for that matter, most careers are based on resolve and energy, their lack can be camouflaged by charm, shrewdness and wit. Berlin did not like camouflage. Only the "real thing" counted. Nor would a single effort do, or a first impression last. In contrast to the Viennese, the Berliner is never grateful or loyal. Even more than the New Yorker, he wants each effort quadrupled and to be impressed each time anew.

In the same diary we read about his stabs at self-education.

> In the forenoon rehearsal of *Scum of the Earth* [a play by E. von Wolzogen], I sounded less Jewish, but am unfortunately influenced and inhibited by Reicher [Emanuel Reicher, a respected Brahm actor]. Very lame. Brahm notices this. I should not let colleagues influence me. When will I finally gain that self-reliance and security that alone can provide the basis for a sound and worthy work? I am swaying like a reed in the wind, listen here,

listen there, accept advice of whose validity I am not always convinced, act against my feelings and convictions, against my individuality; grope in a vacuum. . . . I have not yet identified myself with the part. Am not yet at one with it . . .

About his employer and teacher:

I believe he [Brahm] has a good, noble character. . . . Small weak physique, a Jewish type. Small head, high forehead, face and eyes blurred. His face seems to me sometimes like a big sponge that has absorbed a great deal. One never knows what he is really feeling, rarely what he thinks. . . . The eyes are expressionless. Only his mouth is eloquent, especially when he's not talking. His large, wide lips are always expressing something, mostly an ironical superiority, but also a certain benignity. . . . His movements are gauche, timid, insecure. . . . And yet, behind that high forehead rules a firm, unbending, even obstinate will. . . . He allows nothing to dominate him but his own will and his own opinion, which, however, are not always practical. He has as yet no practice in running a theatre. [Brahm, who had been a critic, took over the management of the Deutsches Theater, his first, only three years before]. . . . He has many enemies . . . but that merely proves his importance.

About another teacher:

Nietzsche . . . I understand him completely . . . systematic suppression of one's individuality and one's instincts for the sake of others. Perhaps I can still change . . .

About one of his heroes:

. . . I admire Bismarck as the greatest man living today. . . . As an Austrian and Jew I ought to be against him. But on the eightieth birthday of such a mental giant it is, I think, permitted to disregard petty party interests. I bought his picture as a memento.

About another hero:

The Tristan and Isolde overture by Richard Wagner had a powerful effect on me. It is painting, sculpture, potent drama, and has a fabulous impact. For the first time since my inexpert maturity [*sic*], a full impression of Richard Wagner.

The avid reader:

In the morning, I cannot resist raiding the bookstore and glutting myself. Tempted to buy books for ten marks. . . . I spent too much money on the books . . .

The avid eater:

. . . Kempinski is Berlin's gastronomical mecca and—cheap. There I realize how susceptible I am to material enjoyments, for I love this restaurant.

Declaration of war against himself:

. . . I see it now, the greatest part of my life will be a struggle, a struggle with myself. I must vanquish myself, overcome that integral part of my nature that inherited laziness, listlessness, shyness. To hell with it. It clings to my resolutions, ideas, my soaring plans, like molten lead. What heat of enthusiasm, what warmth of emotion must be summoned against it! Sometimes this succeeds and then all is well, for the strength, the ability are there, I know that. . . . What good are all the books, paintings, symphonies in the world! I am not advancing in my profession.

On the way to victory:

. . . read all morning at home, later to the cashier to fetch my salary minimum. In the afternoon I go to Runge [Waldemar Runge, member of the group whose erudition and broader experience impressed him]. . . . I broach the plan of founding an experimental stage. We would cast the roles with people hitherto unknown, yet who can be identified with them so that *with many rehearsals and sensitive direction* [italics mine: a new procedure and a new vocation are in the making] exemplary performances would be possible. . . . On weekdays we would have to give matinees so that the actors would be sure to be at our disposal, and we could rent a small theatre for the purpose. . . . Of course, money is needed, the Achilles heel of the whole thing [this Achilles heel would plague him from 1885 to 1943]. Plays must be chosen that would interest and draw an audience. We don't want hypocritically to belie our egoism [!].

. . . We are concentrating on the idea of a club.

And the diary would be incomplete without . . .

. . . *la femme*. Fräulein Schely received me, draped picturesquely on the divan. I rocketed off some cerebral fireworks, and won. Soon, convention,

> etiquette were things of the past and the beast in us broke out and bared its teeth in a lecherous grin. As I was saying goodbye, Fräulein Unger dropped in, pirouetted around her own jealousy, trying to hide it with a transparent, gay cordiality, professing continuously that she wanted to leave so as not to disturb us, all the while remaining firmly glued to her chair. I made my exit and drove to Gertrud Sicker to fetch her for the Wintergarten. I'm interested in her without being in love in the slightest. She'd be pretty, even beautiful, if she didn't have a somewhat misshapen nose. Splendidly built, tall, beautifully white skin, lovely teeth, brown hair, brown eyes, red cheeks. Childlike naïveté, belief in authority, chaste—not very bright. Love is a little game for her. Physically, she attracts me; mentally, I am repelled. She expected me to arrive earlier. She betrays a certain interest. Success in my profession, relatively unusual at my age, my calm and superiority, possibly intrigue her.

I leave it to the reader to decide whether this spewing of a twenty-year-old contains the seeds of a unique career. But he will not have a much easier time of it than I, as we are both, inevitably, drawing on hindsight. To be sure, the powerful urge to give and to take is there. So is the faculty of sharp observation. Even the rudiment of a plan. And a healthy egoism is budding. Then, there is the general dissatisfaction with mediocrity and impatience with all waste of time. Above all, the dissatisfaction and impatience with his own weaknesses. That peculiar mixture of industry and inertia, puritanism and hedonism, which will mark his adult nature, the tendency to total surrender and merciless self-chastisement—they're unmistakable. At the same time, all this is sincerely felt, logically reasoned and prolixly expressed in terms astonishingly immature for his age and for a potential leader. In a way, it seems to me, it is the very immaturity and instability of these diaries that give them their biographical significance. They demonstrate what a long road was still ahead of him and in how short a time he traveled it; again: that the young Max Reinhardt was less remarkable for what he brought to Berlin than what he made out of it there.

But let us take a closer look at that gray, sober, stark, Prussian Berlin where he struck his roots. It was situated in Prussia, no doubt. But *was* it Prussia? Only among other things. Berlin had been for centuries the heart of the Brandenburg March, a rough frontier province of the Holy Roman Empire, long before a Prussia existed, when the Slavic tribe of "Prussians" were heathens, under the sovereignty of the King of Poland, christianized and ruled, at his behest, by those ruthless German colonizers, the Teutonic Knights. The masters of Brandenburg were renowned for their efficient, if unscrupulous administration. It became "Prussian"—more in name than in character—only in 1701, when its Electors wrung from the Emperor the right to call themselves Kings of Prussia, having incorporated the eastern territory—and western additions—into their quickly expanding dominion, eventually reaching from the Rhine to the Vistula—by conquest, trades of real estate and dynastic juggling.

The realpolitik of the Hohenzollern gave Berlin a slightly more exalted status among the older and grander German cities, enriched its population and architecture (badly in need of it) and attracted two ethnic groups: a large French community (about twenty thousand Huguenots to whom the Great Elector granted asylum) and a strong Jewish element, both invited for the purpose of vitalizing the young capital's industry, commerce, arts and sciences—a purpose that was in a great measure achieved. Nevertheless, until 1871, Berlin remained a provincial, though, since Frederick the Great, no longer unimportant, town. The "broad stream of work," indeed, flowed through its center, the air, as my father noticed, was "sharp" and the wind was apt to change abruptly. But this dynamism and unpredictability were still kept within reasonable limits. The Berliner, still, did not suffer from insomnia, much less dreamlessness. With the founding of Bismarck's First Reich all barriers were razed.

The cultural expansion of Germany in which Max Reinhardt took an integral part followed on the heels of the territorial and industrial expansion (which upset a world). Berlin's population tripled within a single decade. The soil of Brandenburg is sandy. The city that, by 1914, would become the world's fourth largest (and, by 1930, the third) was built on sand. In my father's time, very few grasped the symbolic meaning of this fact. He was one of the exceptions. And he was aware of the unrelatedness of the majority of Berliners—who, the joke went, all came from Breslau, and at any rate, like him, were rarely born locally—to their "native" soil. So it genuinely surprised him each time he was accused of being disloyal to Berlin. How can one be loyal to a sand castle?

The steady influx to this "promised land" was motivated by the *promise*, not by the *land*. The incentives for the unending stream of new arrivals were growth and opportunity. And Berlin grew day by day, year after year, and offered a wealth of opportunities. Everything in Berlin grew daily, yearly, including its megalomania. The one million inhabitants, the two, the three, the four and a half million, felt at ease in their perpetual rush hour. Nor did it disturb them—there was really no time to look around—that the urban area became uglier with each new building shooting up (in that regard too, they were brisk forerunners of today's big-city dwellers), just so long as it kept growing and magnetizing everyone and everything within reach, good and evil. A razor-edged intelligence was honed by the constant friction, and a sturdy sense of humor (rare in Germanic soil) was fed by the racial mixture, neutralizing the tension. Yet, these Berlin traits did not give birth to a native Berlin *character*. There is only a Berlin *attitude*. This big-mouthed, big-hearted, tough and tongue-in-cheek attitude is, however, ineradicable, and has withstood the Kaiser's spurious grandeur, republican fusty rectitude, Nazi lie and Nazi bombast, Socialist philistinism, Communist pharisaism and American exhibitionism.

Berlin grew metropolitan overnight, skipping all intermediary phases and catching up in less than no time with the other urban centers of the world. In this headlong plunge, it cared little about what went under or was swept to the surface. It was hypnotized by its own aggrandizement and never had enough leisure to integrate, as its venerable sister capitals had done over long spans of time. The Berliners lived *next* to each other, not *with* each other. (Perhaps this lack of cohesion also explains how it was feasible to divide the city into two hermetically sealed parts, separated by a prison wall, a surgery that surely would have been impossible in London, Paris or Vienna.)

By fiat, then, not through evolution, Berlin had become the nerve center of a great power. That meant consciousness of and lust for power, as well as military pomp and vacuous slogans. But Berlin also served as the amusement center for the landed Junkers around it and for the nouveaux riches inside. That meant fun, prodigality, frivolity. Still, its core remained a solid bourgeoisie, counterbalancing all speculative adventures. That in turn meant parsimoniousness, decency, conservatism. In addition, it was the burgeoning industrial nation's largest industrial city. *That* meant efficiency, worldliness, workers' solidarity and radicalism. Last, but not least, having been promoted to the country's cultural center, the new Berlin stood for knowledge, judgment, liberalism and unstillable curiosity.

A mixture of irreconcilables? It would seem so. How can lust for power get along with judgment and liberalism? Parsimoniousness with prodigality? Vacuous slogans with knowledge? Frivolity with decency? Conservatism with radicalism? They did, and these polar elements coalesced, not so much in the political and social sphere (which, under a surface of behavioral discipline, remained volatile) as in the cultural sphere. The theatre, especially, profited by this and grew metropolitan in no time.

The "gray, sober, stark, Prussian" Berlin is a myth, if, like all myths, containing a particle of truth. I was myself witness to the perhaps not so "golden" twenties, as their posthumous reputation wishes us to believe, but golden enough for me to give firsthand testimony that life in the city of my birth glittered in all colors and gave wide access to every sensual enjoyment; that it by no means suffocated in work—or unemployment—but handsomely compensated the Berliner, with its wealth of theatres, concert halls, opera, operetta and variety houses, museums, galleries, cinemas, bars, dance halls, its variegated prostitutes' beats, its amusement parks and palaces, beer gardens, saloons, lakes, tent cities, excursion cruises and bathing places, for every working hour or every hour on the dole. To be sure, the political polarization and human misery were on an alarming increase, but particularly among young people and between the sexes there reigned a generously unsentimental, unspoiled camaraderie.

Berlin, in the national consciousness of the Germans, probably never figured as their organic capital (or else Eisenhower would not have made the strategic and political blunder of declaring it "militarily not an important enough target for seizure" and Adenauer could have never made out of Bonn a convincing center of government of the Federal Republic). Be that as it may, in my youth, Berlin surpassed all European capitals as far as big-city attractions were concerned. It surpassed them all in terms of ambition, work, protest and pleasure. In order to keep up this round-the-clock tour de force, the Berliner invented the "American tempo." For it existed only in Berlin, certainly not in America, where I sought it in vain as a nineteen-year-old newcomer and where Max Reinhardt, often, was close to losing his wits over the lackadaisical schedules dictated by country-club life or the time limitations imposed by the unions, by the long weekends or when put off until "after Labor Day."

The years in which my father made his way are generally called the Wilhelmine era. But it is often overlooked that in Wilhelm's Reich many of the epoch-making achievements came to pass in opposition to him and were opposed by him. "S.M." (the German initials of "His Majesty," by which he liked dashingly to be referred to) managed to sack Bismarck and to forfeit the "reinsurance treaty" with Russia, protecting Germany's rear. He persevered in erecting the famous kitsch promenade, misnamed Siegesallee (Avenue of Victory), thereby uglifying Berlin a bit more. He built Germany's deep-sea fleet, which cost him England's friendship. He even succeeded in hatching a world war which he did not desire. But he—and his lackeys catering to the majestic taste—did not succeed in running a good theatre. Nor was he able to obtain the dismissal of Brahm, Brahm's production of Hauptmann's *The Weavers,* then considered a radical play, having incurred Wilhelm's wrath. He never forgave the Deutsches Theater for it—not even under new management. His arrogance in foreign affairs cost him his throne; his arrogance in theatrical affairs merely resulted in a family quarrel.

Wilhelm's sons, above all the Crown Prince, did not share their father's bias. Too many pretty ladies on the stage, in the foyers and dressing rooms, precluded that. In any case, the ruler of that domain had a magnetic attraction for the younger Hohenzollern. The heir presumptive was a frequent guest at Kupfergraben. During one of these visits, I recall, I landed on the imperial lap and my father asked me: "Who is that?" I still feel like defending my answer: "The Crown Prince," for both gentlemen burst out laughing uncontrollably. I probably should have said: "His Imperial Highness"—but that was surely asking too much of a five-year-old. My sulks, however, did not cause a rift between the two houses.

One day, the princes plotted to reconcile the two chiefs. Reinhardt's production of *Minna von Barnhelm* by Lessing was set for February 6, 1911, at Bellevue Castle in Berlin (in time to be my father's domicile, then that of Prince Eitel Friedrich). The play's impeccable Prussianness seemed to have been guaranteed ever since Reinhardt opened it in 1905, when the pictorial chronicler of Frederick the Great, the venerated painter Adolph von Menzel, had designed the decor. My mother played Minna. Another participant was Victor Arnold. He, in addition to my parents, is the source of my information about this event—via his pupil, Ernst Lubitsch, who added a little *haut goût* to the tale by relating that he and Arnold, in protest against what they considered Reinhardt's dynastic bootlicking, had their secret fun by smearing snot on the heavy curtains behind which they hid during the command performance between their exits and entrances.

A graver and more conspicuous disturbance took place in the main intermission: As anticipated by the conspirators, the splendorous evening was off to an unmitigated success. Of course, no one had tipped the monarch off as to what troupe was entertaining him. Encouraged by his radiant smile under its famous sweeping mustache, which was trained up to his face by the mustache wax (it was not wax, but sort of a bandage; the German word is *Binde*) symbolically patented under the euphemistic trademark "Es Ist Erreicht" ("It Has Been Achieved"), the sons gathered around him after the third act and inquired how he liked the show. "Capital evening, children! Absolutely capital!" There followed the roguish question as to what theatre, in his opinion, was responsible for what he had seen. "No idea. Absolutely no idea." And then a bomb exploded: "You see, Papa, how unjust one can be? Reinhardt directed it! And all the actors are Reinhardt actors! Now do you find this performance un-Prussian? Antinational?" It *was* a bomb. The Emperor left Bellevue without another word and the last two acts proceeded without him.

It took quite a while before he agreed to a reconciliation with his sons. He never agreed to one with Reinhardt and his theatre. One of Wilhelm's famous verbal gaffes (encompassing social reform and avant-garde art) went: "I've no use for the whole way things are going." The way things were going in the Reinhardt theatres turned out to be much more salubrious for the German people than the trend Wilhelm paid cocky lip service to. Bismarck confidant and Reinhardt supporter Maximilian Harden thought he had drawn a final line under this parody of Prussia's Glory when he said about the by then disgraced, dethroned and deserting Wilhelm: "A coyly marcelled *casus belli* saunters unpunished beneath the elms of Doorn." Not even this political pundit foresaw that only the first, farcical act of a tragedy had ended, that another *casus belli* was about to cause the dismemberment of the Fatherland, the erasure of Prussia from the map and the degradation and dissection of its capital. But until the other mustache took over, no less ludicrous, though masking infinitely more evil designs, the one-sided fecund love affair between Berlin and the Berliner *malgré lui* bloomed.

It is an adage that a Reinhardt opening was an event of more consequence than any political one and that, opening a paper, the average reader would turn straight to the reviews, skipping the headlines, news dispatches and editorials. It is true that escapist concentration on the more pleasant side of German life and disregard for the forces at work to kill it undoubtedly contributed to the killing. Most Germans prided themselves on being "unpolitical" and were forever "surprised" by schemes long in preparation and affecting their very existence. In this respect, the German Jew was no more awake than the Gentile, with Max Reinhardt out front. Berlin's society and intelligentsia scrambled for the best seats. The broad middle stratum filled the remainder, evening after evening. The business community buttressed the operation and backed every new adventure. Artists of every type lent their energies to the common goal. Students monopolized the standing room. The academicians readily gave their counsel and sanction to his treatment of the classics. The workers saw his plays in the union-run Volksbühne (People's Stage), which he added to his string of houses. Except for the small, if vociferous, chorus of carping critics, the press sang his praise and trumpeted his fame. Berlin had only one bone, if any, to pick with its idol: his frequent and manifestly enjoyed absences. Yet the stimuli he received abroad were also to Berlin's advantage. They widened its horizon and established its reputation as *the* theatre city. For wherever he went, he took a little of Berlin with him.

The absences became more frequent and increasingly joyful as he was drawn away not only from the "dreamless" city, but from one of its citizens: my mother. Helene Thimig's attempts, however, to remake him into a Viennese were foiled to a large extent by the Viennese themselves who, being died-in-the-wool anti-Semites and no future historians, did not look on him as one of their own. Still, he might, one day, not have returned, had it not been for his brother Edmund, who was saddled with a business with a daily overhead of twelve thousand dollars, controlling a minimum of five theatres permanently, a sizable stock company with long-term contracts (some salaries as high as forty thousand dollars a year in 1921), firm commitments with a host of dramatists, extended workshops for sets and costumes, Germany's most active organization for touring companies, Germany's most sought-after drama school, a ramified subscription setup and substantial real estate holdings. It was, therefore, unrealistic of Max to try to lure Edmund away from Berlin by surprising him with a renovated and beautifully decorated apartment in the old grange of Leopoldskron. Edmund cleverly reciprocated with a surprise of his own: an exquisite apartment in Bellevue Castle (now the seat of the Federal Republic's President when in the old capital), proving his own prowess as decorator.

With each absence, the competition in Berlin multiplied, both in the Reinhardt theatres themselves and outside. There were new authors (Brecht, Kaiser, Hasenclever, Zuckmayer), new directors (Jessner, Fehling, Engel, Hilpert, Piscator), new ideas (Brecht's alienation), new acting concepts (Fritz Kortner's), new techniques (Piscator's conveyor belt and multimedia effects; Jessner's celebrated, omnipresent staircase). On this kaleidoscopic scene the elder stage man, Max Reinhardt, kept out of stylistic and ideological controversy. As always, he did not prove this or that theory, but purely and simply his talent. And he did this so disarmingly and with such perfection that, with a few explosive exceptions (for instance, Brecht-Weill's *Threepenny Opera* and Piscator-Pallenberg's *Good Soldier Schweik*), all doctrinaire efforts paled in comparison.

I last visited this Garden theatre of Eden in a world steadily growing more sinful and hostile in October 1932. The occasion was a rehearsal of a play by Molnár with Pallenberg. The theatre was, by then, under a different management, but the partners to whom my father had leased it faced the same problem Edmund had: they could not run a Reinhardt theatre without Reinhardt. The play's title, *Harmony,* was ironic. This venture, neither disarming nor perfect, was once more to prove that there is no such thing as a "dead-sure" combination guaranteeing success. My father was, one last time, confronted with typical Berlin humor, when—a regular procedure—he asked his head prop man, old Albert Lau, about the chances of the play. He received a reply in unadulterated Berlinese: "I got a kinda Wieland stench in my nose." (Lau was referring to a celebrated flop of 1911: *Wieland the Smith*, a fairy tale by Carl Vollmoeller.) My father laughed heartily. It was one of the few laughs in an otherwise *triste* comedy. For Lau's prophecy came true. What remains memorable to me, however, about that incident is that it happened on the day I was taking leave of the Deutsches Theater—and of Berlin.

Not of my father. He insisted, in spite of the imminent première, on escorting me with my brother to the port of departure. He—a premonition?—took our separation much more to heart than I did, convinced and determined as I was to return to my beloved Berlin the next year for his sixtieth birthday. My conviction and determination were hardened by the vice-president of the Hamburg-American Line, Dr. Kiep, who kept us company on the boat train from Hamburg to Cuxhaven. We owed his presence to a misunderstanding. Since cabin reservations had been handled by the theatre, the impression had been created that Max and not Gottfried Reinhardt was sailing for the States. My father used the opportunity to pump Kiep, whom he considered an informed man, about the political and economic situation. Kiep, indeed, had the air of a very informed man: The Nazis, he said, had, for the first time (this was a fact), suffered heavy losses in the most recent election, the movement was clearly on the decline, furthermore bankrupt, unable even to raise the necessary funds for their brown shirts; Schleicher (General Kurt von Schleicher, Minister of War)—which meant the Reichswehr—was coming to an agreement with the Social Democrats; he would become chancellor, everything was settled and could not look brighter.

As much as this diagnosis pleased us, sad the long minutes made us this and that side of the railing, when the liner slowly edged away from the pier and the brass band played the obligatory "Muss i denn, muss i denn zu-um Städtele hinaus . . ." ("Must I then, must I then say goodbye, my little town . . ."). The Reinhardts, as befits such an occasion, did not stint on tears, without dreaming that this old German soldiers' song would eventually become an Elvis Presley hit and that the "little town" was Berlin, which the younger son was leaving not just temporarily, and which the entire family would soon have to evacuate forever.

The news that Dr. Kiep—as, by the way, his brother, the German chargé d'affaires in New York too—had been wrong (that Germany's big industry bailed Hitler out, gladly paying for the brown shirts and a lot more besides; that Schleicher—soon to be murdered—*did* become chancellor, but that his rapprochement with the Social Democrats was foiled and he himself toppled by another Papen-Hindenburg intrigue); that Hitler came to power on January 30, 1933—reached me in the subway on my way home from an all-night spree in Harlem. My father, in Berlin, received it a little later. He too had spent a gay evening—with his actors after his last successful première in Berlin. When he awoke, the Reichstag had been burning for several hours.

He left Berlin the following day, never to return, neither of them aware of what they had lost. When I returned to Berlin for the first time in 1954, many of the landmarks of my and my parents' life stood no more. The house where I was born and where my father lived and worked for twenty-odd years was an exception. As were the Deutsches Theater, the Kammerspiele, the Grosses Schauspielhaus, the Komödie, the Kurfürstendammtheater and the Volksbühne. They still stood and are still standing. What was and still is happening inside is another, irrelevant matter. Nor is it made more relevant by the fact that the street on which the Deutsches Theater is located has been named Reinhardt Strasse. I, who always had *every* right to claim "ich bin ein Berliner," did not feel like one any longer. Of course, we also—I was showing my American wife "my" city—had a look at Unter den Linden. The linden trees were gone.

THE DIARY

MONDAY,
OCTOBER 11, 1943

I finally succeed—H. was squashed like an ant—in persuading Foster Kennedy to visit Papa a second time. Have practically to prostrate myself Oriental style at his exalted feet. But it is worth it: after the usual inquisitionary thrusts and jabs at Papa's ego—to give the maestrissimo his due, he's scrupulously thorough—he says we've made it! And Papa's the living proof. He's no longer humbly compliant. If he weren't so courteous, he'd be up to saying: "You don't really give a damn about all this, do you? Well, neither do I! It's behind me!"

Kennedy says Papa can resume work in about a week, provided he doesn't overtax himself. This time, as he leaves, he unbends enough to shake hands with Papa: "Goodbye, sir. Let's hope this is the last time you've seen me." A hope that Papa endorses.

At the elevator Kennedy praises the job his speech teacher did with Papa. Am so carried away by joyous outlook, confess that speech teacher was the one thing that went awry. No comment. He departs another two hundred and fifty dollars heavier.

Call Wolfgang. We're happy as kids—his kids.

In the afternoon to SCPC. Report optimistically to Litvak about Einstein. He's satisfied, but disappointed about Grosz. Promise to obtain good equivalent material from old satirical German periodicals. Try to get out of studio as fast and unobtrusively as possible, but collide head on with Captain [Julian] Blaustein, project officer for our department of engineers. Used to be head of story department at Universal. Nice guy, even nice to us enlisted men. Plays gin and poker with us all night and covers up our matitudinal absences. Therefore cannot afford to breeze off too hurriedly. Unfortunately, he has lots of time to kill, lots of Hollywood molasses on the brain and lots of misguided good will toward me, which is sure death for my precious hours: "Got a great assignment for you, Gottfried, right up your alley. There's this British training film. About German booby traps. Be great if you'd preview it tonight at Monmouth."

Preview an army training film? To test its amusement value? Captain Blaustein seems to have this in mind and my "rich Hollywood experience" appears to make me the ideal man to judge audience reaction and to decide whether the film should be incorporated in the United States Army training program. For once name-dropping doesn't get me off the hook. As Blaustein rightly surmises, Professor Einstein can struggle along without my collaboration at night. It's the first evening I leave Papa alone with Eleonora.

With a private detailed to me I transport the reels to New Jersey and, as ordered, step onstage in the camp entertainment center before the showing to prepare the audience for an unscheduled change in program and to give whatever ladies are present the opportunity to escape. The ladies sit tight.

During the first two-thirds of the picture military men and wives attend with quiet interest as British advance units occupy positions previously evacuated by Jerry and are consecutively blown to bits by charges concealed behind water faucets, doorknobs, light switches, cigarette boxes and other fanciful devices. It may just be my nervous imagination that interest lags, but, shortly, during scene of a Tommy seized by the call of nature, I'm reassured. When he clutches his stomach and presses himself together like a folding chair, the audience howls. Female howls predominate. Dear Captain Blaustein, audience reaction so positive it's earsplitting! Roger. Over and out. And so is audience—over and out—in the aisles, going wilder and wilder as Britisher's frantic search for toilet grows more acrobatic. Dramatic climax: toilet found, soldier relieved, he flushes and the explosion on the screen is a ten-cent firecracker compared to the explosion in the auditorium. . . . Goodbye, Captain Blaustein, maybe I'd better not report tonight? [The U.S. Engineer Corps subsequently decided to pictorialize their own doctrine of how not to be surprised by booby traps.]

Final gag: on way back to New York every few hundred yards along the road an "Is this trip necessary?" sign hits me in the eye. Will let Blaustein answer that one. But some purpose, however unintentional, was served by this trip: Papa convulsed by perfect epilogue to slapstick comedy.

TUESDAY,
OCTOBER 12, 1943

A tailspinning day: Off to chariot races. Helen moving at last. Mail contracts to Korngold and Kohner Bressart. Meet with Liebman [lawyer] to clarify legal questions. Paley's check for twenty thousand deposited. Conference with Irion, Darvas, production manager. We cast, make a timetable, patch up running feud between Irion and me, but right in middle of détente she turns into wing-and-claw monster again: "Your father had a stroke, didn't *he?" My indignant denial is accepted for the sake of our truce. Darvas walks across town with me, urges me to come clean with her. Invite her to tea next Sunday. She will then see for herself that all is well.*

In lobby of Gladstone cousin Eva buttonholes me. She too has heard rumors, wants desperately to go up and visit Papa, but complains that Eleonora keeps turning her away and she has a ton of back correspondence that needs his signature. [Good, devoted Eva, who, with her younger sister, followed her brother into exile in New York, volunteered to fill in as secretary when we were snowed under and, whether paid, paid less or unpaid, could always be counted on. Like all members of his family she revered my father.] Nothing more difficult to discourage than unmotivated devotion. But I finally get rid of her without offending her.

Have a little more difficulty losing Weisgal, who has been lying in wait for me for hours with Silvia trying to divert him. Meyer's way to Papa also barred by Eleonora. Doesn't suspect anything, but is, therefore, less easy to shake. Has plans for Papa that would take a couple of lifetimes to fulfill. Problem: Meyer is not a man to be deflected once his mind's made up. Many dents in many walls testify to his hard head. Even an occasional hole. Hasn't Papa emigrated to America through one of them?

A Dance Around the Golden Calf

MY FATHER EMIGRATED later in spirit and mind than in body. The thought of emigration repelled him, as did any form of compulsion. Free will was to him the breath of life. If curtailed, he fought it by ignoring the interference. This led to a number of faulty and harmful assessments in the period of his exile—a predicament beyond his control he tried to ignore as long as he could.

He was aided in this self-deception by the memory of having quasi-emigrated already once before—from Vienna to Berlin—which led him to underestimate the pitfalls of a basically altered situation. That a voluntary change of residence in one's youth is not analogous to a forcible one at an advanced age and to a land whose language one does not master he rejected emotionally. Encouraged by the early experience, he felt confident that he could make his way or simply continue on it anywhere. His initial successes outside Germany abetted the illusion. Feeling like a fish in international waters, as though they were his natural habitat, it was tempting for him to forget his original springboard and that much more than a springboard was involved. In a letter from Hollywood, following America's entry into World War II, he wrote:

> . . . after the upheaval in Germany, Salzburg was my only safe harbor. I could always return to it, and from it, I could again and again embark anew.
> Vienna, Paris, London, Stockholm, Copenhagen, Amsterdam and many another city were ready to welcome me, even New York. That was not merely economic security, it was also lifesaving artistic security. . . .

He erred. Salzburg had never been his home port, either economically or artistically. There, just as to every other city, he brought with him his Berlin theatre. And after he had lost Berlin, the other cities were ready to welcome him only to a limited degree and success often eluded him. The bountiful spring from which he had been able to draw so generously had dried up. The well-greased technical apparatus was no longer automatically at his disposal. The incomparable ensemble was strewn to the winds, as was the enormously competent office staff, whose efficiency he accepted as a matter of course, even after it was no longer available. In addition, the stamp of origin on his imports was now missing—a factor of uncertainty in any trade, including the theatrical one.

He felt secure in Salzburg? What security was there to be had twenty minutes from Hitler's aerie across a tenuous border? He tried valiantly to disregard the implied threat of this absurd proximity and later forgot that he did not always succeed. In a letter to me from Paris on November 10, 1933, he enumerates some of the

> . . . many worries the upheaval [in Germany] burdened me with. Where I shall go after finishing my work here I don't as yet know. Perhaps to Vienna if by then it hasn't been nailed to the crooked cross. It doesn't look very hopeful. The youth is captivated by "Heil Hitler" and screams and beats it into every head, spreads and pastes it all over the country. Those who govern [in Austria] are still courageously holding out, but the only aid they receive from the rest of Europe are speeches. When it comes to speeches, however, present Germany is stronger and more aggressive. Mussolini, on whom more depends than ever these days [a favorite fata morgana prevalent in Austria in those critical years], remains impenetrable for the time being. In her holy egoism Italy has as yet not made a decision. I can

> hardly go to Leopoldskron. For, apart from being drowned in mortgages and attachments up to its roof [an old treaty between Austria and Germany enabled the Third Reich to slam an impossible-to-meet lien on the castle for trumped-up tax liabilities], the "Führer's" headquarters (in Berchtesgaden) are too close for comfort. He talks and talks and has his ministers talk in every province and into every microphone. From all this it is evident that he's willing to be talked to about everything, even world peace, except about two questions: Austria and the Jews. He wants Austria unconditionally and he doesn't want the Jews at any price. Their ancestry is now being explored all the way down to the great-grandmother and punished mercilessly.

That Hitler was willing to be talked to about world peace was a misjudgment my father shared with politically better-versed people. As to the "mortgages and attachments," he imagined he could make a deal with Hitler's Germany, as though he were still persona grata there and happened to be on holiday of his own free will. Thus, from England he dispatched a noble letter to the Reich's government in which he magnanimously renounced his Berlin theatres and made a "present" of them to the German people. The letter was an empty gesture. How could he give something away that had already been taken from him? And what advantage was there to the victim of a fraud in exchanging amenities with the defrauders? A fraud rebate? In the event, the Third Reich predictably showed no gratitude, neither lifted the lien nor stooped to answer.

But my father was not satisfied with this futile and humiliating attempt. He was to make another one that did more than humiliate him: it almost bankrupted him. From America he transferred good, hard-earned dollars to erase the "debt." He managed to do this exactly six months before Hitler marched into Austria and annexed Leopoldskron outright. Shortly thereafter, a third attempt to save Leopoldskron equally misfired. Ignoring the expropriation, he urged Rudolf Kommer to persuade his flexible friend Princess Stephanie Hohenlohe, then about to be deported from England, to rent the property from him.

The Princess was not born with this name or title. They had rubbed off on her through marriage. Her own origins bore a more prosaic imprint. Fräulein Richter of Vienna, of partially Jewish ancestry, was the proud holder of the Golden Party Badge, personally bestowed on her by the Führer, and, at the time of these negotiations, lived with Herr Wiedemann, Hitler's aide-de-camp and later German consul in San Francisco, where, prior to the United States' joining the Allies, he was ordered to leave the country, having been involved in Nazi machinations. The princess's entry into world politics resulted from her intimacy with the English press potentate Lord Rothermere, who had the *idée fixe* of paving a way back to the German throne for the Hohenzollerns and saw her as an effective intermediary. Her own ideas must have been more practical since her loyalty soon switched from the imperial resurrection of the First Reich to the one that was scheduled to last a thousand years. But she may have had her misgivings about that prospect as well, for she was, at first, not at all opposed to Kommer's approach. Nevertheless, in the end, she found a less complicated way of usurping Leopoldskron—not circuitously through a lease with far-off Reinhardt, but directly by the grace of cozily nearby Hitler.

My father held on to the fiction of being able to keep his options open much longer than the Princess. This produced such painful incidents as when a deservedly respected director of the Reinhardt theatres, Heinz Hilpert, whom Goebbels had designated as Reinhardt's successor, sought approval of *that* usurpation from his former chief by long-distance telephone. Typically, my father underrated the distance (Berlin by then was darkest Africa) and gave his enthusiastic blessing. That propped up Hilpert's own self-deception and gave Reinhardt another opportunity for an empty gesture of generosity in lieu of the curt retort that was surely called for and should have run something like "Don't you think you really ought to clear that with your own conscience?"

In the early years of the Nazi regime, the consciences of those as yet unpolluted Germans who retreated into so-called "inner emigration" (whatever that may mean) needed to be soothed by the approval of the outward—i.e., actual—emigrants. In order to tolerate the ravages suffered by their former friends, benefactors and protégés, they deluded themselves into believing that they continued to live in Germany so that they could rescue German culture from barbarism, prevent greater barbarism, help those of their unfortunate fellow men who had failed to escape or to protect the legacies of the defamed. I believed in these moral alibis as little as in the evasions, vacillations and expediencies practiced by the bona fide refugees, those who, out of blindness, opportunism or mistaken nobility, refused to raise their voices (in absolute safety) about what had been done to them or about the graver inflictions on their trapped brothers. But I represented a small minority. My father was the last one to agree with me that both compromises, inside and outside German borders, decisively helped the Nazis at a time when they were, as yet, anything but consolidated in their own country and still thought they were dependent on world opinion; helped them to consolidate themselves in their own country and to realize they did not have to care a damn about world opinion. Time and again I asked him why Englishmen, Frenchmen, Americans or native Jews, in their host nations, should become excited so long as a Hermann Hesse keeps silent (as a resident of Switzerland he remained so till his death) and a Thomas Mann finds his tongue as late as 1937, so long as a Bruno Walter continues to lead the Vienna Philharmonic even after every Jewish orchestra member has been thrown out and so long as a Max Reinhardt engages in unilateral polite correspondence with his tormentors, seeks to legitimize the thieves who have taken his works and possessions and replies to a reporter's question regarding the political development in Germany on his arrival in San Francisco: "I am an Austrian."

In this respect, I never saw eye to eye with my family. Initially, not even with my "Aryan" mother, who, later, surpassed all Jews in condemning her compatriots and all collaboration with them. At the time of Hitler's (perfectly legal) appointment as Chancellor, she was under contract to Berlin's Volksbühne. Of course, it made sense for the Nazis to pamper the abandoned German wife of the Jew Reinhardt. Only a caustic letter from her son Gottfried in New York, threatening to call himself Goldmann unless she shook the German dust off her feet posthaste, had the desired effect—which does not mean that she would not have done so sooner or later in any case. I was and am of the opinion that, had a man like Gustav Gründgens (that ex-playmate of Erika Mann, a highly regarded Reinhardt actor and director and one of his discoveries) stayed abroad and not promptly left his film location in Spain to kowtow to Hitler and take over the state theatres "vacated" by the Jew Leopold Jessner; had Hilpert resisted Goebbels's lure for a little while and not quickly jumped into Reinhardt's shoes, running his theatres in the Reinhardt style; had Richard Strauss not obeyed a Nazi summons and flown from Vienna to replace the belatedly "indisposed" Bruno Walter at the helm of Berlin's Philharmonic; had Gerhart Hauptmann and Gottfried Benn and Martin Heidegger not flirted with the New Order in its first years; had Sauerbruch, the eminent surgeon, not fronted for German medicine then engaged in inhuman experiments on concentration-camp inmates; had Erich Schmidt, the suave president of Berliner Allianz, Germany's largest insurance company, not rushed to replace Alfred Hugenberg in Hitler's second cabinet; had Nobel Prize–winning physicist Philipp Lenard not debased German science by denouncing Einstein's theory of relativity as Jewish and, therefore, inaccurate; had Wilhelm Furtwängler for once lingered on in his Swiss chalet, instead of "saving" German music and writing high-flown letters to the Propaganda Minister, pleading for the toleration and employment of a small number among the Chosen People, a choice he had made himself and in which Max Reinhardt had the honor to be included—in short: had the elite of

German art, literature, academia, industry, finance and the military not put themselves at the willing disposal of Germany's gravediggers, first of all, nothing would have happened to any of them and, secondly, Hitler and his accomplices would have found it much harder to get a grip on the land of poets and thinkers and to set in motion that of the mass murderers. But the fronts were too blurred, good and evil too interwoven, for a modicum of decency to make itself felt, for the feeblest resistance inside Germany or a halfway united world opinion to form. In the general confusion, vilification, palliation and obfuscation, the scum—to its own surprise—succeeded in grabbing absolute power, after having been presented with bits and pieces of it on a silver platter.

It took my father much longer than my mother to come to this conclusion. When he finally did, he stated categorically that he would never set foot on German soil again. But, in 1933, he managed to overlook that his Salzburg Mephistopheles, in still officially free Austria, was attacked not because of Pallenberg's inadequacy as an actor, but because of his racial inadequacy, and he recast the part. And he insisted that it was purely artistic considerations and not pressure from the prophetic bureaucrats running the Festival that made him give the role to the unashamed anti-Semite Werner Krauss. (As early as 1921, during rehearsals for *The Wolves* by Romain Rolland, Krauss had let himself go in a venomous tirade against the "brothers Goldmann's slatternly way of doing business" on the stage of the Deutsches Theater, because he was irritated by some contractual controversy.) It did not disturb my father that Krauss, before accepting, had to get the permission of Goebbels—which, interestingly enough, he obtained. For my father, *that* facet had to do with those cursed politics, but not art! And that his much-adored Toscanini had preferred to exile himself from Italy rather than conduct the Fascist *Giovanezza* at the start of his concerts, he jocularly ascribed less to Toscanini's political spine than to his refusal to be upstaged by another dictator.

In the same year in which Krauss was allowed to perform under Reinhardt, another, softer-pedaling herald of the *Herrenvolk* came to Salzburg: Furtwängler. What was Toscanini's response? After his colleague's concert, he had himself peremptorily announced backstage and served Furtwängler with an ultimatum: "Next year it's either you or me!" Furtwängler stammered, "Of course, *you*, honored Maestro!" It was not a matter of course. In 1938, Austria was incorporated into Greater Germany and a blasé world calmly watched it happen. Not Toscanini. He stuck to his either/or. And it was not he but the other who reigned from then on over the music in Salzburg. Toscanini took the political consequences, Furtwängler made artistic conquests, Reinhardt suffered the consequences, was artistically in full retreat and politically nowhere.

The "racially tainted" Salzburg performances of *Jedermann* and *Faust* were replaced by racially "pure" ones of a play by Kleist and another one by Goethe. No one took any notice of the fact that of the directors hopping into the breach, one, Erich Engel, had not so long ago put on the *Threepenny Opera* by the Communist Brecht and the "*Kulturbolshevist*" Jew Weill, and the other, Heinz Hilpert, had done *Captain of Köpenick* —with Krauss in a Reinhardt theatre—by kicked-out half-Jew Carl Zuckmayer. The public did not mind the kicking out, since for every face that disappeared, three familiar ones remained. Thus, closing one eye, no one missed the departed. Krauss no longer needed a special Nazi work permit for Salzburg and, although the Thimig daughter had gone to America with the Festival's founder for good, there were enough members of the Thimig family staying behind so that no awkward gap was felt. Furtwängler consecrated the change of scene with the overture to the Kleist play by the "Aryan" Hans Pfitzner, but the all-reaping "Aryans" had overlooked something, nevertheless: Pfitzner had composed and conducted his music to the work for the opening of the Deutsches Theater in 1905 on commission by Reinhardt. Despite German thoroughness, it was, alas, difficult not to keep stumbling over Max Reinhardt somewhere in German civilization.

In America, Toscanini acted the émigré, heart and soul, and Reinhardt not at all. From the very beginning, he had pushed his fate under a more or less comfortable carpet. First, under the carpet of Leopoldskron; later, under those of luxury hotels in Vienna, Venice, Florence, Paris, London, New York and villas in Los Angeles. What on earth, he might have asked, was so extraordinary about this flying carpet? America saw it differently. It saw the prominent victim of a European catastrophe as merely one among a multitude of others, regardless of his frequent previous visits as an honored and welcome guest. A guest, in order to be sure of a hearty welcome, must come from someplace and return to someplace. If he settles down for a longer period, he easily becomes a burden to his hosts.

Another contributing factor to his progressive estrangement from inconvenient reality and his progressive isolation was his ambivalent relation to the Jews. Here, again, he did not see himself as a "case," much less as one of many. He considered his own Jewishness a purely personal matter. He felt no particular solidarity with his fellow believers. He could not bring himself to take his ancestry as seriously as Hitler did. He was, of course, no stranger to anti-Semitism. He had experienced it in his childhood in Vienna when, as he told me, non-Jewish schoolmates had thrown stones at him and his likes in the streets. Any non-Jew in his position and with his record of patriotic services would have been knighted (which he not only desired, but actively worked toward). He never was. The management of Vienna's Burgtheater, which he at one time sought, was barred to him for the same reason in spite of impressive sponsorship. Even the presidency of the Salzburg Festival he had founded eluded him. Hofmannsthal, in a letter to Richard Strauss in 1923:

> . . . and now to Salzburg. I wired you and now I repeat my *urgent* request: please accept this purely formal position which involves no activity on your part whatsoever. Do me and Reinhardt a great favor and preserve for us this field of endeavor. Only in this way will further artistic efforts there be possible. These philistines will never accept Reinhardt as president. They hate him three- and fourfold, as a Jew, as a Lord of the Manor, as an artist and as a solitary human being whom they cannot fathom.

Richard Strauss, needless to say, accepted the presidency, as he had always accepted everything and gone along with everything that was to his advantage. I am convinced Hofmannsthal speaks the truth when he says in the same letter that Reinhardt joins him in his plea. Certain strictures which were imposed even on the most respected Jews my father accepted as inevitable. He resented being made to belong to a "people" whose existence he doubted. A nation of Jews in Palestine he thought a utopia bereft of any attraction for him. When asked once whether he would like to direct a play in Tel Aviv, he said. "I have never liked critics. To play for a public comprised one hundred percent of critics, I am afraid, is not my idea of heaven." Had he become acquainted with today's state of Israel, he would have been most surprised: nowhere, except perhaps in Russia, is there a more naïve theatre to which the spectators adhere so naïvely and enthusiastically as in the Jewish state.

He received a pre-taste of this naïveté and enthusiasm in Paris in 1934, when Meyer Weisgal, a native of Kekol in the Polish province of Plozk, latterly a Zionist journalist in Canada and the United States, left no Zionist stone unturned to lure him to America. My father liked the pretaste. What he did not like was being accosted as a Jew and emigrant.

Weisgal's first sortie into the theatrical field had been a Jewish spectacle, *Romance of a People*, which, in 1932, he had organized within the framework of the World's Fair in Chicago, being in charge of the Palestinian pavilion. He had managed to bring his idol, Chaim Weizmann, the head of the Zionist movement, to the States for this occasion, resulting in a most successful fund-raising campaign. Fund-raising was in Weisgal's blood. But now, for the first time, he tasted blood of a new, more tantalizing type: his nascent love of the theatre. Weisgal was no man of abstract ideals. He needed concrete projects and *propriae personae* to become inflamed. It was his *loyalty* that moved mountains. In Judaism, its object's name was Chaim Weizmann. In the theatre, he had as yet found no equivalent.

Then, one morning, he read in a newspaper that Max Reinhardt had been driven from Germany. He cabled him immediately: IF HITLER DOESN'T WANT YOU I TAKE YOU. The address read: MAX REINHARDT, EUROPE . . . There was no reply. But not because the cable had not been delivered. Rather, my father was as leery of the second as of the first alternative. However, if he thought that this Mr. Weisgal had now been disposed of, he underestimated the zeal and energy of a man to whom silences and refusals are no obstacles whatever. (Once, when Weisgal's booming volubility penetrated Weizmann's bedroom from his salon at the Dorchester Hotel in London, disturbing Weizmann's dictation, the latter inquired the reason for the vocal volume. Secretary: "He's talking to Tel Aviv." Weizmann: "Why doesn't he use the phone?")

With his adjutant, Joe Brainin, Weisgal set out for Europe to induce Reinhardt to direct a biblical spectacle in New York, and learned that Reinhardt was in Paris, rehearsing *Fledermaus*. Armed with a written introduction from Lord Melchett, the son of the well-known British industrialist, statesman and Jewish philanthropist, Weisgal gained entrance to the Théâtre Pigalle only to find himself facing a hydra-headed *cordon sanitaire* whose task it was to shield Reinhardt from approaches of this kind and which did everything to discourage and get rid of unwelcome supplicants —both doomed endeavors in the case of this particular supplicant. Weisgal arranged for the introduction to reach Reinhardt's attention and to be admitted into his presence. There and then, Weisgal discovered his second idol.

My father was sympathetic to Weisgal's personality. He had a penchant for Eastern European Jews. One can put it this way: if Jewishness must be emphasized (which he did not recommend, especially in politics), then let it be the genuine kind! Yet he did not respond to Weisgal's plan. Besides his ideological—or rather, anti-ideological—objections, he had artistic ones: he disliked the makeshift character of the undertaking. He missed the creative impetus. And the manifest speculation on anti-Hitler sentiment by a New York Jewish audience did not sit well with him.

I was worried when I learned of his declining Weisgal's offer. My brother and friends in Europe had informed me about the desolate state of his finances. My own attempts on his behalf in America had all misfired. Hollywood turned its back on him, as did Broadway, hard hit as it was by the Depression and wary of the monumental expenditures associated with him. The patron on whom he had hitherto always been able to count, Kahn, had recently died. On the other hand, there was no dearth of challenges that cried for him. Recently, two mammoth auditoriums in Rockefeller Center (then two-thirds empty and nicknamed "Rockefeller's Folly") had opened: Radio City Music Hall and the Center Theatre. The management of both playhouses, leased to RCA, was at a loss over what to do with them. (One became—and still is—a cinema; the other, after a checkered career as operetta stage, ice rink and home for other perfunctory attractions, is no longer in operation.) As Max Reinhardt seemed to me an obvious solution for them I bent every effort to establish the necessary contact. In vain.

One can imagine my excitement when I was called to the telephone and the secretary of Radio City's vice-president asked me to come and see him the following day—and my disappointment when I learned from Messrs. Aylsworth, Franklin and Beck that they were not interested in Reinhardt but merely in Reinhardt scenery: Were the sets to the Grosses Schauspielhaus production of *Tales of Hoffmann* by any chance still available for a ballet? My suggestion to revive my father's ideally suitable production in the Music Hall fell on deaf ears. The former Broadway producer Martin Beck, a native of Hungary with a smattering of German, had his own artistic beliefs. They propelled him into a flood of verses by Schiller with which he proceeded to inundate me, to the visible dismay of his colleagues. My stomach would have stood this paprikaed literary *spécialité* more readily had I not come with an appetite for a more wholesome meal. Once again, I was an actor in a typical emigration comedy. Perhaps this explains why, nine months later, I chided my father for his lack of interest in Weisgal's venture. He countered:

> The biblical revue . . . would have probably brought me money which I now need more than ever. But Kommer was demanding that I decide without knowing the first thing about the "oeuvre." From what I have heard, it appears to end with the Jews finding a haven in America, after taking us from the creation of the world via the dance around the golden calf to every well-known alpine peak of kitsch. An opportunity for De Mille which, alas, I could not seize for all De Millions in the world.

> I must by now—it is, after all, quite late—remain as I am . . . The entrepreneurs (Zionists of the purest water) called on me in Paris and talked my ears off. I turned them over to Kommer. He and I exchanged agitated and expensive cables. My last contained my rejection and his last dreamed of the "phenomenal success of the biblical revue which would have helped you for many years to come." I am, incidentally, by no means so sure. Every time I have acted against my instincts—fortunately this has very seldom been the case—I have failed. [I was prepared to argue that.]
>
> You really must not be so silly as to believe that the Jewish theme is a stumbling block for me. I have always been staunch in my Jewish convictions. I am even a pious Jew and would be happy if I could help my brethren with what little I have to offer. But I don't believe that they can be helped with scorn or rose-colored trash.
>
> At my suggestion, Werfel is now writing an oratorio and Weill is supposed to compose it. Should it really come to a production, it will be a work of art. I, at least, am convinced of that, for the first chapters of *The Road of Promise* Werfel read to me were grandiose and deeply moving. Whether it will make money is admittedly another question. On that score Charell and company will always have the edge on me. . . .

Well, Werfel wrote no work of art. Nor does the music number among Kurt Weill's inventive and enduring compositions. But at least the poet Werfel and the composer Weill guaranteed my father the *illusion* of occupying himself with a work of art. And this illusion, without which he was incapable of functioning, enabled him to *create* a work of art through his *direction*. Reading the text and listening to the score today without having seen the production, no one would believe that this "biblical revue"—for that, in spite of everything, is what it remained essentially—could have engendered one of Max Reinhardt's masterpieces. But the same impression would be gained by anyone who peruses the scripts of *Jedermann* and *The Miracle*. These commissioned concoctions, concocted by artists, but no works of art themselves, had only one justification: they supplied Reinhardt with a scaffolding and stimulated him to build around it. *The Road of Promise* was another case in point.

What made my father "act against his instincts" this time? (For this happened more often than he admitted to himself.) Was it really the samples Werfel showed him? Was it Kommer's logic, which he usually pooh-poohed? Was it financial need? Perhaps all of these. But they alone would not have budged him, had it not been for Weisgal's single-mindedness. Reinhardt was, however, no less endowed in this regard, and he gave the greenhorn producer some hard nuts to crack.

The first was Franz Werfel. My father had directed his *Juarez and Maximilian* with great success. He esteemed him as a poet. And, like many others, he was in awe of his wife, Alma, the widow of Gustav Mahler. Although her famed beauty had by then wilted, her sharp intelligence, relentless drive, and power over people had lost nothing with the years. I have no way of knowing whether my father was aware that Werfel had become in his heart a fervent Catholic. But he must have had an inkling of it, or he would not have referred to an "oratorio." He was certainly aware of Alma's religious affiliations. She never hid anything under a bushel, least of all her militant Christianity. In Vienna, there were even rumors of her intimate relations with the Austrian Chancellor's father-confessor. At any rate, she was generally credited with being the Egeria of pre-*Anschluss* Austria's Fascist-clerical regime. On the side, she ruled her husband with an iron hand.

With this choice, my father contributed to alienating the project from the character it had been destined to have and which he disliked. The choice of Kurt Weill—the second "nut"—seems even stranger for what was intended to be a religious, patriotic drama. Reinhardt had never worked with him before. Nor would Brecht's collaborator and he have been likely to cross paths in Berlin. Their acquaintance was due to a fact my father, as we know, preferred to play down: their mutual emigration; to the "accident" that they were in Paris simultaneously and had "casually" met. That this skeptical, left-wing materialist would find common ground with the pious, conservative Werfel and the fiercely nationalistic idealist Weisgal was improbable, to say the least.

But there were more *mésalliances* to come: my father enjoined Weisgal to engage for the scenic realization Norman Bel Geddes, by then a man of many parts (scenic designer for stage and screen, industrial designer, architect, futurologist, gadget inventor, lighting pioneer, military cartographer, theatrical producer). Why Geddes was, for once, miscast my father most certainly did *not* know, for Geddes would have been careful not to show him one side of his protean nature: he, Geddes, was not overly fond of Jews, and even less fond of Jewish producers, having had traumatic difficulties with Hollywood moguls, Flo Ziegfeld and Weisgal's predecessor, Morris Gest. In reaping for his Jewish manifesto what he had sown with great tenacity, a Max Reinhardt production, Meyer Weisgal found himself encumbered with the insidious seeds of a zealot of the Roman Catholic Church, a Marxist-oriented atheist and a Waspish American anti-Semite.

I flew from Los Angeles to attend the opening. On the plane, I read an article by Bosley Crowther in *The New York Times* of the day before, relating the tortuous course of what had, in the meantime, become *The Eternal Road*. It was a benevolent account, obviously based on an interview with Weisgal or a press agent in his employ. But some of the items—later corroborated—staggered me: sets rising four stories in height and extending over almost an acre . . . twenty-six miles of wiring strung about the theatre . . . thousands of special lights . . . as much electrical current consumed as would ordinarily be burnt on a dark night on the *Queen Mary* . . . 1,772 costumes . . . a complete mountain, rising from twelve feet below orchestra level to some thirty feet above it, which could be removed to be replaced by the temple of Solomon with its forty-foot columns and Joseph's Egyptian palace with its three-dimensional statues rising to a height of thirty-two feet . . . and so on and on. My mind numbed, I landed in the early afternoon.

Knowing my father's habits, I anticipated a last rehearsal on the day of the opening and took a taxi directly to the theatre. The location of the Manhattan Opera House was far removed from Manhattan's theatrical mainstream. No circumspect producer would have selected it for so costly a show. It had not been in use for many years. The reasons Max Reinhardt was now using it were peculiar: another "nut" Weisgal had been forced to crack was my father's insistence on doing the play in a tent in Central Park. But city authorities had withheld the license for it. A suitable, noise-free substitute in the open air could not be found. Besides, the erection of the giant tabernacle accommodating stage, backstage, auditorium, foyer, dressing rooms, sanitary installations, box-office space, etc., would have exceeded the available capital. My father, however, was stubborn: a tabernacle or no show! Did he prefer "no show"?

Anyway, the tent was an old dream of his. It was in tune with his general urge to break out of conventional enclosures. *Every* enclosure cramped him. "Jacob's tent"—he knew the subjects of his dreams well enough to advocate them persuasively—struck a chord in Weisgal's soul. But when the chips were down, Jacob was more important to him than his tent, and both seemed impossible to merge lucratively in twentieth-century America. Weisgal, therefore, entered into an unholy alliance with Geddes, who, if for quite different reasons, likewise campaigned against the tent idea.

Their first choice was the Center Theatre. Curiously, the Gentile Rockefellers warmed to the Jewish project, whereas their lessees, the Jewish management of RCA, wanted nothing to do with it. The Hippodrome was currently occupied. Finally, Geddes opted for the Manhattan Opera House, because Scotch Rite, the hard-up owners, had no objections to any kind of reconstruction which might be on his mind. Geddes did not say all that was on his mind. What he said was: "If the play is good, people will go anywhere to see it." (The script had not been delivered as yet.)

And more specifically: "Just the people in the [adjacent] Hotel New Yorker will automatically fill the house for six months." (Why the occupants of this commercial hostelry should entertain such neighborly feelings remained one of the Geddesian mysteries Weisgal preferred not to unravel.) Apprised of Geddes's selection, my father sent an uncharacteristically laconic cable from Salzburg: MANHATTAN OPERA LIVING CORPSE REINHARDT.

In the end, Geddes won the battle on the strength of the most provocative argument of all: there was, he claimed, no equivalent theatre available in New York that would do justice to his sets. Should my father wish to wait for a suitable vacancy—which he did—there would be the danger of the play's losing its topicality and the American public's losing all interest. For this interest would stay alive only so long as the Jewish question was on everybody's mind. This would certainly not be the case much longer, Hitler's collapse being predicted daily and necessarily followed by an immediate improvement of the lot of the Jews. So there was no time to waste, and either the decision went to the Manhattan or the project must be dropped forthwith.

With this ammunition—it was 1935—Weisgal pilgrimaged to Salzburg. Arriving in Leopoldskron, and temporarily becoming a close neighbor of the Führer—who, unaware that he was doomed, at that very minute was plotting quite different collapses—the pilgrim persuaded himself and his idol to accept the Manhattan. Simultaneously, he made the shocking discovery that the author of the work he had commissioned was, according to his own report, "intellectually more a Christian than a Jew." Weisgal spared no effort to guide Werfel back to the faith of their fathers. This brought him face to face with a much more formidable adversary: *Frau* Werfel. She fought just as heroically for the soul of her husband as Weisgal, and the few concessions he was able to chalk up for himself were owing entirely to his generous dispensing of her favorite liqueur, Bénédictine. It may be that the monastic origin of this beverage was the source of its power over her; in any event, the "wet nurse of geniuses," as she was dubbed in view of the chain of her legal and illegal companions (Mahler, Kokoschka, Gropius, Werfel), unquestionably became more pliable at the sight of the label on the bulbous bottle. Weisgal pragmatically included one regulation bottle per day on his budget for the duration of the ordeal.

In her memoirs, which flatter this imposing woman less than is her due, Alma herself remembers the occasion thus:

> Max Reinhardt commissioned Franz Werfel to write a sort of Passion according to Saint Matthew, as he expressed it to me, which was supposed to contain the entire Old Testament.
>
> But Reinhardt did not grasp the magnitude of this task.
>
> So Franz Werfel traveled to Salzburg in the summer of 1934 to discuss the whole thing once more with Max Reinhardt and Kurt Weill. A few rich Eastern Jews were also present and Werfel read them the play in its roughest state. After he had finished, one of these gentlemen walked over to Werfel and said: "That was very beautiful, Herr Werfel, but you must write an angrier god—[and here she parodies the Yiddish pronunciation] a god of vengeance!"

Why Max Reinhardt should not have grasped the magnitude of a task he had envisaged and would perform in his well-proven manner is not quite clear. (One explanation: Alma's autobiography was written after her doctors had outlawed Bénédictine for good). And whether or not Weisgal —who, by the way was the only Eastern Jew in attendance and certainly not rich—actually used these words is really immaterial. Having known him intimately, I doubt it. Anyway, he left the gathering with an understandably heavy heart and a pocketbook lightened by several advance payments, bringing with him the fruit of his pyrrhic victory which, among other prices, had been wrung from my father by conceding that the play should have yet another level beyond the two so far planned (of the living and the biblical characters): that of the heavenly hosts, inspiring Geddes to entirely new visions and expenditures.

When, two years later, my taxi drew up at the Manhattan Opera House, I got no impression that a première was being held there that night. The entrance hall was full of rubble: no sign of a box office anywhere. My primary objective was the first accessible toilet. I presumed it was located in the basement and did identify a room suggesting that purpose, though it lacked any kind of relevant installation. I came to the conclusion that the opening had been postponed an eleventh time and that my father had become weary of informing me.

After a hurried visit to the Hotel New Yorker around the corner, I reentered the theatre and made for the auditorium. In the corridors, carpets were being laid. There, I bumped into Weisgal, who, equally, did not look as though any public performance was about to take place. But it soon dawned on me that appearances were misleading. Exceptionally, the opening had *not* been postponed. My reference to the absence of sanitary appliances he impatiently brushed aside, assuring me that these secondary matters were being taken care of. What worried him primarily was the show itself. Despite all theatre superstitions, yesterday's dress rehearsal had disquieted him. It was not the fact that nothing, but absolutely nothing at all, had run right. Rather, the end of the play, or rather, its nonexistence, had shaken him. At about five o'clock in the morning, the rehearsal, indeed the entire play, had seemed to disintegrate, without having terminated in any way. What was more, he had never seen the complete play. So far as he knew, the final scenes had never been staged. That morning, my father had simply broken off the rehearsal at some point and left the house without a word. He had retired to his temporary suite at the New Yorker and remained incommunicado till 2 P.M. when he reappeared well rested and seemingly composed.

I tried to console Weisgal, pointing to the many disastrous dress rehearsals of Reinhardt's that, as a rule, had resulted in great successes and to his occasional inclination to generate deliberate moods of disaster in order to lay, as it were, the groundwork for the famous Reinhardt miracle that would inspire everyone to give his all. Meyer shrugged his shoulders fatalistically and, as he hastened off, was heard to observe: "Tonight the Jews *need* a miracle!" He was not wrong. There hardly existed a Jew in New York with a dollar to his name on whom he had not drawn his Zionist pistol and from whom he had not exacted his tithe. Weisgal had decreed a kind of special levy on the city. Whoever had paid it needed a miracle that night. Weisgal needed it even more. My father needed it most.

When I entered the orchestra, I received a jolt. Here something more malignant than the usual hectic confusion reigned. I was looking at chaos. And, in the midst of it, my father, the only one radiating equanimity, quietly observed the antics on the stage, surrounded by a stirred-up swarm of collaborators, assistants, petitioners, and hangers-on. Stage right, a fanaticized group of dancers in leotards went through ecstatic, angular motions, whipped up by a hand-clapping, foot-stamping, command-rasping choreographer—Benjamin Zemach of Palestine. His style, his persistence, but more than anything, the unmistakable national characteristics of his frenzy, visibly tore at the nerves of the commander, stage center, Norman Bel Geddes.

Geddes's presence surprised me. I knew that Weisgal, in an unaccustomed fit of authoritativeness, had fired him the year before, after having been bankrupted by him. He had been able to skirt my father's veto of this step by replacing him with his assistant, the Reinhardt pupil Harry Horner, whom my father had brought with him from Europe (and who subsequently made a career in his own right as designer and director on stage and screen in America. But, as I learned in the course of that afternoon, my father, in the last weeks of rehearsals, had been unable to resist the temptation to force Geddes down Weisgal's throat once more. His words: "Mr. Horner is excellent. But Mr. Geddes is a genius. What we need now is a genius." Though Weisgal had never understood the Jews' need of this particular genius, he once more bowed to the inevitable.

My concern for my father's economic future, my pity for Weisgal and my clear recognition of Norman's unscrupulousness in no way diminished the fascination which overcame me in that moment. In watching Geddes, I was conscious of witnessing, indeed, a genius in action, a Prometheus unbound. Improvising freely, in supreme control, he cast light and shade on the Jews' exodus from Egypt, from downstage center up through a remote desert and up and up and up toward the Promised Land—an overwhelming experience that, however, ought to have been made at one of the first lighting rehearsals and not several hours before curtain time of the première.

My skepticism about there *being* a première was deepened by the goings-on stage left, when I was told that the pandemonium there had nothing to do with the performance proper, but was caused by a mishap that had occurred that morning: an elevator, constructed by Geddes to raise the columns of the temple, had become irretrievably stuck halfway. The theatre's entire technical personnel joined in the effort to remove the ugly and action-hampering obstruction from sight. To no avail. There was no other way out than to disguise it as best they could and to direct the heavy traffic around it. My father eventually intervened personally and accomplished the unaccomplishable in short order.

Finished with this chore, he strode up the central aisle and stopped quite close to me, presumably in order to gain a perspective of the total picture. A small young man with red hair materialized from a seat nearby and addressed him in Yiddish: "Herr Professor, de Schich sind gekimmen!" ("Professor, the shoes have arrived!")

Without taking his eyes from the stage, my father asked in German: "Wie Bitte?" ("Pardon?")

"De Schich sind gekimmen!" came the answer.

The same dialogue was repeated several times until my father pleasantly turned to his interlocutor, in whom he now recognized the youngest brother of his producer: "Ach, Herr Weisgal! Ich verstehe nicht ganz. *Was* meinen Sie?" ("Ah, Mr. Weisgal! I'm afraid I don't quite understand—*what* is it you are trying to say?")

The other, at the end of his tether: "Mein Gott, Herr Professor! De Schich sind gekimmen!!!"

"*Ah!*" My father finally understood, grinning: "Die *Schuhe* sind gekommen!" and, thanking him for the information, he walked back toward the stage. Whereupon the younger Weisgal threw his arms into the air and dropped back into a seat with the loud complaint: "Ech sprech deitsch und er varsteht mach nix!" ("I speak German and he doesn't understand me!") The entire enterprise had been plagued from the start by such problems of communication.

In the meantime, it had come to open warfare on the stage: the Zemachian battalions were fighting their way to the center in the flickering chiaroscuro, only to collide with Geddes's army. At the top of his voice, he threw down the gauntlet: either Zemach went or he! Stage and auditorium split into two factions whose emotions grew steadily more violent.

My wristwatch read half past seven. Eight-thirty curtain? If I wished to hold on to this chimera and to check into my hotel uptown, clean up, change into dinner jacket and, according to plan, fetch Eleonora at her apartment, there was not a minute to lose. In the general scramble, I cut a path to my father and reached him just as he calmly decided to take over in the general disintegration. "*Herr Weisssgalll!*" His distinctive voice, so rarely heard at such volume, imposed itself over the din. The din subsided at once. Immediately Weisgal was at his side. "Please ask Herr Zemach [who spoke no English] if he would please be so kind as to relinquish the stage," my father continued softly. "There isn't much time left for Mr. Geddes to light the end of Act Three. Besides, the dance number he's rehearsing was cut last Tuesday." Fortissimo, Weisgal translated the request into Yiddish, upon which Zemach, deeply offended, retreated with his flock. Geddes, again, took charge of his Jewish slaves.

I finally greeted my father. He was overjoyed to see me. I did not want to distract him, but could not prevent him from switching his wholehearted attention to me. He insisted on having an instant report of all the more important news from California. When I reminded him how late it was, he looked at his watch and was amazed. "My God," he exclaimed, "it's time for my nap! I must get back to the hotel!" Together, we left the rehearsal still in full swing. Reaching the entrance of the New Yorker, I took my leave with a kiss on the cheek that contained all my hopes and prayers. Then I took a taxi to my own hotel. Through the rear window I saw him waving after me with a rueful smile. I waved back vigorously. He probably did lie down and had a quick half an hour's sleep. Very few people would have been able to do that under the circumstances.

My own nerves were in shreds and whatever capacity I may have retained for believing in miracles was destroyed. It was not merely the catastrophic impression of the rehearsal. What I had witnessed simply confirmed a conviction that had long been hardening within me: too many sins had been committed and had gone unpunished. Despite all efforts to exclude him, the "god of vengeance" had appeared on the scene in a manner unexpected by all.

Even Weisgal had not reckoned with him when Reinhardt returned to the States in 1935 after the Salzburg Festival. He escorted him to Geddes's studio, where the model for the set was awaiting them. The complicated construction, abounding with interchangeable parts, was exhibited on a large table at one end of the spacious room. The dimensions, Weisgal recalls, seemed to him stupendous. Reinhardt was deeply impressed, praised the work and lingered a long while, studying it in silence. Then he backed away a few steps, a move which, according to Weisgal, was bound to reduce the dimensions to the naked eye, and asked Geddes whether the proscenium could not be broadened and heightened a little. He accompanied the question with an arm movement that suggested a swimming stroke, as though he felt somewhat hemmed in. Enchanted, Geddes sprang to his model, dexterously slid several panels aside, eliminated others, and presented the result to the Professor. The Professor nodded in some satisfaction, but in a moment—to Weisgal's apprehension—put some more distance between himself and the object of his riveted attention. There followed the same arm movement, the same request and the same enchantment. This game of cautious questions, exuberant answers and deft manipulations was repeated several times, until Reinhardt had reached the other end of the room and the aperture was twice as high and wide as initially. Only then, by apparent necessity, did Reinhardt give his wholehearted approval. And only then had Weisgal the courage to inquire about the additional expense. "Twelve thousand dollars" was Geddes's brusque retort. With no inkling that this excess of an anyhow generously calculated budget would be the rule rather than the exception, Weisgal consented. The proscenium arch along with the ancient boxes of the Manhattan Opera House were torn down.

The expense turned out to be way beyond twelve thousand dollars. The building's steel girders happened not to run in the direction Geddes had assumed they would. New ones had to be erected, raising the item to sixty-five thousand dollars. As a result of the revamp, another difficulty arose: where to store the scenery not in use at any given time? Geddes, as always, had the save-all solution: one wall of the stage sector could be broken through, thus connecting it with an adjoining parking lot, which would be easy to roof over. By means of a conveyor-belt system, specially invented for the occasion by Geddes, it would be possible to shift the sets to and from the stage at will. To prevent this ingenious stroke of certain ruin, Weisgal conspired with the owner of the parking lot, who obediently turned down the proposal. But in the meantime, this dispute revealed the fact that, even if the play were to have no actors, just sets—and the cast numbered three hundred and fifty—no more than half of the decor Geddes was devising would find a place backstage, and that only behind the proscenium, so abhorrent to my father. In his despair, Weisgal decided to slip out of the Geddes-Reinhardt pincers for once: the scenery was drastically reduced and the proscenium arch reinstalled. A hundred thousand dollars was gone, and the pincers sulked.

While Geddes glumly went about the other architectural corrections of the building, Reinhardt sent from his Nirvana—he had long since departed for sunny California—his assistant, Francesco von Mendelssohn, Eleonora's brother, who, with all his extraordinary and manifold gifts, was still a rabid dilettante in the theatre. He cast the minor parts—the leading actors had been selected by Reinhardt on his way through—and began rudimentary rehearsals. Most of these activities, however, bogged down because of a basic difficulty: there was still no script. Geddes continued to build along the lines of Reinhardt's orders as transmitted through Weisgal, and Weisgal and Francesco acted in accord with a synopsis by Werfel. When the first pages of the play's final version arrived, they brought only limited illumination, the text being in German.

The translation was in the hands of the German-born American writer Ludwig Lewisohn. Literally, the results satisfied everyone—up to a point. Geographically, they did not. For any possibility of conferring with him was precluded by the fact that he lived in Vermont with his mistress in order to escape the wife lying in wait in New York with a judgment against him. Weisgal was not too unhappy about the delay of the English version. Even after it had finally become available, he preferred showing the German text to potential backers. In his own words: "The German language is fraudulent. Its sonorities usually make a greater impression on Americans, especially when the guy doesn't speak it."

It is a moot question whether it was these language problems or the idiosyncrasies of Norman Bel Geddes that caused a misunderstanding which dismayed my father when his arrival on the scene could no longer be postponed and he discovered that the area for a crucial, continuous element of the action was missing: the synagogue. According to the play, a group of Jews flees into its confines from a pogrom. The rabbi calms his congregation with a recital of examples from the Jewish past. In the course of his tales and admonitions, scenes from the Old Testament come to life in the background, while down front the victims of persecution hover, listening to their rabbi's words and debating them ardently. Whatever Geddes's motive, whether the proceedings in this—or any other—synagogue displeased him for ethnic or artistic reasons, no room for those proceedings was in evidence or planned. Only the biblical part of the action appeared to be lushly accounted for.

But my father's canonical neutrality did not go that far. As a matter of fact, he had done painstaking research for the realistic aspect of the play, steeping himself in the hallowed customs and profound emotions of Orthodox Judaism. In his quest for authenticity, he asked Weisgal to take him to a Yom Kippur service. Not aware of my father's purpose, Weisgal assumed he would be fulfilling his wishes by taking a prominent box in Carnegie Hall, where the Conservative rabbi Stephen Wise used to officiate whenever his temple could not accommodate an extra-large number of worshippers. Apart from not being able to gather the impressions he sought in this worldly atmosphere, the hollow pathos of the ceremony went against my father's grain. At the first opportunity, he nudged Weisgal and whispered that he wanted to leave. Outside, he said: "*This* kind of theatre *I* do better!" Weisgal's esteem for Wise was high, but that for his director even higher. He took him to a shabby hall on the second floor of a Lower East Side tenement where poor Orthodox Jews prayed and read the Prophets. This experience was later reflected in the temple scenes—which, for the moment, however, lacked a home.

It *had* to be provided. But where? The stage was fully utilized. The orchestra pit, with the addition of the first nine rows of seats, seemed to offer the only solution. Into this controversy the authors, Werfel and Weill, burst from Europe, inflaming a further, more fundamental one: was *The Road of Promise* a musical drama or a drama with music? The polemic failed to interest my father. But he naturally supported Werfel's insistence on the synagogue set. Weill threatened departure and withdrawal of the score. Weisgal worried about the loss of the most profitable seats. Matriarch Alma's indignation could only be appeased by a double ration of Bénédictine.

The "save-all" compromise came, once again, from Geddes: it was old-fashioned, he lectured—and here he could count on Reinhardt's backing—to have musicians in the pit. On the legitimate stage—and here, in turn, he was sure of Weill's support—there were rarely more than twenty-five at one's disposal, and these usually left much to be desired. He brought up the name of his friend Leopold Stokowski, who was presently experimenting with stereophonic recording. This could be the occasion to bring the results to the world for the first time: "We don't need a live orchestra at all. We'll record the score at the RCA studios in Trenton with a hundred-man orchestra and pipe the music into the Manhattan Opera House via loudspeakers. It will cost much less than paying a band every night for years and it will ensure an incomparably finer rendition."

The proposal was accepted, but had, as everything in this theatrical singularity did, its drawbacks. Not that Stokowski's interpretation or the technical standard of the recording proved disappointing. But neither ever reached the ears of a solitary spectator. Mr. Petrillo, omnipotent boss of the musicians' union, decreed that, whichever music was being used, a twenty-eight-piece orchestra per performance had to be hired and housed. And since a second complication—secretly anticipated by Weill—arose and no one was able to solve the problem of coordinating the singing on the various levels of the gigantic stage with a mechanical accompaniment, Stokowski's discs were abandoned. They had cost sixty-eight thousand dollars.

The excavations necessitated by the building of the synagogue turned out to be even more expensive. While this labor was progressing, my father, one afternoon, asked Sam Jaffe, who played the Adversary, to descend to the bottom of what had once been the pit. Then, watched with grave forebodings by Weisgal, my father climbed up to the two highest dress circles, consecutively, and called down to Jaffe to stretch and crane his neck. Despite Jaffe's contortions, there was no trace of him from Reinhardt's vantage point. Reinhardt nodded in what Weisgal took for satisfaction, which made him even more nervous, as he feared some new idea of the Professor's was going to be put into effect by Geddes, in his inimitable way. But the answer to Weisgal's pertinent question depressed him even more: the Professor had found confirmation of his suspicion that the action taking place in the synagogue would forever be hidden from the upper circles. Nobody had checked the sight lines.

Nevertheless, the digging had to continue, since the only way to enter the synagogue was from below. There came the day—up on the stage, impervious to the racket, the rehearsal was in high gear—when the drillers hit Manhattan's bedrock and a mighty geyser shot up, deluging everything and everyone and submerging the entire undertaking to the last of the four hundred and fifty thousand dollars that it had cost until then. For all participants but Weisgal it meant the death of the enterprise. He went into bankruptcy and moved with his family to a slum hotel in the upper Eighties on New York's West Side. The rest was scattered anew in the diaspora.

But indefatigable Weisgal brought them all back to Zion again. He accomplished the astonishing feat of raising another hundred and fifty thousand dollars, and in 1937 he resurrected his pet project for the *n*th time. It was then that *The Road of Promise* settled down to *The* (more apt) *Eternal Road*. This obstinacy almost cost him a harmony he had never jeopardized so far: with his family. Although his wife, Shirley, had resigned herself to their ruination and to the probability that the second-generation Weisgals would have to do without a higher education, she had issued one ultimatum: her brother's stamp collection, on which he had toiled a life long, must under no circumstances be touched! But during one of their frugal family meals, Meyer and his brother-in-law sat facing each other in an electrically charged atmosphere. The eyes of the brother-in-law restively tried to avoid the fateful stare of his vis-à-vis. The observant Mrs. Weisgal harshly admonished her mate: "Stop that, Meyer! Stop it or you'll never see me again!" Meyer did not stop, and did not say anything. His eyes pierced the sporadic glances of his brother-in-law—until the latter had enough, put knife and fork aside and gave up with a shrug: "All right, take it already, Meyer!" Shirley's outcry did not influence the transaction. Nor did she remove herself from Meyer's presence. He liquidated the collection and at once began to rebuild the temple. On Kommer's insistence, Weisgal was compelled to take on a co-producer, the experienced Crosby Gaige (whose experience was no match for Weisgal's determination).

Recasting became necessary. Isaac's son, played by Sidney Lumet, had outgrown his costume. And the diligent efforts of my father to teach him the right inflection of the word "Father!" for the scene of the sacrifice, the only line in his part, had been for naught. The costume could have been altered, the untimely growth of a beard concealed by makeup, but what to do about the change of voice?

All these scenes, none of which I had witnessed and probably would not have believed if I had, had been whirling in my head since I said goodbye to my father a little more than an hour earlier. When I approached the Manhattan Opera House with Eleonora among a multitude of taxis and chauffeured limousines and saw the bejeweled crowd *en grande toilette* streaming into the theatre, I thought for a moment that this scene too was part of the phantasmagoria. Once inside, a pleasant surprise awaited me: there was a box office, there were carpets and drapes, there were ticket-takers and ushers. Programs, on the other hand, were missing. (Later on, I also had occasion to ascertain that urinals, toilet bowls and sinks had been installed where I had looked for them in vain that afternoon.)

Until intermission, I was happily spared the knowledge of a further disaster, one which could have prevented the show from opening at the very last minute. Half an hour before curtain time, the fire department turned up, banning the performance because regulations had been flouted outrageously. These ill tidings reached Weisgal in the hotel room next door, which he had rented for the night. Just about to change into a dinner jacket, he was preoccupied with a different, though no less vexing problem: Shirley had forgotten to bring his patent-leather shoes, and he had the highly original idea of lining up all the bellboys of the New Yorker in order to try on their footwear. Whether he solved *this* problem I do not know. The other he did: within twenty minutes, he located Mayor Fiorello La Guardia, tearing him away from one of his joyrides on a fire engine. Accompanied by Fire Chief John J. McElliott, La Guardia arrived at the theatre just in time to wage a spirited battle and give the green light to the curtain after taking due notice of the cultural significance of the occasion, masterfully pleaded by Weisgal. To appease his experts, he ordered that forty additional firemen must guard each performance—another unforeseen and considerable item of the weekly budget.

Meanwhile, the opening-night audience, representing New York at its most elegant, waited with merciful patience for the lights to dim. I was not patient. Nor was I impatient for the verdict. Eleonora waited devotedly for the miracle. And lo and behold, among persistent coughing spells—to round it all out, the grippe was raging in town—and after a few waves of goading applause, it happened: the curtain rose. The miracle lasted three whole acts. (The play had four.) They were of extraordinary power and poetry, moving and uplifting. The Jewish destiny was captured to its very core and, yet, the overall effect was universal. Although the musicians had been assigned a room far removed from the stage and out of sight of it, and the conductor was able to maintain contact with the players only by way of an intricate relay system, man and machine worked with unmatched precision.

The climax was the end of the third act: Moses leading his people into the Promised Land—and it looked as though they were mounting into the sky. It was breathtaking, the audience so engrossed that it forgot the hour. It was midnight by the time of the main intermission. Eleonora and I walked the corridors, out onto the bustling sidewalk and back inside again, as though in a dream. The evening so far was plainly a triumph. True, there had been indications of a certain restiveness in the balcony, as the audience up there could not follow the recurring scenes in the synagogue, but the hypnotic effect of opening-night excitement prevented an eruption. New York's smart set luxuriated in unmitigated enthusiasm.

What ensued after the much-too-protracted interval is far more difficult to describe. Weisgal had attempted it, but not done justice to it. It was not just that, suddenly, absolutely nothing seemed to go right any more. The action dragging across the plethora of platforms and ramps and struggling along in the cavernous depths seemed to lose all contour and context. Where was the ax, I asked myself, my father used to wield so deftly? The night advanced relentlessly without reaching an end. The audience was drained, physically and mentally, unable to absorb another single impression. The viscous flow of the final scenes—were they really the final scenes?—made it, at last, conscious of time, of colds, of empty stomachs. Both play and performance melted away in a sort of haze. Entrances and exits seemed no longer lit, the actors no longer alive, the doings no longer to make sense. Stage and auditorium were in a coma, but somehow resisted the relief of death. What, at last, charitably put a stop to it I do not remember. At some undetermined time, around 2 A.M., the play silted up and the last spectator fled. Backstage, no one spoke to anyone else. When I fetched my father, we too were silent: Weisgal stood transfixed among the debris of the second temple, which the public had never laid eyes on.

The wake was held at the Colony restaurant. During the intermission, Raimund von Hofmannsthal had called the headwaiter and arranged for it to stay open. I was annoyed to find further confirmation of the distance my father had steadfastly maintained between himself and this venture. Contrary to the custom of a lifetime, not one member of the company, not even Weisgal, had been invited. Max Reinhardt's friends at the table had never looked upon this Jewish venture as one worthy of him. Kekol's schnorring inroads on Czernowitz's jealousy guarded castle *privé* had turned Kommer into an enemy of Weisgal. (He actually dissuaded some of his prize "customers" from investing in his client's show.) Nobody bore my father any grudge for having wandered off onto "the wrong side of the tracks," because he was Max Reinhardt. But they were tactful enough to ignore *The Eternal Road*. It was not mentioned once during supper.

At 5 A.M., the persistent ringing of my telephone woke me from a leaden, alcohol-weighted sleep. What was going on at the other end of the line was, at first, hard to make out. But one thing was clear: wherever it was happening, alcohol was still flowing. Francesco's tongue was so thick and his soul so full that I could make neither head nor tail of his message. The few words I thought I did understand were swallowed up by the bacchanalian noise in the background. And then, all was drowned out by the earsplitting, unmistakable word-made-flesh. Weisgal was attempting to gain the others' attention at the highest pitch of his badly impaired voice. Finally, he came to the phone and croaked: "Come on over to the New Yorker, Gottfried! We're all here, your father too! We're celebrating!" I groaned.

Half an hour later, I entered the hotel's banquet rooms, which an incurable optimist must have reserved way in advance. It was a lunatic asylum. Or had I made an error? Was it New Year's Eve? Weisgal, every strand of his frizzy hair galvanized, stood on a long table strewn with empty glasses, half-empty glasses and turned-over whiskey and champagne bottles, both arms stretched wide, in each fist a bundle of newspapers, brandishing them wildly. One could see that he was still bellowing, but one could not hear him. For once, even *his* vocal organ was on strike. Every morning paper had been panegyrical. The dean of New York's critics, Brooks Atkinson, wrote in *The New York Times:*

> After an eternity of postponements *The Eternal Road* has finally arrived at the Manhattan Opera House, where it opened last evening. Let it be said at once that the ten postponements are understood and forgiven. Out of the heroic stories of old Jewish history Max Reinhardt and his many assistants have evoked a glorious pageant of great power and beauty. Call it pageant, if you will, or call it opera, spectacle, fantasy or profound religious teaching, for it is all of these things in equal measure. It is fundamentally the mystic story of man's heritage under the laws of Almighty God. For God is the hero of this imaginative telling of the Torah and Old Testament fables about the ancients who learned through suffering and anguish how the earth must be trod.
>
> Always the votary of grandiose theatre conceptions, Dr. Reinhardt has found in the Bible stories a subject that fits his hand. Franz Werfel has molded the great episodes of early Jewish history into a large-scale script. After tearing out about half of the venerable Manhattan Opera House, Dr. Reinhardt and Norman Bel Geddes, who is a superman in his own right, have constructed an enormous series of ramps and platforms that rise in supplication to the portals of heaven. In what must have been an orchestra pit in the sober days of old, a synagogue is now in session, crowded with Jews who have huddled there while a mob of persecutors howls outside. At the reading table stands their rabbi who is comforting them with stories of the agony their forebears passed through. On the plains and hills that fill the depths of the opera house these stories are acted, danced and sung.

> The rise of the stages symbolizes the periods in the history of mankind's relationship to God.

The *Daily News* accorded the show four stars. Both reviews would have sufficed to guarantee that *The Road* would be truly *eternal* on Broadway. But the afternoon press was no less flattering. *Time* magazine heaped praise on Reinhardt and Bel Geddes. Joseph Wood Krutch had this to say in *The Nation*:

> . . . it is the spectacle to which everything else is subservient and which demonstrates again that the reputations of Reinhardt and Bel Geddes are actually based upon a great deal more than the showmanship of the circuses. For one thing the crowds are never merely crowds, and no matter how complicated the groupings may be one never loses the sense of form and organization. For another, there is inexhaustible variety; so that spectacle, which ordinarily grows so quickly monotonous, seems continually fresh. . . .
>
> In derogation I have heard it said of *The Eternal Road* that "the movies do this sort of thing better." Nothing could be wider of the mark for the simple reason that such spectacles as this have no relation whatsoever to the realistic spectacles in which the moving picture excels. Nothing could, as a matter of fact, be less realistic. The ancestor of *The Eternal Road* is the medieval mystery play, and the method is the method of convention and symbol. What we see represented is not a person or an event. It is always an idea. And the measure of the art is the adequacy of a very special iconography.

Of course, there were also the few dissenting voices, and, as was Reinhardt's lot everywhere, they came from the ultra-intellectual corner. Stark Young in *The New Republic* gave reluctant approval, feeling that "Reinhardt's expert engineering" crowded itself between play and audience. And George Jean Nathan—taking up, as it were, the cudgel for Alfred Kerr, Karl Kraus and Herbert Ihering of yore—postulated that "a true poet like Werfel cannot be guided by other men's fancies" and concluded that he was far too good for hackwork à la Hollywood. But the overwhelming majority was eulogistic. How had it been possible for the miracle to have happened this time?

After rising a second time on January 5, 1937, I was given the simple explanation: In order to get their copy in on time, most of the critics had left the Manhattan Opera House after Act III. Whether this telling fact was the immediate cause for cutting Act IV or whether, for that matter, anybody ever gave a specific order for the elimination (my father declined to commit himself), it is a matter of record that no one ever saw Act IV again.

The delivery, then, had been hazardous, but wondrously successful. Keeping the child alive proved much more hazardous and much *less* successful. At 4 P.M., with the next twelve performances sold out and the advance sale booming, Weisgal rolled up his sleeves to save it. The computation was as shattering as it was simple: The maximum gross per week amounted to twenty-six thousand dollars, the weekly "nut" to thirty-one thousand dollars. Theoretically. In actual fact, *The Eternal Road* was condemned to lose seven thousand dollars a week, rather than five. And not because audience interest subsided—the show remained sold out till the last performance—but because every evening and every matinee the two "blind" upper circles revolted and demanded their money back.

The all-but-sucked-dry investors refused to donate more blood. Many of them had contributed unwillingly in the first place, having been bludgeoned into doing it by Weisgal's powers of persuasion. An example was a Mr. Strelzin, a hypochondriac of means who, when in bed—a frequent location of his—promised Meyer the fulfillment of nearly all his wishes. But, hardly back on his feet—which, too, happened occasionally—he regularly suffered from amnesia. Meyer put it this way: "Horizontally, the man is worth a million. Vertically, not a cent." Luckily, during his horizontal phases, Strelzin used to be draped with conspicuously beautiful ladies whose desire to appear in a Broadway show Weisgal knew expertly how to convert into cash. On that score, however, he ran into strong interference from Reinhardt, who barred the stage to these attractive, but invariably talentless, creatures. Weisgal found a solution: Since males and females in an Orthodox synagogue are separated by a heavy grill, why not place Strelzin's harem behind it? Weisgal's answer to the irate question as to where his protégées had been at the première did not satisfy Strelzin. This tap, henceforth, stayed turned off.

Weisgal raised the money to cover the deficit week in, week out. For eight months. He talked Cardinal Hayes, archbishop of the New York diocese, into lifting the ban on Catholics attending the theatre during Lent. He paid fewer and fewer salaries and royalties and borrowed cash from the unlikeliest sources—including a waitress at his flea-bag hotel. The collected unions, suppliers, technical and office personnel, actors and authors went into litigation against him. So, even, did Max Reinhardt.

A Catholic organization had declared its readiness to take over the house, for one performance for a fixed sum. So, one gray afternoon, three nuns visited Weisgal's office to finalize the agreement. They could not have chosen a more inopportune hour. The unpaid-for interior decorations were being hauled away by court order at that very moment. Weisgal, face buried in his hands, his elbows resting heavily on the desk—with the chair on which he sat the only two remaining pieces of furniture in the room—was still racking his brain over how to raise the curtain that night. It was, therefore, not too surprising that the nuns got a reception they neither expected nor deserved. His language was always extremely colorful. This time, it embraced the entire spectrum. Aghast, the ladies fled—colliding with the moving men on their way back for desk and chair.

New visitors. For a change, delegates of a Jewish organization. They were lugging in a heavy plaque which they wished to present to Meyer Weisgal in honor of his accomplishments for the People of Israel. By now, his directives were more precise: in unambiguous terms he conveyed to them what they could do with the plaque and where they could do it. But the consternation of the injured emissaries promptly brought him back to his senses. Apologizing profusely for his behavior and for not being able to offer them a seat, he picked up the receiver from the floor, called Maurice Levin, one of his embittered angels, and congratulated him on receiving so exalted an honor. It took him no time at all to fix an appointment with the increasingly "angelic" object of his flattery and to arrange for the solemn presentation of the plaque—but not before securing a firm commitment for the now obviously due check. A second call to the head of the organization that had selected him for the accolade resulted in a quick remelting process, changing the name on the plaque from Weisgal to Levin. *The Eternal Road* had just been granted another reprieve when the three nuns returned to face a much more amenable Weisgal. They told him they had sought consolation in a nearby church and prayed for his soul—with the desired result. A further reprieve.

But there arrived the day when *The Eternal Road* ran out of reprieves. Even Weisgal could not raise another penny. Every third New Yorker was his creditor. Every fifth New Yorker was trying to drag him into court. It was the irrevocable end. But first, all the damaged participants organized a final matinee for charitable purposes and donated their services. The beneficiary: Weisgal. It was one thing to litigate against him, another to see him totally destroyed. This last performance, too, began with a rebellion and ended with an ovation. Weisgal was called before the curtain time after time.

The curtain calls, the applause, the jubilation never stopped. A stage manager appeared with a telegram from Hollywood. The sender was creditor and plaintiff Max Reinhardt. After a cascade of tears, Weisgal collected himself sufficiently to read the message aloud; then—the final blow—all the lights went out. Only one person knew that the cause of this Reinhardtian effect was not a short circuit: the broken man stage center. The Department of Water and Power had sent long-enough reminders, had sued, and now patience and current were exhausted. Sam Jaffe lit a match and handed it to the next actor, who passed it on to the next, and so forth. More matches were lit and a long chain of tiny flames was relayed to Weisgal, who, in their light, and in a choked voice, read the following words to the hushed, motionless house:

> MY DEAR FRIEND, THE GREAT WORK THAT YOU AND I BROUGHT TO LIFE NOW LIES RIGIDLY, MUTELY ON THE DARK STAGE. YOU SUCCEEDED, EVEN THOUGH TEMPORARILY, IN INTERRUPTING THE DANCE AROUND THE GOLDEN CALF AND RAISING THE TABLETS ANEW. BUT NOW WE MUST RESIGN OURSELVES. THE LIGHT THAT WE LIT TOGETHER IN THE MANHATTAN OPERA HOUSE WILL SHINE UNDIMMED IN THE HISTORY OF THE THEATRE AND OF THE JEWISH PEOPLE. IN FRIENDSHIP, MAX REINHARDT.

Max Reinhardt had made his peace with his own fate.

OCTOBER 12, 1943
(continued)

The light that Papa lit in the heart of this man still burns today. [It went out, finally, in 1978.] But I have a sure way to get his two-track mind onto a third. Surprise him with news that Meehan and I have drafted comedy based on his frenzied producership. Read excerpts aloud. Weisgal is so taken with his own zany image he forgets his resolution to get through to Papa.

Lovely, long evening with Papa. He completely at ease and, for a change, the one to initiate conversation. We become his confidants about people and things significant in his life, about creators he idealized, above all Shakespeare and Rembrandt, tragicomedy and dramatic chiaroscuro, with man always as focal point. In music Bach receives the highest honors. Unmatched depth with unmatched clarity. Content and form in perfect union. And what about living artists? Who are his ideals among them? Few. Very few. Frankly, he must say, his has been a lean time for original creation. Good for adaptation. What originality did emerge came, conversely, through dehumanizing the artist's subject—a destructive development according to his lights. Abstraction, atonality go against his grain. In music, too, Papa's has been more a time of brilliant interpretation. Conductors outshone composers. Take Toscanini: naïve, passionate, exacting and virile, head and shoulders above all others. Rarely are the exacting passionate, the passionate virile, the virile naïve. An awesome combination.

Together we remember when Papa bought me a standing-room ticket in the Berlin Opera for an astronomic sum while he sat, white tie and tails, in the orchestra. [It was a guest performance of Milan's La Scala with Toscanini conducting Il Trovatore. Impassioned bravos shook the walls after Lauri Volpi's stretta, went on to ten thunderous minutes of handclapping, cheering and stamping in the hope of an encore. Toscanini, who permitted repetitions only when prescribed by the composer, stood immovable as Gibraltar. Helpless, the tenor bridged the embarrassment by gesturing apologetically toward the glowering maestro until, like a knife slicing through Bel Paese, he cut off the ovation and stormed on with Verdi.] Papa follows up with the reminiscence of when he and Toscanini stood chatting idly [in French, which neither of them could really speak, but which was an acceptable compromise for a non-German-speaking Italian and a non-Italian-speaking German] in lobby of the Salzburg Festival House. And Toscanini, without preamble, grabbed his arm, pulled open the center door of the auditorium and propelled him into a rehearsal of Bruno Walter with the Vienna Philharmonic. Like mechanical toys, one musician after the other stopped playing, eyes fixed on grandstand play in the back. Baffled by the orchestral freeze uncalled for by the score, Walter turned around and discovered the culprits. On cue, Toscanini yanked my father back into the lobby, not, however, before hissing out—this time in distinct German: "WEAK!" A tale made to order for Eleonora: her two heroes united in one anecdote!

Eleonora serves Papa his "special": grapefruit juice spiked with a thimble-ful of gin, me a king-sized scotch. . . .

What about other acting greats? Ah, there's that actor of absolute, original genius: Chaplin. Again: laughter and tears, sense and nonsense, side by side. Among Papa's colleagues no one made a deeper impression on him than Josef Kainz [the Viennese David Garrick]. He says he learned more, in every area, from this fascinating, complicated personality than from anyone else he met in his formative years: from fencing to locution, from understanding to helping others understand.

But transcending the art of acting was—the godchild's heart flows over—Duse, Eleonora's godmother. Not because her dramatized emotions were superbly controlled, her pauses impeccably timed or her gestures thoughts come to life and every word in her mouth pure poetry, but because on the stage she bared her soul. And her soul was divine. What an irony, he thinks, that it should have left her body in a most undivine terminal: Pittsburgh, Pennsylvania.

Papa is pro Duse, anti Sarah Bernhardt; pro theatre, anti theatricalism. Curiously enough, tonight, he takes, for him, quite vehement stands: pro Wagner, anti Brahms; pro Dostoevski, anti Tolstoi; pro Stendhal, anti Balzac; pro Twelfth Night and The Winter's Tale, anti The Tempest and Coriolanus.

The name Michael Chekhov comes up again, his dream Hamlet. Chekhov's teaching, however, is another cup of tea. Papa hoots with laughter at the recollection of our six-foot-six friend Count Friedrich Ledebur [glamorous black sheep descended from Holy Roman Empire nobility], a student in the Chekhov drama school at Ridgefield, Connecticut, advancing his courtship of heiress Beatrice Straight, substantial sponsor of the school and starry-eyed amateur [since matured to an Oscar-winner] by enrolling as a pupil. Chekhov is a Stanislavski disciple. Ledebur, a gentleman horse trainer, trailer dweller and nonconformist who bathes by rolling in desert sand. When Papa asked him what he was doing in class, he answered: "Growing." The first exercise Chekhov prescribed for him was to stretch until he felt himself reaching to heaven. [The method didn't work. Ledebur didn't gain an inch—physically or artistically—and he didn't marry the heiress.]

And Stanislavski himself? A unique director and a remarkable stage personality. Never would Papa forget the impact of the guest performances of the Moscow Art Theatre in Berlin. A perfectly integrated troupe, a most profoundly thought out interpretation and a meticulous reliving of human emotions, complete dedication to art.

And Stanislavski's "method"? "Methods per se are sterile. What is good for one is bad for another. Genius finds imitators, not heirs. Spark cannot be generated systematically." Papa is all for exacting rehearsal—calls himself a fanatical rehearser—but not as an objective in itself. Unlike Stanislavski and the fraternity to whom his method is sacrosanct, Papa does not subscribe to arbitrary exercises in concentration or to a general approach to specific aims. He veers away from the group-reading rehearsals, improvisations and theoretical discussions that were Stanislavski's precious stuff, because he, Papa, has no need of them for his be-all and end-all.

Papa does not pave a long, winding road in order that, at its end, the actor may "find himself." He maintains it is the director's task to guide the actor in the desired direction. The director's presence at rehearsal and his contribution to it—if he is a craftsman—make the involved explorations and time-consuming experimentation of a Stanislavski superfluous. Having started as an amateur of means, Stanislavski came naturally to his protracted method. He needed to find himself and he could afford it. Then he came to believe in it and had admirable results with it. Stanislavski: no one else. His own approach—surely not one to imitate, either—being of a more pragmatic nature, varies constantly with the respective personalities and problems encountered. "Jump into the water and swim!" has always been Papa's credo, not: "Try out every conceivable style of swimming and then adapt yourself to the one most suited to your individuality."

His favorite scenic designer? There are two: Oskar Strnad and Norman Bel Geddes.

Enemies? Critics at large. Karl Kraus was the most dedicated. Was the hatred mutual? No. When he heard of Kraus's death in 1936, he was struck by a feeling of loneliness. Dedicated enemies are even less easy to replace than friends. And Kerr? Clever, a bright littérateur, dialectically effective, a feeling for the theatre—especially for its distaff side—but intolerably affected and erratic.

And, between us, what about his clash with Brahm? His forehead clouds.

His differences with his discoverer, mentor and predecessor shadowed his life. To branch out on his own, he firmly believes, was his prerogative, more, was vital to his development. But it was a knife in his conscience that Brahm suffered by it. Because he did not deserve to be repaid with pain. Naturally, the pain wasn't willfully inflicted. Still, it was sharp and lasting.

A talk cutting across so many boundaries on an October night in 1943 must ultimately touch on politics: Zionism runs counter to his deep-rooted belief in assimilation, though Weizmann is very close to his heart. He finds Roosevelt superior to Churchill, moral values to rhetoric. Here we differ. To my way of thinking, Churchill's rhetoric is sublimated action, Roosevelt's morals often politics. We're in accord that the most intelligent commentator on the current political scene is Walter Lippmann.

It's four o'clock in the morning, an hour when my mind starts feeling mosquito-bitten. But Papa, fresh as a lettuce leaf, starts expounding his theory of individual rhythm: Everyone has, arising out of his nature, his own rhythm in life. It must be recognized, felt and obeyed. To resist it is to swim against the stream of one's existence, a foolhardy and futile effort. This is not to say that one should drift. One must move with the stream, take advantage of fast currents and always keep in a position to seize the chances that, accidentally, are swept one's way. Accident is the architect of life.

Intentional Accidents

. . . In the afternoon I go to the Café Monopol. In the back, several tables have been bunched together. That's where the actors sit. Heaps of newspapers are piled up on the chairs. The fat, black newsprint is being burrowed through. One's daily information is being amassed and later serves the boasts in the saloon. Empty phrases and stale jokes whirl about in stage Esperanto, that strange brew of old plaster-and-greasepaint wit and spoofed familiar quotations. Always at the expense of others, the jokes ambush from the rear, flying like snowballs into the back of one's neck. After an opening a paper is impossible to get. Bad reviews are, of course, read more than once and when the target arrives, he is received with sarcastic reserve. One leaves the paper in question on the table for him, smiles meaningfully and keeps silent. A well-known anecdote has an actor sitting in such a café, triumphantly poring over a gazette. His colleague asks him: "Why are you so cheerful? Did you get a rave?" "No," is the characteristic answer, "you're being panned."

THUS, MY FATHER VENTED his aversion to the institution of the coffeehouse, entering these remarks in his diaries of 1896. The "Berliner" Reinhardt remained hostile to this Viennese, Turkish-imported tradition his life long. Except for its variations on the Piazza San Marco or on the Champs-Elysées, where the setting is the attraction, I never saw him in such surroundings. He hated talk for the sake of talking, the talking to death of problems that cannot be solved that way, of tasks that need doing, not debating. Nevertheless, as a young actor, he spent several hours every day sitting in one of the cafés around Unter den Linden and Friedrichstrasse (a busy intersection). How come?

Well, first of all, an actor needs to "abreact," to simmer down emotionally and mentally, after a rehearsal or performance. If he does not drink or play cards or indulge in other habits resulting in hangovers or loss of irreplaceable funds, the Central European coffeehouse is an ideal place for the purpose. He does not want to be alone, yet he wants to be *left* alone. In his furnished flat, he might start to brood or be driven to work or to sex. No relaxation there. (Once relaxed, he has nothing against these preoccupations.) The reluctant young coffeehouse habitué, Max Reinhardt, does not care to listen to himself or others. Oh, he likes to listen, but not to professional talkers, no matter how amusing now and then. He has not yet reached the stage where he can afford the luxury of amusement. His instinct tells him he must use his time well. He seeks no distraction. Nor will he grow into the type of artist who is all wrapped up in his roles, lives in garrets, works in a studio, will attain immortality at his writing table or, for that matter, at the coffeehouse table (where some of the best Central European literature was born). He will produce art through *others*. He does not as yet know how, nor even which art. But he has the premonition and the will. And his premonition probably tells him that he is going to need people. People will be his medium and he will be dependent on their cooperation. The coffeehouse is full of people.

He waits. Not altogether passively. (He is never passive. Even his gift for listening is not passive. It has often been said of him that he used to listen dynamically.) He hopes himself to *bring about* the tasks in store for him; the tasks, he feels, are *in the air*. He hopes to catch them on the fly, as it were. In the coffeehouse it is possible simultaneously to remain anonymous and be on the *qui vive*, without necessarily being bored (he abhorred boredom). It is possible to submerge, while remaining ever-ready to surface and spring to the occasion. The young actor Max Reinhardt—a pupa existence—sits among acquaintances and strangers and keeps to himself, itching for the accident he is determined to attract magnetically, the accident, he is fiercely convinced, that will happen and bring him luck.

He was surely not the only one yearning for the big chance. But perhaps he was the most awake, the most concentrated and, when the moment came, the most persevering. He was obsessed with potentiality. His diaries of that period differ little from the reminiscences of the other neophytes in the theatre around him. His growing pains, dreams, impressions are similar to theirs. It is, then, not surprising that in the years 1895 to 1900 it was left completely open as to *who* in the circle, if any, would solve the problems, realize the dreams, sublimate the raw material they were all so deeply engrossed in. There exists contemporary testimony as to his marked acting talent and personal cachet. But that he might have the stuff for more than a competent actor's or effective actor-manager's career no one guessed. It was, indeed, impossible to guess, since he himself had not, as yet, discovered in what extraordinary way and measure his gift would exceed the others', much less found the opportunity to prove it. For he would, after all, not exceed his peers as actor or actor-manager, but in a vocation he first had to create for himself.

I have said in another context that my mother, with love's flair, was the first to detect his hidden qualities. Even as the contours of his leadership became more sharply defined, his closest collaborators were not really aware of the process taking place before their eyes. When it could no longer be overlooked, the majority deemed it inexplicable. This led to the oddest theories and accusations: there was something fishy about the entire thing; Reinhardt had not always been aboveboard. It was said that he had appropriated—or misappropriated—everything from others who were too slow or too maladroit to exhibit their talents or, as one would put it today, to "sell themselves." Circumspection and shyness were interpreted as craftiness and deviousness.

His "betrayal" of Otto Brahm, to whom he admittedly owed his start, remained the talk of the town for seven years (till the embittered Brahm died after a heroic, but hopeless rearguard fight against his former ward and triumphal successor) and never completely subsided. The case of the actor Friedrich Kayssler is another one in point. Kayssler was Reinhardt's best friend and closest colleague, of the same age, but intellectually more mature, better educated, firmer in character and poise and, being North German, more at home in Berlin. He started out as the leader of that younger flock in Brahm's stable and Reinhardt looked up to him. Kayssler's tragedy, which he could never understand or reconcile himself to, was that his protégé would eclipse him, a source of continuing repressed acerbity between the friends and of malignant gossip about Reinhardt's ingratitude and ruthlessness, even though Kayssler remained a respected, if somewhat colorless, pillar of the Reinhardt ensemble for decades.

A particularly dark blot on Reinhardt's ascent was, in many eyes, his relationship with another comrade of his earliest days, a fellow actor who left Brahm's company and joined the group openly before Reinhardt: Richard Vallentin. Because of this seniority, he was the nominal director of the group's initial productions, including its first hit, *The Lower Depths,* in which both he and Reinhardt played. Another member of the cast, the actor Eduard von Winterstein, recalls in his memoirs, *My Life and My Time*:

> One thing is certain: Even though Reinhardt did not direct this play officially and even though none of us had an inkling of his directorial talent, in his quiet, unobtrusive and modest, but therefore all the more persuasive manner, he had the strongest influence on the genesis of these performances, without our and perhaps even his being conscious of it.

Once free of his contract with Brahm, Reinhardt also began directing "officially" for his company. He was promptly charged with relegating Vallentin to second place. When he refused to let the disgruntled Vallentin go, people said he feared the other's competition and preferred to drown him in his wake. When he finally accepted his resignation, they pointed their accusing finger at another "betrayal." The fact that Reinhardt's star was on a spectacular rise and Vallentin's steadily declining had no effect on the legend that Vallentin was the real directorial talent of the time. If that had been so, Reinhardt could no more have suppressed him than Brahm could have suppressed Reinhardt.

Ever since those salad days, a slight whiff of charlatanism has hovered about my father. In that vein, in 1913, Friedrich Freksa, author of *Sumurûn* (who resented that Reinhardt never put on one of his "serious" plays), wrote a vitriolic, frankly anti-Semitic roman à clef about him: *Erwin Bernstein's Theatrical Mission.* In it, Bernstein/Reinhardt is depicted as a virtuoso in mental thievery, as a sensation-seeker and callous exploiter of erotic liaisons for profit and career, shrinking from no scandal and, in particular, defrauding a kind old lady enamored of him, thereby ruining her. A roman à clef with no secret drawers to unlock? No, it is not that simple. The attack was below the belt, but the target was vulnerable.

No denying that he learned from everyone and absorbed everything stirring around him. And if some of those he observed and listened to spoke and acted more sophisticatedly than he, it was, nevertheless, he who would succeed in making something more unusual and effective out of what was being said and done. Was it his fault that few expected leadership from him and that he surprised the others as well as himself?

The scandal Freksa takes aim at concerns the talented, pretty actress Camilla Eibenschütz, one of my father's leading ladies (Ophelia, Juliet, Lysistrata) and leading lady-friends. (My mother accused him of having "possessed this creature during rehearsal in the proscenium box.") In Freksa's exposé her thus-besmirched replica was wed to the seducer's chief financial backer and the shameful act ruined both the marriage and the prosperity of the theatre. In sober fact, lovely Camilla met son and heir Wolfgang of German newspaper-chain tycoon Adolf Huck, main shareholder in the Reinhardt corporation, after achieving her double leading-lady status. Wolfgang Huck demanded she renounce her stage career as a condition of marriage. The condition was accepted and the Deutsches Theater lost a star (and, I suppose, sooner or later, my father was looking for someone else to share the proscenium box with). In any event, the theatre's financial resources flowing from the Huck fortune were never endangered. On the contrary, Wolfgang Huck remained a staunch supporter of Reinhardt's Berlin enterprises to the bitter end, a record that came in handy in an awkward de-Nazification proceeding after World War II.

The real name of Freksa's "poor, duped, kindhearted old lady" was Emmy Loewenfeld. She played an important part in Max Reinhardt's life, having contributed twelve thousand marks needed to pay the stipulated penalty for his breach of contract with Brahm. She also invested in his first independent efforts. According to my mother, she was very rich and very ugly. Judging from his history in this particular regard, the latter circumstance alone should have precluded the affair suggested by Freksa. Enthusiastic as she undoubtedly was about the young visionary—and perhaps even smitten with him—she probably did not desire an affair either, since, from all reports, she was a very clever woman. That my father encouraged her generosity and generously used his charms, I do not doubt for a second. And it is also true that her husband balked at her extravagance and excessive infatuation with the theatre and sued her in court. The author concludes his two-volume diatribe with the "deserved" collapse and squalid end of the evil megalomaniac. It is a conclusion the subsequent course of events failed to confirm.

It was also an accident, though not intentional, that enabled Max Reinhardt, as junior member of Brahm's ensemble, to find himself in that jumping-off position in the first place, a position which for most other actors meant the top rung of the ladder. To get there, it usually took even the most talented a quarter of a lifetime, by a trek which, in the professional lingo of German-speaking countries, led "through the provinces." During his first engagement of this kind the twenty-year-old Reinhardt had the fabulous fortune to be singled out by Germany's foremost producer. Instead of having to earn his acting spurs in countless mediocre road companies, he got the chance to put that obligatory phase in an actor's maturing process behind him under ideal conditions. Having to prove himself among an elite, benefiting from the advice and demonstration of the best in the profession, he was spared the common drudgery of trial and error. (Too many errors in this exalted company would have precluded further trials.)

Essentially, however, this autodidact learned only through doing it yourself, and under Brahm, doing it yourself for the likes of him was limited to acting, which did not quench his burning thirst. A well-rehearsed part leaves little latitude for accidents. So he established contact with the university, not to enroll in any seminars (he could not matriculate as a student because of insufficient schooling), but to appear in performances put on by an academic association open to nonstudents. The offerings were, in the main, Greek tragedies under the aegis and in the translation of the eminent classical philologist Wilamowitz-Moellendorff. It was not the translation that enthused the young Reinhardt. Many years later, Hofmannsthal wrote about the inception of his *Electra*:

> . . . the impetus to put the play down on paper I received suddenly, when the young theatrical manager Reinhardt talked me into doing it. I had told him he ought to produce classical drama. He excused his reluctance by citing the "plaster-cast" nature of the existing translations and adaptations . . .

What excited Reinhardt was the cradle of European theatre. But he was not satisfied with reading or hearing about it. He wanted to lie in it bodily, to *participate* in the Greek plays. They were to play a vital part in Max Reinhardt's repertoire ever after. In 1911, after having produced Hofmannsthal's (anything but "plaster-cast") versions of *Electra* and *Oedipus*, he directed Vollmoeller's adaptation of the *Oresteia* and the critic Siegfried Jacobsohn, who, likewise, had taken part in these academic functions, wrote:

> We were students at Berlin University, glowing with passion for "art and literature," and we belonged to the Academic Union, in which we could

> give or listen to lectures about our favorite subjects. Here, the theoreticians soon parted company with the pragmatists. I, for my part, kept writing [about the decline of the theatre and the need for a rude awakening] . . . and we decided to shame the sleepers among the theatrical entrepreneurs and to put on our own productions. . . . Suddenly, things began to stir around us. It seemed as though all our young energies were being instilled with a new courage. For an actor who in the *Oresteia* had been assigned nothing more than the report of Iphigenia's sacrifice discovered himself overnight, took a mighty step forward and became the deed of our intent; the innovator and ruler of Berlin's theatre. His name was Max Reinhardt.

"The deed of our intent . . ." Well put and in no way derogatory, I think. To ascribe to Max Reinhardt the originality of every *thought* he put into action would be as unreasonable as trying to prove the originality of every one of his *actions*. It is sufficient definition of his achievement to credit him with having been the theatrical expression of the *Zeitgeist*.

The coffeehouse was the crucible in which new ideas were bandied about, plans forged and formulated, a springboard for initiative. Max Reinhardt, the initiator, the organizer, was born among its spindly chairs and marble-topped tables. The university widened his horizon intellectually. But there recurred the summers when the Deutsches Theater was closed, the coffeehouse empty and the university in recess. There was no recess—and never would be—for Reinhardt. In his calm zeal, he saw to it that there would be no recess for his cohorts either. Why should the younger contingent of the Brahm ensemble, during summer vacation, not tour on its own? But Reinhardt did not stop at the level of his cohorts. He sought to interest several veterans in joining them—and succeeded. At first, his own role in these improvised summer engagements was subordinate, commensurate with his status as minor member of the cast. What made him so eager to bring them off? Could it be that he hoped for something to happen on these tours that would make them worthwhile? An accident, perhaps, that was unlikely to occur in the normal routine of an actor's existence? If that was indeed his hope, his intention, he was not to be disappointed. We have an eyewitness account of these early tours, the previously introduced Eduard von Winterstein:

> Under the guidance of Reinhardt, whose superior position among us none of us was aware of [including Reinhardt], the preparations for the Vienna tour began. . . .
>
> Today, in retrospect, I am of the opinion that Reinhardt, even though

> he was not directing at that time and nobody had an inkling of his directorial genius [including Reinhardt], exercised an enormous influence on us. . . .

He would hardly have been able to do that under the benevolent but stern scrutiny of Otto Brahm, within Brahm's perfectly organized system of production which excluded, if possible, any unforeseen happening. The summer sallies from Brahm's fortress were so successful that Brahm, after two years, considered it prudent to legitimize them by leading them, henceforth, himself. The luster remained, but the spark was gone. Yet it lasted long enough for Max Reinhardt's name to appear, in 1900, for the first time on a program (for Ibsen's *Love's Comedy*) as official director.

A new staging area for these longed-for happenings had to be found, another outlet for his frustrated, unfocused energies. A brush fire that had started on Montmartre and quickly ignited the other bohemias of Europe provided them: the cabaret. It was inexpensive to run, required only part-time contributions, lent itself to collective effort and, being novel, did not have to meet too exalted standards. It was probably more these practical considerations than Reinhardt's affinity for this form of entertainment that attracted him to it. He was about as fond of the cabaret as of the coffeehouse.

It all started with Die Brille (The Eyeglasses), a club founded by his coffeehouse circle with the aim of ridiculing rampant philistinism, every member donning super-sized spectacles and, in a grotesquely solemn initiation ceremony, being dubbed "Clairvoyant Knight." I am certain that he was more responsible for and intrigued by the ceremony and its props than by the programmed symposia. The first public performance, for a charitable cause (the collection for a member of the group, the eccentric, profound, language-juggling poet Christian Morgenstern, who suffered from advanced tuberculosis and was badly in need of funds for a cure in Switzerland), proved such a success that the club "went public" thereafter. Before long, actor after actor of the Deutsches Theater deserted to Die Brille, soon to be renamed Schall und Rauch. It was as though most of the younger actors of the Comédie Française had changed their envied status for membership in the Moulin Rouge.

What prompted all these fine actors to take so unlikely a step? Fascination with cabaret? Hardly. They must have been aware that something was brewing in the Kleines Theater (to which the cabaret had moved in order to accommodate ever-growing audiences) which the traditional stage, even at the highest level, could not offer them. The origins of most revolutionary movements are obscure, as are those of their leaderships. Reinhardt's were no exception. This blur is annoying for the historian, convenient for the zealot and, for the skeptic, an opportunity to fish in muddy waters. Indisputable, however, is the fact that, almost unnoticeably, the cabaret turned into a legitimate theatre and that *one* of its less prominent founders revealed himself *spiritus rector*. Those who gathered around him did not even realize at first that it was he whom they were gathering around. What drew them together was that they all wanted the same thing or, rather, that they all wanted to get away from the same thing (naturalism and bathos) and sensed instinctually where the initiative lay for the hoped-for change.

Reinhardt's long behind-the-scenes existence and his slow development as leader were only partially due to his timidity. The determining factor was martinet Brahm, who flatly refused to let him go. Reinhardt was one of the last dissenters to make the break official, and the only one not permitted to do so amicably. Perhaps Brahm sensed a potential rival before anyone else and sought to delay the contest. If so, his obstruction was a blessing in excellent disguise to the Young Pretender. It enabled him to grow with his responsibilities, to gather invaluable experience before exposure, and it prevented the group's many failures from dragging him down with them—as was the fate of many of his fellow aspirants who attempted many of the things he did, before he did them, and were never heard of again.

For the Kleines Theater was by no means the first to play the "new authors." And though its productions kindled more interest than the previous and competing ones, the financial situation in its first years was most precarious. Oscar Wilde's "indecent" *Salomé* (closed to the general public by order of the police), Wedekind's *Erdgeist*, Strindberg's *Rausch*, Maeterlinck's *Pelléas et Mélisande* (with Reinhardt, for the first time in Berlin, as acknowledged director) and Hofmannsthal's *Electra* were the most provocative productions in town, but did not make their producer rich. The smash hit of the Gorki play brought the change. Thereafter, the Little Theatre became too little. Reinhardt, now a full-fledged theatrical manager, rented a second house, the Neues Theater, adding Shakespeare, Schiller, Offenbach as well as Beer-Hofmann and other contemporary dramatists to his repertoire. The most promising actors of the younger generation flocked to him. He became a magnet for authors and lured the best painters (among them Nolde and Corinth) and musicians to his lair. The time when accidents would determine his future was nearing its end.

But one more accident, and, indeed, the most decisive in my father's working life, was still due: his take-over of the Deutsches Theater itself.

He did not aspire to this unique honor and responsibility: he would have never had the arrogance. There was only one—the remotest—possibility for it to happen: if it fell into his always-strategically-placed lap. It did. The theatre's wealthy owner, its founder under this name (emulating Paris's famed Théâtre Français), Adolf L'Arronge, an all-around showman, had a remarkable flair for trends in show business. Twice before, he had made some startling and fruitful decisions: In 1883, when he smelled that Berlin audiences were ready for a change in their theatrical diet, which had become either too shallow or too sterilely solemn, he transformed an operetta house into a legitimate playhouse, with himself as *primus inter pares* of an all-star company. Then, in 1894, when he concluded that Berlin audiences were ripe for more intellectual entertainment, he dissolved his company, leased the Deutsches Theater to the critic Otto Brahm, who had made a name for himself—in association with several other figures of Berlin's intelligentsia—by founding the avant-garde Freie Bühne (Free Stage, modeled after Antoine's Théâtre Libre), where Ibsen and Hauptmann had their say. Along with somewhat stilted productions of the classics, it was Ibsen, Hauptmann and their followers who continued to have their say during Brahm's remarkable eleven-year tenure. Now, in 1905, when the time came for the contract to be renewed—everyone assumed it a mere formality—it was not. L'Arronge, at the height of Brahm's career, decided naturalism had had its day and handed over his theatre to a well-known writer-producer who was, however, even more passé than naturalism. An unusual case of miscasting for L'Arronge and a dilemma. Naturalism or not, there was simply no available substitute of comparable producer status for Brahm. But something had recently occurred in Berlin that greatly reduced the importance of ordinary—or, for that matter, extraordinary—producer status. L'Arronge at once saw its practical consequences. His nose, once again, steered the old fox, against his own taste, in the right direction and unexpectedly opened a precious door to a newcomer *waiting* in the wings.

Max Reinhardt was actually an unlikely choice for L'Arronge, his *commercial* record being far from impressive. So far, he could boast of only two bona fide hits: *The Lower Depths* and *A Midsummer Night's Dream.* But the second had some amazing features. To begin with, that it *was* a hit. What, at the time, Germans generally looked down on as a tedious fairy extravaganza, a minor work by the Bard (enjoyed mainly by ham actors behind the footlights and cultural pharisees in front of them), had previously been banished to matinee performances for the benefit of schoolchildren and pensioners with a higher education. What had made out of this tired war-horse a winning racer? How could this drug on the repertory market suddenly transform itself into a smash hit and make its producer Europe's number one theatre man? Certainly not the text, as has just been indicated. Not Mendelssohn's score. It had escorted this play regularly and, given the musical standard of the Neues Theater, probably better. Not even the actors. Reinhardt's cast was excellent, but in no way special or of star caliber—anyway, one with which Berlin was well acquainted. Nor the set design, although the grass carpet (especially imported from London) and the replica of a real forest on a revolving stage, forever conjuring up new vistas, were novel—and risky: one of the scenery changes was so complicated as to necessitate an intermission lasting an hour and a half. What, then, created the sensation? It was the *sum total* of all these elements or, to put it another way, the new element that made out of all of them a conceptual whole; the single idea to which all participants bent plus the generating force behind them; the unfamiliar ingredient of a new type of *direction.* The woods *acted.* The actors were a botanical part of the woods. Trees, shrubbery, mist, moonlight intermingled with the lovers, the rehearsing artisans, the trolls, the elfs, the spirits. The music, the wind, the breathless running, the clowning, the fighting were all of one key and came from one and the same source. So did the calm, the sweep, the dream, the poetry. Nothing was background, nothing foreground. Passion, humor, lyricism, bawdiness, nobility, fantasy did not have their allotted moments side by side or consecutively. They were ever-present, simultaneous, feeding on one another in multiple symbiosis.

Siegfried Jacobsohn wrote:

> Does anyone remember having experienced in the theatre such a degree of exultation—not on the part of single individuals, not of certain groups, but of the entire mass of the audience? Here, for once, the notion of theatre materialized as a democratic art of the highest rank, without causing a shudder to the most sensitive nerves. For the means are altogether aristocratic. Sound and color and light form a perfect triad . . . the illusion of a world of spirits. Moonlight shimmered and the morning light dawned splendidly. Here and there a glowworm shone. Leaves rustled, you could almost smell the moss, twigs cracked, and the forest seemed immeasurable. . . .
>
> It was a perfect illusion because, in purity and greatness, Reinhardt had preserved his understanding of Shakespeare's poetry and of his players' individualities. . . .
>
> With one flexing of the fingers, Reinhardt masters his instrument. There are no interfering noises. Technique is transmuted into art and art into a higher form of nature . . . the elves and the humans begin to merge, as do the loving couples and the louts. If there are wreaths to be distributed . . .

one of them ought to go to Heims [my mother, playing Helena] . . . and one to Arnold [playing Bottom]. But, in the end, their tribute too must be shared with their, our Reinhardt, who, with this Shakespeare cycle, has embarked on a project undreamt of in German theatrical history.

I am not suggesting that L'Arronge necessarily perceived the historical significance of what had happened at the Neues Theater: the entrance of the modern director. He may not even have been particularly appreciative of that single artistic feat. (His taste was cautious-conservative.) And the managerial aspects of Reinhardt's *Midsummer Night's Dream* must have worried the seasoned practitioner: its production cost and running expenses were so high that only a run of over six months could recoup the investment, something unheard of in the repertory Berlin of those days. (The number of performances, transferred in time to L'Arronge's own theatre, was to exceed that hurdle by the hundreds.) Yet he offered Max Reinhardt his Deutsches Theater on the spot. The decision stunned Berlin. It broke Otto Brahm's heart. Deepest resentment, but also deepest conviction, made him publicly predict the direst consequences for the temple of culture he had worked so hard to erect.

And so the novice actor who had entered the venerable house eleven years before suddenly found himself at its helm. He was thirty-two and ready for the challenge. Less than six months after signing the lease, he would be the landlord. A golden period of the German theatre had begun. And, unlike the nation, it won its place in the sun. This conquest, of course, could obviously no longer be left to accidents, intentional or otherwise. And though they continued to be the prayed-for miracles of my father's religion, he no longer waited for them. For a long time to come, he would be too busy to wait for anything—least of all in a coffeehouse.

THE DIARY

WEDNESDAY, OCTOBER 13, 1943

Thirteen is Papa's lucky number. Or fateful number? The combination of a thirteenth falling on a Friday is his dream. Whenever possible he schedules his openings on this coincidence. Wolfgang was born on the thirteenth of December, I in the year 1913 in a house whose back entrance bore the number 13. The address of the Deutsches Theater: Schumannstrasse 13. In point of fact, the numeral 3 by itself is decisive in Papa's life: He was born in 1873; discovered for Berlin in 1893; his first major success was in 1903; and his enforced departure from Berlin was in 1933. And now we're in the year 1943. What is in the cards for the balance of this year?

Heavy thoughts. Shake them off and go up to his apartment. We chat, order his breakfast, my lunch, from room service and, while waiting, I deliver news of Italy's declaration of war on Germany. Like all Austrians, Papa loves Italy, but doesn't set much store by her military prowess.

Have determined to make this my lucky day. Call Corbett, make a date with her for the evening, the second since Papa's illness I won't be with him. In afternoon, drive to Princeton to see Einstein again. On phone he agreed to appear in the film. Said reason for doing so was he'd never forgive himself if, on his account, I ended up in a Himmelfahrtskommando [German soldier's term for punitive detail that assures ascension straight to heaven]. Asks if I brought the text for his speech. I suggest he jot down a few lines of his own. He demurs: His thoughts may very well not be acceptable to army brass. I guarantee him no one in my army would dream of questioning anything he felt inclined to say.

He sits down and starts writing. Long, uneasy minutes go by. The "few lines" I suggested become a dissertation that indicates no intention of coming to an end. Shudder to think what they will add up to on the screen. Albert Einstein on the cutting-room floor! At last he looks up at me with a: "Nervous? Yes, yes, you are. It's too much, I know. But you can cut anything you want." He hands me the page:

> Why is the great struggle you're engaged in an inescapable necessity? The reason lies in the nature of the German state and of the German masses.

> *This state is dominated by a minority that for centuries, but increasingly since Bismarck, willfully pursues its goal of subduing other nations just as it succeeded in subduing its own people. This minority consists of opulent landowners, army elite and big business together with intellectuals who, via the universities, are in a position to manipulate all teachers and thereby the entire nation. They stop at nothing so long as they believe there is nothing or no one to stop them. Specifically, they have trained the population to be submissive and to obey to the point where, at their command, it is capable of the most heinous and inhuman crimes. Since they smugly ignore the rules of international conventions, the only weapon against them is naked force. Only by this means can tolerable living conditions in the future be created on our earth.*
>
> *It has been given into your hands to carry out this task. If the danger that menaces civilization is not extirpated, before long there will not remain a single corner in the world where freedom-loving people may live in security.*

He cuts my compliments off with a deprecatory gesture: "All truisms, all truisms!" Which, I say, too few people seem to be aware of. And that's what makes his comment so valuable. I cough. When I'm lying or trying to be tactical, I always cough: "It might be judicious, Herr Professor, to delete a few lines for . . . cinematic purposes." "Please, Herr Reinhardt, I'm not proud of my prose. I told you you can cut or change as much as you want." First of all, I say, I must translate. And, he adds, I must get a final okay from my superiors. I brush this aside. He insists: "I know the thick-headedness of goyish officers!" Assure him we have nothing to fear on that score. Our unit's password is "nebbish." He grimaces: "Jewish officers? They're even worse! On top of everything they're afraid!"

Walks to door with me, expresses hope everything will work out and that I'll come back again soon. In car cannot resist another look at my new screenwriter's script. Unfolding page, discover other side covered with mathematical equation in his hand. All very impressive. All the baffling numerals, symbols, parentheses, powers, fusions, separations adding up to . . . zero. But an Einstein zero! Difficult decision: to steal or not to steal? Retrace my steps, ring bell. He's surprised that his invitation for me to return should have been acted on so promptly. Draw his attention to what he undoubtedly overlooked and might have need of. He smiles: "No, no, that's what I have a head for." And as if this statement needed corroboration, he taps his magnificent head. I stare fascinatedly at the vault of such unique treasure. He misinterprets my stare, apologizes for seeming braggadocian: "You see, my friend, emigrations are easier on physicists than on *theatre people. We're not dependent on language—only on what's inside our heads. Once again,* auf Wiedersehen. *My very best wishes to your father."*

A Ghetto Under Pacific Palms

FOR EIGHT SUCCESSIVE YEARS, from 1934 to 1942, Max Reinhardt lived between the Hollywood Hills and the Pacific. This, if one excludes his childhood in Vienna, was the longest he spent anywhere next to Berlin, longer than he lived in Vienna as an adult, and, if one considers the briefness of his seasonal sojourns, longer than he lived in Salzburg. Viewed from this standpoint alone, it is one of the most important stations in his life.

But settling there permanently in 1934 was not his first acquaintance with California. As early as 1926, the *Miracle* tour brought him to San Francisco and Los Angeles for recasting and refresher rehearsals. In contrast to Toscanini, who christened this stretch of land *Italia senza anima* ("Italy without soul"), my father fell in love with the landscape, the climate, the openness of the inhabitants and a future which he prophesied (and which has, meanwhile, come true to an extraordinary degree). This love, which lasted the rest of his life, remained, however, largely unrequited, if only for the fact that the film capital was situated there, and film for Max Reinhardt remained all his life an unrequited love. And the theatre, despite the steadily increasing population and its urbanization and despite Hollywood's strong attraction for writers and every other kind of artist, did not take root there, at least in Reinhardt's time.

In 1926, this problem, if he ever gave it a thought (and I was astonished at how little thought he did give to matters of survival), in no way clouded his passion for this corner of the earth. He learned to ride horseback, Western style, made friends among the owners of the great ranches in the hinterlands of Carmel, Monterey and Del Monte, and saw himself surrounded by beauty, not the least of which was feminine. Some of these beauties he had brought along himself: his Madonna, Lady Diana, and his Nun, Rosamond Pinchot. Originally Lili Darvas had been slated for this role. But her husband, Molnár, had talked her father into vetoing the venture. Max Reinhardt embarked for America in 1924 without an actress set for the second lead. Onboard ship, he met Rosamond Pinchot, made love to her and cast her, a complete stranger to the theatre, in the part. In wresting her from the shelter of an affluent society existence, he, in the long run, did this zestful dilettante no favor. For without him, her stature as an actress—once hooked, she could not tear herself away from the stage—was insecure. (Soon, she would belong neither here nor there, neither to the theatre nor to society—certainly she was not meant for the arms of Mephistophelian Jed Harris—and removed herself from both by suicide.) Her understudy alternated with her in life as well as on the stage: Iris Tree was the youngest daughter of Sir Herbert Beerbohm-Tree and a lovable creature of many talents, all delighting my father. Her greatest talent was for human relationships.

All this femininity was, of course, not exclusively preoccupied with the work and person of Max Reinhardt—*he* was much too preoccupied for that. Around him buzzed other sundry suitors. Two of them, familiar to us, were to become fixtures in my father's life: Friedrich Count Ledebur, and Raimund von Hofmannsthal, who parlayed the part of a silent penitent in *The Miracle* into sinning with the Madonna, a springboard for ever more exciting adventures. It was an adventurous, romantic, glamorous period all round, although it also had its humorous side: When Noël Coward, after a show, once stopped for a bite at the Savoy Grill in London, he found himself sitting next to the table where Diana, equally alone, was having her supper. They had never met. After a while, she turned to him and asked: "Noël Coward?" "Yes," he answered. "You wrote *Private Lives?*" "Yes." "Very funny." Waiters were serving. After they had gone, Noël Coward turned to her: "Lady Diana?" "Yes." "You're playing the Virgin Mary?" "Yes." "Very funny." End of dialogue.

At San Simeon, my father was the guest of William Randolph Hearst, who had never given up his intention to worship his mistress, Marion Davies, as the Virgin in a *Miracle* film. Neither her talent nor her notoriety predestined her for the assignment. But the despot ignored all that, just as he would not accept the fact that every effort, so far, had failed to publicize her to stardom. Nor did teaming her up with Clark Gable or Bing Crosby help. Even a Hearst genuflection before Louis B. Mayer, expert in launching stars, did not bring about the desired result: Marion Davies could be launched, but would not float. The *Miracle* film with her never materialized.

In 1923, a year before the première of the pantomine at the Century,

Hearst had invited my father onto his yacht anchored in New York Bay to offer him a hundred thousand dollars to direct a *Miracle* film with his sweetheart in the lead. True to a well-proven Reinhardt practice, my father answered that he never carried on business negotiations himself. When, subsequently, Rudolf Kommer, expecting a compromise, asked for a hundred and fifty thousand dollars, Hearst broke off negotiations with the statement that he was not in the habit of bargaining. It was the first of many Anglo-Saxon business surprises for the newcomer from Central Europe. The deal was dead. In 1923. In 1936, negotiations were renewed and the agreed-on payment of two hundred thousand dollars was made to my father for the same project. But Jack Warner—in whom Hearst now placed the hopes that Mayer had dashed—called the film off.

Everything about Hearst seemed to my father oversized: the giant body; the millions he earned, spent and owed; the beach house in Santa Monica, whose grounds could have accommodated three hotels; the old-master fakes on the walls; the color photos of Marion Davies covering whole pages of the Hearst newspapers every Sunday; the historic buildings he bought in Europe, dismantled into myriads of components, packed into crates, shipped to America and partly rebuilt in San Simeon, while the rest stood around for years unopened; the dimensions of the ranch which my father, on long horseback rides, could not begin to explore; everything about these rides when all the guests of the palace—which was never finished, because the landlord clung to the superstition that if he ever ceased building he would die—had to follow the ruler of San Simeon over hedge and ditch, up hill and down dale, and were able to rest their sore behinds only when he stopped and asked his caretaker whether this or that mountain in the distance still belonged to his estate, a question that was invariably answered in the affirmative; the permanent intoxication of the lady of the house (consumption of alcohol on the property was expressly forbidden), which, on these excursions, seriously endangered her balance in the saddle; the vast private zoo outside his windows. I myself had occasion to gape in astonishment at this colossus with wedge-shaped head and chirping falsetto, a bass fiddle with a piccolo sound, at the party he gave for Reinhardt after the première of the *Midsummer Night's Dream* film in 1935. The rooms of the beach estate had been supplemented by a huge tent extending over three tennis courts. Two large bands, one for jazz, the other for light classics, alternated without pause. Circular bars surrounded the poles, and champagne—or whatever beverage was desired—flowed in proverbial streams. The barrels of caviar never remained full—or empty—for very long.

The Hollywood that had received my father nine years before had been less industrialized, wilder (in its mores and its gambles), less citified and more exotic. The stellar fixtures were Douglas Fairbanks and Mary Pickford, Charlie Chaplin, Lillian Gish, John Gilbert, Mae Murray, Rudolph Valentino, Ramon Novarro, Gloria Swanson. Of course, Reinhardt, the star from a faraway galaxy, was greeted with the proper respect. In the course of this visit, he made the acquaintance of Joseph M. Schenck (Nicholas's younger brother), then president of United Artists. They agreed on a film to be made with Lillian Gish with a subject still to be decided on. Since religious fare had triggered this first trip to California, it was not too farfetched that another religious subject suggested itself. In any event, we know that the treatment which Hugo von Hofmannsthal subsequently collaborated on had Therese von Konnersreuth as the central character, a young Bavarian girl with the stigmata of the crucified Christ, which began to bleed from her hands and feet in her moments of ecstasy. My father's interest in this theme was not merely based on his conviction of its dramatic effectiveness and suitability for Hollywood (where he was mistaken). It also touched on a question forever in his mind: what is the true nature of the actor? He tried to answer it in his Columbia speech:

> With the lantern of the poet he descends into the as yet unexplored abysses of the human soul, his own soul, in order to transform himself mysteriously and to re-emerge with his hands, eyes and voice full of wonders. He is at once sculptor and sculpture. He is the man at the farthest borderline between reality and dream and his feet are firmly planted in both realms.
>
> The autosuggestive power of the actor is so great that he is not only able to affect inner, psychic changes, but, without technical aids, physical ones as well. And if one thinks of those much-discussed miracles which have occurred at all times and in many places, when simple people relive Christ's passion with so strong a force of imagination that their hands and feet show wounds and they actually weep tears of blood, one can appreciate into what mysterious regions the art of acting may lead. It is the same process Shakespeare describes when he says that the actor utterly changes his accustomed visage, his whole being, and can weep for Hecuba and make others weep.

In order to bring the Konnersreuth project off, my father went to Hollywood a second time in 1927. Again, he was enchanted. And, this time, he was counting on the longed-for breakthrough into films. Not that he had had his fill of the theatre. That could never be. But he felt that, on the beaten path he had so far trodden, he had achieved what was humanly achievable. He craved new paths. Hollywood looked a desirable goal. Above all, it appeared to promise much-needed money.

The Konnersreuth film never materialized. The superficial reason seemed obvious: Hollywood was in the throes of changing from silent to talking pictures. It was not a smooth transition. Solid firms suddenly faced ruin, gamblers received an unexpected chance, stars disappeared, new ones with voices were not yet on the scene, others who managed the leap had not yet proved themselves—nothing but scarcity of money, huge required investments, insecurity of the market and of hitting on salable subjects. The Reinhardt film, a silent film envisioned in more stable times, had cultural pretensions and an offbeat theme. It therefore had no appeal at the moment.

But did this international theatre man hold no attraction for the new Hollywood? He felt he should. In his settling of accounts with Kommer, fifteen years later, he wrote: ". . . never had I been more necessary here [in California] than at the birth of sound pictures and never did I wish to participate more passionately." And a few lines further on:

> The question of my work and my income in Hollywood at that time played a much weightier part than any momentary inclination. It was the time when my brother was retiring from business and I had to think of giving up my theatres. I did that much too late. At the time the chances for my staying here and leaving Berlin would have been incomparably more favorable.

In that he was unquestionably right, but there were much tougher obstacles to his "staying here" to overcome than he suspected, tougher than what he reproached Kommer for:

> You left me here stranded with children, among whom the always gay and pleasing Raimund guarded his father's script, but did not know enough English to tame the unruly executives with his charms.

My father believed that the Konnersreuth project, or another, might have jelled, had Rudolf Kommer condescended to abjure for a few days his continuous tête-à-tête with big money and high society in New York and join him in Hollywood, so contemptible a locale from Kommer's coffeehouse point of view. He was wrong. Of course Raimund was no Hollywood agent. But neither was Kommer. He had no knowledge of or interest in film. And he lacked the connections and all ammunition for persuasion. He spoke better English than Raimund, but that would not have helped him with the "unruly executives," most of whom did not. Perhaps a professional agent or an experienced motion-picture lawyer could have mediated (in which case my father would have, at least, been paid off, which did not happen). But the main hurdle was not lack of adequate representation. The real gulf between Hollywood and Reinhardt lay in their respective mentalities.

My father by no means scoffed at Hollywood's creed, which is so discredited today and even then was condemned by many. He even showed a certain reverence for its first commandment: Thou shalt have no other gods before me ("me" being the god of the box office); but he was not a reliably true believer. Reinhardt's own system functioned according to a similar, if not so strict, commandment. His theatre and those of his predecessors were, after all, also purely private enterprises, geared toward profit and dependent on it. The comparison may shock theatre historians and Reinhardt fans, but it is a fact that the Reinhardt theatres were run according to economic principles analogous to those guiding the Hollywood studios in their heyday. Both had a fixed annual program, a salaried stock company, their own workshops, stockholders, manifold means of distributing and production, an immensely varied repertoire extending from spectacle to the most intimate script, from culture to light entertainment. Plays were not only accepted and produced, but commissioned and readied under supervision for home consumption and export. My father never voluntarily pursued a project if he was convinced that it would result in a financial loss. Of course, circumstances, at times, forced him to produce succès d'estime—or distinguished failures—but that was true of Hollywood too.

When my brother, after Edmund's death, gave up his art-history studies in order to jump into the breach and follow in his uncle's footsteps, my father was not happy about the decision. For him, as he never tired of pleading, everything happening backstage and outside of the auditorium reeked of prostitution. Yet he gave in to Wolfgang's wishes, though urging him first to learn every single branch of the trade. For example, he recommended that he spend time in the box office, the material hub, in his opinion, of the theatre, and to study the attitudes of its consumers. Along this line, he wrote to me in 1933:

> Wolfgang is in Italy and hopes to drum up pictures there, unfortunately not in the only way that seems to me right, that is *from bottom to top*, but from top to bottom, by founding companies. There is an endless exchange of letters and high-sounding exposés. But so far no film has materialized.

> Sternberg and Thalberg started differently (and in better times to boot). I myself have, once again, seriously flirted with films in Paris, but, alas, as platonically as ever.

It is significant that my father singles out Sternberg and Thalberg as shining examples for a motion-picture career. For both were antitheses of his own talents and tastes. The one, a vain and arrogant, pseudo-learned expert technician of the silent-picture school, with a painter's eye, but neither ear nor heart, a wizard with the camera, totally inept with actors, one of those film directors farthest removed from living theatre. The other, *the* Hollywood Caesar, the inventor of the producer system, the archenemy of the creative director, for whom art and artists were something to juggle with to achieve complete domination of the medium, who treated writers like well-paid and interchangeable servants, directors like pampered puppets, and who would think nothing of remaking two-thirds of a film if he was not satisfied with the results or thought the cash customers might feel likewise. (Ironically, my brother's first job in Hollywood was as one of Thalberg's assistants, the first step in a quick "bottom to top" career, heartily approved by his father.) Uninfluenced by his personal affinities and predilections, Reinhardt never condemned the founders of the Hollywood religion: Louis B. Mayer, the messianic go-getter and hamming hypocrite; Jack Warner, the shrewd manipulator of clownish unscrupulousness; his brother Harry, of gloomy unscrupulousness; Harry Cohn, the coarse, brutal, professional lowbrow; Sam Goldwyn, at war with the English language, but at peace with the best of taste; Jesse Lasky, the gentleman among thieves; old Laemmle, the early primitive, with enough zest to found another sect.

My father did not condone their lack of education and their aversion to educating themselves. But he understood their problems, esteemed their unbridled enthusiasm (unbridled except by box-office considerations) and admired their pioneering accomplishments. He forgave them their lack of manners. Their elbows did not hurt him. The joy of children at play, no matter how cruel, the indomitable urge to invest in products of fantasy, the firm determination to become rich, even though the wealth was more hoarded than enjoyed, compensated in his eyes for all the many faux pas. What mattered to him was that these were steps *forward*, even if they stopped at nothing. The jokes circulating at Hollywood parties about the illiteracy and the boorishness of the despots would evoke smiles from him, but no agreement. When I would give a parodistic report of this or that of my bosses' monstrosities, I could be sure of his laughter, which, however, was always followed by gentle reminders that I should never forget the importance of promoters in show business; it did not only live on artists. For example, Richard Wagner, in his opinion, owed more to the theatrical entrepreneur Angelo Neumann (whom my father had met in Prague on his early tours) than to all the princes, princely managers and clever critics. Angelo Neumann, he said, was one of those—often Jewish—temperaments uniting intense enthusiasm for art with an equally intense enthusiasm for business, willing—unlike more conservative and better-mannered individuals—to take extraordinary risks in both fields. Without those risks, he insisted, the theatre would stagnate in convention. In his own life, he told me, the gentleman impresario Cochran and the upstart impresario Gest had played similar roles. He had been on the lookout for such a connoisseur of the market ever since. In vain.

The men who built Hollywood were of the same type. But they did not have the empathy for Max Reinhardt that he had for them. Hollywood was not aware of any kinship with Reinhardt, and actually distrusted his respect. To be taken so seriously by one of the theatre's greats left Hollywood's rulers with the vague suspicion he wanted to pull a fast one on them, exploit them for his own ends, rob them of hard-earned money. They could somehow understand—and were willing to use—unworldly artists or artists who sought recognition or wealth according to their own rules. He, apparently, did not belong to either category. He, moreover, presented them with another puzzle: Where they expected elbow, he seemed astonishingly malleable; when they made jokes, he was in earnest; what was sacred to them, he found funny; when they thought they could simply run over him, they ran into a wall.

He was less troubled by the uncouth and the uneducated than the slick and the half-educated. The latter, as he heard them, spoke the same vulgar language and had the same vulgar thoughts, only they mouthed them under Van Goghs and Picassos, framed by first editions and Georgian silver or supported by rococo furniture or Chippendale. He never turned up his nose at self-made upstarts. He was one himself. But, with him, the education had kept pace with the career. The more he accomplished, the more he learned, the more he wanted to learn. The pocketbook bulged, but so did the cultural challenge. He wanted money so that he could spend it, could produce something with it. It was a means to an end. For Hollywood it was the end; or the means to achieve what Hollywood, in truth, craved: neither art nor luxury, but power. For Reinhardt art was everything and luxury a great deal. Power did not interest him. In the *setting of the goals* lay the principal discrepancy, which my father, whenever he flirted with films, hoped would go away, but which those he wanted to ensnare felt in their guts: Reinhardt made money with art; Hollywood made money with or without art. More frequently without. To the heresy "Art before box office," instead of the orthodox doctrine "Box office before art," the hierarchy reacted most allergically. That kind of fun, they knew, could cost irretrievable millions.

In Max Reinhardt, Hollywood saw this kind of heretic. He was right in believing that when motion pictures learned to speak, Hollywood needed fresh blood from the theatre. But motion pictures learned to speak *English*. Films had become, overnight, national. (Foreign-language versions, synchronizations came later.) Besides, the film moguls felt threatened by the invasion of the word merchants they needed. So they degraded them to highly paid serfs. Max Reinhardt did not fit into this scheme. (At George Cukor's housewarming party my father met Irving Thalberg and expressed his gratification that, in Hollywood, a director could afford such comforts. Thalberg concurred spiritedly: "I encourage personal extravagance in the talent working for me. It makes them dependent!")

It took my father three months before he realized that Mr. Schenck did not intend to produce the Konnersreuth film. The closer their relations, the deeper the abyss between them. That is how it was always. Shortly after World War I, Paramount czar Adolph Zukor looked my father up in Berlin and offered him the direction of Milton's *Paradise Lost*. The preliminary talks came to nothing, because neither had read the work. But after my father made up for this gap in his erudition and submitted written proposals, they were turned down. The paradise was lost once again. Equally, the sporadic negotiations with UFA and other German companies as well as with the self-appointed "gypsy" Gabriel Pascal, who had been clever and eccentric enough to wangle out of George Bernard Shaw the film rights to his plays, which he had refused to every other producer, led nowhere. He did shoot—in his spare time, brightening up his summer holidays—two silent pictures in Italy, but they were of no particular consequence. A "Max Reinhardt Film Company" was founded on the strength of them but never produced a film. Eventually, his relations with Warner Brothers would not be so different: the promising *Midsummer* honeymoon was followed by a barren autumnal marriage and, finally, a hibernal divorce.

For three months my father literally was sent into the desert. He spent them at La Quinta, a hacienda hotel he loved, near Palm Springs. I have a letter from him about those months, in which he rhapsodizes over the moon landscape in the background and the Elysium before his bungalow.

Friedrich Ledebur rode with him through Joshua trees into dramatic sunsets, Iris Tree taught him English and all waited for Raimund von Hofmannsthal's daily bulletin from United Artists. It inevitably boiled down to two words: "No news." They became a familiar quotation. Mostly, the engaging messenger did not even get to pronounce them: the recipient anticipated them with such mocking boredom, half chuckling, half fatalistic, that everyone present would break into spontaneous laughter.

My father was genuinely fond of this shy Casanova, Raimund, as he was drawn to most Hofmannsthal characters. Raimund had inherited most of his father's nature, except the creative side. He lived his own life as though it were a product of the paternal imagination. On July 5, 1929, shortly before his death, the elder Hofmannsthal wrote to his friend Carl J. Burckhardt about this "product" of his:

> A week ago, sunburnt but rather slim, swinging a delicate cane and exclusively concerned with two monkeys which he bought in India for Reinhardt's Leopoldskron menagerie, Raimund appeared. It is like a miracle to me that he has been here for only eight days and that we have spoken of so many things and heard so much. His descriptions are excellent and the flow—a chain of strange meetings with sailors, Russian ships' doctors, madmen, Javanese sugar magnates, Hindu savants, Australian sheep breeders, all Conrad characters—is unending.

As to the inner life of Hofmannsthal's live products, he maintained an odd detachment regarding them. He followed their adventures, joys and woes as dramatists do when watching their characters from a theatre loge. Once, he shocked the puritan in Max Reinhardt when he told him pridefully that Raimund was being kept by a prostitute in Paris. I have no way of knowing whether this confession reflected the truth, fatherly wishful thinking or just poetic license. In any event, Hofmannsthal senior had to pay for this fascinated indifference cruelly: Raimund's older brother, Franz, who worked as a waiter at the Hotel Continental in Berlin—without his father giving it much thought—visited his paternal home at Christmas in Vienna's suburb Rodaun. Franz came—one is tempted to say, deliberately—to shoot himself. The rifle shot came, for his parents, out of the blue, for himself out of a very dark sky. The confrontation with ugly reality in his own stronghold was shattering to Hofmannsthal. The funeral had already begun and Frau von Hofmannsthal had gone ahead; the ringing bells from the adjacent cemetery could be heard through the open windows. As Raimund proffered his father a top hat, the elder man suffered a fatal heart attack, eyeing himself in the mirror, as he correctly continued to place the hat on his head—his final action. My father could not attend the obsequies of his great friend and closest collaborator, for, on the same day, he suffered the loss of another friend and collaborator: his brother.

Max Reinhardt's California escapade in 1927 concluded in a lighter vein: Hollywood's uncrowned king, Douglas Fairbanks (né Ullman), an Austrian half-Jew and, therefore, in a position to communicate with my father in remnants of a common mother tongue, and the "queen," Mary Pickford, made a last effort to mediate between Max Reinhardt and films. They invited him for dinner to the "royal castle," Pickfair, along with a young industrialist with motion-picture hopes, a certain Howard Hughes, who, by prearrangement, fetched my father at his hotel. Both gentlemen, it was thought, should smell each other out on the way. Neither my father nor the interpreting Raimund have, since, explained satisfactorily what actually happened during the car ride; which of my father's words, whether in Raimund's English or my father's German—incomprehensible to the monosyllabic driver—offended him. The fact is that he dropped his passengers abruptly outside the gates of Pickfair and sped on without another word.

The dinner, in the absence of its cause, showed a dubious gain: Before bidding the guest of honor goodbye, Fairbanks led him into the longest dressing room he had ever seen. Fairbanks opened one of the corridor-like closets and asked him to pick any in the endless row of suits as a farewell present. My father first hesitated—his wardrobe, though not comparable to that of his host, was well stocked—but then, not wanting to seem impolite, bowed to the foreign custom and selected a garment at random. This symbol of all past and future misunderstandings between Reinhardt and Hollywood adorned his clothes rack, unused, for a long time, for Douglas Fairbanks and Max Reinhardt may have had many things in common, but not their figures.

By 1934, the face of Hollywood had greatly changed. The romantic, effulgent period belonged to the past, everything was systematized and went like clockwork. Sound-film Hollywood had succeeded in subduing the world and sat smugly on its undisputed throne. The era for heroes was past. It was the heyday of the super-manager. An even more hostile wind was blowing in Max Reinhardt's face.

During my year-and-a-half novitiate in Hollywood, I had found my way about without too much difficulty, first with Lubitsch, then Metro-Goldwyn-Mayer. Being the son of a famous man has its advantages and disadvantages. On the one hand, I had an easier entree than the average applicant. On the other, one expected too much of me: the more I gave, the higher the expectations. Moreover, nobody ever believed that I was broke. Max Reinhardt a have-not? Inconceivable. I could never convince anybody that he was and that I had even less. When Lubitsch "engaged" me in New York, he thought my desire to work in films was a whim. The only way I could attach myself to him was to volunteer without salary. (This most unsatisfactory arrangement paid off handsomely later, as I had calculated; the "job" proved to be an invaluable reference.) Once this "deal" was made, he was friendly enough to ask me to fly to California with him and was put off when I told him I lacked the means for that type of transportation.

That I could afford the trip to Hollywood at all, even by the slowest train, and that I had the subsistence minimum for a few months there without pay, I owed to the same misconception about my father's pocketbook. In New York, my social contacts had almost exclusively been Kommer's friends—which meant millionaires. Frequent guest in the most feudal households, I sometimes did not have the money for the bus or subway fare home. One evening, having been invited for dinner by Bill Paley, I found myself in the company of, among other tycoons, Bernard Baruch, Gerard Swope and Harrison Williams. At table, the conversation centered on Roosevelt's most recent attempt to stop the economic collapse of the United States: the temporary closing of all banks across the country. The subject left me more or less cold, as I had never seen the inside of an American bank. But my temperature rose abruptly when our host took an impressive wad of bills out of his trousers pocket and explained he happened to have withdrawn a large sum in the nick of time. Was anyone present in need of a little cash? It was theirs for the asking. He went the round, giving each of his guests an opportunity to accept or decline the offer. My turn, thank God, came so late that I was able to allay the excitement gripping me and decide on a strategy. I rapidly added up the rent owed to my landlord, the debt at the drugstore, the train ride, three months in Hollywood. Without, I hope, batting an eyelash, I yielded to the gentle pressure and availed myself of—the smallest amount changing hands that night—three thousand dollars. The return of the money proved much more awkward and complicated—and less prompt—but, in the meantime, the evening over, I enjoyed the taxi ride from Beekman Place home.

My relations with Lubitsch were cordial from the beginning, but not altogether without friction. On one of the first evenings of my apprenticeship, after we had finished shooting, he took me along to Hillcrest, the

Jewish golf club of Los Angeles, where Emil Ludwig was giving a lecture about the ever-darkening world situation. Though no friend of alcohol, the unaccustomed intellectual strain drove Lubitsch to a few glasses of whisky. Their effect caused an awkward incident when he raised his glass to me and drank a toast: "To all the parts your father never gave me!"

Another obstacle in my way was that, time and again, I ran into Europeans who had found employment in Hollywood on the basis of an alleged previous connection with my father. In fact, there was no German-speaking person in Hollywood who, rightly or wrongly, would not claim a Reinhardt past. When I reported at the Paramount studio gate in Hollywood for the "job" Lubitsch had promised me, the studio policeman—I had the feeling I was seeking admittance to a military camp—called Lubitsch's secretary, a Miss Trondell, and, after a few words, handed me the receiver. She was German. My question as to whether her boss had told her of my arrival was answered in the negative. Anyway, she informed me, the scheduled film had been postponed and Herr Lubitsch had gone to Arrowhead for a two-week vacation. My thorough familiarity with the German translation of the works of James Fenimore Cooper enabled me quickly to identify "Arrowhead" as the English equivalent of "Pfeilspitze," an Indian character in the third volume of his Leatherstocking Tales, but gave me no clue as to the lake in the San Bernardino Mountains where I might, otherwise, have been in contact with Lubitsch personally. Miss Trondell asked me whether I had anything to do with *Max* Reinhardt. My reply seemed to try her patience to the breaking point: This was too much! An impertinence! There wasn't a person coming from Europe who didn't pester her boss for a job on the basis of having God knows what to do with that name. Reinhardt actors, pupils, assistants, collaborators, cousins, nephews, nieces and uncles were slowly but surely coming out of her ears. But that someone now had the gall to pretend he was the son was the end! She hung up. Winning Miss Trondell's benevolence was the first of many tests I had to pass in Hollywood.

In the summer of 1934, these lines reached me from Paris:

> At the end of August I am supposed to travel to California to do *Midsummer Night's Dream* in the open air at a festival sponsored by the Chamber of Commerce. San Francisco, then Berkeley and perhaps also Hollywood. The results would certainly be meager and actually I have had just about enough of the old *Midsummer Night's Dream,* which I did in Florence for last year's festival with an Italian cast, and in June '33 in

> Oxford with an English one, both times in a marvelous ambience. But perhaps, somehow, an autumnal beauty will still result. And besides, I'm not being honest: one can no more have enough of this magnificence than a conductor can of the Ninth or the Bach oratorios. Above all, the main result of this California trip would be a *Wiedersehen* with you, which I long for. Who knows when the opportunity will arise again?

The "old *Midsummer Night's Dream*" not only became an "autumnal beauty" but could have brought him total financial security for his autumn years, had he husbanded the money.

The next message I received from him was a telegram in which he urged me to secure Charlie Chaplin (Bottom), Greta Garbo (Titania), Clark Gable (Demetrius), Gary Cooper (Lysander), John Barrymore (Oberon), W. C. Fields (Thisbe), Wallace Beery (Lion), Walter Huston (Theseus), Joan Crawford (Hermia), Myrna Loy (Helena), Fred Astaire (Puck) and so on.

That the project did not become a source of mourning was entirely due to a force my father could seldom match: the energy of a persevering female.

Catherine Sibley, the daughter of the president of the University of California's Alumni Association, had theatrical aspirations and pursued my father all over Europe. She became his assistant in Florence by making a perfect pest of herself and eventually succeeded in getting him to California—which, quixotically clinging to straws in Europe, was the last thing he wanted. One day, two tried collaborators (Felix Weisberger, assistant director, and Einar Nilson, in charge of music) arrived with Miss Sibley to lay the groundwork. It was a risky, not to say irresponsible, delegation of authority. Purely in physical terms, the three staging areas (the Greek Theatre plus a campus meadow at Berkeley, the San Francisco Opera House, and the Hollywood Bowl) confronted the director with a tremendous challenge. Neither his envoys nor I was up to it. Nor had my father any right to expect that we would come up with the cast that we did. (It included, among others, the discoveries of Mickey Rooney, Reinhardt's best, pagan-wildest Puck, and Olivia de Havilland, a temperamental and bewitching Hermia.)

My father pushed his luck to the danger point when he delayed his arrival till thirteen days before the première. That he dared to do this in the film capital, in close-up, as it were, before an array of the world's best-known actors, directors and producers can, in my opinion, only be explained in one way: He was relying once again on the miracle drug without which he could no longer function. In these thirteen days, with actors who were unknown to him, in a language largely inaccessible to him, it worked again.

But my point is not the artistic side of this performance, which combined poetry and slapstick, grandeur and tenderness. That Max Reinhardt knew how to put on *A Midsummer Night's Dream,* after all, surprised nobody. The most astonishing feat was the technical *coup de main.* I remember how, intrigued by the natural coulisse, he worked out a torch parade for the last act, stepping to Mendelssohn's Wedding March, from the heights of the Hollywood Hills to the bottom of the valley, across a specially built bridge onto a scene that seemed suspended in free nature. (The shell had been removed.) It did not concern him in southern California's tinder-dry vegetation, that this constituted a fire hazard of the first order. How difficult people found it to deny him a wish is proved by the okay from the Los Angeles Fire Department.

At the dress rehearsal, the torchbearers reached their destination two hours after the play had ended. They could not find their way through the pathless brush in the dark. All participants begged my father to renounce such manifest lunacy. But lunacy and miracle seem not to be too far apart: at the opening, the torchbearers arrived on the terrace of Theseus' palace on the dot and, with the final bar of the march, assumed their prescribed stance.

How he could endure that kind of suspense is still a riddle to me. But this time, he was not spared a shock: The final applause of the fifteen thousand spectators (the Angelenos filled not only the escalating rows of seats, but had made themselves comfortable on the grass slopes above) was so thin that my father was not even called to take a bow. The reason for this was that, after the epilogue, no curtain fell. The stage simply went dark and spotlights blinded the audience. No stimulus to acclamation. Also, Los Angeles, even in 1934, had a traffic problem that other cities were to learn to live with much later. Whatever the enthusiasm for the performance, it was stifled by the hurried exodus to the automobiles, while my father, perplexed, stood around in his dinner jacket, convinced that he had, at last, received the comeuppance for his evergrowing recklessness.

But the comeuppance turned out to be of a different nature. Contrary of the gloomy prophecies of the film moguls who, most unenthusiastically, had yielded to the pressure of Harry Chandler, publisher of the *Los Angeles Times,* to underwrite a one-hundred-and-twenty-five-thousand-dollar guarantee for the venture and who had warned that the average public would stay away from it, since the Shakespearean language was incomprehensible to them (at the party after the opening, Columbia president Harry Cohn needled me with: "Next time we're gonna play in Latin!"), the undertaking became an unprecedented box-office hit. One hundred and fifty thousand people saw Reinhardt's *Midsummer Night's Dream* in the Hollywood Bowl. The guarantee was never called upon. Warner Brothers made a one-hundred-and-eighty-degree turn and gave my father a three-picture deal, the first of which was to be *A Midsummer Night's Dream.* Salaries: a hundred and fifty thousand dollars for the first, two hundred thousand for the second, two hundred and fifty thousand for the third. Max Reinhardt settled comfortably in Hollywood.

In the meantime, half of European and four-fifths of the German-speaking civilization moved into this Californian coastal strip. The area that received them, though absorbing only a few, extended not much further than ten square miles. First the German wave swept in, then its Austrian counterpart. They were followed by the French (along with those Hitler refugees who had sought grudgingly granted asylum in France and in the other countries swallowed one by one by their bane) and, finally, by the English (who took their pacifism so literally that they took up residence in still peaceful, if otherwise, at least at first, unbeloved, America). It was the mass migration of a thrown-together elite unprecedented in history, the volume and force of which is hard to grasp even now, only forty years later. Even for me who was witness to it.

One might imagine a splendid center of the arts and sciences amidst alien surroundings, erected by Richard Neutra, the trail-blazing architect from Vienna, decorated with the sculptures of the Russian-American Alexander Archipenko; with lecture halls where one could sit at the feet of the Frankfurt sociologist Max Horkheimer and the Berlin philosophers Ludwig and Herbert Marcuse; with concert halls where one could listen to the violin of Russian Nathan Milstein, the celli of Russian Gregor Piatigorsky and German Emanuel Feuermann, the piano of Polish Arthur Rubinstein, accompanied by an orchestra consisting of the foremost instrumentalists from the Berlin, Vienna, Warsaw, Paris and London philharmonics under the direction of Berlin's Bruno Walter and Otto Klemperer, playing works, as though they had been especially composed for it, by Austrians Arnold Schönberg and Ernst Krenek, Russian Igor Stravinsky, German Hanns Eisler; with theatres putting on operas by Austrian Erich Wolfgang Korngold and operettas by Hungarian Emmerich Kálmán, starring Polish tenor Jan Kiepura, German soprano Lotte Lehmann and Berlin's queen of the musical (from Vienna), Fritzi Massary; where Berlin's Marlene Dietrich sang her countryman Friedrich Hollaender's "Falling in love again . . ."; where Berlin's Lotte Lenya sang her husband (from Dessau) Kurt

Weill's songs from his *Threepenny Opera;* where the new plays by Augsburg's Bertolt Brecht were brought out by Budapest's Melchior Lengyel (inventor of *Ninotchka*), Paris's Jacques ("Tovarich") Deval and Mainz's Carl Zuckmayer, interpreted by Paris's Charles Boyer and Annabella, Mannheim's Albert Bassermann, Berlin's Else Heims and Vienna's Fritz Kortner; where Lübeck's Thomas and Heinrich Mann would read excerpts from their most recent novels, followed by Munich's Lion Feuchtwanger, London's Aldous Huxley and Christopher Isherwood, Prague's Franz Werfel and Vienna's Vicki Baum; with sound stages in which Vienna's Fritz Lang, Otto Preminger and Billy Wilder as well as Berlin's Henry Koster and Robert Siodmak (from Alabama) and Paris's Jean Renoir shot their films under the aegis of (Berlin's Irving Thalberg) Erich Pommer, with Berlin's Karl Freund as cameraman (responsible for *Camille* and *The Good Earth* and, for that matter, Max Reinhardt's 1912 and 1913 silents *The Isle of the Blessed* and *Venetian Nights*), featuring Vienna's Hedy Lamarr and Peter Lorre, Berlin's Lilli Palmer and Felix Bressart and Paris's Jean Gabin—a list that can be expanded at will, without limit. Though most of them had not necessarily been good neighbors at home, often, except for insults, not even on speaking terms, they were now, at least geographically, close neighbors in exile and learned to speak with one another with silver-alloyed tongues.

It was a crazy quilt enriched by visiting strands from the east like Freud's pupil and deviator Alfred Adler; the German musico-sociologist Wiesengrund-Adorno; the English poet W.H. Auden; Vienna-Berlin-London's stage star Elisabeth Bergner; the Berlin banker Jakob Goldschmidt; the German architect Walter Gropius; the Russian pianist Vladimir Horowitz; the Polish violinist Bronislaw Hubermann; the German writer Emil Ludwig; the French writer André Malraux; the English playwright and novelist Somerset Maugham; Republican Spain's Joan of Arc, La Pasionaria; the Austrian pianist Artur Schnabel; the Polish-Austrian pianist Rudolf Serkin; the German tenor Richard Tauber; the Italian–New York maestro Arturo Toscanini; and a Jew, born in Russia, then a notable chemist from Manchester, England, on and off head of the Jewish Agency, Chaim Weizmann, not knowing then he would be the first president of the state he helped so much to create. Add to them the less known, but no less distinguished, list of educators, scientists, doctors, psychiatrists, lawyers, journalists, fiction and nonfiction writers, draftsmen, photographers, conductors, singers, musicians, actors, architects, bankers, art dealers and other merchants, chess and bridge players, collectors, statisticians, politicians, technicians of every kind, and masters in every conceivable craft—

and you have, on the one hand, the result of the most suicidal bloodletting of a civilization since Spain's expulsion of the Jews and Moors in 1492 and, on the other, the most extraordinary influx of knowledge and talent to another continent.

Since the Jews in this community of exiles were, for once, not in the minority, it is, I believe, permissible to call it a ghetto. No ghetto, to be sure, where anyone was forced to live or that one could not leave at will, much less one that threatened naked survival. But then, there is a theory according to which the Jewish ghetto was initially formed voluntarily, because its inhabitants were inclined to stick together in foreign lands and to continue obeying their own laws, even when they were not forced to.

Very few of the Californian exile community (I was one of these exceptions) had come of their own free will. But most were tempted to see the inevitable through together, preferably in a place where motion pictures beckoned to offer a means of livelihood—real or imaginary—even for people who had no experience in films (in accordance with the old saying: everybody has two professions, his own and the movies), where there was no need for heating, for winter clothing, and where the widespread illusion was that one was superior to the natives (most of whom were recent settlers themselves).

The ghetto was so imponderable, its contours so amorphous, that many occupants did not perceive it at all. My father's wishful imagination, as well as the fact that he had visited this land of milk and honey and orange juice many times before *without* political motives, completely blurred this actuality for him. And does a ghetto lie right on the beach? Does it have palms, night-blooming jasmine, bougainvillaea and rows of citrus trees? (There is one Jewish settlement which fits this description, but it is a state, and it wasn't in existence then.) Does every ghetto dweller, normally, own a little house with a garden and a car? My father enjoyed the view, his home, his closer family, a few friends, his dog and whatever work he conjured up for himself. In his fellow settlers he saw no fellow sufferers—rather, individuals living the same way he did. Either he was glad when he met an old acquaintance or else he avoided him, as though a chance meeting had occurred during a joint trip on an ocean liner or in a dining car.

I was, in a way, a link between the ruling powers outside and the inmates. In view of what happened in the more evil ghettos and camps of those days, this sounds sinister. In a less evil sense, it actually could be. There were immigrants who received jobs in which they were supposed to shield their employers against other job-seeking immigrants. These used to lose all heart when they heard that a luckier companion of the common misfortune had been consulted about their aptitude. When their forebodings were confirmed, I would try to console them with a parable by Molnár: "I was often asked: 'Why doesn't the National Theatre in Budapest put on your plays?' My answer: 'Because the National Theatre doesn't put on plays by Jews.' Inevitable next question: 'But the manager of the National Theatre is a Jew!' My stereotype answer: 'The best restaurants in New York have Negro doormen to keep the Negroes out.' "

I was not one of these doormen. I was too young to fear the competition of elders and my job was secure enough to allow me to help the newcomers I esteemed. And I was able to help a good deal. Only in one case did I remain ineffectual: I could not help my father.

Many of my pictures were written—in collaboration with indigenous talent—by refugee writers, the music composed by refugee composers, and some of the best European actors played in them. One day, even Bertolt Brecht honored me with a visit. Only years later did I learn what he thought of such visits. In his "Bukow Elegies" he writes:

HOLLYWOOD

Every morning to earn my bread,
I go to the market where lies are bought.
Hopefully
I line up with the salesmen.

This time, salesman and hoped-for buyer had little confidence and agreed that the former was out of place. This creative, shrewd, crew-cut head admittedly stuck out like the proverbial sore thumb in my "culinary" den. In his unadulterated Bavarian accent, he fascinated me for an hour and a half with a proposal for a film about the production, distribution and consumption of bread. It had as much chance of being accepted by MGM as *Gone With the Wind* would have had of being put on by Brecht's Berliner Ensemble. I do not know whether I should be proud or ashamed of my quixotry in actually trying to persuade my executives to buy Brecht's "lie." MGM, not enjoying a particular rapport with the Knight of the Rueful Countenance, thought me mad and pitiable, but not funny.

These unbridgeable gulfs in the ghetto were widened further by those of its surrounding country: California boasts both the highest summit in the continental United States and its lowest point (below sea level), only twelve miles distant; snow-framed desert alternates with subtropical flora, mountain lakes with seashore, and architecture imitating every style in the world; pine woods and arid canyons are peopled by urbanites who cling to air conditioning. Made-up, powdered, costumed, the inhabitants roast in the burning sun. Theatre people without theatre. Colossal wealth is amassed by individuals who basically have no use for what it can buy. Branded as sybarites, they in fact live only for work. Filled with provincial inferiority complexes, the Hollywoodian is (at least, was at that time) hospitable, but very sensitive to criticism. And everyone criticized. Particularly the immigrant. Laughing Hollywood does not tolerate laughter, is incapable of self-irony. Its symbol is Buster Keaton: deadpan in all situations.

The greatest contrasts collided in the salon of Salka Viertel, intimate of and scriptwriter for Greta Garbo. It *was* a salon. In her house in Santa Monica, George Sand, Chopin, Liszt, Musset, Delacroix would have felt comfortable. Now it was where Greta Garbo elucidated to Max Reinhardt how she intended to play Hamlet: where Chaplin rounded out his universal gifts and recruited his musical ghostwriter, the brilliant sycophant Hanns Eisler; where the happy-go-lucky virtuoso in the grand tradition, Arthur Rubinstein, was polite to the unhappy and unlucky, tradition-trampling Arnold Schönberg; where the brothers Heinrich and Thomas Mann, estranged for decades, were reconciled after many weeks of delicate Ping-Pong diplomacy at a festively decked-out Ping-Pong table where, on other occasions, Schönberg would try to get the better of his more tonal colleagues, but the twelve-tone system, for once, failed him; where Garbo knelt before Stokowski and listened, enraptured, to such tales as when he spent an entire day—from sunrise to sunset—with a native sage on an Indian mountaintop, gazing at the landscape spread out below and discussing the eschatological problems of the world, only to realize, after taking leave of each other, that his interlocutor had spoken no English and he did not know a single word of any Hindu dialect, and yet they had understood each other completely; where Max Reinhardt, for the first time, made the acquaintance of his former *Dramaturg* (literary adviser) Bertolt Brecht—whose early dramas, even though not frequented by the landlord, had had all their Berlin openings at the Deutsches Theater—and discovered, admittedly somewhat late, the genius of their author. The same discovery in reverse came to the author equally late (prompting him, a few years hence, to tell Elisabeth Bergner during a rehearsal of *The Duchess of Palffy*: "Everything I know about the theatre I learned from Max Reinhardt and the Chinese").

Salka herself was an empathic and uncalculating hostess. She was a friend. Not only to her friends—and she had many (Max Reinhardt and Helene Thimig among them)—not only to the numberless individuals she helped because they were friends in need, but to the ghetto as a whole, for she was one of the few who knew and faced the fact that it was a ghetto. Hers was one of the few clearinghouses between the inmates and the guardians. It was neutral ground where, for a few hours, everything was allowed and many an opportunity was created.

Other centers of attraction were Lion Feuchtwanger's Mexican-style mansion with an Alexandrian library, where the language was Marxist; Heinrich Mann's shabby living room, where Germany's next government was being formed (without any consequences); Alma Mahler's in every sense Catholic hospitality; and, not to be forgotten, the Clover Club, the gambling casino on Sunset Boulevard. There, one evening, being the only non-Hungarian at the roulette table except me, the agglutinative language got on Otto Preminger's nerves and he brought his fist down on the green baize, shouting: "Goddamnit, guys, you're in America! Speak German!"

What my father did not understand was why each member of this star cast considered himself happy to be invited to his house under the Pacific palms for dinner, for conversation and for the best of memories, when hardly anyone came to see his performances at his Workshop. The Max Reinhardt Workshop, curiously, was *no* center of attraction to the ghetto. Its activities took place practically behind closed doors.

> I think it might interest you to see a modern version of *Jedermann*, the final production of this semester; it introduces a good many talented young people. I would be very happy if you and Mrs. Lubitsch could come today, tomorrow or the day after. Warmest regards,
>
> Max Reinhardt

A draft for a telegram to Lubitsch to be typed by my father's secretary. Similarly to Greta Garbo:

> Please come to the Workshop today or tomorrow and take a look at the old *Everyman* in a modern version with a number of young talents. It would make me very happy to see you again. Cordially yours,
>
> Max Reinhardt

Identical messages were drafted for Charlie Chaplin, Sam Goldwyn, Harry and Jack Warner, Joe Schenck, Darryl Zanuck, Aldous Huxley, James Hilton, Harold Lloyd, Cecil B. De Mille, Joe Pasternak, Frank Capra, Walt Disney, Walter Wanger, Norma Shearer, Charles Boyer, Bette Davis and many, many others: "I would not dare impose on your precious time if I were not convinced that it would interest you . . ." etc. And a P.S.: "The addresses are easily obtainable A.S.A.P. As a last resort use Gottfried Reinhardt."

But nobody came, nobody was interested, nobody sacrificed even a little of his "precious" time. The Europeans would rather wallow in a rich Reinhardt past than enjoy a more modest Reinhardt present (that so many of them had demanded of him back home). The Americans followed his own example, and ignored his ghetto existence.

Following the surprise triumph of *A Midsummer Night's Dream* in the Bowl, which had taken Hollywood unawares, but had not dispelled its prejudices against Reinhardt, the filming of the play was the last opportunity for Hollywood to come to terms with him. Thereafter, the dialogue broke off for good. Today, the film looks better than it did at the time. What then seemed inadequate is accepted today as normally antiquated. What survives are the first-rate performances of most of the actors and—as I notice each time I see the picture on television and noticed especially during a recent showing for young students at an American university—even those viewers who have no inkling of Reinhardt, and particularly none of his Shakespeare productions, are inadvertently captivated by the magic spell that once captivated a world.

Santa Monica, November 13, 1934

Dear Papa,
Since our last nocturnal discussion many thoughts have gone through my head about you and your work here.

You are leaving the arena where you fought and had your glory—the theatre—and are entering, as you yourself know best, an entirely new field. Its perils for you lie less in your underestimation of it than in your overestimation. Film is, as you theorize yourself, a form of the theatre, of playing. It is not a new art—insofar as it has so far developed into an art at all—it is a child the theatre had to sire in a wholly and quite suddenly technicized world. . . . Three-quarters of the sound-film makers stem from the stage. I don't allege that every theatre man can make films; but then, not every theatre man can make theatre either. I don't even allege that you, the master of the theatre, and of every kind of theatre, will revolutionize motion pictures. Nor do you want that. But I am convinced that you, today, can give motion pictures as much as they can give you. There is only one thing that can prevent it: too much modesty on your part.

If you don't succeed in films, it will be your own fault, and not because you are not equal to the job in any way, but because you might not attack this new medium with the pleasure, energy and grasp it deserves and which you have applied to every other artistic endeavor.

> I have seen people making films here under the best and the worst conditions. I have observed good and bad directors, good and bad writers, good and bad supervisors at their work. . . . And I tell you this: Papa, don't make any compromises, they make no sense. When you return from Chicago, gather your collaborators and tell them what you have in mind and how and when you want to start working. Be hard. Only that way will you get anywhere with the hard people here and with the soft delegates who represent the big shots and are, therefore, doubly cautious.
>
> Believe me, all artists who have made careers here, and especially those who, in the beginning, had less to show than you, have forced their intentions on the merchants, as you call them, in the way I am now suggesting to you. For art—there is no other way—has to be forced on the people running Hollywood.

His reaction to my letter—I was twenty-one and had a year and a half's experience in Hollywood behind me—may be imagined. Anyway, he had settled for compromise. Ignorant of modern cinematographical technique as it had developed since his last picture in 1913, and not particularly interested in it, he had entrusted himself to the routine hands of William Dieterle, his former Brutus and Good Fellow (in *Jedermann*), who had become staff director at Warner Brothers and had been instrumental in bringing about the deal. The partnership was cordial, but not congenial. The atmospheric component of the film several times comes dangerously near to kitsch. My father would never have stood for Dieterle's optical effects in the theatre. He stood for them on the screen because he saw them for the first time only after the picture was completed. Except for the immediate work with the actors, he was, this time, a captive, not only of his co-director and the camera he did not control, but also of his employers, who saddled him with a cast chosen almost exclusively from their contract players. These in no way lacked talent or box-office appeal. But they had made their mark in gangster films, musicals and low comedies.

Max Reinhardt's film career was at an end. The projected *Danton* ran afoul of Jack Warner, who missed the *inferno* in the script. Not that he had expected a comedy. Not even a Divine one. But the French Revolution was too inflammatory for his taste.

The industry's total boycott of him, the fact that, from one day to the next, he could earn neither the one hundred and fifty thousand dollars per film that he could yesterday (and of which nothing was left) nor the hundred, two hundred or three hundred dollars a week which he needed so urgently today, was incomprehensible to him. Sitting on the fence between his needs and his prospects and observing both areas (and earning fifteen hundred dollars a week), I understood the problem, but could do little about it. I did arrange meetings for him with Louis B. Mayer, but they resulted in not much more than the gift of a box of cigars.

In a way, Mayer acted a role in my father's life which my father had put on the stage most effectively. He never forgot that Sunday afternoon when he took "His Mayersty," as he referred to my lord and master in a telegram once, to a *Jedermann* performance in Salzburg. He had anticipated that his guest would relate "the play about the life and death of the rich man" to himself. What he had not foreseen was the violence of this egocentricity. I am sure Mayer's antics in the audience made all efforts on stage pale by comparison. For days, the arm against which his neighbor had pressed with all his might for one and half hours was too sore for my father to use. Mayer's reaction, however, produced no catharsis: in Hollywood he continued to behave toward him more callously than Everyman toward the Debtor.

"I won't let that son of a bitch into my studio—until I need him!" That was Mayer's motto. He did not need my father. The industry had no place for Max Reinhardt, and he had no place in the industry. In 1942 he wrote:

> It is wonderful here on the Pacific and life is a thousand times better than in New York. But I grew up on the fourth balcony of the Burgtheater.

Around the same time Thomas Mann wrote to Agnes E. Meyer:

> Max Reinhardt's house is furnished like a veritable stage set: ours is all sober function by comparison. We spent a companionable evening there yesterday, while everyone was propagandizing for a theatre Reinhardt hopes to open in New York. He is going there now, eager to be permitted to practice his magic again. But the means that will probably be at his disposal will be just enough for an ascetic theatre of conviction, not for the magic and opulence he loves and he produced in richer times. I fear he is not the man of the hour. But in any case he will have more chance in New York than here.

Had Thomas Mann gone to more performances at the Workshop, he would not have committed the error of calling Max Reinhardt's style in 1942 "opulent." (One year later, in New York, my father failed with an "ascetic play of conviction" but succeeded with a pretty "opulent" operetta.)

In the beginning, the Workshop attracted scholarships from the major studios, the most promising graduates receiving contracts. Several successful motion-picture actors, even stars, were born of it (Robert Ryan and Nanette Fabray leading the long parade), but for the Workshop this practice proved to be a boomerang. My father—he stressed it often enough himself—had never been a pedagogue. He did not believe that acting could be taught by imparting knowledge. All one could do, he maintained, was to hand the aspirants the tools and to explain their use to them. Playing could only be learned by playing. The true teacher could, in effect, only be a director. So he *directed.* His "courses" were rehearsals, his "exams," performances. When, after the first year, the studios did not renew the scholarships, the Workshop had to rely exclusively on tuition fees. But the Professor cast the parts in his productions strictly according to the talent of the student, and acting talent does not seem to bloom among the rich. So, in the main, he worked with recipients of scholarships, which soon became a euphemism for non-paying pupils. The ones who paid, after a while, ceased to take this discriminatory treatment lightly. With the result that they too stopped paying.

Even the most frugal theatre performance costs money. To my father, the Workshop performances meant as much as any he had directed in Berlin, Vienna, London or New York. During the final rehearsals, educational considerations were completely forgotten. No one dared to remind him that, by demanding things way beyond the requirements of a school, he was only hurting his own pocket. The only one who might have dared to remind him was I, because I had to foot the monthly deficit. But for this very reason, perhaps, nothing of the kind crossed my lips.

From a historical perspective, this self-delusion of "business as usual" was no delusion whatsoever. Outstanding work was done in the Workshop. In a way, my father reverted to his very beginnings, when he still lacked the means which later, erroneously, became his trademark. The mixture of serene maturity and enforced asceticism produced small jewels: Maeterlinck's *Sister Beatrice* (a chamber-orchestrated *Miracle* with John Huston as priest); a chamber-orchestrated *Everyman; Six Characters in Search of an Author* (at one of whose unforgettable rehearsals my father showed Bob Ryan how literally to collapse after the discovery of his daughter in a brothel, how to fold up like a jackknife and to exit, his torso bent horizontal, a destroyed human being). The bleak hall of the no-longer-in-use radio station on Sunset Boulevard, without a podium, without sets, with two lamps, a minimum of props and a maximum of debts, was no programmatic turning away from the sensual, the illusionistic, the ornamental. He simply bowed to necessity, enjoyed it and made the best of it. And it was the best. There was as much magic on this Reinhardt stage as there ever had been on his previous ones.

But no matter how moving the performances were, their aftermath was dismal. The playing sector was often more crowded than that of the seats. After the curtain dropped, one went out into the street, took a breath of fresh air and drove under palms to the Pacific. And one forgot the ghetto—until one was shaken awake by letters like this one:

> You don't know what it means to wait even a *single* day for one's daily minimum, calculated down to the last cent. It is an incomprehensible and, moreover, quite senseless torture to be forced to run into debt with domestics (over and over again!), at the market or anywhere else, not to be able to pay the bills for water, gas, telephone, electricity, and to have to drive with threadbare tires. . . . I must speak to you urgently about the subscription theatre which I have discussed at great length with Thomas Mann, Werfel, Huxley and people from the university. Perhaps this would be the last legitimate chance for me—perhaps! I don't know. I'm tired. All my love,
>
> Your father

Drop by Papa's apartment. He's napping. Leave my evening itinerary and phone numbers with Eleonora. Corbett's apartment, later Maisonette Russe at the St. Regis. Before taking off, celebrate my "lucky day" in anticipation with dry martini at Gladstone bar. My first in—can't believe it—three weeks! Rousing welcome from Beverly Hills Commandos. Martinis triple and quadruple. All present and accounted for delighted to hear Papa quite recovered (from dogbite).

Corbett, champagne, caviar—Silvia is ten safe city blocks away—candlelight and soft music on Mr. Menelaus' gramophone. This is no dream!

On to Maisonette for good, expensive drinks and bad, expensive food. And dancing. Too close? Realize from gawking on all sides, even an old-fashioned square dance would be too close for a GI in company of a Broadway star on public dance floor. What will tomorrow's gossip columns say? And remember "21." The night Papa and I dined together there and I had my run-in with Oscar [Levant: radio star, eccentric pianist and acid-tongued wit. As he always did at the sight of my father—regardless of place or time—Oscar yodeled gleefully, full voice, across the crowded room: "*J-E-D-E-R-M-A-N-N!!*" That night, I wanted nothing more than to disappear under the table, which Oscar, at this moment, was approaching. A beautiful Chateaubriand with sauce Béarnaise and pommes soufflées was being served. The meat was charred on the outside, pink in the middle and of a size to feed an army. But not, it struck me—and this is what got me off on the wrong foot—a sergeant in the U.S. Army. I laughed up into Oscar's face. First mistake. Never inaugurate fun with a professional funnyman. Second and fatal mistake: "You see, Oscar," I said, "this is how you'd be eating too if you were in the Army!" He took my self-irony as a sting at him for not wearing his country's colors, slapped my face, sprinted across the room and down the stairs. I felt no offense. I knew the neuroses of this poor, driven, brilliantly gifted enfant terrible only too well and I would gladly have let the matter rest, had not the entire restaurant been waiting, breathless, for some kind of Luxembourg-at-dawn reaction. Yet army regulations put me in a mortifying bind: Brawling in uniform was a court-martial offense. On the other hand, not to brawl after being publicly insulted would condemn me to a life of shame in the one eatery in New York where, on

Uncle Sam's sixty dollars a month, I could still gourmandise like a millionaire. On the cuff. For the duration. I shoved the table away, tugged myself free of my father's restraining hand and caught up with my "assailant" at the cloakroom, struggling into his coat while making a for-dear-life dash toward the exit. For the first and last time in my life I swung with a stiff uppercut to the chin. Mack Kriendler, brother of proprietor Jack, threw his weight valiantly between us—thereby separating nothing more obstreperous than me from the quivering handshake Oscar was offering me. Peace concluded and Oscar fled, I made my excuses to Mack for the disturbance and congratulated both of us—for different reasons—on there having been no spectators at my pugilistic exhibition to give us publicity. Mack corrected me: There was one deadly exception—John O'Hara! He had taken a good look at the battle on his way from the men's room to the bar. John O'Hara, gossip-on-the-town and friend of Walter Winchell, Mack warned me, had to be stopped and the only way for me to do it was to glue myself to his side till he rolled into bed drunk. Mack went upstairs to my father to explain. I went to O'Hara in the bar, went along with his drinking until "21" palled, went step in step with him until we reached Winchell's haunt, the Stork Club. No Winchell in sight. Went to the men's room with John, went back to our places at the bar, went almost to the verge of DT's, but didn't let go, went home with him, poured him into bed and went home to my own. Cost: world's worst hangover. Gain: good news—i.e., no news in the morning papers].

A page walks around Maisonette carrying a blackboard. On it written in chalk: "Message for Sgt. Reinhardt." Apologize to Corbett—all the time thinking I shouldn't have left him, I shouldn't have left him—and go to the telephone booth. Eleonora on phone: Bad news. Papa woke up from his nap complaining of headache. His speech hesitant and confused. He looked ill. Say I'll be there at once, hang up and return to table. Cannot tell Corbett truth, cannot, while signaling waiter, trying to pay check and hustling her out of chair, convey that, although I adore her madly, have to drop her on her head forthwith. Deposit her in taxi. My Belle Hélène is a hellcat. Slams taxi door in my face. I take next cab to the Gladstone.

Papa is pale and mute, but otherwise no sign of change for the worse.

THURSDAY,
OCTOBER 14, 1943

So yesterday was not my lucky day! Nor his. Just as Papa always says: You can't force luck, you have to have a talent for it. And even talent fails sometimes. My morning visit to him a shock. The right corner of his mouth sags. I pretend not to notice. Again the exhausting game of father and son eyeing each other suspiciously, each searching for an apocalyptic response in the other. Which of the two knows more? Which will weaken first and tell? Neither yields. Just as on Fire Island, Eleonora, once the first blow is past, becomes composed. Nun-like she accepts what will be will be.

H. pays his daily call, is not unduly dismayed by "slight facial paralysis." Says Papa unquestionably had another spasm. But we're not to be discouraged. Recommends consulting another distinguished specialist, a Dr. G. in Boston. Revolting leeches applied to Papa's temples again. Report bad news to Hollywood. Urge Wolfgang not to influence Thimig pro or con trip. The time has come when she must make her own decision. No one has the right to keep her away from her husband—not even her husband.

Oppressive evening with Papa and Eleonora. Silence. Side glances that speak lugubrious volumes. Think of a wonderfully happy evening in same room a thousand years and forty-eight hours ago. And now gloom, like a jungle vine, chokes out a fruitful life. A life that knew no barriers is again, suddenly, imprisoned within the four walls of a hotel room. Within a damaged brain box.

FRIDAY,
OCTOBER 15, 1943

Facial paralysis less marked than yesterday. Was it a false alarm? I must stop seeing ghosts. And so must he. He forces himself à tout prix to enunciate faultlessly and, by shrewd substitutions, compensates for inability to find the right words. Wants to go over Helen libretto with me again, finds some of the repartee banal. Beg off till evening, as have asked for conference with Litvak about scheduling Einstein interview. Papa raises no objection, says in interim he'll make notes which we can discuss on my return. I do an immediate about-face: Litvak's not important, tomorrow will do. Let's talk libretto now. My implication not lost on him, second round of our tacit duel has begun.

Have been thinking that perhaps it was a mistake to overprotect, to isolate Papa. Decide on radical experiment: to bring in new company and distract him from his introversion. Pick John Meehan. John has no curiosity about anything, is interested only in horse racing, drinking and the job at hand. Also, he is very polite and friendly. It works. Papa welcomes another face, a change from Eleonora's, his doctors' and mine.

When he retires for his afternoon nap, I ask Eleonora to call me the minute he wakes and go down to bar with Meehan. Not more than ten minutes pass. An apparition: Papa is crossing lobby and waving blithely to me through the glass doors. Behind him Eleonora shrugs helplessly, gestures that he wants to go for a walk. On their return I accompany them upstairs. We have dinner. The duel is resumed. I parry with words, he with measured silence, with quick, stabbing looks. "Papa . . ." No use going on. Eleonora, however, is still in easy communion with him: She reaches over and strokes his hand. He smiles at her gratefully. When his eyes travel to me, his smile dies.

Dinner is over. The climax is reached: he stands up abruptly, crosses to his desk and sits, his back to us. Nothing I say makes him look at me or receives an answer. Eleonora proposes listening to records. He now turns his anger on her: "N-no m-music t-tonight!" A hiatus. Then he picks up his pen, dips it in the violet ink and holds it poised over a sheet of paper. Is he challenging me? Or his destiny? I plead with him not to push things now, not to be impatient, not to . . . The muscles of his face twitch. He flares out at me: "L-leave m-me in p-p-peace!" I have no choice. Neither I nor anyone else can stop the considered self-destruction churning within him. He has won the duel. And we are frightened, Eleonora and I, as we sit and watch him slowly, deliberately put his pen to the paper, see the pen scratch erratically across the page, then halt ever so briefly, scratch on again. The hand that moves it must be moved by supreme will alone, for in the loose sprawling strokes all control seems to be gone. Finally, he pauses thoughtfully, replaces the pen, recaps the inkpot, removes his glasses, slips them in their case and pockets it. All very neat. A ritual of orderliness. He rises, crosses to me and puts his arms around me. His tears wet my face. He holds me in a tight embrace. I kiss his cheek. Press him close—hoping to transfer my hope. He kisses me hard—as he used to do when I was small and he would say goodbye. Then he walks to the bedroom and closes the door after him. We hear the key turn in the lock and we understand: It was goodbye. When we look at the page in its folder, we see an illegible scrawl.

SATURDAY,
OCTOBER 16, 1943

Paralysis has spread to the right arm. H. pessimistic for the first time. Another first time: telephone Thimig directly. It isn't only beginnings that happen for the first time. Feel I must, and stress gravity of the moment to shake her. It hits her. Of course, like all of us, for a while she had a reason to hope for the best. Yet Wolfgang never softened the facts. Maybe she didn't want to believe them. Maybe she still doesn't want to. Maybe she can't make up her mind to face them. Does not commit herself about arrival, but asks me to let her know further developments. I promise them through Wolfgang.

During dinner Papa has difficulty cutting his meat. Without fuss Eleonora does it for him. It's the most natural thing in the world. He accepts it in the same spirit. The music we play when our meal is ended, his favorite records, he tolerates indifferently. Only a week ago today, he was in transports over the discovery of Manhattan from the back seat of my Buick! Onto what strange planet did this unquenchable curiosity disappear?

Phone rings. Reception clerk announces a visitor for Professor Reinhardt in the lobby. Ask the name. He struggles over it. Can't make out what he's saying. Clerk coughs discreetly: "The gentleman says the Professor knows his name. He made the appointment [cough cough] months ago!" Papa is looking at me questioningly. Light dawns with the first four letters: Beer! [Richard Beer-Hofmann, playwright-poet member of what was often referred to as the "old-modern" or "neo-romantic" school of literature in turn-of-century Austria. Forming a Viennese triumvirate with the spiritually related Hofmannsthal and the more down-to-earth Schnitzler, he, along with the former, played an influential part in Max Reinhardt's intellectual growth, and his two most important plays—The Count of Charolais and Jacob's Dream—were brought to the stage by my father. Out of inspiring collaboration blossomed a lasting friendship. In 1938, the Beer-Hofmann family fled Vienna, leaving behind a library that any university would have been proud to own. Without any means or hope of earning a livelihood, the Beer-Hofmanns crowded into an apartment on New York's Upper West Side. Belles lettres settled gratefully for a daily loaf of bread.]

Papa smiles at me knowingly: What are you protecting me from now? Hand over mouthpiece, I say: "It's no one. It's for me." Into phone: "I'll be right down." Easier said than done. Don't know how to face this imposing and gentle figure of my childhood.

Confronted in lobby by sight of the stooped seventy-seven-year-old whose serene Talmudic features tremble with outrage, my routine alibis stick in my throat. Not that they would have served me. Am drowned in a lava flow of complaint about Max Reinhardt's imperious forgetfulness of time, about his infuriating unawareness that other people schedule and keep their appointments by the civilized means of a clock and that, at least, with *old friends and fellow sufferers in emigration he might have made an effort to curb his insufferable unreliability and that—heartbreaking topper—despite these and all the other maddening Reinhardt egoisms he has put up with a whole life long, he traveled by bus from 110th to 52nd Street and walked all the way crosstown, from Broadway to Park Avenue, to see him—at ten o'clock at night! Because he respects the fact that other people's night is Reinhardt's day. And because he loves him. His eyes fill with tears. As mine do—because his hurt is for once so unjustified and I cannot explain to him why. Although I try: "Papa isn't feeling very well today. He's terribly sorry but . . ." He pats my arm, not believing a single word, but exonerating me from Papa's sinning and, shaking his head incredulously that the sinner should be so incorrigible, turns and leaves.*

Collaborators, Allies, Adversaries

We were sitting in the Café Monopol . . . in a large company of friends and acquaintances. Suddenly Reinhardt beckoned to me and motioned me to follow him to a nearby table. . . . He told me he was looking for a dramaturge and why he thought I was the right man for him; and when I joyously accepted, without thinking twice, he continued: "What I envisage is a theatre that, once again, fills people with joy. . . . I sense how tired people are of finding their own misery mirrored in the theatre again and again and how they long for brighter colors and uplift.

"That does not mean that I want to renounce the great accomplishments of naturalistic dramatic art! I couldn't do that even if I wanted to. I went through this school myself and I am glad that I had the chance. Our evolution is unimaginable without this severe education toward an inexorable truth. . . . But I want to continue this evolution . . . beyond the smell of poverty and the problems of social criticism, to apply the same high degree of veracity and genuineness to pure humanity, through a profound and sublimated art of the soul. . . .

"I would not dream of committing myself to a definite literary program. . . . I feel the growth everywhere of new, young energies, exploring new avenues. Wherever there are new talents in our time, from whatever direction they may stream toward me, I shall welcome them. Nor shall I shun experiments if I believe in their worth: what I shall not do is experiment for the sake of experimenting, literature for the sake of literature. . . .

"The theatre, after all, is more than an auxiliary art form of other art forms. The theatre has only *one* purpose: the theatre. . . .

"I am going to set the highest standards for my actors . . . a cultivated art of speech, as the old Burgtheater knew it, before the bathos of the last years . . . until, once again, the music of the word is heard.

"I am thinking of a small ensemble of the best actors. Intimate plays . . . cast not only with good, but with the best actors, down to the smallest part, and so carefully tutored that the strongest and most centrifugal individualities will harmonize as though in a single chord. . . .

". . . What I have in mind is a sort of *chamber music of the theatre*. . . .

"And then, when I have developed my instrument far enough to be able to play on it like a violinist on his precious Stradivari . . . then the time will have come for the essential: Then I will play the *classics*. You're astonished? Yes, I see in the works of the classic poets the natural, basic stock of the theatre. . . . You have no idea how intrinsically easy it is to perform naturalistic plays. . . . To call himself a real actor, a man must first prove that he can play Shakespeare. . . . Of course, I know the aura of tedium that clings to classical plays. . . . This dust must go. One must play the classics . . . as if they were contemporary creations. . . .

"The classics will engender new life on the stage: color and music and grandeur and splendor and serenity. Theatre will revert to being a festive act. . . . I intend to attract the best painters: I know they are impatient for me. . . .

"Actually, one ought to have two stages next to one another, a large one for the classics and a smaller, intimate one for the chamber art of the modern poets, if for no other reason than that the actors won't become frozen in a single fixed style. . . .

"And, actually, one ought to have a third stage, in addition. Don't laugh, I am absolutely serious about that and I am visualizing it at this very moment: a grand stage for the grand art of monumental effects, a *festival* house . . . a house of light and consecration, in the spirit of the Greeks . . . in the form of an amphitheatre, without curtain, without wings, perhaps even without sets, and in its center, relying on nothing but the word, the actor, in the midst of the audience, the spectators becoming co-actors, included in the action, becoming part of it, of the play. The frame separating the stage and the world was never important to me. . . .

"In between, it goes without saying . . . we must travel a great deal; must let other cities, other countries, other continents confirm what we have evolved in a small circle. . . . The performing arts, when they feel they have reached maturity, must conquer the world. And, by the way, there's another reason: I, personally, feel nowhere as comfortable as when traveling."

All this young Max Reinhardt told me in our first talk . . . 1902. Exactly this way; I have not forgotten a single one of his thoughts or added a single one. He spoke quietly, clearly, conscious of his will. Not a shade differently from the way he would speak today. . . . For man never changes, as Reinhardt likes to say.

IT WAS THE AUTHOR of this memoir, Arthur Kahane who drew my father's attention to the existence of *The Lower Depths.* My father told me that Kahane had only read a review of the Moscow opening, and that they decided, on that basis alone, to acquire the play, without waiting for a translation.

With his long beard, his kind eyes and long, beautiful hands, profoundly learned Arthur Kahane looked like a Jewish prophet. He contemplated the life his friend *lived.* He was no go-getter. The man who filled that part on Reinhardt's staff, who actually *got* the money, who did the shouting, running and arm-twisting for him, is described in Werner Krauss's ghost-written autobiography, *The Play of My Life,* where he tells of his very first meeting with my father. The "Professor" circled in silence about him in his office, measuring him nonchalantly from top to bottom, as they waited for "two gentlemen." Krauss continues:

> And then came the two gentlemen, Reinhardt's "right hands," Kahane and Hollaender. . . . Felix Hollaender was vital, alert, witty, a sharp poser of questions, who lisped a little, and was most absentminded and distracted. They say that once the telephone rang and he picked up the inkpot, bellowing, "This is here, who's that?" All the actors imitated him.

The actors were not the only ones to make fun of Hollaender. So did his writer colleagues on the outside, who saw in him, Kahane and their likes nothing but glorified press agents—which, in truth, they partly were.

Who was this comic figure, Hollaender? According to my father, emphatically, the most indispensable of his early associates. A popular novelist, he held the formal positions of dramaturge and director (by unanimous consent, not a very good, though an eagerly busy one). But it was not in them that he made his indispensable contribution. His stirring up things between the lines of duty was what distinguished him. His wide connections, an iron conviction and a conspicuous lack of inhibitions made him an ideal drumbeater. When the Deutsches Theater was up for sale, Hollaender succeeded within twenty-four hours in getting enough financiers to break down Reinhardt's doors and vie for the chance of becoming shareholders. Thanks to Hollaender, Gerhart Hauptmann entered into an exclusive contract with the Deutsches Theater after Brahm's death. He became one of the very few allies with whom my father was on a first-name basis and whom he addressed with *Du.*

He was not on a first-name basis with Hofmannsthal, Beer-Hofmann or Carl Vollmoeller. Yet they, more than other "house writers," could be called his collaborators. It was not only that he produced, at times inspired, commissioned or edited their plays, that he was the first, at times the only one, to produce them. Their literary prestige, particularly that of the first two, was to him what Hauptmann's had meant to Brahm, what Chekhov's had meant to Stanislavski and O'Neill's to the Provincetown Players and the Theatre Guild. They translated, adapted, worked with him on scripts, and Hofmannsthal, in particular, lent his pen and his name to many manifestos inaugurating Reinhardt projects.

Those to whom the name Hermann Bahr (1863–1934) still means something know him as the Austrian author of a number of "well-made," diverting and, in their day, popular plays, of which *The Concert* heads the list. He was a herald of naturalism (and, as such, an ally of Brahm, in which role Reinhardt first met him), then gravedigger of naturalism (which made him an ally of Reinhardt), a diagnostician of expressionism (which let him hope that someone would appear to succeed Reinhardt and, when he saw no one appearing on the horizon, that Reinhardt would rejuvenate and succeed himself). His essays on the theatre of the twentieth century are profound and prophetic.

When, subsequently, Bahr was approached to contribute to a Reinhardt *Festschrift,* he sent in the following text:

> . . . Paradoxically, one could say of Reinhardt that his personality's actual attraction consists of his not having any, but that he fashioned out of every personality of his generation his own. . . . Reinhardt himself did not bring a personal note into German art, yet, through his peculiar power to magnetize and to absorb every personal note audible anywhere and everywhere in his generation, he became their collector. And as all these personal notes, otherwise widely scattered and foreign to one another, were gathered within him, something new, something proprietary, something personally Reinhardtian was made of them. And it is through this process that he became the great director.

The article was not incorporated into the *Festschrift.* This was petty, and Bahr revenged himself for it by publishing his analysis in *Die Weltbühne* (where it reached many more readers). Bahr was only repeating, though in a more benevolent tone, what my father's adversaries had been preaching all along. I hope I have been able to convey that Reinhardt did not become the great director that way. The image of the sponge signals a momentum-gathering, Richard Wagner–inspired anti-Semitism that denies to the Jews originality and true creativeness, relegating their talents to scenting negotiable values, economically and artistically, and being ingenious middlemen. In a time and a country where some of the creating was being done by an Einstein and a Freud, this attitude was fatal—and not only for the Jews.

If Karl Kraus was Reinhardt's most obdurate adversary, Alfred Kerr, Germany's most esteemed critic, writing not for an esoteric periodical but for Berlin's most influential morning paper, was the most effective. So long as Reinhardt and his company were struggling, Kerr, the great booster of Gerhart Hauptmann, used to sting his former colleague and Hauptmann sponsor, Otto Brahm, with occasional Reinhardt raves, playing one against the other. But when, to Kerr's—and everyone else's—surprise, his occasional protégé dethroned the mighty Brahm, the latter became teacher's pet and the "usurper" the butt for his mannered wit. He called him a "relatively simple man" whom he anything but "hated." But he admitted to being allergic to the "noise" Reinhardt was making, at the core of which he sensed an "appetizing mediocrity."

> I am not playing along. As clear as it is to me that Reinhardt, as a rich talent and able chief of operations, skipped over the unoriginality of many a theatre addict, as clear it is to me that he is serving the noblest kitsch we have had for a long time; things that are almost indistinguishable from art.

But with the years, Kerr's campaign spent itself, as a younger generation began to catch his jaundiced eye—in particular Piscator and Brecht ("A play by Brecht is by no means meant for primitive listeners, rather it is a play by a primitive author"). Finally, Hauptmann succeeded in effecting a rapprochement between Reinhardt and Kerr, for whom the former target now served as a bulwark against what he perceived to be an ever-increasing vulgarization and brutalization of German culture.

While Kerr's animosity stemmed from a literary suspicion of the Director's Theatre, Kraus's, in my father's view, was pathological, going back to a trauma in their early days as aspiring actors. Well-heeled Kraus had leased the suburban theatre, where my father was appearing, for one evening in order to star in a scheduled performance. My father played a smaller part and earned applause. Kraus was hissed. His arrogant incompetence provoked a colleague to slap him backstage, an incident that was repeated on other occasions, and all of which he blamed on my father.

Another unsuccessful actor turned writer was the internationally known publicist Maximilian Harden. He was one of Reinhardt's earliest fans and most vociferous extollers. His friendship with Rathenau opened the door to finance, through which Hollaender found his way to some of the capital required for purchasing the Deutsches Theater. In the *Festschrift* denied to Hermann Bahr a letter from Harden to Reinhardt was reprinted:

> If you were a purveyor of pomp, I would be your most adamant adversary. That you are not and never have been I want to bear witness to loudly. . . . Not through lavish display have you taught us, a whole group of disappointed lovers of the theatre, to fall in love with it again. But through your earnest intentions, your sense of the relevant, your fanatic love for a cause.

The "display," lavish or not, was, nevertheless, very much part of the game. Before it was won—and for a long time after—it rested securely in the hands of a key collaborator, the scenic designer Ernst Stern. In his *Diary* he wrote:

> Today in his office, Reinhardt showed me an oil painting by the famous Norwegian painter Edvard Munch. It depicted a room whose characteristic feature was a large, black easy chair. The room was intended for Ibsen's drama *Ghosts*. Munch's picture, painted in his typical style, gave me only very few hints for the scenic conception as such, and I said as much to Reinhardt. "Maybe," he replied, "but *the chair says everything!* [Italics his.] Its black reflects the whole mood of the drama. And then the walls of the room," he continued, "they have the color of diseased gums. We must try to find a wallpaper that has this shade. It will put the actors in the right mood. Mime, in order to become free, needs the right room, modeled by form, light and, above all, color." *To take into account the psychology of color*! [Italics his.] Reinhardt showed me the way to it.

The galaxy of friends and foes my father gathered in his orbit seems to contradict a judgment I made before: that he was not good at choosing people. It does not. He hardly chose any of them. He attracted them. He could not help it, for better or for worse. This also applies to his alter ego, whom he called in a letter to me "the completely unexpected and most overwhelming boon in my life: my brother Edmund."

This second oldest son of his family was the first he sent for. In Berlin, Edmund worked in a goldsmith's shop and then went into bankruptcy in the leather business. Around the same time, he became involved in an unhappy love affair. Max, one night, came upon him as he was putting a revolver to his temple. He wrested the weapon from his hand and made him swear on everything that was holy to them never again to contemplate suicide. This traumatic experience laid the foundation for a unique interdependence that bound the two brothers to each other for life.

Max had just moved into the Kleines Theater. The company was struggling for economic survival. It was not easy for him, when he still had to find himself and make his own way, to lend material and emotional support to someone else, no matter how eagerly given and direly needed. I mentioned earlier that it was my mother who suggested giving Edmund a job in the theatre. There was, however, no indication whatsoever that the fledgling enterprise had enough vitality to save him or that he might be at all useful to it. Though both turned out to be true beyond all expectations, at that stage Reinhardt's partners could not have been very happy about this additional burden on the budget. To them, hiring a complete stranger to the profession who had very little else to offer than his unprepossessing self reeked of shameless nepotism. To my mother, for whom Reinhardt was no longer one of a group, but its head, such an odor was not offensive. An extenuating circumstance may have been that Edmund was discretion personified, that he abhorred being conspicuous and never was. When death suddenly exacted its long-announced claim on him at the age of fifty-four, Adolf Paul, a playwright who remembered him from the days he had a comedy running at the Kleines Theater, wrote:

> The man in the shadow entered the realm of the shadows. . . . And Berlin, without having been aware of it, discovered all of a sudden that in Edmund Reinhardt it had had its mightiest theatre man. People became aware of it only now that he was gone.

He recalled Edmund's beginnings:

> Before curtain time a young man used to stand next to the box office, humble and self-effacing, a small memorandum book in his hand, writing out passes for friends of the establishment. . . . That was Reinhardt's brother.

Edmund Reinhardt was soon doing much more. Soon he became the "soul of the business" (in the literal sense of the phrase). He imposed parsimony on all transactions and acted as Max's devoted and effective mouthpiece in the sharp negotiations for expansion that followed each foothold gained. He was no promoter, no money raiser, nor a born leader. But seldom has someone understood so well how to plan the procurement of capital, to husband it in the face of overwhelming temptation—and an irresistible tempter—and to run a multiform operation through others. Above all, he knew exactly when one had to give in to Max Reinhardt and when it was crucial he be dissuaded. And there was only one person by whom Max let himself be dissuaded: Edmund. His yes was always a hard-fought concession, registered with relief; his more frequent no was just as hard, but delivered with such charm that even the most disappointed found it difficult to be angry with him for long.

Unhesitatingly, he delegated tactical authority and sought for each sector the best expert available. He was a master at evoking loyalty and the reins never slipped from his delicate hands. The strategic decisions were solely his. At such times, the shy introvert would not shy away from looking his opponent straight in the eye. And whenever he was maneuvered into a corner, there were those two magic words that extricated him from it, diplomatic and truthful words: "my brother . . . ," whom he insisted he must first consult—and rarely did—and for whom he insisted he was acting exclusively—and always was. What made Edmund my father's ideal collaborator was that he relieved him of two particularly hateful duties: administrating and saving.

Edmund drew up the blueprint for a stock corporation (in which Max, with his talent as his only investment, held the majority). In the first years, he saw to it that the necessary credit was on hand when the big bills fell due. Later, when such crutches were no longer required, he saw to it that the bills did not match the splendor for which they were incurred. The Deutsches Theater paid anything but splendid fees or salaries. Edmund's rationale for his notorious niggardliness in business—increasingly hard to uphold considering Max's notorious prodigality in his private life—was simple: the honor of working for the Reinhardts justified financial sacrifices.

These "sacrifices" on the part of artists, technicians and administrative personnel to whom the brothers Reinhardt offered but a scanty living were a source of constant irritation which the victims vented sporadically. It was a common occurrence that this or that member, having attained prominence, left the Reinhardts in a huff, litigated against them, even took public stands in the press. Edmund remained unimpressed by such rebellions and unembarrassed. He knew what power he represented and waited patiently for the renegades to return to the fold, either on his terms or accepting what he deemed a tolerable compromise. And that is what the majority of them eventually did—forever grumbling, but rarely denying Edmund the respect due him.

The reactions to his death alone furnish ample proof of that. A flood of condolences from within the trade was of course to be expected. But not from every nook and cranny of it and not the tidal wave that inundated my father with heart-stirring professions of fidelity, not only to him but to the memory of the deceased. The messages from high and low were remarkable for their understanding of the man gone and, therefore, of the defenselessness of the man left behind. Even more significant, however, seem to me the lines from a source in no way obligated or even involved:

> My dear Herr Professor,
>
> When you were about to achieve greatness, your brother was in search of an apartment for you in a house on Königsplatz [the house in which my brother was born] whose landlord I was. To my inquiry about your financial circumstances and what security you could offer for the considerable rental, he replied:
>
> My brother is a genius.
>
> Earlier than others he recognized this quality in you and believed in it unshakably. His belief convinced others and, in hours of weakness that surely you, too, must have gone through now and then, probably yourself.
>
> He was capable of all this, for he was himself a genius and a man of character. Whoever knows this, as I do, does not attempt any words of consolation now, but simply presses your hand in mute commiseration.
>
> Since my name, by itself, will not mean much to you, I should like to remind you of . . . the help I was able to lend you in obtaining the Komödie.
>
> With assurances of my high esteem,
>
> Yours sincerely
> Lion

Except for the sender's name and address, no more is known about him than what the letter contains. But that, it seems to me, is quite a lot. And though, I am sure, my father did not have the vaguest notion who Mr. Lion was, he must have been moved to the core by his tribute—more than by those of such sympathizers as Frederick Leopold, Prince of Prussia, Luigi Pirandello cabling from Sicily, David Belasco from the United States; as the Moscow Art Theatre, whose manager, Leonidov, speaks of the "loss of your venerated brother . . . whom we esteemed both as a human being and theatre man"; as the director Heinz Hilpert, who mourns "the best brother, the most noble human being, the most modest servant of creative work"; as the president of the Deutsche Bank, Emil Georg von Stauss, who wires: "I shall keep this splendid man of whom I gained an excellent impression in frequent negotiations in my faithful memory."

In other words, Edmund made *his* way not just as a fraternal adjunct, although that is precisely what he wanted to be. He had become a fascinating, loved and attacked, highly esteemed personality in his own right. The polish, education, aesthetic judgment and self-assurance Max acquired through professional traffic with the best literature and art, hobnobbing with the best brains and talents and the necessity of making independent decisions about matters of taste and worth under the scrutiny of jaundiced eyes, Edmund, ever on the fringe of these activities and associations, acquired in his spare time on his own. He read profusely, regularly visited theatres and concerts, traveled widely and maintained affairs with women of high intellectual caliber. And yet, the more important Edmund's role in the steadily expanding operation, the less visible his existence to the outside.

Even the two brothers saw each other seldom. There was little social companionship between them. And since Max, wherever possible, stayed clear of management problems and Edmund, unless he or Max considered it absolutely necessary, was averse to mixing in artistic questions, their contacts were kept to a minimum or reserved for long telephone calls (preferably long-distance), even longer telegrams and love letters. In these communications, each, but especially Max, professed over and over his desire for the company of the other and for an end to their separations. Yet I believe that both nursed more tenderly the *idea* of being close than actual contiguity. They lived, after all, in the same house (on Kupfergraben) from 1911 onward, but even the hours they kept made meetings between the night owl and the early riser all but impossible. In the theatre their offices could not have been more distant from each other. And then, Edmund's cardiac defect forced him to take care of himself in the few leisure moments his strenuous working schedule permitted. This ever-lurking danger precluded the long nights, improvisation and irregularities so commonplace in a theatre man's life. The brothers' intimate relations and, at the same time, odd lack of personal contact seem best illustrated by this ritual: Directly following the final curtain call at an opening in the Deutsches Theater, before exchanging a word with anyone else, my father would hasten to my uncle's office—which was connected with the manager's box by a private stairway—to receive the fraternal blessing. There may have been opinions he valued more highly or more expert prognoses to be had; nevertheless, Edmund's sanction was, if not the most weighty, certainly the most pressing item on his agenda. These meetings were invariably brief; so brief in fact that the Professor's absence was hardly ever noticed backstage and the ritual known only to the fewest. A kiss on the cheek would seal it and, immediately after, the two brothers would resume their different ways, the one taking his place in the worldly melee, the other retiring from it to the most private of private lives. Next morning, as Max's bedtime hour approached, Edmund would be at his desk, founding, building, arranging, mediating, shielding, braking, steering. Under the gently tenacious aegis of this true *éminence grise* the empire grew, his presence hardly in evidence, yet always felt. Somewhere in the shadows there was always "my brother."

But, as we know, Max was not Edmund's only brother. There were two others and there were sisters, parents, uncles, aunts, cousins, in-laws, legitimate and illegitimate offspring. (One afternoon in the Rosenberg apartment on Kupfergraben, I was fascinated, as an adolescent, to find myself looking unexpectedly into the eyes of my father, even though they were embedded in another head and a female one at that. It was the head, as I learned later, of my older half sister, his illegitimate daughter, Jenny. I don't remember ever having seen her in our part of the house, though it was not my mother who kept her away from us. It was she, in fact, who explained the astonishing resemblance to us, which was, however, very partial, the rest of her features apparently going to the credit of a Miss Kornfeld, a meek lady my father had had an affair with in his, so to speak, pre-respectable days. My mother made no such distinctions and was sorry for the girl. Financially, of course, Jenny was taken care of—including her education [in England]—even after her marriage, even after my father's death, as a legatee. But, as long as I lived in Germany, he almost never saw her. Edmund, as usual, was glad to be his proxy.)

For everyone, Max was the revered head of the family and, as token of their reverence—as was the custom those days in Jewish families one of whose members had made good—every able-bodied male had automatically stopped working, leaving the responsibility for their and their dependents' livelihoods in the lap of the lucky one fate had clearly chosen for this purpose. But just as my father was becoming more and more the figurehead of his theatres, so he acted as a figurehead in the role of paterfamilias. In that domain too, the man to talk to was Edmund. It was a thankless task which he performed with intelligence and tact and, unless he was riled, with warmth. The wives of his charges had a habit of riling him:

Dear Edmund,

. . . I am afraid you have a false picture of my marriage and of my relation to my wife. It is not at all "henpecked." On the contrary: My wife suffers a great deal under my unfortunate character. . . . I think she often regrets having married me. . . . I give you my holy word of honor that I give her nothing but housekeeping money. . . .

I am most thankful to you for the promised raise and if you could augment it to 250 or 300 marks, you would make me very happy. . . . I wish it were possible to talk to you longer than five minutes. . . . Love,

Yours, Siegfried

This brother, whom we have met before, was married to a Gentile. She was to save his life: Together, they emigrated to Holland, where, after the Nazi invasion, he went underground and hid throughout the war. The remuneration his benefactors asked for this service she earned by knitting for the Master Race.

In a letter from the Hotel Majestic in New York, in 1923, Edmund writes to his youngest brother, Leo, who had gone to Switzerland to convalesce from pneumonia:

With Max's approval I have relieved you for the time being from your duties in the Deutsches Theater for the period of one year. . . . I am able, in addition, to give you news which will probably be most welcome to you: I have asked Max to send you the monthly amounts . . . directly from now on. . . . You needn't, therefore, address yourself to me in the future any more and I need no longer occupy myself with your affairs.

I continue to wish you well. Adieu. I don't expect an answer to this letter.

E.

I am convinced that Edmund still frequently occupied himself with the affairs of this ailing, touching brother and of his family. Leo, a most kindhearted person, who could boast of few gifts, felt discriminated against in the sinecure he had been assigned in the theatre. When his wife chided him for it at home, he used to compensate for the humiliation the next day in his office, bringing down his tiny fists on his desk, assuring everyone willing to listen: "I have *yes* talent!"

And in Berlin Uncle Rosenberg:

Dear Edmund,

Please light this candle tomorrow, Monday evening, for Jahrzeit [Jewish anniversary of the dead] of dear, God-blessed Papa [my grandfather] and keep it burning till Tuesday evening.

Wednesday night we are expecting you for dinner with dear Max, as also on Thursday after fasting.

Love,

Hermann

Besides running a big business and a large family, Edmund—and that was perhaps his most exigent function—also ran Max's private life. Edmund purchased or rented Max's houses, apartments, cars; he engaged the domestics and paid all bills. For smaller, daily expenses Max received pocket money from him. Max's progressive alienation from normal monetary dealings assumed grotesque forms. Paying checks in restaurants became ever more awkward transactions. Every bill was turned over three, five, seven times to make sure that it was the desired one. And coins seemed to throw him into such bewilderment that, after strenuous examination, he would part with them full of disgust, dropping whatever number happened to be in his hand, as though they were poison and he could not rid himself of them fast enough. I remember a particularly ludicrous moment when the incredible came to pass and Max Reinhardt in the company of his sons used a streetcar (apparently the driver could not be found and no taxi was available). I believe it was his first ride in a public conveyance in thirty years. His protracted search for the demanded change, the conductor's refusal to break proffered notes of high denomination scraped together from every conceivable pocket, the steadily mounting confusion on one side and anger on the other—the whole performance made such a comedy hit with the other passengers that a hasty getaway from the devilish vehicle seemed advisable and was duly executed at the next stop.

That so excessive a dependence on another person and a virtual declaration of one's own incompetence had to be paid for dearly, once this person was no longer there, was obvious to all but my father. The penalty exacted from him for his self-indulgence after Edmund's death was, indeed, heavy. He knew, of course, that no one subsequently trying to take Edmund's place could possibly match his fidelity, circumspection and honesty, but he acted nevertheless as though they did. He was no longer able to regenerate his atrophied faculties for dealing with life's trivia. Consequently, the ensuing years were a field day of incompetence and crookedness. The nadir of the rapid decline in the quality of managerial and legal assistance was reached the day my father called me during office hours in Hollywood and insisted I drop everything and come straight over to the house: He had reached the end of the line. Ruin was staring him in the face.

It was the first time that he permitted me to look into his financial situation, as he had hitherto feared that, because of my loyalty to my mother, she might get wind of his assets. Entering his lovely villa on Outpost Drive with the many rescued treasures, the glorious bird's-eye view of Los Angeles and the lush subtropical garden, it was difficult to grasp the full meaning of what had happened to the grand seigneur and his consort: They were penniless, without a single possession in the world. Not a piece of furniture in the house belonged to them, not a painting, not a plate, not a knife or fork, no suit of clothes, no dress, no button. Their private car was in hock and so was the truck of the Workshop. My father's shares in the Workshop were impounded as collateral for personal loans and his residence was twice mortgaged—all in favor of his California attorney to whom he had given unlimited powers. Alleged unpaid fees and debts had surrendered my father lock, stock and barrel into this man's clutches. The predicament was all the more incomprehensible as my father had been a big earner until recently. But not only was there nothing left of these earnings (almost four hundred thousand dollars in five years), not even the taxes had been paid on them. Mrs. Thimig, in addition, discovered that her personal savings, kept in a private bank account, to which the lawyer, as to everything else, had access, were gone. My father's right-hand man of yesterday was today demanding immediate cash payment, else he must foreclose the mortgages and liquidate all movable property.

With the aid of expensive legal advice, by threatening disbarment and in extended, unsavory haggling, I finally reached a settlement my father could barely live with. But that—*barely living*—was as far as it went. I could not save his beloved house high in the Hollywood hills. It became the home of his erstwhile collaborator, who, for reasons Reinhardt never had any inclination to explore, preferred the role of deadly adversary.

It is not hard to imagine the forlornness in such distress of one accustomed to collaboration and bulletins of another sort:

My dear, dear Max!

You are showing such infinite love and kindness to me that I could not be happier or prouder. Your last dear, dear letter I could not even finish reading in one session, I had to interrupt continuously. . . . It has been at all times, since my childhood, my most ardent, unspoken wish to be able to work with you and to be with you. And even today that is still my one and only wish. And therefore I take it as a given that I will work with you and for you as long as you have need of me and as long as you permit me. . . .

In the Circus [the Grosses Schauspielhaus in the process of reconstruction] things are advancing at an awfully slow pace. . . . Kratz [a building contractor] sent a bill for overtime in excess of eleven hundred and fifty marks and I approved payment in full, although I could easily have deducted a thousand marks for the bonus he had received. . . .

I have repeatedly negotiated with Wolf [former owner of Leopoldskron] . . . He became disagreeable when I mentioned the carved coat of arms and demanded that the objects he had verbally agreed to at the time be included in the contract. . . .

Of the new caretaker whom you wish to hire I would demand that he knows how to handle horses. . . .

I have taken a look at the stage of the theatre in the Royal Academy in Berlin with Knina and Dworsky [my father's crack stage technicians]. It is thirty-six feet wide and twenty-seven feet deep, has flies, iron curtain and a most primitive lighting layout. . . .

Please give Mama, Gottfried and Adele my warmest regards and be embraced by your ever-loving, old

Edmund

P.S. Please wire in what adaptation *As You Like It* is to be played. I would like to order the material.

THE DIARY

SUNDAY,
OCTOBER 17, 1943

The expression in Papa's eyes has changed: no longer searching, no longer pleading for clarity, no longer fearful, no longer wavering between scorn and gratitude, no longer interested in challenge. No longer innocent. With adulthood thrust upon him and childhood no longer in his pocket, he refuses to go on playing.

MONDAY,
OCTOBER 18, 1943

Dr. G. from Harvard makes his appearance. The intellectual conductor. Refugee riding the American waves high on his excellent reputation in Germany. A personality directly polar to our formidable K.'s. But his self-assurance isn't one bit less than the other's and his vanity simply a rose by another name—with the Scottish thorns tactfully tenderized by a condescending smile. The vanity is in his thoughts, not in his deportment, which is modest. Have no quarrel with that. Have no quarrel with anyone who can help Papa. But Papa's back is up. This big, smooth specialist with whom he can talk in his mother tongue, who keeps assuring him at frequent intervals—too frequent—of his admiration for the artist he is, irritates him all the more. For his examination is no less disagreeable than Kennedy's and—thanks to the complimentary asides—takes twice as long. The diagnosis: not altogether crushing, but depressing enough.

Translate Einstein text, cut it, receive permission for shooting. Run into Junior Laemmle. Wants to sell me a "terrific mausoleum" in Brooklyn—without, naturally, having an inkling how ill-timed the proposed bargain is, because, alas, it is so well-timed. He grows lyrical over the beauty of the site and deplores lack of appreciative occupant—his mother, former occupant, having been reinterred by his father in an even grander mausoleum in Hollywood, where she now rests in peace beside him. Regret I can't entertain Papa with latest Schweik story.

TUESDAY,
OCTOBER 19, 1943

Marked deterioration. Speech very difficult to understand. H. explains that new little strokes occur every day. Papa, he says, intensifies them by trying to force solution.

The meat now reaches the table cut up in small pieces, as if for a child.

Meet gossipy Gessner and mate in elevator. This time their questions are needle-pointed. My answers, conspicuous by their absence. But they are quick to get the message, these two. And so considerate. No further questions. Just soulful expressions and commiserating nods. What beneficial brew can be stirred out of a famous friend's death? [I was soon to find out.]

Wolfgang calls: Thimig left California by train. Why not by plane? Tell him am sending money for his flight.

WEDNESDAY,
OCTOBER 20, 1943

Third visit with Einstein. He approves of the translation—does he really understand it?—and of the cuts. We speak about God and the world, the Jewish God and the non-Jewish world. He fulminates against the quota system in American universities. "The Jewish academician in America is walled up in a ghetto." Einstein's solution: Jewish universities. Like Papa, he's no Zionist. But, unlike Papa, he's a militant Jew and believes in Jewry's fighting for its rights wherever it has settled.

"Professor, what made you leave Germany so early—so long before Hitler and violent anti-Semitism?" "I saw no reason to wait until it became violent." "But you went back and became the Kaiser's most prized scientist, didn't you?" "Ja—but with a Swiss passport! You see, as a scientist I'm an opportunist. Professionally, I was happy with the company I kept in Berlin. Politically—what shall I say?—I was never comfortable with Germans. Or they with me." "Still, the arch-German Kaiser Wilhelm Society did invite you to become its director." [The forerunner of the present Max Planck Society, Germany's highest-ranking institute of natural sciences, its membership then limited to German nationals.] "Because there are no greater opportunists than the Germans. When I refused to give up my Swiss citizenship they closed their eyes to the statutes." "And you left before they opened them again?" Wicked grin: "I told you I was an opportunist."

Hitler came as no surprise to him. He concedes that the majority of Germans may not have wanted Hitler, but, all things considered, they certainly deserved him. And that goes for all the Deutschland-über-alles Jews who were more chauvinistic than their Aryan persecutors. Ask him what drew him to mathematics originally, because if appearances count for anything he should rightly have been an artist. Unhesitating reply: "Its lovely simplicity." I laugh. He emphatically does not! Have to explain myself: "Coming from you, Professor, someone who's discovered something that only a handful of people in the entire world understand, it sounds pretty funny, don't you think?" He doesn't: "I have heard that 'handful of people' nonsense too long. It's a journalistic lie! Any halfway knowledgeable mathematician or physicist understands the theory of relativity!" The artist in him is moved to give me an example of this "simplicity": he points to the pristine beauty of Euclid's proof—surely I remember it from my schooldays—that primary numbers are infinite. I do not remember it from my school or any other days and must confess that what I do remember never struck me as simple or beautiful. But, sudden miracle, with Albert Einstein as guide, it becomes both. Thank him for thrilling revelation: the kinship of mathematics and art. Einstein laughs: "Not only in theory. Also in practice. Your father and our good friend Meyer Weisgal even got me to schnorr for The Eternal Road!"

Back in Gladstone, find half a dozen urgent messages from Eleonora in my box. Hurry upstairs. Ashen-faced, she tells me Papa has not emerged from his room until now—it's four in the afternoon—and he hasn't given any sign of life. She was terrified of going in. . . . I knock on his door. No answer. I turn the knob, enter. Papa is sitting on the side of his bed. His eyes thank me for an eternity of waiting ended. But he makes no move. Fire Island's horror film now plays in slow motion: The fastidious Max Reinhardt is wearing no jacket, his shirt collar is unbuttoned, his tie, perfectly well within his reach, lies next to him on his bed, his shoes next to his slippered feet. He cannot dress himself. Help him, take his arm and walk him into the sitting room, where Eleonora has long set the table for breakfast.

He eats with his left hand, Eleonora helping him when he fumbles or spills. Suddenly, he stops, tries to tell us something. With difficulty we gather it is something he wanted to do when he woke up in the morning, but he wasn't able to bring it off. His delivery is thick, yet he finds most elaborate circumlocutions for what he apparently could not perform and cannot convey to us directly. We try guessing: "You wanted to get dressed? To shave? To telephone?" And so on and so on. "N-no n-no n-n-no!" He *pretends to be astonished at our denseness, then, growing increasingly restless, tries to ridicule his despair. He laughs, shakes his head in self-mockery: "I-it's grotesque! Everybody does it, everybody can do it!" Eleonora makes another stab: "You wanted to brush your teeth, Max?" He nods vigorously, closes his eyes and leans back. Later in the day, I ask him whether it might not be a good idea to have someone else help him until he's better. I don't say "nurse." He doesn't ask who this "someone" is. He's relieved.*

THURSDAY,
OCTOBER 21, 1943

H. gets a nurse for us. She doesn't wear a uniform, simply turns up daily to "assist." But the increasing razor nicks on Papa's face call for additional assistance. I arrange for a barber from the Ambassador to come in every morning. Papa's growing need for assistance doesn't disturb him any more. Once it's there—and we always manage to make it seem providential—he leans on it. Again, he is immaculately soigné—except his right leg is dragging. And so our life goes on. It's a great effort for us to deny to each other that Papa's condition is worsening fast, but as he speaks less and less, subterfuge with him is not much of a problem. Tell him en passant of Thimig's arrival day after tomorrow. No response.

FRIDAY,
OCTOBER 22, 1943

The day of certainty. No more hope for recovery. His right side almost totally paralyzed. Hospital-room routine replaces illusionary improvisation. Nurse wears a white uniform. Eleonora spoon-feeds him. Not a word crosses his lips. His glance comes from a distant world, goes through me, into another distant world.

Cancel everything: Korngold, Bressart, Corbett, Irion—without, of course, giving the real reason. Call off Baker and Meehan as well. Leaden emptiness.

Wolfgang wires he will be here on Sunday. Tell Papa. His face is expressionless.

SATURDAY,
OCTOBER 23, 1943

Have grown accustomed to the fact that, by entering his apartment, I enter the past. Paralysis has extended to his left side. He's no longer able to leave his bed.

Three nurses around the clock. Darvas and I fetch Thimig at Grand Central Station. Though she is mentally prepared to meet the worst bravely, her unyielding will power makes it impossible for her to accept it. Somehow she feels her very appearance on the scene must change it. But the deployment of her remarkable energy comes too late. Her stream of proposals is out of date. The bedside reunion is without union. The fervor of clasped hands is all hers. She calls to him softly. He doesn't answer. Not with his lips or his eyes. Hers fill with tears of frustration and sorrow. His are dry and remote.

I leave them alone and only now discover that Eleonora has vanished, leaving no trace that she's ever been there, but also no trace of anything personal belonging to Max Reinhardt. I can't even find the page with his last scribbles. A new administration has begun—with nothing left to administer.

H. makes his dire medical report to Thimig. She insists on calling in a new doctor—a Dr. Elias, who has been recommended to her. Although he thinks it's futile, H. doesn't object. Neither do I.

SUNDAY,
OCTOBER 24, 1943

Fetch Wolfgang at La Guardia. On way back to Gladstone, bring him up to date about Papa. He's terribly down.

Papa's bedside: Wolfgang sits beside him. Kisses his brow, tries to reach him—as we all do—but, defeated—as we all are—leaves the room with me.

Lunch with him at the Plaza. Oak Room. One of the last masculine bulwarks against female invasion of the sacred right of men-onlyness over a noonday martini or two. Atmosphere very old New York. Sentimentalize about its sad passing, but suddenly realize Wolfgang's almost a stranger here. Actually, he is a stranger in America. His adopted country is Hollywood. I'm the only member of my family to have taken root.

People, many from the theatre, stop by our table, ask about Papa. I introduce Wolfgang. We become a twin target of questions, maintain a noncommittal united front. But, quite honestly, I don't know what the deep secret is we're guarding. Something that doesn't exist? We both know Papa is no more and that the world will still go on, as it always did, when it hears of it. Well, not quite as it always did. After the first shock the loss—in a time of such immense losses!—will not leave a scar. But it will leave a gap. A taken-for-granted spark will have flickered out. Only in the darkness will it be missed. There has always been—and there always will be—art and entertainment, showmanship, low comedy and high style in acting, love of classics and the avant-garde, literary, spectacular and intimate theatre, circus, pantomime, ballet, opera, the round, the half-round, the square, the arena and the box, drama and farce, box office and succès d'estime. But all in a single life's work?

Why am I writing all this down? I guess, like Papa in the last year or two, I prefer occupying myself with what I want to think about, and not think about what is facing me, what I have to face.

For Wolfgang and me, of course, the spark can never disappear. And when we think of him, we're not just reaching into the cornucopia of our own memories. A living picture of him is ours, painted by the world that surrounded him, of the world that made him and that he made. Some of the images passing before our eyes on this autumn day in New York we have never seen ourselves. Yet they couldn't be clearer and brighter in our consciousnesses. For example, as far back as 1908, his audacious, almost socio-critical concept of The Merchant of Venice *with Shylock, Shakespeare's Semitic butt of jokes—thereafter for years played as a conventional heavy—as the victim of unscrupulous, beguiling Venetian playboys! None of the characters are propelled purely by their own volition, all are driven by environmental prejudices and prides. Wolfgang and I smile: How "modern"! [I'm still smiling today.] It's a funny feeling to sit in this room fragrant with the Americana of lamb chops, corned-beef hash, porterhouse steak and french fries where, from neighboring tables, snatches of stock-market talk and last night's grosses drift over to us and to dwell, as we do, on the esoteric theme of German Shakespeare. Not that, as so many Europeans, we turn up our noses at Americans' so-called obsession with money. We're well aware that in our former fatherland what one shrank away from was not the joy of making money, but the "indelicacy" of admitting it at table or any place else. Ours was the "superior" land of* Bildung. *A magical word meaning education, culture, refinement, breeding. To have it, set you apart from the average man, the nouveau riche, the underprivileged. Its strongholds were the classrooms where stiff-collared pedants dispensed higher learning, the bourgeois* gute Stube *[front parlor] and the classical theatre.* Bildungstheater*—no bones about it—was not intended as lively entertainment. It was a guaranteed-not-to-fail soporific, its lulling effect interrupted only by the occasional burst of a starring performance—that was Germany's pride. You had to be bored by Goethe, Schiller, Kleist or something was wrong. Distinguished boredom was what made the classics classic. Yet Papa turned these dreary musts into intoxication for ear and eye,* Bildung *into box office. His one-man show was a college's entire curriculum of German, Spanish, Italian, French, English, Latin and Greek. We two* Bildungs *alumni wonder whether he would have made it so exciting if he had gone to college and learned the classics by rote instead of discovering them for himself.*

By now, all the other lunchers have left. We pay our bill, but linger on in the deep, roomy chairs. No wonder that our thoughts go back to another oak-paneled room, similar deep, roomy chairs.

Muted Strings

ONLY ONE YEAR after Reinhardt had been granted the rental of the Deutsches Theater—on condition he give up his other two houses—and six months after he had become its owner, he added a second house to it by acquiring a run-down ballroom next door and rebuilding it into an all oak-paneled, "drawing-room" theatre for a selected clientele. Borrowing from the language of music, he called it Die Kammerspiele (The Chamber Playhouse), a term so expressive that it was at once adopted by Strindberg for a series of his intimate plays and, subsequently, became a common name for small theatres in most German-speaking cities. The stage was elevated so little above the orchestra—no more than three steps connecting them—that, with a mere suggestion of a proscenium frame between them, it was hard to say where the one began and the other ended. Prompter's box (found in all Central European theatres) and pit were eliminated. The simple, rectangular enclosure had the acoustic effect of a Stradivari. In this delicate shell actor and audience were merged as one.

> On November 8, 1906, the Kammerspiele opened with Ibsen's *Ghosts*. But after this first sentence I am already disgusted with my dry tone. I shall not hold myself in check, act the critic, sift or weigh pros and cons. Whoever doesn't rejoice over this is falsifying his impression or is insensitive to art. I, for one, have never and nowhere felt such an impact—on myself or an entire audience. A review that measures what is achieved in the light of what could be achieved has, for once, nothing to measure. It can merely seek to discover the secret of this phenomenal impact.

Thus the rejoicing of Siegfried Jacobsohn. "Not a breath is lost," he went on, ". . . here only the creature of the poet exists, not the person of the actor."

The Danish novelist and essayist Hermann Bang describes a dress rehearsal at the Kammerspiele with its "self-absorbed crowd of celebrities" in the foyer and its drama students (the school was on the top floor of the theatre) "perched outside on the steps, like fledglings in a nest." Bang registers the entrance of Hofmannsthal: ". . . lithe, straight lieutenant's shoulders. . . . Small, elegant, with a body at home in the works of great tailors." And about the "host" he says:

> The eyes are awake—no, more than that: vigilant. . . . A man who waits and is at his post, but now as he smiles his face suddenly grows young, which it actually is, and shines with I don't know what—yes, it shines with a jaunty, irresistible bravura.

A dialogue develops between the two. Bang detects hidden problems in Reinhardt "which perhaps no living soul knows, but whose depths one can guess." He sees "a leader of troops casually changing his gloves in the hail of bullets." He doubts that "in all the world there is so beautiful a room for a theatre." He speaks of "wonderful harmony."

And then the day of the opening. He spots Ferenc Molnár in the audience. He wishes he were able to see his face, but:

> He doesn't reveal it to us. His mask wears a monocle.
>
> While everyone knows everyone else and the satin waistcoats of the men shine and the ladies flash their diamonds or drape them in sable . . . one feels transported in this oak-paneled room to the billiard room of an elegant country manor. . . . But when the candelabra high on the walls dim, the house lights go out and the velvet curtain parts . . . Max Reinhardt speaks. His is the only voice heard.

In the Kammerspiele white tie was the prescribed etiquette (but soon abandoned) and applause after the curtain's fall ruled out. All his glorification notwithstanding, Bang calls the final impression "glacial." Yet he concludes his piece with the sentence: "Where Max Reinhardt reigns, there is the center of theatrical art." These two observations would seem to be contradictory.

They become less contradictory when one considers that the Kammerspiele did not survive long as the center of Reinhardt's theatrical art. The "glacial" ceremonial ran counter to the times (but, interestingly, for once, not counter to the critics). Moreover, perfection in live close-up on an assembly line cannot be perpetually sustained even by a genius. Nor did the output of literary masterpieces—which alone made possible the symbiosis of performer and onlooker and alone justified the microscopic exposure of the human soul—hold up. Soon, the exquisite environment was void of animate existence. After Ibsen's *Ghosts,* Wedekind's *Awakening of Spring* (probably Reinhardt's greatest success with a contemporary play; over five hundred consecutive performances, not counting the many revivals), a triumphal *Feast of Peace* by Hauptmann and an enchanting *Aglavaine and Sélysette* by Maeterlinck, the Kammerspiele gradually lost its raison d'être and the *director* Max Reinhardt his zest for the ever sparser *spécialités de la maison* he served. Other directors for them were not easy to find. In time, the Kammerspiele under the *management* of Max Reinhardt became the fifth wheel on his cart of Thespis. The muted sound of a fine violin is special and bewitching. But not for too long a duration.

THE DIARY

OCTOBER 24, 1943
(continued)

The tables around us are now being set for dinner. We move into the noisy, jam-packed bar adjoining [the way we used to do from Papa's office at the Kammerspiele to the Deutsches Theater]. *It amuses us that Molnár's "mask wearing a monocle"* [so baffling to Hermann Bang] *probably concealed nothing more baffling than contented snooziness.* [Molnár's own story told at the drop of a hat about another opening in the same theatre would seem to confirm this: ". . . So at last, after eleven hours on the train, I arrived in Berlin—all the way from Budapest—just two minutes before the curtain went up on Reinhardt's première: It was at the Kammerspiele. My favorite theatre. The seats are like clouds. I sank into mine—as I say I was exhausted from the trip—and leaned back. Bliss. On the stage—it was very, very dark; for me a dark stage is anyway better than a sleeping pill—an old retainer hobbled around, jingling a bunch of keys. The next thing I heard was a bunch of keys jingled in my ear by the night watchman trying to wake me so he could lock up the empty theatre. For me, it was one of Reinhardt's dreamier performances."]

"Want to go up and see the old devil?" I ask Wolfgang. "Up where?" "Not heaven, that's for sure." Reverse myself: "The stop before." Wolfgang is mystified. Explain: the Hotel Plaza is now known as the well-heeled émigré's retirement home. "By the way, Mosheim's a star boarder" [Grete Mosheim, graduate of Reinhardt's Berlin drama school, later a leading lady in his ensemble]. *Wolfgang protests that she's still young. Give him the whole macabre story of why she decided differently* [how this un-Germanically provocative German actress escaped her homeland and landed in London frightened—frightened of new shores, a strange language and, therefore, the specter of failure. In her dressing room, she met doddering American zillionaire Howard Gould, accepted his glistening offer of marriage—on condition she give up acting—and lost everything that made her own life glow. While the premature dowager faded within her multi-chambered gilded cage on Central Park South, her septuagenarian spouse grew bouncier by the day. His daily boost: to sit at his window every afternoon with an old crony, look down at the panhandlers in the street below and estimate their haul. But on Sunday—Grete's once-a-week rebellion

day—when she held her salon for my father, Lili Darvas, Otto Preminger, Oscar Karlweiss, Walter Slezak and other of her real-world friends, the panhandlers became bosom pals who helped distract him from the nerve-grating German conversation around his tea table].

And Molnár? Leaves the Plaza almost never. Its room service, barbershop, restaurants, newsstand, coffeehouse-type music in the Palm Court and his writing desk with a view of the most beautiful square in Manhattan are paradise enough for the most unbudgeable ego between Budapest and the Bronx. But occasionally he can be lured away by Max Reinhardt and son's invitation to Neugröschl [exile offshoot of Vienna's best Jewish restaurant, almost as famous for its kreplach as for its proprietor's deathless words to errant waiters: "What is it I see again on all the tables? No salt!"]; or when his dog-devoted mistress, whose pert little nose he keeps in its proper place in a grubby one-room hideaway in Washington Heights comes to pick him up for lunch—not at the Plaza; or when, in summer, the city heat becomes unbearable and he sheds it—and lady friend—for the cooling breezes of Montauk Point, Long Island. [One hotter-than-usual summer, the entire Hungarian colony rose up in arms against the cool cynic's abandonment of his hot and understandably bothered lady friend and plotted an end-of-vacation revenge: "Ferenc," they confronted him in a body on his return. "Vhile you vere gone vee have slept vith Vanda. ALL!" His summer tan unpaled, Molnár replied triumphantly: "Ahh, but for money she sleeps only with me!"] That the Belgian dramatist Maurice Maeterlinck should also be an "inmate of the home" and that Molnár should be able to rub shoulders daily in the elevator with the Nobel Prize winner (whose plays Max Reinhardt put on in preference to his own) without having to be bored by his fey stage dialogue is a special pleasure for him.

Through the wide windows we see darkness has set in. Central Park's autumnal colors have blurred into a shapeless smudge within its massive stone frame shot through with lights. We telephone the Gladstone. Situation unchanged. We go on talking, order a bottle of wine.

Vintage Year

ON DECEMBER 27, 1911, the London correspondent of the *Berliner Tageblatt* reported:

> On Saturday a genius invited the inhabitants of this city to his home. As a Christmas present, he had promised them he would make them forget for a few hours the grayness of everyday life and introduce them to a realm of purest beauty, a wonderland conjured up by his magic wand. The genius kept his word.

In the words of the reporter, the shivering Londoners are, of a sudden, transplanted out of the damp fog into a subtle, mysterious light that cuts through the semi-darkness of a Gothic cathedral. He writes about the pious tones on the organ, the pious nuns who enter the main nave with the public, the murmured prayers and the glorious treasure of the church: the wonder-working statue of the Virgin Mary. He depicts the opening of the great portal, granting the spectators who have taken their seats in transepts a view of a spring landscape on the Rhine. Led by a nun, a host of devoted believers is trooping in . . .

> . . . Marian songs are heard. Pilgrims are praying their litanies, children are waving green branches. Ever new flocks of people crowd their way in, ladies-in-waiting in splendid medieval costumes, peasant women, knights in heavy armor, beggars, acolytes swinging high their incense bowls, an exalted arch-bishop and many invalids seeking recovery. On a stretcher a lame man is carried in. More dragged than supported, the agonized cripple approaches the Virgin. . . . With increasing passion the "Ora pro nobis" rings out. Then a shattering scream, the cripple shoves his friends aside and, with arms stretched wide, he stands on the steps of Mary's throne. He is cured.

There follows an account of the rejoicing, the flood tide of the multi-tude, an exultant Te Deum, the procession out into the open, the closing of the doors to the cathedral and the lonely Nun remaining behind. The author's words remind us of the famous *Reinhardt upbeat.* Before the action proper begins—of the Nun's being seduced by the Piper's lures and the dancers of his retinue, her falling into the arms of a trespassing Knight, the evil winning out over the good, her breaking her vows and following the call of worldly love—we have been given a preliminary impression of the ensuing event's meaning and of the elementary force that will engulf unsuspecting London and the unsuspecting world that evening.

> The statue of the Virgin is alone. A ray of light flutters over the lithe figure. Suddenly, Mary rises and, with divine love and deep pity for the fallen maiden, she turns the palms of her hands toward the door. Love for the sinner makes her descend from the throne with movingly pathetic gestures. She doffs her crown and her cape and wraps the Nun's veil around her, assuming her part.

Reading on, we follow the progression of the story in captivating pictures, the ups and downs of the Nun's path in the hustle and bustle of worldliness, until her return to the abbey in shame and penitence and her collapse before the Virgin's statue, back in its place, as though by a miracle, now that the good deed has been accomplished.

> A sustained tone on the organ trembles on, and a deep, devotional stillness reigns in the cathedral. And all at once, a new jubilance, an ovation, shouts and clapping. We are called back from the realm of beauty so we may pay homage to the genius who, quite up to date, yes, quite humanly, stands in the center of the cathedral. He does not wear the frock of a sorcerer, holds no magic wand. In modern evening attire the small and yet so great sorcerer faces us: Max Reinhardt.
>
> The joy was indescribable. People shouted, waved and crowded into the main nave, calling for Humperdinck [the composer], Vollmoeller [author], Stern [scenic designer], for Mme. Truhanowa [the Nun], Max Pallenberg [the Piper], for Maria Carmi [Madonna]. German art, German spirit and German enthusiasm achieved a gigantic success. With one sweep, they conquered London, not with a sword, no, with a nobler weapon: art.
>
> Even in the frame of a review as extensive as this, it is impossible to relate what Reinhardt and his troops have accomplished. Once again, Reinhardt violated all traditions. He did not lead us into a theatre or into a modern circus. In Olympia [London's big exposition hall], only in Olympia, he was able to bring off this tremendous event.
>
> . . . the effect of this play is not disdain of pious faith, but genuine religious devotion. Or as an English colleague expressed it more frivolously: "The Catholic Church should thank Reinhardt for the propaganda."
>
> Again: Reinhardt worked a miracle. In less than four weeks the cathedral

> was built, the lighting fixtures installed, the big stage trap (the biggest ever put into a theatre) dug out, the machines for it brought into place, the portal erected and the gigantic hill with its pine trees which, twice, was rolled into the center of the hall, the choir, the orchestra of 200, the great mass of extras (2,000) drilled and seventy thousand pounds sterling expended. It is difficult to say what is more admirable: Reinhardt's artistic audacity or the financial audacity of the firm Cochran and Tayne, to which, putting their trust in Reinhardt's art and name, in the face of an enormous risk, London may give thanks for *The Miracle*.
>
> The press today matches the enthusiasm of the public. From two to four columns are dedicated to *The Miracle*, which is called "Reinhardt's great triumph," "Reinhardt's greatest spectacle," "the sensation of London," "a marvelous living tableau."
>
> The performance, all in all, was an immense success with public and critics . . . and Germany, especially Berlin, owes a great deal to Reinhardt.

The rave in the London *Times* was headed 'THE MIRACLE' AT OLYMPIA. PROFESSOR REINHARDT'S GREAT SPECTACLE.

In the *Athenaeum*'s opinion:

> . . . it is difficult to avoid superlatives in speaking of Prof. Reinhardt's production of *The Miracle*, the mere bigness of it all is so impressive. . . . Obviously, the larger his material, the more completely he is inspired. It looks as if his imagination had taken fire at the sight of the vast building . . . at any rate, he has handled it like a magician.
>
> Again and again as this panorama of incidents moves under our eyes, we are struck by Prof. Reinhardt's mastery of stage crowds, his skill in grouping colors and costumes harmoniously, his knowledge of what can be done with stage-lighting, and his instinct for effects that are grandiose and dramatic, as well as by his feeling for beauty.

It is no exaggeration to say that for any director—before or since Max Reinhardt—putting on a show like *The Miracle* would have represented his main effort of any one year, if not his only one. In Max Reinhardt's vintage year, 1911, it was merely the concluding climax. What is more, that year's climate favored all crops, every type of yield, in all locations. It even favored Dresden, where the bureaucracy of the Royal Opera, but especially its resident director, had fought tooth and nail against my father's collaboration on the debut of *Der Rosenkavalier*. Having no interest in embarrassing the local hack, he did not appear officially on the program and did not go onstage during the initial rehearsals, working with the cast, singly and in groups, in the foyer. Nevertheless, as time progressed, his steadily growing involvement could not remain a secret for long and the *Berliner Tageblatt* wrote on January 21: "It is being authoritatively reported here [Dresden] that Max Reinhardt has assumed a large share in the direction of *Rosenkavalier*." Thus, more or less against his will, my father pioneered yet another development that has since become the order of the day: the preeminence of the stage director in opera. (In a Viennese newspaper I recently read the review of a Mozart opera at the Salzburg Festival with a stellar cast, a conductor of world renown and a director of whom perhaps 10 percent of the audience had ever heard. The review devoted 1 percent of its space to the composer, 9 percent to the conductor, 10 percent to the scenic designer, 20 percent to the singers, and 60 percent to the director.)

Reinhardt's contribution to *Der Rosenkavalier* was more important to the development of operatic performance than to his own. His reluctant involvement came about because the hypersensitive librettist, despite the surefootedness of his composer, did not dare risk this step onto the operatic stage with so unconventional a script without the protective hand of Reinhardt—a hand that had protected his vulnerable creations for the legitimate theatre so many times in the past. He practically forced Richard Strauss to use his considerable power to make Reinhardt's participation a condition.

No one would assert that one of the three most popular operas of the twentieth century would not have reached its destiny without Reinhardt's help—or, for that matter, without the help of that fine scenic designer Alfred Roller, whom Gustav Mahler had recruited to the Vienna Opera from the drawing boards and who had worked for Reinhardt in Berlin since 1905. Still, it might have taken *Rosenkavalier* longer to win a place in the hearts of audiences had it come into the world under routine circumstances. As it was, it became an immediate popular and critical success. The state railways had to schedule extra trains from Berlin to Dresden to accommodate the avalanche of the capital's spectators.

How important the *authors* of *Der Rosenkavalier* deemed Reinhardt's contribution to their efforts is reflected by the fact that he stood as godfather at the baptism of several of their brainchildren, if not actually at the *birth* of the alliance itself. Although Hofmannsthal's dependence on Reinhardt was infinitely greater than Strauss's, Reinhardt's influence on Strauss predated that on his partner. Strauss may have read Oscar Wilde's *Salomé* before seeing Max Reinhardt's production of the play in 1904. It is even possible, though unlikely, that he saw its first performance in Paris with

Sarah Bernhardt. If he did, neither impression moved him to productivity until he attended the Berlin opening at the Kleines Theater, a performance famed for its sensuous interpretation, its high tension and optical innovations. (For the first time, three-dimensional sets—designed by Max Kruse—were employed, giving the tiny stage an unwonted depth and leaving much more to the audience's imagination than met its eye. But, more crucial, it was the first time that the art of the actress Gertrud Eysoldt came into bloom in the title role, shocking and exhilarating Berlin with her electric emotional charge, exploding uninhibitedly.) The result was that he dropped everything else and wrote an opera on the subject as revolutionary as *Parsifal* had been in its time, shocking contemporaries through its sophisticated eroticism. Strauss and Hofmannsthal had met for the first time in 1900. Subsequently, Hofmannsthal sent him a scenario. Strauss refused it. But then came Hofmannsthal's *Elektra*, again produced by Reinhardt at the Kleines Theater, again with Eysoldt in the lead. That event forged Strauss's artistic partnership with the poet, starting with their opera *Elektra*.

One year after *Rosenkavalier* Reinhardt directed in Stuttgart the first performance of the team's *Ariadne auf Naxos*. Richard Strauss's music accompanied Reinhardt's *Bourgeois Gentilhomme* by Molière. My father, to whom these musical excursions were marginal efforts and who followed operatic activities only cursorily, was not aware of his historic contribution to the Strauss-Hofmannsthal oeuvre and would have been most surprised to learn that it was one of his lasting achievements.

With *The Miracle* crowning it and *Der Rosenkavalier* ringing it in, the year 1911 also saw the first performance of Hofmannsthal's *Everyman* in Berlin's Circus Schumann—with Moissi in the lead and Roller as scenic designer. If only because of the quadriga, Reinhardt-Hofmannsthal-Moissi-Roller, reuniting in 1920 in Salzburg, it is permissible to say that its festival had, in a sense, been founded nine years before. *Sumurûn* was another 1911 event in London. Stockholm first saw Reinhardt's *Oedipus* in the spring of that same year, and the correspondent of the *Berliner Tageblatt* reported:

> . . . the chorus, of great significance to the production, had a stunning effect. The sold-out house [a circus] applauded enthusiastically. Finally, spectators carried Moissi and Reinhardt through the crowd. The Crown Prince and Prince Eugene attended the performance.

After Sweden came Russia. Fritz Kortner, then a juvenile choragus, who was to become one of Germany's most profiled and popular actors and who, though making his career in open rebellion against Reinhardt, stepped into his shoes, ending up in Germany as his directorial heir after World War II, writes in his memoir about the Moscow opening:

> They came in tails, dinner jackets, *grande toilette*, as it befits the nobly casual reserve of the metropolitan public. . . . Two hours later . . . they were bewitched, a drunken crowd, surging down the steps, toward the stage, mingling with the youth of the balcony. . . . Through all this I kept watching Reinhardt. He was quiet and yet moved.

The extras in these traveling engagements (among them St. Petersburg, Kiev, Odessa, Budapest) were usually recruited from the academic youth at the various stopovers. In many places, but especially in Hollywood, where a great many White Russian émigrés made up the supply of Central Casting, I have met former students who did not fall in love with Reinhardt in orchestra or box seats, but by taking part in his performances on stage. They retained their love all their lives.

The fruity bouquet of *La Belle Hélène* during the Munich Festival, in the summer of 1911, we have already savored.

When one measures Reinhardt's output, that year seems to embrace the work of an entire decade. According to a newspaper report, before the end of June his Deutsches Theater and Kammerspiele had presented nine new plays. Five modern German authors had their say, and six from abroad. The classical repertoire included new productions of Kleist's *Amphitryon*, Molière's *Forced Marriage*, Shakespeare's *Comedy of Errors* and *Othello*. But the list before the middle of the year would be incomplete without mentioning the first performance of *Jedermann* and the most far-reaching undertaking any German director could embark on: Goethe's *Faust II*. It alone could have filled a whole year in the life of any other theatre man. That this much-admired production, with a cast of one hundred and eight, twenty scene changes, lasting eight hours (with a one-hour intermission), was part of the packed schedule of 1911 and enjoyed eighty-five performances between March 15 and June 11 surely nobody would have considered possible. Nor has the feat been duplicated since.

The Reinhardt-spoiled Berliner took the year's program with twenty-seven of Reinhardt's own productions (ten of them new) in his stride. But the theatrical world abroad was shaken out of its complacency. Witness an editorial on page one of the Paris newspaper *Le Temps*, normally dedicated to political issues: "Max Reinhardt is a master of the artistic 'jiu-jitsu' and makes himself master of his audience without effort. His power and acumen are extraordinary . . ."

But even vintage wines turn sour in some mouths.

Siegfried Jacobsohn:

> *Jedermann:* A sterile affair that can have no consequences whatsoever. Reinhardt is slowly, or perhaps no longer so slowly, losing his touch. . . .

THE DIARY

OCTOBER 24, 1943
(continued)

On our way home, we cross Fifth Avenue to the Savoy Plaza [since elbowed out by the General Motors Building], where Wolfgang stayed with Papa during the winter of 1927–28. Wolfgang, a true Reinhardt, isn't much of a talker. But when he does talk, he talks well. He is also a true Heims. It's her iron will that helps him overcome his Reinhardt inhibitions. However, this gives him an inflexibility foreign to his father. He may change his always intelligent opinions, and very often does, but his highly personal motives for them never change. Unfulfilled ambitions, resentments, prejudices early developed and never abandoned, a Heimsian tendency to self-righteousness and a Reinhardtian tendency to wishful thinking are their source. He is almost never relaxed and, I believe, has seldom really been happy. Although we've been separated by long months and private worlds long years ago diverging, I find my affectionate feelings for him once again confirmed. He can be utterly charming, but not warm; sharp-witted, but not deeply probing; insecure, yet enviably composed; immensely inquisitive and uncommunicative; proud and, in so many ways, helpless. We've always been close, but never at ease with each other. When we were boys, he dominated me. When we were grown, mine was usually the helping hand. He's thin, I'm fat. He suffers in the shadow of his father, while I, no greater inheritor of paternal gifts, have evolved one of my own: to bear this burden cheerfully. Is Papa's death a relief to him? He talks more freely today than usual.

The Apostle of Peace

IN NOVEMBER 1927, Else Heims-Reinhardt and her two sons were making their annual plans for the winter holiday. As usual, the intention was to spend the boys' Christmas vacation at Arosa in the Grisons, Switzerland. I was looking forward to staying at my cherished Waldsanatorium, which Mama did not choose owing to any tubercle bacilli in our midst, but because she knew the proprietor and because of its superb site. My own eagerness focused on (bad) skiing, (inept) flirting and, given the diverse local preoccupations of the adults, on availing myself of the (premature) opportunity to play the adult in the hectically erotic atmosphere of Hamsun's *Last Chapter* or, when I felt particularly fanciful, of Mann's *Magic Mountain.* Of course, the overshadowing presence of my nineteen-year-old brother did not smooth my entree to these castles in the air whose newest dream inhabitant was a lovely, clever brunette three years older than I, with sparkling eyes and febrile cheeks, who titillated me, during long, undisturbed, convalescing afternoons, from the cozy pillows of her solitary bed. My relief, then, may be imagined when something most extraordinary occurred in our down-to-earth family routine: Mama received an extremely friendly letter from Papa, insinuating all kinds of rewards for her if she would give him permission to take Wolfgang to New York on his forthcoming tour there. He argued convincingly that introducing the young man to the New World under such felicitous auspices might provide him with a start in life not likely to be duplicated so soon. But it was not these auspices that moved me to back this request with whatever weight my opinion had with Mama. Though not yet fifteen, I was working on my own start in life. I wanted to move it up.

As always, Mama was torn between her genuine concern for our well-being and her own strategic interests, a conflict she remained unaware of, since both, in her mind, were identical. This time, they actually dovetailed: Her firstborn's record during his last years in Berlin's Gymnasium and his initial semesters at Heidelberg University had not been very encouraging. It was mostly a record of absences. A change, any change of environment, would do Wolfgang good, she thought, even at the side of the devil, his father. And, as accepting the obvious and the reasonable could be couched in terms of a painfully generous concession, she earned by her reluctant consent a contract for two appearances in the Reinhardt theatres otherwise barred to her: as Mistress Page in Shakespeare's *Merry Wives of Windsor* and the Mother in Shaw's *Misalliance* (neither, however, under Reinhardt's direction). She imposed only one condition: "Madame" must not be found in the same city at the same time as Wolfgang. This was agreed to. When Mama and I arrived in Arosa, a wireless reached her from the ship on which Papa and Wolfgang were sailing: I TAKE OFF MY HAT AND BOW LOW TO YOU . . . EVER GRATEFULLY MAX.

The auspices under which my brother accompanied my father to America were, indeed, felicitous. He was to witness an exciting first meeting. For the Reinhardt who docked in Manhattan on November 14, 1927, was a total stranger to America; as he was to every country he had not visited with his original German-language productions intact. The unexotic, indigenous Reinhardt who was an integral, even emblematic, part of his civilization's mainstream, the Reinhardt about whom Thornton Wilder wrote to me in 1967: "How I would love to spend hours and hours studying the various regie-books. *Der Schwierige* [a play by Hofmannsthal which Wilder had viewed in Salzburg in 1927], the most perfectly realized production I have ever seen on any stage. Goldoni's *Servant of Two Masters,* the various *Midsummer Night's Dreams* and the Berlin productions of Shakespeare and Kleist and Strindberg that I never saw," was unknown outside his country except to a few travelers. *That* Reinhardt, with a major part of his company, was about to make his debut on the international scene.

That Reinhardt had two sides to him. The managerial mantle fell on his shoulders in the natural course of events. He simply followed in the footsteps of his distinguished predecessors at the Deutsches Theater, Adolf L'Arronge and Otto Brahm. Where he differed from them was in the oddity that he acted as his own chief director. This duality of function and ambivalence of attitude led to many misconceptions:

> I don't know whether, in some quiet hour, you will ever have the desire, surely not to reply to me, for there is no reply to facts, but to talk things over frankly with me. This is of course entirely up to you and has nothing to do with my enduring esteem for your talents. But, in order to avoid further misunderstandings, let it be stated here at once and categorically that I would not be in the position to accept a letter from anyone but you personally, the only responsible manager of the Deutsches Theater and the Kammerspiele so far as I am concerned. Farewell, dear Mr. Reinhardt. I am sorry.
>
> Respectfully yours,
>
> December 24, 1909 Arthur Schnitzler

And a telegram from Gerhart Hauptmann to Professor Reinhardt, Berlin, April 21, 1932:

> MANAGEMENT WITHHOLDING MY PROPERTY NAMELY ROYALTIES DUE ME. YOU MAX OF COURSE HAVE NO INKLING OF THIS. BUT I MUST NOT HIDE FROM YOU THAT MY PUBLISHER AND I WILL EMPLOY ALL LEGAL MEANS IMMEDIATELY. FORGIVE MY DISTURBING YOUR PEACE. YOURS
>
> GERHART

Normal quarrels between producer and author? One, perhaps, about the nonacceptance of a play or a disagreement regarding its production, the other simply about money? On the face of them, undoubtedly. But the manner in which the two foremost German dramatists of their day take this particular producer to task connotes a more complex relationship. Schnitzler, in a letter of resignation, obviously deeply offended by both substance and form of some slight, feels induced to mention Reinhardt's talents and leaves the door respectfully open. Hauptmann is equally angry, even threatens to go to court, but takes care not to let the controversy spill over into the personal sphere. How to explain *their* ambivalence?

By the very same duality. For it is the same ambivalence. They are addressing one person, but hoping to reach two people. Accustomed to the exemplary business conduct of Brahm, they expect similar treatment from his successor and complain bitterly about not getting it. With every other producer, that would have been the end of the respective associations. But this one had an ace in the hole: namely, his chief director, who was under very personal, exclusive and internal contract to him and whom no author could afford to pass up lightly. To any play directed by him, after all, success was practically guaranteed. In other words, no matter how irritated they were with the manager, they kept wooing the director.

Conversely, director Reinhardt, in the intimacy of collaboration, was prone to make promises manager Reinhardt found difficult to keep. And whenever manager Reinhardt approached a playwright (or star), he kindled hopes in them that he would also direct their plays. When this was impossible, either through unwillingness or overwork, even the closest relations became severely strained at times. What is more, the manager employed a most unpredictable and willful chief director over whom he had very little influence. The former knew no sectarian prejudices, was constantly on the lookout for projects in the remotest corners, never too finicky not to give a halfway promising one a try, ever ready to weather droughts by means of commissions, accepting works, if not indiscriminately, still, in the eyes of quality-conscious critics, not always up to his theatres' standard, generally preferring productivity to selectivity. The director, on the other hand, was an unashamed favoritist and full of idiosyncrasies. He had to fall in love with a play in order to want to direct it—and to direct it well. He did not fall in love with Schnitzler. And only on and off with Shaw or Maugham. While Schnitzler felt rejected, Shaw and Maugham did not care who directed their plays, just so long as he was competent. Maugham did, in fact, object strenuously to the musical treatment of his *Too Many Husbands,* involving the addition of a part he had not written. Since the inadvertent "musical" was a little gem, Reinhardt regretted this reaction sincerely and invited Maugham to come to Berlin to see for himself. Maugham did not come. When I met him years later, he told me with a chuckle—the chuckle further impairing the t-t-telling—that the royalties he collected from this play in Germany, exceptional for that market, had reconciled him to the outrage. My glowing description of the performance impressed him less. It was the manager that had reconciled him with the director.

Shaw was used to earning more money in Germany than at home. Like Shakespeare's, his plays were more popular there than in England. *The Apple Cart*, for instance, flopped dismally in London and New York, while breaking box-office records in Berlin and Vienna. The cynical idealist took this unexpected present in his stride. My father, the superstitious idealist—two hits in a row with a playwright whom, as director, he had hitherto neglected seemed to cry for a follow-up—suggested to Shaw a drama on Christ. Shaw answered that Christ would not make a good dramatic hero, because he always fell silent where he would have to talk and because his appearances had essentially been undramatic. Christ, according to Shaw, was less the hero of a drama than the creator of numberless dramas. For Shaw, managers were a source of money, not inspiration. For Reinhardt, contemporary authors were a source of the theatre's raw material—in need of money, to be sure, but sometimes of inspiration as well. What he thought of his own role in this give-and-take, Philip Carr of *The New York Times*, who interviewed him at Leopoldskron in 1927, just prior to the New York tour, reported:

> The position of the producer was one of the first subjects of our conversation, and it is interesting to note that Reinhardt regards him as a provisional or rather a transitional figure in theatrical development. The ideal state of things, he thinks, would be one in which the author should perhaps be an actor, as Shakespeare and Molière were, and should at least be sufficiently a man of the theatre to produce his plays. . . .
>
> Both, knowing the theatre and its ways, could not only put their plays on the stage, but *could alter them and allow them to grow in rehearsal* [italics mine], according to the circumstances of their theatre and, above all, the personalities of the actors. . . .
>
> If the producer is necessary today, says Reinhardt, to bridge the gulf between the authors and the actors, it is really because the authors do not know their business. They write their plays in the solitude of their study. . . . They leave it to the producer to translate these plays into theatrical expression, whereas they not only ought to be capable of doing such translation

> themselves, but *should compose and adapt and modify their plays* [italics mine] in such sympathy to the theatre that no translation is necessary.

This "translator" made his employer a millionaire. But the millionaire could not budge the "other" to "bridge the gulf between the authors and the actors" when he did not feel seduced, by the living authors as well as the dead. Of some poets and masterpieces he could never get enough. To others, in no way inferior, he gave a wide berth. His appetite for most of Shakespeare was insatiable.

To understand this, I think, a word about the German Shakespeare cult, of which Max Reinhardt was a high priest, is needed. The Germans' "special relationship" with England's *poeta poetarum* is well known, but to anyone whose mother tongue is English slightly incomprehensible, if not comical. How can a German claim Shakespeare as a *German* author? And how can German directors and actors interpret him more congenially and do him more justice than his compatriots?

Perhaps the neutral voice of Danish critic and historian, and Shakespeare scholar, Georg Brandes can help us understand the phenomenon:

> Having acquired complete mastery of the style, Schlegel [August Wilhelm Schlegel, with his partner Ludwig Tieck, the definitive German Shakespeare translators] . . . opened his hand, and between the years 1797 and 1801, let fall from it into the lap of the German people sixteen of Shakespeare's dramas, which . . . might, in their new form, have been the work of a German poet of Shakespeare's rank.
>
> Let us consider what this really means. It means not much less than that Shakespeare, as well as Schiller and Goethe, saw the light in Germany in the middle of the last century. He was born in England in 1564; he was born again, in his German translator, in 1767. *Romeo and Juliet* was published in London in 1597; it reappeared in Berlin as a new work in 1797.
>
> When Shakespeare thus returned to life in Germany, he acted with full force upon a public which was in several ways more capable of understanding him than his original public though it was spiritually less akin to him and though they were not the battles of its day which he fought. He now began to feed the millions who did not understand English with his spiritual bread. Not until now did Central and Northern Europe discover him. Not until now did the whole Germanic-Gothic world become his public.

And concluding that particular chapter (about Schlegel, in his *Main Currents in Nineteenth-Century Literature*):

> . . . a small thing, the translation of a poet who had been dead for two hundred years, it yet provided the most precious spiritual nourishment for millions, and exercised a deep and lasting influence on German poetry.

The German "public" Shakespeare had thus gained (and to which the eighteenth-century language was more easily accessible than the sixteenth-century one to their English contemporaries) was a reading public. It remained for Max Reinhardt, a century later, to muster millions of spectators. It is no exaggeration to declare that what Schlegel-Tieck and Count Baudissin (who was to complete the team) had done for German poetry, Max Reinhardt did for the German theatre. Through him, Shakespeare became by far the most often performed author on the German stage. Was it Shakespeare's Shakespeare or Reinhardt's Shakespeare?

Georg Brandes (writing in 1909):

> It would be ridiculous to stress the simplicity of Shakespeare's stage and decor against these [Reinhardt's] efforts. The way the play [*The Merchant of Venice*] is played here [at the Deutsches Theater] is perhaps the way it lived in Shakespeare's imagination. His stage could only give a lithograph of the multicolored, radiant picture he visualized and has, therefore, nothing exemplary for the present. What is decisive is that at no point where Shakespeare's unadulterated humanity and high sagacity break through the erratic movement of the fairy tale, were his words drowned by the noise from the performance. Reinhardt's assailants imply that he lets the director crowd out the poet; it is not true; he supplements the poet.

England's most distinguished critic of that time, William Archer, a most unneutral voice:

> I have seen only one of Max Reinhardt's Shakespearean revivals at the Deutsches Theater, Berlin; but that struck me as a marvel of good taste in mounting. The play was *The Winter's Tale*. Almost all the scenes in Sicily were played in a perfectly simple yet impressive decoration—a mere suggestion without any disturbing detail, of a lofty hall in the palace of Leontes. For the pastoral act in Bohemia, on the other hand, a delightful scene was designed, for all the world like a page from a child's picture book. . . . The whole effect was charmingly fantastic and admirably in keeping with the action of the scene.

It is a great pity that Reinhardt's Shakespeare reached so few qualified English eyes and ears. They, thus, missed not only his *pièces de résistance*, but many facets of Shakespeare until then never illuminated anywhere. They missed another thing: the sense of having themselves actively contributed to this Shakespeare renaissance beyond their shores. English publications at the beginning of our century abound with laments about the woes of the London theatre and the need for someone like Reinhardt to reform it. Very little, if anything, is said about Reinhardt's debt to the London theatre, which was substantial.

I have already mentioned the inspiration he received from Gordon Craig. Reinhardt's use of shafts of light to replace a built decor (best exemplified in his *Danton* productions) goes directly back to Craig's principles and experiments. But, equally, the novel and daring magnitude of his sets' dimensions owed its impetus to him. So did the focus on controlled *space* as a visual frame for drama. Finally, the importance Reinhardt attached to the stage set itself, giving it a role as vital and autonomous as that of the spoken word, of music, of mime, of all the other legitimate elements of theatrical expression, fulfilled Craig's demands. Where he did not follow Craig was in the subjection of the actor to the visual image. Craig's *Über-marionettes* could not fit into the scheme of a man who had proclaimed: "It is to the actor and to no one else that the theatre belongs." In his own country, Craig shared the fate of most prophets: He was largely ignored. On the Continent, he was recognized, but his influence remained confined to living on in the work of others. His own attempts to test his theories—two efforts for Brahm, one in collaboration with Stanislavski and a production with Duse—were all luckless. His negotiations with the Deutsches Theater fell through, since Reinhardt would not entrust him with a mise en scène and offered him "only" that opportunity where he thought Craig's strength lay: in scenic design. That was unacceptable to Craig.

Neither Stanislavski's inner naturalism nor Meyerhold's stylized formalism, neither French realism nor Vienna's classicism could have sparked what the British playwright-actor-producer Granville-Barker called (in a contribution to *Fortnightly Review*, 1911) Reinhardt's "gift of seeing things in a mass, as a child sees them," a gift which, according to Granville-Barker, enabled Reinhardt to "find in Shakespeare full scope for the childlike vision which he possesses and which is really indispensable in a producer of Shakespeare comedy." If there was an external source from which my father scooped inspiration, he found it, according to his own words to me, in Granville-Barker's and, above all, Beerbohm-Tree's productions (especially in the latter's *Hamlet* and *A Midsummer Night's Dream*). The Germans used to approach Shakespeare in congealing awe.

Perhaps the English, in those days, showed too little respect for their national treasure, took too much license with it, but they encouraged my father to disregard tradition and to obey nothing but his own instincts. That is why Granville-Barker could express astonishment that "there is nothing academical or literary" about Reinhardt's Shakespeare. He need not have been so astonished. He had the right to pat himself and his confrères on the shoulder.

When the Hamburg-American liner S.S. *Deutschland* docked at the West Forty-sixth Street pier on November 14, 1927, marking, as producer Gilbert Miller stated in *The New York Times*, "the first time that an entire theatrical plant moved across the Atlantic," the reception was not auspicious. The *Times* commented:

> Max Reinhardt . . . arrived yesterday from Germany with his son Wolfgang, thirty-four members of his company and forty-seven trunks. . . . As the impressive-looking theatrical director walked down the gangway . . . papers were served on him in a suit for $1,000,000 by Philip Miner of Cleveland for alleged breach of contract.

It is not the merit of that case which makes the incident worth recording. (As it turned out, the judge was to decide against the plaintiff.) What matters is that such embarrassments plagued my father throughout his professional life, particularly away from home when Edmund could not hold his protective hand over him. At fault was his promiscuity in forging business contacts. He lent a sympathetic ear to anyone managing to approach him with a proposition, made all sorts of promises, was apt to forget them as soon as his back was turned, even after preliminary papers had been drawn, and often did not bother to inform his regular aides, especially when he knew they would frown on the contact in question.

Except for this sour note, the German *stagione* was one triumphal hymn from beginning to end. It took Manhattan by storm, theatrically, socially and, in a measure, one might even say, politically. New York's mayor, Jimmy Walker, greeted Reinhardt and the leading members of his company at City Hall. There ensued an unbroken string of banquets in the great hotels and mansions of the city, in the homes of New York's rich, powerful and talented. The Empire Theatre was the scene of a gathering in his honor at which its chairman, Nicholas Murray Butler, president of Columbia University, spoke of "art and science as two great binding forces that bring men and nations together." New York, he said, was a "great capital of men" to which Reinhardt, "a great captain of drama," had brought the "contribution of essential beauty which lies at the base of everything." John H. Finley, to whom Butler yielded the chair, reminded the audience that there had been other "great capitals of men. But," he added, "how impossible it would have been for a Persian director to have put on a drama in Athens eight or nine years after the battle of Plataea." (Only five years later, that "Persian director" could not even put on a drama in "Susa" and had trouble finding backers in "Greece.") The Reverend Karl Reiland called him an "apostle of peace" and declared that in ancient Rome it was the custom to confer the title "Benefactor" on anyone who contributed greatly to the happiness or well-being of the people. He said he would demand that the Church confer that title on Professor Reinhardt. My father answered in German. He said his heart was full. And whenever that was the case, he had to use his mother tongue. He said he was not a speechmaker and explained that, in the theatre, he had a hundred eyes, a hundred voices, a hundred faces to express what was in his heart and mind. "But," he is quoted as having continued, "if I had a thousand eyes, a thousand voices and a thousand faces now, I could not express what is in my heart." Then in English, he concluded: "I thank you very, very much." The audience is reported to have risen and cheered.

It kept rising and cheering for eleven weeks. The original schedule calling for seven plays in eight weeks had to be extended to satisfy popular demand. A second house (the Lyceum) was leased to lighten the burden of the Century Theatre. According to *The New York Times*, hundreds of people were turned away at each performance. In the final weeks it became necessary to add a third matinee. The weekly gross at the Cosmopolitan Theatre (to which the company moved for the more intimate plays) averaged thirty thousand dollars. "The Reinhardt engagement ended in what is customarily referred to as a blaze of glory. Laboring under terrific expense, the German company lost only a negligible few thousand dollars," ran the gossip of the Rialto. And after the irrevocably last performance, the column recounted, the audience gave the guests from overseas an ovation lasting thirty minutes. Alexander Moissi made the farewell speech for Reinhardt, promising to be back soon.

Moissi was the undisputed star of the glittering ensemble (so much so, and, what is more, in his own eyes as well, that he refused to attend the rehearsals called by my father on the boat), which included the "German Barrymores," as the New York press christened the family Thimig, Lili Darvas, Vladimir Sokoloff (who defected to Reinhardt from the Taïrov company during its recent German tour), the comedian Hans Moser, the heroic protagonist Paul Hartmann, America's own Rosamond Pinchot and the dance teams of Ernst Matray and Maria Solveg (who doubled as actress and would, one day, become Reinhardt's highly efficient assistant on Broadway), and Harald Kreutzberg (one of the finest dancers of his day) and Tilly Losch. The latter pair gave a number of separate exhibitions of their art, forming the basis of Tilly's American stardom.

The choice of plays offered fairly representative samples of the Reinhardt repertoire: two German classics with Schiller's *Love and Intrigue* (". . . it shows off the Reinhardt company at its legitimate, classical, dramatic best"—Atkinson, *Times*; "Helene Thimig gave the daughter irresistible pathos"—Woollcott, *World*) and Büchner's *Danton's Death* ("The most rousing and stupendous piece of stagecraft ever contrived within a theatre"—Gabriel, *Sun*; "Tremendous as a rhapsody of the eternal mob, quick and throbbing as a dramatic spectacle"—Woollcott, *World*; "Titanic"—Hammond, *Herald Tribune*; "Overwhelming"—Mantle, *Daily News*); medieval morality in Hofmannsthal's new adaptation of *Everyman* ("A gorgeous rite"—Hammond, *Herald Tribune*; "My God what a man! Moissi can play in Hindustani for me"—Hall, *Evening Telegram*; "Miraculous"—Atkinson, *Times*); commedia dell'arte with Goldoni's *Servant of Two Masters* ("Kept the house in an uproar transcending all knowledge of any language. Sublime slapstick. A sardonic and hilarious presentation"—Woollcott, *World*; "Hermann Thimig created a character as funny as some of Charlie Chaplin's"—Hall, *Evening Telegram*); contemporary drama with František Langer's *Periphery* ("Sharp, fantastic . . . brilliantly played"—Woollcott, *World*; "Extraordinarily fine bits of acting, plenty of action, plenty of excitement . . . moments of sinister brilliance"—Littell, *Evening Post*); the international scene, concluding the engagement, with a virtuoso part for Moissi in Tolstoi's *Living Corpse* (". . . perhaps the finest of all performances which the visitors have given"—Atkinson, *Times*); and Shakespeare, of course, as a starter, with *A Midsummer Night's Dream*, the most controversial offering owing to the issues I have touched on before ("One of the wonders of the modern stage . . . a lovely thing has come to town and it is time to ring the bells in the steeples"—Woollcott, *World*; "Nothing that we have evolved in our wildest imagination equals the Reinhardt production in its physical perfection and completeness. An event in the theatre, believe me"—Mantle, *Daily News*; "So in the beginning there was *Midsummer Night's Dream*. Not Shakespeare's but Reinhardt's *Dream*, as the lighted signs said precisely"—Gabriel, *Sun*; "As for *A Midsummer Night's Dream* that was most cruelly butchered, the Oberon was so far from fairylike that he might have been Hamlet. Beautiful lines were deleted to introduce dances of a calibre one would expect to find on a four-a-day vaudeville program. The four beautiful lovers were turned into idiots . . ."—George Whitney, in a letter to the editor of the *Times*; another letter to the same editor: "Reinhardt has made two distinctly new contributions to Shakespeare's play. One is the handling of the lovers. By turning them into comics, almost buffoons, he has removed them from their usual realms of utter bores . . . and the other new contribution . . . is the interpretation of Oberon. . . . Interpreted by Reinhardt and Moissi, this character becomes the key of the play, as it should be. . . .").

No other foreign company, prior to Reinhardt or after, has earned a like degree of popular and critical acclaim in America. The impression was deep and enduring, a stunning confrontation with an art that had been as ballyhooed as it was unfamiliar.

> Perhaps *The Miracle* has given us a distorted image of Dr. Reinhardt's theatrical genius. Far from being a ringmaster as *The Miracle* seemed to indicate, he is a versatile director, as able in staging drawing-room comedy for an intimate theatre as he is in organizing *Everyman* for an out-of-door production in a square before Salzburg Cathedral.

Thus, Brooks Atkinson, in a summary of the entire engagement. In his specific review of *A Midsummer Night's Dream* he says:

> Dr. Reinhardt's image of the *Dream* appears to be Shakespeare's, too. One hopes that the dull fact of mortal death does not now prevent Shakespeare from enjoying this refulgent dream in modern theatrical wizardry. . . .

On March 1, 1928, Mr. Atkinson's paper announced that Max Reinhardt had sailed for home on the S.S. *Hamburg* of the Hamburg-American Line, "accompanied by his young son, Wolfgang. He said he will return in the fall." He did. But for that wild-goose chase in Hollywood and not, as had been suggested not only by Mr. Atkinson, but by many members of New York's theatre community, to prove his wizardry in English on Broadway proper. The apostle of peace had won a blitzkrieg. And, like most victorious blitzkriegs, his was denied lasting rewards. When he revisited American shores six years thereafter, he came as a refugee. Again, he brought with him his oldest son. His hope, in 1927, that my brother would set down roots in the New World had been dashed. Wolfgang did not share the enthusiasm for what the apostle called the "promised land" and decided to go back with him, back to what was then an old, sick world. Granted, his stay had not been altogether paradisiacal. One day, as could have been expected, "Madame" joined the troupe and Wolfgang had to leave town in accordance with the parental agreement. He spent the rest of the sojourn alone at Lake Placid. I suppose he would have preferred a little more company in Arosa.

As for my own hopes, it also took another six years till Arosa's lovely, clever brunette and I were united. In America. And Hitler had something to do with that too. The delayed union, though, had no lasting consequence either. Great events sometimes leave small traces.

THE DIARY

MONDAY,
OCTOBER 25, 1943

Papa no longer moves, a sculpture on a sarcophagus that only comes to life when there is an effort made to swallow, an effort that finally fails. Intravenous feeding begins. Eleonora, wearing a prim stranger's face, makes a formal visit, does not encroach on Thimig's proprietary suffering or protest when her entrance into Papa's presence is strictly verboten. Proud Eleonora sitting here—her home for four weeks with Max who was hers—need not struggle for status. She yields to her exclusion as if she had expected it, finds it perfectly consistent with Thimig's Weltanschauung. Nonchalantly the victor wraps her faded sable cape around her shoulders, smiles and leaves what's left of the field to her pyrrhic antagonist.

TUESDAY,
OCTOBER 26, 1943

Liebman tells me of rumors around Broadway that Max Reinhardt is dying; of feelers from New Opera Company about whether I'd be willing to do Helen without "the old man." Thank God, Papa will never know—thank God or Nature or whatever cruel force keeps the human life alive after it has ceased to live, yet has the charity to make it oblivious of what can only offend.

Our eyes don't leave him. His never leave the ceiling. Around the deathbed no word is spoken. "Four walls" can "a prison make" and thoughts can be more constricting than "iron bars." I stare at him and think of a letter he wrote me once from California in which he grieved about the loss of "the irreplaceable treasure of Leopoldskron" that was, for him, "a pure love affair." "Yet," he went on, "one doesn't die when love is lost. Certainly one can exist without marble halls and eighty rooms." And this sentence stays with me: "With a view to one's last lodging it's perhaps wiser to accustom oneself in time to limited space."

Wolfgang and I cannot accustom ourselves to him in that "limited space." We prefer the wide past to the narrowing present. In my room we continue our tour d'horizon. "*Victories, victories,*" *I say.* "*Only victories? Never bad years?*" "*Oh, yes,*" *says Wolfgang.* "*1920/1921.*"

"Admired Much and Much Rebuked . . ."

. . . I pursued my path. And if I enjoyed the one and the other vexed me, neither one nor the other was able to lead me astray.

THE FIRST FIVE WORDS are by Goethe, spoken by Helena in the second part of *Faust*. The follow-up is by Max Reinhardt, who said it when he addressed Berlin's actors in 1930. They were no exaggeration—with one exception; and even then he fought the all-out assault for nine years before, for the first time in his career, he admitted defeat and quit. Having run a theatre for the many in his Deutsches Theater, and a theatre for the few in the Kammerspiele, he embarked in 1910 on a theatre for *all*. He found it in the round of the circus. That this place ordinarily displayed acrobats, clowns, animals and animal trainers, whereas under Reinhardt it gave life to antique tragedy and comedy, medieval mysteries and moralities, had, of course, no thematic connection. But the word "circus" with all its associations was too tempting for the critics not to lard their polemics with it in every conceivable variation. They accused Max Reinhardt of Caesaromania, excess and the prostitution of cultural values. Today, it is almost incomprehensible that notions like amphitheatre, arena, round, half-round, circus ring, mass direction could generate such revulsion. But they did. The writer Franz Ferdinand Baumgarten went so far as to publish his diatribe against the "Circus Reinhardt" in book form:

> . . . the crudest case of modern art demolition. The opinion that one can cleverly conjure up spiritual effects by the technical means of orchestra play [in the Greek sense] reflects the ignorance of the intellectuaille [*sic*]. The waxworks-cabinet idea of unrolling what is timeless and not spatial, the essence of the ideal drama, among the spectators like an occurrence in the street, is the annihilation of art through material clumsiness.
>
> The servant wants to be master. The megalomaniacal director annihilates the drama.

Siegfried Jacobsohn called Reinhardt an "imperialist" and wrote: "The people need bread, not circuses." Why not? one might ask. Are the two needs incompatible? Are entertainment and uplift privileges of the sated rich? Who was the real imperialist here? The progressive left insisted on a class-conscious proscenium theatre. The "capitalist" with the "Wilhelmine ambition," as the publisher of the *Weltbühne* labeled Reinhardt, insisted on the theatre of the masses for the masses, was determined to place the actor in the center of the public and to involve the "public, having become an acting populace in itself," in the action.

Only in one other instance did Max Reinhardt face comparable resistance: in his unwavering drive to get the actor Alexander Moissi accepted —this time, against a united front of critics. Julius Bab later called this effort "Reinhardt's highest moral achievement." Moissi had attracted the attention of the great Josef Kainz at Vienna's Burgtheater when he was an understudy. Kainz took him to the Direktor, Paul Schlenther. Together, they secured his education. Prague gave him his first chance. Then Reinhardt adopted the young man whom the embittered press branded as a "tenor," "Italian," a "miserable speaker," whose "oddly alien, soft movement of limbs" repelled. Just as with the arena, so in this struggle for the survival of a highly sensitive personality there arose a mighty ally of Reinhardt: the public. Moissi became its hero. The opposition finally threw in the sponge in 1910, after Reinhardt's first decisive victory in both fights. Moissi played Oedipus in the Circus Schumann. From then on, his unique position on the German-speaking stage was assured. He became the only German actor of his time to gain an international reputation.

The other fight did not reach an equally happy outcome, though while it lasted, Reinhardt succeeded in leading his *other* star to triumph: the crowd. It was promoted to an equal partnership with the protagonist, confronting him on equal terms; no customary static chorus, no actor-led units—going back to the Meiningen tradition—triggered to illustrative movements on cue; it was animated by giving each member a physiognomy of his or her own, even his or her own spoken text, and then again forming whole groupings that expressed themselves with deliberate uniformity through stylization of voice and gesture. In other words, this was not pantomime (except in pantomimes), not ballet (except in ballets), it had no ornamental functions, nor was it a realistic mob miming the emotions of "plebs," "retainers," of "spear-carriers" or other conventional human clusters on the stage; instead, it was an autonomous, freely expressive, dynamic element of the drama. Photographic reproductions of scenes rarely reflect the life that once was in them. But I find that some of the "stills" of the *Oedipus, Miracle, Danton* and *Eternal Road* productions do largely succeed. What they, of course, cannot impart is the acoustic effect. Julius Bab wrote:

> Just as Reinhardt, in his work with the individual actors, knew how to achieve extraordinary tensions through leaden pauses, mute walks, sudden confrontations, steep crescendi of sound and movement, the same faculty extended to his choral direction. As the great tragedienne Charlotte Wolter [Burgtheater star] was famous for her scream, so Reinhardt created something like a "Wolter scream" of the crowd. No element of the theatre inspired Reinhardt's temperament and creativity in so uninhibited and revolutionary a way as the treatment of the extras, the choral direction. . . .

That extras ought not to be "extra," is a directorial commonplace today. In the first and second decades of the twentieth century it was, however, considered radical. These crescendi of mass ecstasy, these huddling diminuendi, the ritardandi of dawning, slowly paralyzing horror, the breathlessly expectant accelerandi, the catatonic rests and vivaciously surging alla-breve passages, the muted fade-outs of predestined doom were symphonic. But Reinhardt was not only the conductor of this unwritten symphony. He was its composer.

The effect of this polyphonic and polygestic theatre on spectator and listener was elementary and overwhelming. The nay-sayers had no influence on the crowds either inside the arena or surrounding it. How was it possible then to claim: that the throng crushed the individual, that the word of the poet was stifled in the circuses, amphitheatres, rotundas, exposition halls, courtyards, town squares, gardens and meadows? Because the mob loves pageantry? Is titillated by sensation? For the sensation-hungry and pageant-addicted there were enough fireworks of every kind thriving outdoors and in to satisfy their craving without a Reinhardt. That they stormed the arenas and open-air box offices to see Aeschylus, Sophocles, Shakespeare, Hofmannsthal, the Old Testament, the French Revolution, Marian plays, Moralities and the *Arabian Nights* was unprecedented and must, after all, have had something to do with the spirit of these works. The truth is that competent actors stood their ground against the counteracting multitude without effort. More, they were stimulated by it. So why the relentless paper war against it?

We live in a time that worships the future. Reinhardt's time worshipped the past. The conventional forms of playing had congealed in the brains of thinking people. The arrival of the literary theatre affected only

Max Reinhardt with Helene Thimig, his second wife, California, 1936.

Eleonora von Mendelssohn. *Left*. Eleonora as a child, with her mother and her godmother, Eleonora Duse.

Left. Helene and Hermann Thimig in Goldoni's *A Servant of Two Masters*, Vienna, 1924.

Below. Eleonora von Mendelssohn with Silvia Reinhardt, 1937.

Left. The author, Gottfried Reinhardt.

Below. Franz Werfel's *Eternal Road*, New York, 1937. Scene design for the Manhattan Opera House.

Eternal Road. The revolt of the slaves in Egypt.

Max Reinhardt in Hollywood, with William Dieterle, Mervin Le Roy and Michael Curtiz, 1935

Thornton Wilder's *The Merchant of Yonkers*, New York, 1938. June Walker, Percy Waram.

Caricature of Norman Bel Geddes by Emil Orlik, during rehearsals of *The Miracle*, 1924.

Norman Bel Geddes working on set models for *Eternal Road*, New York, 1937.

A *Midsummer Night's Dream*, Hollywood, 1935. *Above*. Anita Louise as Titania and James Cagney as Bottom. *Right*. Mickey Rooney as Puck and Olivia de Havilland as Hermia.

Reinhardt at work on the set of *A Midsummer Night's Dream*.

A Reinhardt Workshop production of Goldoni's *At Your Service*, 1939. Nanette Fabray, Robert Ryan and others.

Above. Gottfried Reinhardt directing Clark Gable in *Betrayed*, 1953.

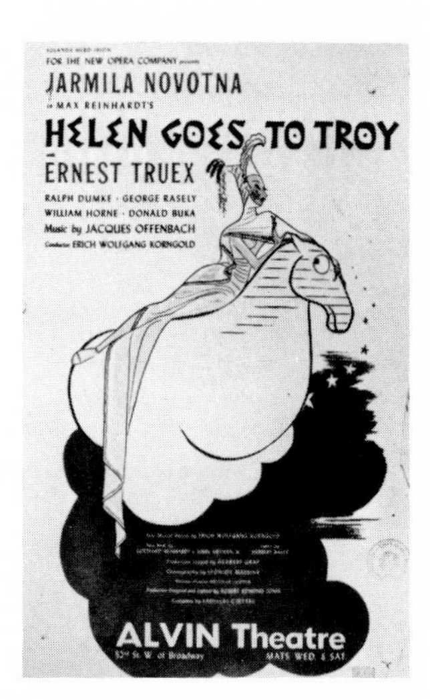

Helen Goes to Troy, New York, 1944.

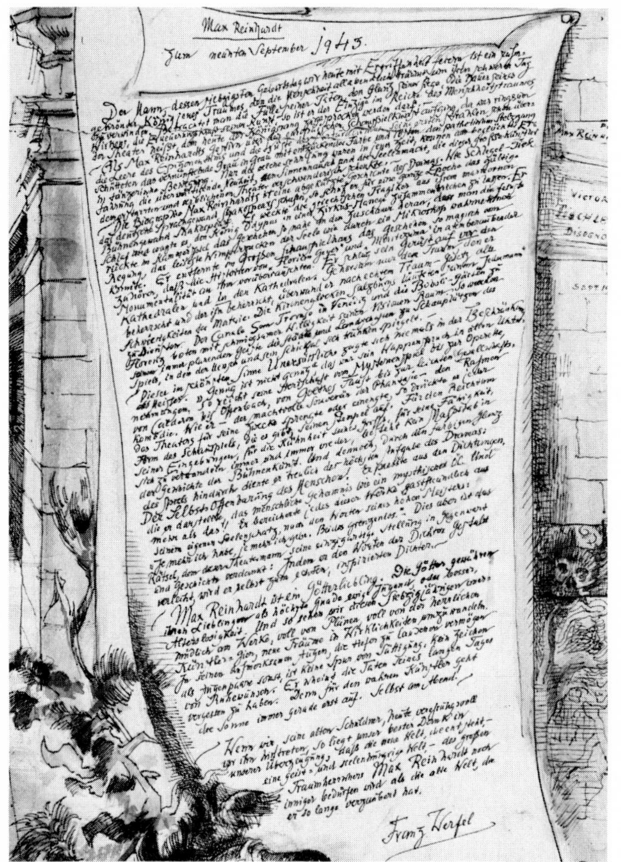

Max Reinhardt

Zum neunten September 1943.

Franz Werfel

Left. Inscription of the plaque honoring Max Reinhardt on his seventieth birthday, September 9, 1943.

Max Reinhardt in Los Angeles.

the *content* of its offerings, not the *framework*. On the contrary, in that regard, it actually favored the status quo. The same is true of the political theatre. The more rebellious the themes on the stage, the more traditional the structure of the building as well as the (upper) class structure of the audience (and the investors). The literary theatre, by necessity, addressed an educated elite and was, therefore, conservative in the socially behavioral sense. Writers, directors, actors paid dramatic lip service to the plebs, but the plebs did not become theatrically respectable thereby, either in the eyes of parlor leftists or in those of bona fide Marxists. To cater to the primeval desire for spectacle in man—which contributed so essentially to the birth of the theatre in antiquity and to its renaissance in the Middle Ages—on a high literary level seemed a sacrilege to the advocates of twentieth-century progress. Max Reinhardt, on the other hand, felt that the *composed* movements and *melodies* of the crowd, far from distracting from the poet's word or from individual drama, were a legitimate component of the art form on a par with the others. And he was convinced that the revolutionary undercurrent of the age, which he felt keenly—in his way just as keenly as, for example, Brecht or Piscator (both faithful subscribers to the proscenium stage and its feudal audience structure; whenever did they perform for the working class as Reinhardt did?)—should make itself felt not only in the realm of ideas, in new staging techniques and new acting styles, but in freeing the theatre of obsolete partitions, restrictions, and wonted comforts.

So long as his flirtation with the *demos* kept within what were considered reasonable limits, the attacks did the same. But when, in 1918, believing he perceived the democratic spirit of the time finally coming into its own, though misjudging completely the practical possibilities of the young democracy (and its stability), he bought Circus Schumann and rebuilt it into the so-called Theatre of the Five Thousand (it had three thousand seats) in the hope of establishing a *permanent* home for his people's theatre, the scribes declared total war on him. And for the first time, his most reliable ally, the public, abandoned him. The future, which for my father was always the present, had, alas, not yet begun. The social strata the giant theatre attempted to reach simply lacked the means for attending it. The intellectually embattled undertaking lacked an economic basis. The Great Playhouse became a poorhouse.

The tragedy of the Grosses Schauspielhaus, however, lay not in the material sphere. The revolutionary élan of the Reinhardt theatre went under with it. Up to then, he had been an iconoclastic reformer. That period of his life had now come to an end. Henceforth, except for occasional breakouts, he resigned himself to the conventional form and conventional customs. Up to then, he had built in the modern style. The fact that the architect of the Grosses Schauspielhaus, Hans Poelzig, was represented by several impressive modernistic structures in Germany did not save his renovation of the Circus Schumann from condemnation by the modernists. Contemptuously, the interior was tagged the "stalactite cave," as though these tourist attractions the world over were excesses of ugliness! The acoustics were a continuous target for censure. Every reviewer complained about not being able to hear the actors in the "mammoth" auditorium. The very opposite was true. All actors playing in the Great Playhouse, including my mother, were united in their praise of the effortless projection of the spoken word. Every whisper, they would tell anybody who was still listening, could be heard in the farthest and highest row. But the men who lived by their pens pretended to be deaf and blind. (The Nazis went them one better: Thinking that Poelzig was a Jew—he was not—they simply hacked away the "stalactites," thereby, at last, indeed ruining the acoustics. The Communists eventually solved that problem by turning the house into a variety showplace, which it is still today.)

Weimar Berlin's illuminati, finally, achieved what they wanted against their own interests: Reinhardt abjured his faith and was "led astray," his "desertion" to Vienna being all the more resented.

I mourned it perhaps more than anybody because it coincided with his desertion from the family (an additional motive for the decision) and because the days when the Grosses Schauspielhaus was being rebuilt numbered among the happiest of my childhood. Amidst iron bars and mortar, scaffolding that grew into the sky, bridges over innumerable chasms, from Olympus to Hades, the six-year-old poked and stumbled as if in paradise. No première, no matter how exciting, could rival it. When the job was finished and the housewarming guests, in 1919, marveled at the *Oresteia*, Cassandra compensated the downcast boy for his lost paradise: "Apollo! Apollo!" came the voice of his mother, unforgettably, from high up in the contested vault. And when, at the end, three thousand throats burst forth with the obligatory "Reinhardt! Reinhardt!" and the father showed himself on the battlefield of the Atridae, it was not only the son who was deceived that another victory had been won. The *Berliner Tageblatt*'s social column stated: ". . . the [freshly-baked republican] audience, including Prince and Princess August, in their box, and numbering several thousand heads, among them the true heads of academe and the arts, was spellbound and, at the end, it was the young people especially who called their beloved Max Reinhardt into the ring over and over again with thundering enthusiasm."

But the following morning the Furies cared little for the young people and only stepped up their persecution, albeit not of Orestes, but of his landlord and director. In self-righteous unison they pointed to their many warnings in the past, and now let him have it full force. Rebuke had won out over admiration. In the face of this hostility in the postwar misery, it was clearly a hopeless undertaking to educate a new mass audience to the finer arts. Even to the author of *Masse Mensch* (Mass Man), Ernst Toller, who was represented by his *Machine Wreckers,* a play about the industrial revolution in England. Its climax was the lynching of the Foreman. The actor who played him could not take a bow after the opening. He lay motionless in the arena, surrounded by the cast mingling with the public. Being the victim of so vast a mob out for blood had been too much for him. A doctor had to be called to revive him.

Julius Caesar. Werner Krauss. Embodiment of the monumental ego, wounded, tumbling down, step by step, from mediocrity to mediocrity, clinging to them only to receive further wounds, betrayed, suddenly small in stature, but losing nothing of his mental greatness, finally breaking down under the last dagger thrust from his friend who towers over him and trembles in fear of his own deed; Caesar, almost astonished, not completing his last words (as he did not complete his life's work): "Et tu Brute? Then fall Cae . . ." And then the awakening of the little people, the shock over the petty crime, their dread of the terrible repercussion—a breathless happening in time and space: the first stab, still not quite real, happens on the stage, far up and far away; but, from stab to stab, step by step, the catastrophe not only dawns on the dictator, it comes nearer to the spectator, with each stab, with each faltering step, until the seducer of the people dies in their midst, palpably close, before their very eyes, in the arena which they encircle.

A *Hamlet* with Moissi, all in black, in stylized modern dress, is ahead of its time as much as the building is.

Büchner's (followed by Romain Rolland's) Danton moved John Mason Brown to write in *Theatre Arts*:

> It is Danton, composed in the face of death, who makes the mob look small beside him. He has been one with his people who are accusing him. . . . He has outgrown his belief that liberty can be bought by blood alone, just as he has grown to hate the men who prosper by roaring its cant without sincerity.

> Confronted by this mob and with the executioners before him, this Danton laughs. At first, in the low and single chuckle that resounds in that breathless Tribunal. It begins to grow and fills out into a long laugh—a solitary comment on man's dreams and ambitions. Suddenly, someone else is carried away by the daring and contagion of his comment. The laugh swells slowly but susceptibly from the rabble onstage to the mob in the auditorium, enlarging, including more and more people, until the theatre rocks with a Gargantuan roar, and everyone laughs, at first without knowing why, but continues nonetheless heartily on, discovering that this derision is aimed at the whole futility of life, laughs hoarsely, madly, for what seems an age of disillusionment, and keeps on laughing until the stiff backs of the enclosing soldiers remind the crowd all too harshly of the world we live in.
>
> This scene comes as the supreme moment that the Reinhardt season . . . has so far revealed, and as one of those experiences in the theatre that burns its way into the memory of those who have been part of it.

The "Tribunal" is Reinhardt's. The time of his revolutionary programs is over. There follows a time of concentrating on the perfect single performance.

THE DIARY

WEDNESDAY,
OCTOBER 27, 1943

Pneumonia has set in. H. tells us Papa has only a few days, at most a week, to live and, all things considered, the complication is a blessing in disguise.

THURSDAY,
OCTOBER 28, 1943

Two specialists awaited: Professor Elias and, again, Foster Kennedy. Elias arrives first. Brilliant conductor? Middling? Mediocre? Immaterial. He cannot prove it. The score defeats him before he has a chance. Both doctors confirm H.'s prognosis. Kennedy sits between Wolfgang and me on the sofa in my apartment like an iceberg between two sinking ships. Wolfgang —not yet aware of the Kennedy charisma—tries to forestall being "told the worst" by involving him in a discussion of perhapses and maybes which the latter finds superfluous. He cuts it short with a jolly slap on Wolfgang's knee, rises: "Well that was it. Last time I saw your father in this world!" His good cheer undiminished, he picks up his overcoat and leaves.

FRIDAY,
OCTOBER 29, 1943

Can't stand the staring and the waiting. Make a date for lunch with ostracized Eleonora. Want to let her know what is her right to know and to console her for being shut out. Both unnecessary. She knows and she doesn't feel shut out, because they parted when he was still conscious. What happened thereafter—is happening now—touches neither her nor him. Describes the seventy-six-year-old Toscanini's indignant reaction when she told him Papa was dying: "That's ridiculous! One doesn't die this young!" We have to laugh. We're not indignant. But, of course, we're not so old. We're unhappy. However, having witnessed his decision to die, we agree we must accept it. We know that once he has struggled to a decision he'll follow through meticulously. But we also know his im-

patience with last acts that don't know how to end. And again we agree that if he were still in command he'd cut these superfluous final scenes without a second thought. But he no longer is in command. We talk about when he was.

Dialogue at Voisin

WE REMEMBER, interrupt each other—our spilling-over talk has no pattern, but it runs something like this:

"Eleonora, I think I'm a big enough boy now to stand an answer to something that's been on my mind for a long time."

"Oh, dear. I've done something horrible. What?"

"Nothing all that dire. It's just—do you remember when Papa and Wolfgang and I stayed at the Hotel Hajek in Mödling [a resort in the Vienna Woods] and you and Fischer [the pianist, Eleonora's first husband] came to see us?"

"Of course. After your father opened the Josefstadt." [Vienna's Theater in der Josefstadt reopened in the spring of 1924.]

"Right. And out of the blue Fischer asked Wolfgang and me to go for a walk. He dangled some kind of lure—like 'retracing the footsteps of Beethoven.' I don't remember exactly. But I do remember you stayed behind with Papa."

Eleonora quivers like an expectant bride.

"I was young and innocent then, but not innocent enough to believe you and Fischer hadn't cooked up that educational tour between you."

Eleonora's smile is the smile of a satisfied bride: "Is that *all* you wanted to know?"

"No. I want to know whether it's true that you offered my mother a deal: If she'd seduce Fischer—make a man of him or whatever—and give you a few pointers on how to seduce Papa you'd try to get him away from Thimig for her."

"Are you shocked?"

"Bewildered. What did she hope to accomplish? Or you, for that matter? If Mama was such an expert on sexual enslavement why didn't she advise herself?"

"Maybe she did. Maybe the advice wasn't taken. Besides, don't underestimate your mother. She handled your father cleverly—with all his wanderings—very cleverly for years. She only lost her grip when she ran up against someone just as possessive as she was. And ten years younger! If your mother had stuck to our original bargain I could have prevented the whole mess. Don't forget I was ten years younger than Thimig!"

"You mean she'd enjoy losing her husband to you more than to Thimig?"

"I didn't want to own him. I just wanted to love him. And she knew it too. Why else would she smuggle me onto the same train to Stockholm with him [Reinhardt's tour to Sweden with Strindberg's *Dream Play* in 1921], telling me he was alone and that it was my one chance to trap him? . . . Except in the end I was the one who was trapped. I could never let go of him."

"The Mendelssohn-Reinhardt curse. We don't seem to be able to let go of each other, do we?"

"That's why my poor sister killed herself."

"Because of Mama?"

"Angelica loved your mother desperately."

"That was way over my head then. All that got through to me was whenever Angelica came to see Mama I was dragged along on their ferny, gladesy walks in the Grunewald."

"Oh, Gottfried, everything—bad or good—held us together. . . ." She reaches for my hand. I feel a ground swell of nostalgia threatening to drown us both.

"Eleonora," I urge. " 'Leave it with the rest'!" [Exit line of the Valet in his scene with Lady Milford in Schiller's *Kabale und Liebe* when he spurns the purse she presses upon him as a reward for telling her that the diamonds he brings her from her princely lover cost him nothing more dear than the sale of his devoted subjects as Hessian mercenaries.]

"Ah, that line! Night after night I sat on the edge of my seat until he made his entrance."

"Or didn't."

"Or didn't. How well I know. It was wicked of him. Imagine waiting until the fourth act for Max Reinhardt to appear and to have that idiot of an understudy walk on instead! I hated him."

"Not more than Papa hated acting."

"It wasn't easy for him. Don't forget it was the first time he'd been on a stage in twenty years!" [Since 1906, when Reinhardt played Engstrand in Ibsen's *Ghosts*.]

"Whatever the reason, I can tell you I used to shiver every time the hour approached for his driver to pick him up in Mödling. Such moans and groans—you'd have thought he was being led to the guillotine. I wonder why he did it at all."

"It was *her* fault. Papa did it for *her*!"

"Come, come, Eleonora! She's not that bad. Or that good."

"Oh, yes she is! Both! He would never have left Berlin if it hadn't been for her. And never, never would he have sniveled around those anti-Semites at the Burgtheater, humiliating himself the way he did, if she hadn't egged him on. All those high and mighty guardians of Austrian culture conspiring against the Jew Reinhardt. With Helene's father leading the parade!"

"That parader must have been double-jointed. He got on the Reinhardt bandwagon awfully fast!"

However emotional Eleonora's judgment is about those three years, it undeniably confirms certain facts: Hugo Thimig, progenitor of Austria's histrionic royal family and onetime head of the Burgtheater, was far from a Reinhardt fan, privately or professionally. Contained in his memoirs, for the year 1903, is the comment: "The much-praised Reinhardt is a mediocrity." Two decades later, when both Hofmannsthal, who was eager to see his plays inaugurated in the city of his birth by the director he esteemed above all others, and Richard Strauss had persuaded the Minister of Culture that Max Reinhardt was needed to infuse new life into the ossified Burgtheater, Hugo Thimig denounced the move as "Reinhardt's threatening invasion of Vienna's cultural institutions." And he wrote:

> Berlin's stage-effect man has now managed to wipe out the last vestige of art in the Viennese theatre and, what's more, in its own house.

He was precipitous. Reinhardt never got the chance to commit this dastardly deed. The Hofmannsthal-Strauss démarche was neatly sabotaged by Hugo's friend Anton Wildgans, poet of passionate verse, dramatist and current manager of the Burgtheater. Wildgans called Reinhardt ". . . the wily window decorator from Pressburg who was made a professor" and deplored "this entire Reinhardt fad" as "the symbol of artistic immorality in the theatre." Invidious rumors were launched: Reinhardt had been booted out of Berlin; America wanted no part of him; he was persona non grata practically everywhere and the only alternative left him was to close in on poor Austria, sponge up her meager resources and use them for his own reclame. The two years of his negotiations with the Burg led to nothing more than a few invitations for his former Berlin ensemble to perform in a ballroom of the Imperial and Royal Palace. Once again Wildgans summed it all up succinctly in a draft to the Minister of Culture:

> All this one can risk without shame in Berlin because the rabble there, bereft of taste and tradition, will buy anything. . . . I don't say that Vienna hasn't its share of this human scum as well. I simply say that one shouldn't encourage and breed these mass instincts and that, in the last analysis, nothing is to be gained by transplanting the Reinhardt swamp flora to Vienna.

The "swamp flora" included the finest German-speaking actors, among them Helene and Hermann Thimig. An awkward situation for their papa, as may be gathered from this passage in his memoirs:

> Wildgans' main concern was to assure me there was no personal animosity intended toward my children should it come to the regrettable possibility of his resistance also being directed against them. . . .

In the end, my father was forced to give up his dead-end infatuation with the anti-Semites and to accept salvation from a Semite:

War and inflation profiteer Camillo Castiglioni started out in life as the son of a poor Triestine rabbi. He died shortly after the most astounding coup of his brazen-as-brass career—the successful negotiation of a United States–Yugoslav agreement after World War II. In the years between, he parlayed Austrian automobile tires—of which he had been a salesman—into a gigantic conglomerate of automobile and airplane works, mines, banks, steel and paper mills, chemical and electrical industries, all of this accomplished by acquiring, at the highest market price, capital goods the value of which increased from day to day with borrowed money that decreased in value from day to day, thus benefiting at both ends from monetary devaluation—as long as it lasted. His rises and falls gained him the name "the Austrian Stinnes" and the temporary pleasure of being next-door neighbor to the Viennese Rothschilds, in a palais ornamented with Tiepolos and Guardis, rare Chinese porcelain and Renaissance furniture, where, in true Renaissance style, he played the patron of the arts. As coincidental incentive, his young, beautiful wife Iphigenie burned to play leading roles on the stage. Though her talent was tiny, his purse was large. He bought Max Reinhardt an old theatre—for whose original opening Beethoven had composed *The Consecration of the House*—and put sufficient means at his disposal to restore it in regal gold and red, brocade and velvet, with Venetian chandeliers and ceiling frescos by old masters and an asbestos curtain displaying the oversized reproduction of a Canaletto view of Vienna. It was (and remains today) a perfect jewel of a theatre, set in one of the seedier quarters of then impoverished Vienna on the verge of revolt. He called his latest enterprise "The Actors in the Theatre of the Josefstadt under the Guidance of Max Reinhardt," rejoining their ranks, not merely in name, but by casting himself in a small part.

Helene Thimig's well-known perseverance made her father's reconciliation with her lover, sooner or later, a foregone conclusion. Beyond that, what actor ever refused a good part for the sake of principle? Or what anti-Semite ever declined to make a profitable exception in the case of "his" Jew? Ultimately, the Thimig family en masse became the nucleus of a troupe that initiated a series of felicitous performances with Goldoni's *Servant of Two Masters,* executed in commedia dell'arte style—actors, costumed for their parts, putting up and changing the naïvely painted screens that served as scenery, the stage vibrant and gay with slapstick romance, dancing and singing, Egon Friedell (Dottore) talking Hugo Thimig (Pantalone) into a comatose state and Hermann Thimig (starved Truffaldino) stuffing himself witless in a noodle orgy; and our old friend *Kabale und Liebe,* memorialized, if sporadically, by Reinhardt's rendition of "Leave it with the rest."

"Berry!" Eleonora exclaims with joy at sight of S. N. Behrman, who has stopped at our table on his way out of the restaurant.

"Eleonora! Gottfried! How mah-velous to find you two together. You saved me two telephone calls today."

"We wouldn't have answered them, Sam."

"Oh God, have I alienated you too?"

"Not at all. But telephone calls that are never made cannot be answered."

"To tell you the truth, dear boy, I'd have been on to you the whole week long. But my secretary was out sick. And I was in sick."

Eleonora pulls him into the chair next to her, kisses him: "Sit a minute, darling. You know what we were just talking about?"

"The actual context eluded me from across the room. But the overall impression was Schiller at his most *Sturm und Drang.*"

"You just won a prize! We *were* talking about Schiller—the only time Gottfried ever saw his father on the stage."

"*Were* you! Was he mah-velous?"

"Well, I was only eleven and hardly objective."

"I know objectivity is not your forte, dear Gottfried. This I expect only from Eleonora."

S. N. Behrman, playwright, biographer, *New Yorker* contributor, Hollywood scriptwriter and Eleonora's and my good old friend whose friendship made him little more accessible to us than to members of his family, Broadway stars, collaborators, editors, studio executives or the host of business and social acquaintances whose names crammed his address book and diary—and left his daily schedule as blank as he could possibly make it. Sam's daily schedule revolved around two basic principles: avoiding things and running away from people. In his home from his wife and his telephone; in the theatre from his co-workers; in Hollywood from Hollywood. My efforts to entice him away from New York to assignments at Metro-Goldwyn-Mayer rarely involved less than four to six months of tortuous negotiations through his agent, Harold Freedman, whom he evaded more assiduously than anyone else, and invariably ended the first or second day after he was installed in a Metro office with my discovery that he had already booked his return to New York on the next Super Chief out. On studio orders I would then, far from ungratefully, accompany or follow him to my favorite city, where, over the years, we collaborated on many screenplays. Sam's rabbit run from human approach was matched in compulsiveness by his curiosity about people. No paradox. He liked people very much—but not today, tomorrow. Eleonora and I belonged to the select group of his friends from whom he scampered away at a slower pace, using us as spyglasses to satisfy his curiosity about the world around him. Another "no paradox": Sam was an asocial snob, bored to extinction by celebrities whose attention flattered him no end. One who tickled his vanity especially and from whom he fled consistently was his wife's brother, violinist Jascha Heifetz. I nicknamed Sam "*der Schwierige*" ("the Difficult One") after the title role of Hofmannsthal's comedy. He was absolutely delighted with the comparison. Raimund pronounced it an inspiration and concluded that Behrman would be the perfect adaptor of his father's play. To this end, he spent long years wooing him. But I think even Raimund wouldn't have called them misspent. For never would the character of "the Difficult One" be portrayed more faithfully and with more finesse than by Sam in his ingenious resistance to Raimund's overtures. Predictably, Sam was inflamed to ecstasy by Max Reinhardt from the first moment their paths crossed. In 1966, he wrote me:

> Your letter arrived in the nick of time. I was just going to send a protest over your uncommunicativeness to the *Salzburger Nockerl* or whatever that local journal of yours is called. I am so happy that you have finally settled down [a euphemism] to writing a biography of your father. He is a fabulous subject—haven't I always told you so? What a panorama of twentieth-century life in Europe he dominated and of course in England and America, too!

For this panorama Eleonora and I were his keenest "spyglasses." He could never get enough of the view. It excited and intrigued him and filled the pages of his *Burning Glass*, a book only thinly disguised as a novel, in which he incorporated my father as one of the characters, the only one referred to by his true name. Obviously, Sam considered Max Reinhardt too fixed a historical personality to be tossed off fictionally. But when it came right down to it, he preferred rubbing elbows with this fixed historical figure on the printed page or, vicariously, in conversation with Eleonora and me to being directly exposed to it. Although my father was a virtuoso in escapism himself, he couldn't understand Sam's feints at getting together as soon as possible or hopefully working together on promising projects only to meet, when they were reacted to enthusiastically, a disappearing back. I, of course, understood why. The greater my surprise when, in the summer of 1937, I heard from Kommer that Sam had taken off for Austria "to pay homage to the great king of Leopoldskron, one of the few whose 'throne is secure' " (as he wrote in *The Burning Glass*). What was unsurprising was Sam's rapturous reaction to his first sight of the "king's" domain. My father's letter recounting it I could have prophesied in my sleep six thousand miles away: "Heaven! Professor, I envy you. What beauty! What peace! I'd give anything to have a place like this to work in." As usual, my father took Sam at his word, invited him to stay at Leopoldskron, to write, not write, do anything or nothing—whatever he wanted to do in "peace." It was agreed that my father's chauffeur would collect Sam and his luggage that same evening at the hotel in town where he was staying. That same evening, my father's chauffeur went to Sam's hotel in town and returned without Sam's luggage and without Sam, but with the intelligence that Mr. Behrman had left town a couple of hours before. For the States, according to the concierge. Which precise state in the Union was not clear. But if it was a matter of necessity to know, Mrs. Behrman could be reached in the maternity ward of the city hospital. *Mrs.* Behrman? The news stunned my father. Like so many of Sam's friends, he had no inkling that Sam had married and kept a wife under wraps for a number of years. The following morning, word reached Leopoldskron that the houseguest manqué had become father of a boy so eager to meet him that he entered the world two months earlier than scheduled—an impatience Sam did not share. He too was anxious to meet his son. But not today. Tomorrow.

Sam is now focusing—through us—on a facet of Reinhardt that kindles his inquisitiveness: "I've encountered most of the lamas of our theatre—Olivier, Gielgud, Lunt, Noël Coward—the lot. And in every one of them

—the cleverest and the most ponderous—there's a touch of the ham. But not in your father. Somehow I can't see him putting on makeup, struggling into tights, spouting the same fatigued lines with relentless conviction."

"He couldn't have agreed with you more. As a matter of fact he threw the whole ballast overboard the minute he could afford to."

Eleonora is in her element: "And that's the reason, Gottfried, why he behaved so ridiculously backstage in *Kabale* . . ."

"Do I hear treason against the sovereign from those fair lips?"

"He did it deliberately. Because he didn't really want to do what he was doing. So he made all kinds of silly complications. In protest. Like a bad child. Well, just for example, he insisted on having his own valet as a dresser. Everyone else got ready in half the time. Less."

Sam finds this "delicious": "The Great Sorcerer playing the Sorcerer's Apprentice!"

"And not always without enjoying it. Eleonora, you must admit that no child—bad or good—ever had more fun with a toy than Papa had with the Josefstadt chandelier."

Sam zooms in like Sherlock Holmes: "*The Josefstadt Chandelier*! What a title! Ah, I can just see the high jinks that went on beneath that glittering chandelier!"

"Sorry, Sam. No high jinks. The glitter went on and off. It's a terribly unlibidinous story. My father was crazy about that chandelier—it was an eighteenth-century one—and he hung it on a long silk cord as low as he could get it. Because he felt it would be in bad style to stick it smack up against the ceiling. When the other house lights dimmed *it* dimmed and ascended to the top of the house. [It still does.] A concession to the twentieth century: allowing the paying customers in the balcony and boxes to enjoy a view of the stage unobstructed by a luster—no matter how rare an *objet de cristallerie* it was. When he demonstrated its ups and downs to Wolfgang and me, the more ups and downs we clamored for and the more fun we had."

"That fun is exactly what bothered your Uncle Edmund. Actually not the fun but that it was going on in Vienna. *Berlin* is where he wanted him. Their theatres were falling apart without him. Good old Edmund. He knew his Max. There was only one way to get him back . . ."

Sam grins: "By giving him bigger and better chandeliers to play with?"

"Clever Berry. He gave him three entire *theatres* to play with! Better still—two of them weren't yet *built*! *That* did it!"

Eleonora's recollections are volleyed back by mine, with Sam, spectator at a mah-velous tennis match, swiveling his head from her to me and me to her, cheering us on with questions, applauding our answers:

Le Malade Imaginaire. At the Komödie. My father sits Wolfgang and me in a box directly above the stage—unexpectedly on the *stage* side of the proscenium. We're bowled over. He disclaims any credit for the invention of the unusual location, explains its origin goes back to the time of Louis Quatorze when the privileged wanted to be on more intimate terms with play and players than the more plebeian audience.

Sam pounces: "Aha! So you were the privileged! Even then! Now I understand everything. It was *tradition* that entitled you to your own bath and toilet at MGM while I had to pee with the proletariat in the men's room. What a father to have!"

Next over the net: Pirandello's *Six Characters in Search of an Author*, a forerunner of the theatre of the absurd—putting the lie to the charges that Max Reinhardt turned his back on contemporary literature.

"Even though my father practically took the play apart—something he almost never did—and put it together again his way, Pirandello was overjoyed."

Sam: "As I recall, Mr. Pirandello's enthusiasm was not shared by New York audiences."

Eleonora: "New York audiences didn't see his version. *Six Characters* wasn't really a success anywhere except with Reinhardt." She describes the Komödie's naked stage where amorphous characters bare their naked psyches. Max Pallenberg plays the—greatly expanded—part of the Director. Theatre in the theatre. Pallenberg's larger-than-life performance, made up as Max Reinhardt, is theatre in the theatre in the theatre, which leaves no way of telling who inspired whom: the actor-Director the man who directed him or vice versa.

Next: Hofmannsthal's subtle social satire *Der Schwierige*.

Sam: "Ahhh! How I'd adore to adapt that!"

Even Sam has to laugh.

Next: Galsworthy's thriller *Loyalties*.

Sam: "Thriller? Come now. That mediocre revel in anti-anti-Semitism boxed up in the tea and tweed of an English country house?"

A dedicated duo, we give alternate proof of how under Reinhardt the "tea and tweed" thriller becomes a subtle social satire (and the subtle social satire, thrilling theatre).

Sam: "Next?"

Eleonora: "Max disentangled him!" She explains how the shrewdly carpentered plot was limbered, how the scenes floated on air and on the wings of music—composed by Mischa Spoliansky, who, seated at a piano in the audience, sparked the dialogue with rhythmical accents. [In Hollywood—Robert Ryan was a member of the cast—my father repeated the stunt with equally congenial music by Bronislau Kaper.]

Knut Hamsun's *Gone to the Devil*—delivered by the good Lord into Reinhardt's hands. And blessed. Visually, acoustically, psychologically, an impressionist painting. A chiaroscuro canvas of moods, a harmonious concert of heterogeneous souls.

"Given the choice, dear boy, I'd have *seen* those souls a thousand times in a row rather than read about them once. It's the dullest play I know."

"That's probably what intrigued my father."

"Boredom?"

"Challenge. He told me—a long time ago—the only plays that really interest him are the ones that *need* him."

"That's odd. Then why did he never direct one of mine?"

"I admire your modesty, Sam. And he admires your writing. Enormously. That's why."

"Oh! I'm touched and by the way eternally grateful for what he did for me once. Just an announcement in *The New York Times* that Reinhardt *might* do my *Second Man* so increased my prestige on Broadway I never again had to wait for a table at Sardi's. I tried to thank him for it. Darling man. He said he'd like to read my play. That, I told him, would be *too* much. If he'd just keep on announcing it."

"In any case, Sam, he put you in the exalted company of George Bernard Shaw."

"He never did their plays either?"

"None of Schnitzler. And only two of Shaw."

Eleonora comes through with her ace: "Yes, but *what* Shaw! *Saint Joan* with *Bergner*!"

Sam: "Hallelujah! Now you're talking about a *play*, about perfection—but that would seem to eliminate Reinhardt's interest, wouldn't it? What was the pull? Bergner?"

"No, no, not at all. She was Shaw's condition for my father's doing the play. He *did* on occasion close his eyes to a play's merit, you know."

Bergner, an actress of calculated femininity contained in the body of a boy, half elfin-gay, half melancholic, full-time flirtatious, hoarse-erotic-voiced, an Austrian-Jewish composite of lightning intelligence and lingering charm, did not, as we know, quicken the pulse of her Austrian-Jewish compatriot, Max Reinhardt, with these qualities as she did her Germanic devotees'. The keenness of mind, epicene allure and flirtatiousness that sent them spinning were precisely what put him off. My father was, without question, overly critical of her. Bergner's hold on an audience—and, especially, her Berlin audience—had a magnetism that could not be explained away merely by calling it "technique." Bergner was her own director and her own critic, her presence eclipsing every environment—from which she received no stimulus. She fitted into no ensemble, least of all one shaped by the will of another. Happily, the gulf between director and leading lady affected neither her memorable performance of *Saint Joan* nor his memorable direction of the play. This dichotomy actually enhanced the performance's effect. For Shaw's virgin is a "loner" who never becomes part of the fabric around her.

But with *Romeo and Juliet* came the parting of their ways. Insistent on groping toward her own concept of Juliet, Bergner collided with a special relationship between author and director. The rest of the company—Czech-accented Romeo, handsome novice Francis Lederer, excepted—all graduates summa cum laude of the Reinhardt school, formed a homogeneity repellent to the Bergner instinct, the Bergner brain. Not at one rehearsal did she act with full voice. The only directorial pressure he brought to bear was to inquire mildly at the end of each day's work when she was going to put her full voice to use. Each day her answer was a beguiling, enigmatic smile. After dress rehearsal the question was repeated. And answered, as it had been in all the weeks before. After opening night—still without full voice—question time was over. The Reinhardt "alumni," having come through brilliantly, merely pointed up the fact that the greatest lovers in history had died, not a Shakespearean death, but a trivial one caused by an embryonic Romeo and an isolationist Juliet. Richard Beer-Hofmann's comment: "Two intelligent Jewish children from Prague discussing love."

"Mah-velous! So it's not only we crippled authors who need the Reinhardt crutch. I hope you've conveyed that message to your temperamental La Corbett! When are you going into rehearsal with *Helen?*"

I look at Eleonora. Tears stream down her cheeks: "Oh, Berry," she says, "Max is dying."

He turns to me. I nod. There is no more repartee. Sam, the master of it, answers simply with tears.

THE DIARY

SATURDAY,
OCTOBER 30, 1943

Up bright and early so as not to be late for SCPC. Through Greenie grapevine have been warned that our company commander is thirsting after Beverly Hills Commando blood. Mine particularly, because of my apparent disrespect for the sixty dollars due me monthly as a GI. My absences on a day free of all duty save the obligatory one of arriving at the post at the appointed hour, falling in with other stuporous GI's, inching forward toward an armed captain and top sergeant to accept the cash, salute smartly and depart, are bitterly resented.

Before leaving, look in upstairs for a moment. Papa's nurse opens the door. Even before she speaks, I know it is the moment: "The coma has begun." Go in his room, hear his heavy breathing changing gradually to a struggling rattle. I never thought it would be like this. The nurse wakes Thimig. I call Wolfgang, tell him, say I'll return as soon as I'm dismissed.

On my way out of lobby, am handed telegram from Hollywood, addressed to Max Reinhardt:

> DEAR PROFESSOR: CAN'T TELL YOU HOW SORRY WE ARE TO LEARN OF YOUR ILLNESS AND WE PRAY YOU WILL SOON RECOVER. WANT YOU TO KNOW OUR THOUGHTS ARE ALWAYS WITH YOU. KNOW YOU WILL BE HAPPY TO LEARN THAT WOLFGANG IS RETURNING TO OUR STUDIO AND WE ARE VERY HAPPY TO HAVE HIM BACK HERE. HE IS A LOVELY GENTLEMAN AND AN ABLE CRAFTSMAN AND THE LORD KNOWS THERE ARE NOT ENOUGH OF THEM AROUND SO WE CAN ALWAYS USE A MAN OF HIS ABILITY. EVERY GOOD WISH TO YOU YOUR WIFE AND SONS. ANN AND JACK WARNER.

With a month's pay in my pocket, am free to return to Gladstone, to Papa's room. Sit there with Wolfgang and Thimig until late in the night. Waiting. Numb. Suddenly, above Papa's rattling, hear Thimig's voice: "Gottfried, would you mind if I talked to Wolfgang outside—just for a few minutes?" And once again I'm alone with Papa. Not closer again, but am grateful just the same. I don't think of the end. I think of beginnings.

Birth of Direction

SHORTLY BEFORE 2 P.M., the semi-darkness of rehearsal. In the orchestra, just a few visitors and members of the theatre. Here and there, a human outline in a box. The stage is lit by a work light and bare except for rows of chairs, a table or two, a sofa and screens substituting for a set. Actors in mufti, some carrying their role booklets, consulting them every now and then, but otherwise, almost mechanically, moving about, grouping, dispersing, sitting, exiting and entering according to a manifestly preordained, tacitly-agreed-on plan. Stage left, a small table with a desk light; on it the script; on a chair before it, the prompter unfailingly, monotonously filling the gaps in the text. Stage right, a larger table with several chairs—unoccupied. Stage center, arms akimbo, the contour of the inimitable, much-imitated back of the *Regisseur*. It is not the *Regisseur*. It is one of his assistants. It does not matter which one. Like all of them, he is irritating the players, among them, world-famous names. It takes all their self-control to accept his a-little-too-authoritative corrections—pardon, reminders. The intonations, movements have an underwater quality.

A sudden beam of light, neither disturbing—there is not very much to disturb—nor arresting: one of the grudgingly tolerated interruptions interrupting nothing. To the right, in the rear of the auditorium, a double door swings open and—only an old hand would grasp the significance—the master of the house saunters in, followed by his staff. With the exception of those who must have been waiting for this opportunity to break through the cordon at last, to get their word in while he is in relatively accessible transit, the decisive entrance is ignored. Only the deputy on stage, for a split second, peers nervously over his shoulder. His moments are numbered. Otherwise, the stage is as concerned with the new arrival as he is with the stage.

An aide helps him off with his coat; the lamp on the director's lectern wedged in between two of the front rows is lit; he sits beside it. While the rehearsal acts as if it were continuing, he is shown some scenery designs. After a laborious search for his eyeglasses, he puts them on and studies the designs, nods, mumbles alterations. From his briefcase he takes a sketch of his own, compares it with its equivalent, weighs the pros and cons of each, suggests a compromise and impulsively leaves the bunch of drawings and the decision—which has been made—in the hands of the designer. The private secretary hands him several letters for his signature. He takes his time reading and signing. In turn, he entrusts her with a pack of handwritten, book-sized telegrams to be typed and dispatched. Imperceptibly, the gravitational center of the proceedings switches from the stage to the orchestra. One of the actors decides to participate no longer in the scene, ostentatiously seating himself on the sidelines and waiting. The tiny rebellion is overlooked. The assistant director jumps into the breach, reads the lines and acts for the striker. The cause of the disarray, for the first time, takes fleeting notice of what is transpiring on stage and is amused by the dissonance. But before things can get out of hand, as though obeying an inner alarm clock, the apparently so uninvolved "outsider" takes off his glasses and, suddenly, gives the actors his undivided attention. At once, the swarm of hangers-on about him edges away; other interests take second place.

"Please, once more from the beginning!" sounds the assistant's voice. Max Reinhardt has risen and surveys the action with his omni-ranged eyes. The mutineer quietly slips back into his role. Unhurriedly, briefcase under his arm, Max Reinhardt mounts the makeshift steps leading to the stage and takes his seat at the director's table. Without interfering with the dialogue, as if they were part of it, a number of—sarcastic?—"good mornings" are heard and echoed with a half-swallowed "morning . . ." The change of command takes place without friction. Automatically dethroned, the scapegoat sits next to Max Reinhardt.

The briefcase produces the prompt book. It is nonchalantly opened, leafed through, the eyeglasses ceremony is repeated—Max Reinhardt is reading. Between every page of the text a piece of paper is inserted, encompassing the direction of the play in every detail. On the pages themselves, the margins and spaces between the lines are covered with additional annotations in several colors of ink, with subsequently added comments in pencil. Self-drawn blueprints determine the areas of action. Every walk, every position is painstakingly recorded. Treble clefs announce musical accompaniment. Fermatas designate pauses. Cuts are indicated. The desired emphases, intonations and gestures are marked: "Shakes his head." "In playful earnest." "Elegiac melodies from the piano." "Swings herself onto the grand piano and lets her legs dangle." "Dramatically exclaims." "Curtly exploding." "Softly imparting." "Irritated again." "(She laughs in mocking imitation, brightly.) Hihihi." "He raises his finger." "Scratches his head pensively."

"Herr Professor!" The glasses come down. He looks up. "It's somehow hard for me to say this sitting down. Something must go on inside me first. I feel like taking a step or something, thinking, I must—I don't know. Struggle with myself . . ." Max Reinhardt rises. The book remains on the table, the page with the entry: "Thinks a moment, reaches peremptorily for her arms and draws her down to him; presses her close to him," remains opened. The assistant director studies it, then scrutinizes the actor with barely concealed contempt. Meanwhile, Max Reinhardt is walking up and down, up and down, reaching a decision. The actor watches him. The actor has become the spectator, the spectator the actor. The actor does not see Max Reinhardt, he sees himself. The transformation is uncanny. Max Reinhardt stops, "struggles with himself." "Something goes on inside him." Without transition, he submits softly: "Perhaps you try it this way once?" and promptly slips out of the role. "But how do I get back to her then . . . ? His inner resistance is too strong!" "Why don't you try it?" The actor does. Several times. It doesn't work. Max Reinhardt puts his arm around his shoulder and steers him to one side. He whispers to him. The actor laughs. Max Reinhardt nods encouragingly. They have a delicious secret. They return. They pace the floor together, Max Reinhardt's hand firmly gripping the actor's arm. After a while, he loosens the grip, lets go altogether, steps back and observes the actor growing more and more convincing, stirring. Max Reinhardt's face, expectantly, savoringly, duplicates every expression of the actor, his brain visibly duplicating every one of the actor's thoughts. But the actor does not find his way back to her. Each time he attempts it, something paralyzes him; he is rooted in his tracks. His inner resistance is too strong. Annoyed, feeling he is on the right road, yet not able to walk it, he looks to Max Reinhardt for help. In vain. Max Reinhardt is no longer at his side. He has crossed to his partner, seizing her arm and pulling her gently, but determinedly, forward. He leads her toward the actor. She obeys like a sleepwalker. She appears frightened and, at the same time, totally attracted. She does not "ape" Max Reinhardt. He does not "act out her part" for her. They are both one person. The actor turns away. But it is too late to block the dynamics. Both halt directly behind him. He feels them breathing down his neck. He spins around, his eyes piercing hers—or Max Reinhardt's? The actor, enraged: "But the pause is much too long!" "Shhh! Nothing's too long!" hisses Max Reinhardt. He presses the pair into an embrace. At first, somewhat mechanical, it becomes a need. The embrace seems endless. Not to Max Reinhardt, who will not let his two victims part. But to the prompter. She enunciates the overdue line. With an impatient gesture, Max Reinhardt orders her to be still. "Yes," says the actor dryly, "it'll work that way. Except . . ." "The line is cut," decrees Max Reinhardt.

The scene is repeated, repeated, repeated. Is it a scene for two or three people? Two, obviously. One forgets the presence of the third person . . . and then, again, not. The duo, in this phase, would be incomplete without the third. The pair feels almost naked when he leaves them to their fate. While they are groping for the next move and arguing with the confused prompter, Max Reinhardt reclines on the sofa, his arms locked behind his head, feminine seduction personified. Has she seen it? She kisses her partner and, collecting herself, crosses to the sofa. "Lines! Lines!" she demands abruptly. "Goddamnit, what do I say here?" Not the prompter, but Max Reinhardt feeds her the line almost inaudibly. He is preserving the mood. She isn't. She repeats the line dryly, without expression. Reinhardt does not mind. He has yielded his place to her and she stretches out on the sofa, her arms locked behind her head. Mood wins over mechanics. And, eventually, the actor "finds his way back to her."

Nine-thirty P.M. Stomachs are growling, extremities aching. No wonder. The cast have, after all, been on their feet for twelve hours without a break, Reinhardt only for eight. But "on his feet" would be an understatement. The stage is crowded, the stage is empty, he acts along with the others, plays their parts, is their audience, laughs tears, cries, prompts, muses, listens silently, tongue pressed against cheek, temple resting on extended index finger. He is in the melee, he keeps out of it. He hugs an emoter and admonishes: "You're playing this as if it were a disaster. But it's just a misfortune!" And to a comedian who insists he always gets a laugh with a certain piece of business: "My dear, up here you only hear the laughs. But down there, I see the people vomit." Like a sonic boom, he rends the air with a single word, in the middle of a spoken line, to set the tone, to awaken. To one he says hardly anything, to the other everything. Here he gives the melody, there just an accent, unlocking a whole new train of thought. And when asked about the sense, the purpose, the motivation of a speech, a scene, a character, he is careful to let the author explain, in the author's own words. He not only knows them by heart, he has taken them to heart. Understanding the author's words, according to him, means listening to them, not arguing about them. The truth must be found within them, not be injected into them. When he listens, he seems in a trance. He is deeply in love . . . but with whom? The men and women with whom he plays and who play with him? Hardly. Soon, he will leave the theatre and he is unlikely to meet any one of them again until the next rehearsal. Their personal lives leave him untouched. They know this and hate it. But they are enslaved. Why? Because he is in love with the characters they are playing—to which they are chained. By their talent, which enables them to do it. He wallows in it . . .

. . . till someone plucks up the courage to remind him, in a whisper, how late it is. Then he nods, his thoughts elsewhere, where it counts, continues to rehearse a bit, separates himself unnoticeably from the doings, consults the prompt book once again, closes it, puts it into his briefcase, laughs loudly at a well-delivered line, encourages someone with an incisive "Excellent!" as he descends the steps and is immediately surrounded by his retinue in the auditorium waiting to gain his attention, signs a paper, answers a question, slips into his overcoat and, before anyone is aware of it, has disappeared through the double door to the right, in the rear. Onstage, the act is played to the end under water, the deputy having taken over the reins. But no one waits for his "Thank you, ladies and gentlemen. Tomorrow at ten o'clock, Act III with the following . . ." He sees only the fleeing backs of an exhausted, edgy, exhilarated troupe.

A great friend of his—he shared the honor with Nietzsche, Freud and Rilke—Lou Andreas-Salomé, wrote about a Reinhardt rehearsal:

> In the winter months I used to yield to the temptation of spending my days in Berlin. The lure was Max Reinhardt's invitation. . . . It became such a pregnant experience in my life that everything else I received from him, including the contact with the rich circle of people around him, became secondary, and—that is saying a lot. I am thinking not of the controversies about the Reinhardt problem, neither the glory nor the blame, not even of the productions themselves, but of his uniqueness as a working man. . . . As actor, fighting shyness, in social intercourse equally insecure, Reinhardt, in his work, is so enraptured that it explains his unbelievable endurance and freshness: a will to dream and an almost brutal will to action. . . . When Agnes Sorma [the German Duse], in Ibsen's *Ghosts*, sobbing and suppressing her sobs, listened to her son's confession, without seeming to be able to hit the note Reinhardt demanded, the rehearsal ended in general exhaustion. Leaving the theatre, the overstrained woman was overcome by a crying spell.
>
> I will never forget how Reinhardt sprang up at this, arms extended, and exclaimed in ecstasy: "That's it! That's it!"—whereupon the crying spell became part of the instantly resumed rehearsal.

Most of this is today—if, perhaps, not with the same intensity or a comparable series of results—everyday theatre routine. Still, had an actor, producer or author read this account of a rehearsal in 1900, he would have thought it absurd. For although, ever since the inception of drama, there have been authors, players and managers who, besides their own special acumen, had this gift of helping their colleagues, their troupe, their interpreters, to greater theatrical effect, each in his own peculiar way, no one, before Reinhardt, made out of this specific gift an autonomous profession. How did it come about that he gave up all functions in the theatre, including acting, for something so imponderable?

Had my father chosen a new designation for this new, "imponderable" activity, he would have done a great service to clarity in the history of the theatre. By simply adopting a familiar one—familiar in connection with a relatively menial task—he caused a conceptual muddle never completely unraveled. The muddle is, in addition, linguistic. In England the person who does—at least, did in Reinhardt's days—the actual staging of plays is called producer. In America this title is applied to someone bearing the responsibility for raising financing for and, thereafter, running a show—functions the English call a manager's. London's "producer" became Broadway's "director." To confuse matters further, the German "*Direktor*" parallels the English "manager"—and the American "producer"—whereas the Englishman's "producer" and the American's "director" are the German's "*Regisseur*," the role Max Reinhardt conveniently, but not in fact, slipped into. It is, incidentally, a term borrowed from the Frenchman, who, however, prefers instead the designation "metteur en scène."

We know that Reinhardt did not conceive, did not even seek this role; that he grew into it by helping others. That seems to have been more important to the young man than acting himself. We have witnessed his first steps. They were small, cautious, tentative. It was not he who forced his ideas on the others. The others, vaguely sensing a superior sensitivity and unwonted conceptual clarity in their midst, apt to express itself in highly practical—i.e., helpful—terms, welcomed the muttered hints—actors will always welcome tangible help and have welcomed it long before the "modern director" was eager and expected to give it, regardless of where it came from: whether from a (more experienced) colleague, a (theatre-wise) author, or a (talented) manager. They encouraged the young busybody who was taking such an interest in their problems, began asking for his advice, effortless demonstrations and, finally, came to count on this novel crutch, sometimes unaware that it was novel.

Winterstein remembers his first confrontation with Reinhardt, rehearsing *Pelléas et Mélisande*:

> We sat in the green room and waited for our scene, waited and waited. It turned twelve, one o'clock. As far as we could tell, not more than two pages of the play had been dealt with. That was, in itself, something entirely

> new and unexpected. This scene would formerly have taken a director a quarter of an hour to block out. Reinhardt needed four. At first, we simply shook our heads until it was our turn, and we understood what Reinhardt meant by "rehearsing" . . . I realized what it was that constituted Max Reinhardt's directing talent and his artistically pedagogic accomplishment. It was not that he imprinted a preconceived notion on an actor. He actually fused the personal peculiarity of the actor with the picture of the character he had drawn for himself.

Now, picture a man with this really indefinable talent: a fine actor, but not one of the greats; a soul passionately dedicated to poetry, but no poet; eyes and ears that devour music, painting, sculpture, architecture, without producing them; bent on translating everything he sees, hears and esteems into his own language, a language he must largely invent; an ambitious, awake, emotional, pondering, not very young man (about thirty) who sees no reason why he should not adapt the achievements of electricity and all other technical and economic innovations of his era to his field of endeavor. Whether it was he who did away with the footlights and lit people and objects from above, from the side, and front, is not essential. That he did not invent the revolving stage, but revolved it more skillfully—what is more, not hidden from the audience's eyes—is a known fact. But not essential. That—not in theory, but in practice—he expanded the two-dimensional stage to the three-dimensional stage is not what made him per se the director. The cyclorama, the Fortuny sky—none of them Reinhardt's. But without Reinhardt, they would not have ushered in a new era of the theatre. That era began, as I have pointed out, in 1905, with the opening of his first *Midsummer Night's Dream.* Never before in the history of the theatre was a person who had not tangibly taken part in the production—by writing, acting, designing, making music—ad hoc discovered by the audience and called before the curtain. When it dropped, the audience wanted to see the person it hadn't seen. Max Reinhardt was the first of his kind to take a bow. Hermann Bahr wrote on that occasion:

> The public's enjoyment was like a child's . . . they screamed ecstatically . . . and now it was: Reinhardt! Reinhardt!, roared at full pitch, storming through the house. Reinhardt, Reinhardt, and no end in sight!

This clamor for "Reinhardt!" to show himself after every Reinhardt opening, this fervent evocation of the reigning spirit, rang on in my father's ears throughout his life. It soon felt as natural to him as to those who had demanded and responded to curtain calls for centuries. When the performers and, sometimes, the authors had received their due and the bidding for the absent "Reinhardt!" grew almost insulting to the others present, they would first beckon to him, then shrug their shoulders to the audience in embarrassment and finally pull him onto the stage, first sharing it with him, riding happily on the new waves of enthusiasm, then yielding it to him in solitary splendor. There was nothing coy about his reluctant performance. The glint in his eyes and his (formal) attire were proof that he was fully prepared to give it, and, what is more, that he enjoyed it. No, he not only played his part with gusto, he also knew, as usual, how to direct the scene. It became a ritual that everyone was familiar with and delighted in.

Well, not everyone. Not all the established stars, who resented the sudden encroachment on their age-old prerogatives. Nor did that merely apply to taking bows. It included at times, as we have seen, taking direction. He would have to build new stars—and did.

Nor was the delight shared by all the critics. Those who lost no time in joining battle with the "new star" and what they considered his star allure and excesses grasped as quickly as he did that this regular, vociferous adulation, beyond bolstering an ego they wished cut down to size, gave him real power. What was the use in picking bones with a culprit who had already been acquitted by popular consent, nay, put on a pedestal? How was a public to be discouraged from lending support to a man and his methods when its elite had already openly pledged it? The legendary glamour of the "Reinhardt première" indeed developed into a formidable weapon in his hands. It overshadowed every negative voice in print.

Finally, alas, his competitors were not happy. Did he, then, have competitors? Ironically, it was he who bred them in profusion. In the arts inventions cannot be patented. By fashioning for himself a new function, he had opened a floodgate through which a multitude of challengers and imitators streamed. In the next several years, there were few managers or actors of note who did not make a stab at *directing* (in the new sense of the term). The majority did not succeed. But some did. What was granted to none of them, however, not even to the most gifted or temporarily *en vogue*, was that perpetual love affair with the audience that, with each opening, eagerly awaited an almost always frenzied climax.

OCTOBER 30, 1943
(continued)

Thimig and Wolfgang return, reseat themselves. The death watch is resumed. But the dying die in their own time. And the grieving living feel hunger and thirst while they wait. Wolfgang and I go downstairs for a bite. Ask him what Thimig wanted "outside." He says she asked him to call Paul in California and to instruct him to remove everything valuable from Papa's house immediately and to store it elsewhere. People may die, but their wars survive them.

SUNDAY,
OCTOBER 31, 1943

Two A.M. It's over. The last sign of life that, for eighteen hideous hours, rasped on stubbornly—detached from the signs and wonders this life had been composed of—stops as it began: without any discernible cause or sense. Papa's nurse makes a routine entrance, instantly grasps the changed situation, makes a routine check of pulse and heart and closes his eyes. All routine. And that's good. Emotion would be superfluous. Papa shut out his own sight days ago.

Legends, Characters and Walks

AN EPILOGUE

IT TOOK MY FATHER five weeks to die—according to my diary. It doesn't seem possible to me now any more than it did then. I had had no feeling of the passage of time from the first day to the last. For the most part, my feeling was of being caught up in a relentless wind machine.

When it stopped, another kind of tempest swept in on me. My apartment at the Gladstone became VIP transit rooms with the telephone ringing nonstop and a doorbell pressed so frequently I finally left the door open—to the flood of tactful condolers who gripped my hand in silent sympathy and left after a minute or two; of embarrassed condolers who sat mutely on the extra chairs moved in by the hotel manager and cast significantly doleful looks in my direction; of old-friend condolers who embraced me and wept unashamedly; of condolers totally unknown to me, commiserating shadows floating in and out. How, I wondered, had the news flashed to so many, so fast, on a New York Sunday? Death apparently has its own grapevine.

If grief were to be measured actuarially, my seventy-year-old father's death should have added up to a sad, philosophic acceptance of the fact that a rewarding life had reached its normal expectancy or to gratitude that illness and misery had, mercifully, come to an end quickly. Yet it struck me that the wave of emotion sweeping through my rooms meant something more than mourning for a man, something more tragic than the loss of an old friend. What it was, what no voice expressed, I thought I knew: This man symbolized a splendid era that had been steadily declining, a decline, however, which people only became conscious of when one of its pillars fell away.

Three years later, my impression was confirmed by a letter from abroad in which I learned that one day after the death of Max Reinhardt, when radio waves had carried the news across the embattled Atlantic and the BBC had transmitted it to Germany (where tuning in on these broadcasts was a capital crime), the members of the Deutsches Theater—except for a few Nazi diehards—assembled to commemorate their proscribed leader of other days. In a Berlin more than half destroyed and inured to staggering casualty lists, they braved denunciation to express their sense of loss for a single man or, rather, like those gathered in my hotel rooms, for the era this man symbolized—one that, in their country, had been officially buried eleven years before. The courageous ceremony was repeated in Vienna. No more significant commentary is needed on a fidelity so strong that Dr. Goebbels deemed it circumspect to ignore it.

Someone—I don't know who—had ordered a death mask made. In the making, my father's lower lip suffered a distortion which, with every attempt to right it in plaster, grew worse. The final model was the likeness of a cynical, disillusioned man. A false legend perpetuated in plaster.

A *New York Times* reporter came to interview me. For hours. But the detailed biography I racked my brain to give him never appeared in print.

The next morning's two-column page-long obituary perpetuated a time-worn legend in newsprint.

We had long grown accustomed to every kind of medium propagating —with truth or fantasy—Max Reinhardt's image in his lifetime. But the announcement sprung on us the next day (Monday) by self-elected do-gooders that he was to be honored in two weeks with a testimonial evening —which, judging from the fact that tickets were already printed, had to have been ordered while he was still alive—floored us. True, he was then breathing his last. But still breathing! Our alert Gladstone neighbors, the Lothars, had used their elevator reconnaissance to good advantage: Carnegie Hall had been booked and Bruno Walter approached to conduct the New York Philharmonic Orchestra in a memorial concert and Herr Lothar had generously designated to himself the role of eulogist. Obviously, our thoughts were far distant from the pomp and ceremony proper to Max Reinhardt's exit from this world or the personal glory to be finagled out of it. Had we been consulted beforehand, the last commemorators we would have chosen were the ones submitted to us as a fait accompli. To lead him out musically, our natural choice would have been Toscanini, the conductor whose genius had always thrilled him and with whom he was in clandestine league against mediocrity, rather than Bruno Walter, with whom he had been at odds more than once. And for literary comment our preference would have been for that other friend of singular stature, Thomas Mann, instead of the minor novelist with theatrical ambitions. Toscanini took it as an unforgivable affront that the Reinhardt family passed him up.

Meanwhile, preparations for the funeral—to be preceded by memorial services in the Free Synagogue with Rabbi Stephen Wise officiating—went forward. With caution, since Rabbi Wise was as eloquent as he was admired—but not necessarily for his eloquence. As his words tended to string out in an unbroken chain from the Free Synagogue to heaven, Meyer Weisgal, the perennial solver of the insoluble, undertook the job of snipping the chain before it became airborne.

Only the immediate family and close friends attended the simple ceremony. Rabbi Wise cooperatively limited himself to Orthodox prayers and a few quotations from Shakespeare, and Bach was played by the Busch Quartet in front of his black-cloth-covered pine coffin. What a furor the selection of that plain pine box had aroused! Our morticians, men of elegance and fine judgment, maintained that the famous Max Reinhardt could not be transported to his resting place in anything less than a gorgeous brass-handled mahogany casket. We eventually won out, but were immediately embroiled in another contest: Our morticians of elegance and fine judgment could not be shaken in their conviction that so illustrious a corpse must be cosmeticized and the coffin left open for public view. We, however, refused to have his defenseless features peered at by inquisitive eyes. Once again, we were pitted in combat against the polished diplomats of death. And, once again, we were victorious.

The service over, we were ushered outside at a slow and decorous pace, past a line-up of funeral-parlor functionaries whose grief-stricken features put ours to shame, toward a row of black Cadillac limousines posted behind the hearse. Pace and gloom were prepackaged. But then something splendidly extemporaneous met our eyes: The street was choked with people, from Central Park West to Columbus Avenue, shawled heads, gray beards, the unmistakable stoop of Jewish shoulders (the pre-Israel stoop)—the entire emigration of New York or as much of it as could crowd into that long city block was on its feet. And from that mass of people came a silence so united it drowned out the din of New York traffic. It was as if the Professor himself were indicating that by family insistence on privacy at his rites we had staged only half the play. For the play *Max Reinhardt,* he might have been saying, was not only intimate, but of the masses for the masses.

He was laid to rest in a Jewish cemetery near Hastings-on-Hudson. A receiving vault is what the people at the cemetery called the tight, eerie stone structure his coffin was lifted into. "Receiving," meaning temporary, fit into our plans perfectly, as it was to have been a provisory arrangement—our intention being to maintain it only so long as the war lasted and until the situation in Europe cleared sufficiently for us to decide on the place of his final interment.

The war has long since ended and the situation in Europe has become as "clear" as it will ever be, but not so far as Max Reinhardt is concerned. At least not sufficiently to justify his remains being returned there. The decision to do so—with which I was faced a number of times—was all the more difficult as he had stated emphatically that he never wanted to go back to Germany or Austria. While I have little doubt that, with changing circumstances, he, like so many other émigrés, would have changed his mind, I didn't feel it was my right arbitrarily to act in contradiction to his wishes. Perhaps, had Berlin, Vienna or Salzburg shown a sincere desire to make up for the years of his exile and had they overcome my reluctance with persuasive demonstrations, I would have yielded to the pressure. But in the end I was always spared that tussle with my conscience. Nazi memory-lapses outlasted de-Nazification for many years.

Admittedly, the cultural climate in the German-speaking world has become warmer toward him in recent times. A new generation has taken over, free of its grandparents' hostility and guilt feelings vis-à-vis the Reinhardt era and of its parents' *à tout prix* opposition to it. Its curiosity about the past is unencumbered by fear of being judged obsequious or of appearing to lack independent judgment. Today, Max Reinhardt is remembered, is the subject of study and is even celebrated. However, here, too, moth-eaten legends too often distort the truth and the jubilees tend to enhance the glory of the jubilants. Nevertheless, constructive efforts have been made. Prominent among them is the founding of the Max Reinhardt Research and Memorial Center in Salzburg. To any hiker in the hills it would be surprising to find a muddy pool as the source of a fresh stream. Yet the man responsible for initiating this flow is one Heinz Kindermann, an octogenarian Austrian professor who, under Hitler, edited a book of poems by Reich Youth Leader Baldur von Schirach and who published a history of the theatre in which he recommended that "Max Reinhardt's contribution to the theatre be mercifully forgotten in the Orcus of silence."

At the same time that so fervent a patriot of the Third Reich was thus urging that Reinhardt's polluting influence on German *Kultur* be obliterated, a fugitive from that *Kultur* was hailing him—in New York's Carnegie Hall—as a model of pure Austrianism. A legend ill conceived, ill timed and in unfortunate taste. I skirted thanking Ernst Lothar for this flight-of-fancy valedictory by writing him a short note, assuring him that he had revealed a totally new Reinhardt—even to those near and dear to him. By return mail came his humblest thanks for so touching a compliment from the son of one of the greatest *Austrians* it had been his privilege to know. A burnt ironist, I sent Bruno Walter an uncarping message of appreciation, avoiding any reference to his tastefully selected program—which had not the remotest connection with Reinhardt's taste in music nor contained a single note reminiscent of the rich range he had drawn on for his productions. And with great effort I overcame the temptation to tell him that the obfuscated tribute, crowned by contralto Kerstin Torborg's recital, with himself, a pianistic Valentine, as her tender accompanist, would have made my father —had he been given the choice—flee the hall. (Nothing made him more uncomfortable than emotive *Liederabends.*) The major irony—in which I had no part—was that in the first posthumous Reinhardt presentation he could not fill more than a quarter of the house.

As things turned out, his probable reaction to the clumsy spectacle was made exquisitely graphic through one of Fortuna's mischievous darts. The dart—unwittingly—was Harry Horner, his devoted pupil. Had Horner foreseen the event in its most dismal light and determined to convey a Reinhardtian riposte to it, he could not have done so more effectively than in choosing for his decor a stage bare of everything but a photograph of Reinhardt blown up to heroic size, his head turned indifferently away from the goings-on. Yet, through the evening's mishmash of opportunistic motives and confused concepts one honest emotion filtered through: In my own flight at the first possible moment I was stopped short in the lobby by a hand stretched out to me. The hand was old and it trembled. I took it in mine. It was the hand of Richard Beer-Hofmann. There was biblical simplicity in his way of asking pardon for anger so terribly unjustified.

The twenty-year battle to the death between Else Heims and Helene Thimig over Max Reinhardt was in no way resolved by Max Reinhardt's death. If anything, the two contestants gained more ferocity in battling over the possessions he left behind than they ever had in their struggle for possession of the man. Armies of big-brain lawyers from two continents were recruited (their big-gun fees made them, after the smoke had cleared, the main beneficiaries) and, as always, in the middle, Wolfgang and I, two weary couriers, trudged between the lines with cease-fire proposals and armistice conditions. When my father's will leaving all theatrical memorabilia to his wife, Helene, was read, my brother and I felt no resentment. Understandably, this actress to whom the theatre was life and breath seemed to him a more plausible guardian than his two motion-picture producing sons. As the legacy included the entire body of his hand-annotated *Regiebücher* (prompt books)—the only testimony existent of his talent in action—we felt it fitting that it should go to someone who would cherish it always.

Always. . . . Just a few years after my father's death, on a late November afternoon, a Hollywood auctioneer telephoned me, apprising me of "a very interesting collection of Max Reinhardt stuff" which he felt it was his "duty to give Max's son first crack at before putting it up for public auction." An hour later, I was led into the auction house's treasure trove in back of the salesroom where, on a long wooden table surrounded by used-but-still-in-nice-condition washing machines, refrigerators, radios, beds, lamps, rolls of carpets, overstuffed sofas and assorted knickknacks, the larger part of my father's oeuvre was strewn about—roughly one hundred and thirty prompt books, handwritten diaries and personal letters. Los Angeles lawyer Frederick Mahl, Jr., Mrs. Thimig's last American strategist, had received them from her in lieu of his fee. Mr. Mahl was a man with a heart of gold. It was he who had advised the auctioneer that the lot should rightfully be offered—spot cash—to Reinhardt's younger (gainfully employed) son. My resources were no match for the gold in Mr. Mahl's heart —even less so for his hallucinate presale asking price. Yet I could not sit back and see my father's legacy sold, perhaps scattered as single items among souvenir hunters. My only alternative was to bid for it. To lessen the risk I telephoned the entire German refugee colony in town and pleaded that no bid be made against mine.

As wonders go, the response I met was a perfect one. Auction night arrived. The refugees, turned out in full force, had come only to cheer me on and there was nothing between me and Mrs. Thimig's inheritance but a small voice caroled out a second before the wooden hammer was banged down. Harvard and UCLA, my only serious competitors, had gone as high as their budgets allowed and had bowed out before the small voice—Marilyn Monroe's—suspended the auctioneer's hammer in mid-air. To match her bid would have beggared me. So M.R. belonged to M.M. The world press whooped up stories about "Sex Symbol Goes Intellectual."

There wasn't a man alive who wouldn't have given his eyeteeth to end up with Marilyn Monroe. Alive. But in my father's circumstance her lure remained open to question. I believed I had the answer: Meyer Weisgal—who else?—would advance the wherewithal and I would appeal to Miss Monroe's better nature to give up this folly, give up the Reinhardt *Regiebücher* for the price she had paid for them. A part of my letter to her ran: "Surely you will understand, dear Miss Monroe, that, aside from monetary expenditure, these books belong to Max Reinhardt's son and not to you." She answered very promptly and affirmatively. Whether her better nature was genuinely touched or whether the whole thing had been a publicity stunt that had served its purpose, I couldn't say. Didn't care. All that mattered was that the books were rescued and, some years later, were to become the nucleus of the Max Reinhardt Archive at the State University of New York at Binghamton—a worthy monument to him.

The story has a moral. The moral is never mail a check in haste. For I was just on the point of mailing Meyer's to Miss Monroe when the auctioneer telephoned me. He said he was glad I had "bought the stuff after all" and added that it could be picked up at his place any time with a check made out to *him*. Monroe had not collected it or paid for it.

In March of 1944, Silvia and I were, at last, lawfully wed. Until the summer of 1945 she shared me generously with the United States Army. In September the war was over, with probably the most futile contribution to its victorious end being my Einstein sortie and subsequent capture of him as a prize to be filmed at the Signal Corps Photographic Center.

Our marriage was a compromise. Silvia wanted to marry. I did not. She

took great umbrage at this. My solution was that we marry and keep it a secret. At this she took even greater umbrage. But we married. And her umbrage swelled with each day of secret matrimony. It was Einstein who gained for her the status she seemed to set such store by.

Before leaving the post, the morning I was to drive to Princeton to fetch him for the big day, I called Silvia and asked whether she'd like to come along and meet Einstein. "Einstein! Ein-stein!" she gasped with varying modulations of ecstasy. "Oh God, EINSTEIN!" Her heady sense of becoming part of history in meeting "EINSTEIN!" reached its peak when we arrived at his house and saw at the top of the stairs a familiar Brillo-haired figure hugged in a pepper-and-salt outer garment of non-committal shape waiting for us. "There he is! There he is!" Silvia shouted. The figure descended. There he was not. *There* was his sister, slightly shorter of Brillo-hair than he and wearing, I soon perceived, a skirt, not a frock. Several hesitant steps behind her, my film star followed. His smile of welcome was warm and gentle as summer rain. So pure. And here I wa with my dark secret on the seat next to me, palpitating to be introduce I jumped out of the car, heard my voice saying: "Professor, I would like introduce you to my wife." The "wife" part came out like thunder thro fog. Silvia's surprise was no greater than mine. I guess, maybe, when are face to face with a discoverer of ultimate truths, you do not lie.

Another thing you do not do with him is to drive away in a car you have sworn a solemn oath to his sister that he will not be give opportunity of coming within smelling distance of salami, a vict hankered after as much as his gall bladder rebelled at it. On the ri to New York, he kept staring out the window. Spring had suddenl rambunctious, come up with a blustery wind that sent the you trembling nervously on the trees. He said he loved the feel of th his face. Would it bother me to have the top down? As Silvia given up her seat inside the car to him—was receiving spri revel full in her face from the rumble seat and had not demurre I certainly couldn't. I stopped and put the top down. The delighted him. Life was a joy, he said, if one recognized the There was something poignantly evocative about this state sophisticated a scientist. I asked him how he, who exam nomena so dispassionately, could believe in wonders. B answered. Because the more one knows, the more one re of the connecting-all. It was my chance, my once-in-a-li learn about this "all." I put modest feelers out, which course you can understand the theory of relativity. Ye

it to you. Very simply. I shall start by putting you in a large carton which is being pulled through space at an ever-accelerating speed, say, on a string. You, however, are not aware of this, because the carton has no windows and you can't see out. Consequently, you know nothing about what is going on outside. But you sense a force—in direct opposition to the direction in which the carton is moving—which pushes you against one of the walls, and you, accustomed as you are to that sensation on earth, ascribe it to gravitation. However, in this instance, the phenomenon can be explained much more plausibly by the law of *inertia*. You see, what is normally presumed to be valid on earth need in no way be valid in another reference system. As far as the earth and our whole solar system is concerned, Newton established laws of astonishing accuracy. But they don't suffice for other reference systems. Now, I happen to have arrived at a little more accuracy and a little more universal validity. But someday, I am sure, someone else will come along who can achieve an even greater degree of accuracy and whose formulae are universally even more valid. Until then, my friend, mine will have to do." He smiled. The gentle summer rain was gone. An aurora borealis shined on me.

At the Hotel Great Northern on West Fifty-seventh Street I pulled up, went inside to telephone the post and announced my arrival with Einstein within the next half hour. Silvia had a date elsewhere, but volunteered to keep him company until I returned. Her reward was the opportunity of listening to him reflect aloud on the fleetingness of fame: "*Ja*, so few years ago it would not have been possible for me to sit in an open car in New York without crowds all around me." It wasn't quite clear to her whether he was relieved about or regretful of this development. However, when we were stopped by a red light at the next crossing, I noted that he acknowledged with a courtly bow the casual "Hi, Prof" called out by a pedestrian.

When word spread that Einstein had arrived, the SCPC turned into a beehive of officers, enlisted men and civilian personnel, swarming to get a closer look at the fabulous visitor. The crush of gawkers had been anticipated and dealt with—as we had in Hollywood when shooting Garbo—by closing off the set with black draperies. We posed Einstein at the rail of a ship moving past the Statue of Liberty. In reality, of course, it was the Statue that moved in back of him on a process screen. The mysteries of back projection inflamed his curiosity as much as, if not more than the mysteries of relativity inflamed mine. At any rate, he asked a lot more questions than I had. My new superior officer—Litvak had long abandoned our puny project for grander war-effort films and was, at the moment,

vigorously pushing his plan to restage the Normandy invasion complete with LCT's, bombs bursting, guns spurting fire and soldiers swallowed up in the foaming sea, for the all-American Litvak unit (an Anglo-American team had divided the honors of photographing the genuine landing); it took a hurried trip to Washington by Colonel Frank Capra and the direct intervention of General Marshall to prevent this second invasion—Major Anthony Veiller asked me whether I would ask Dr. Einstein please to comb his hair. "No," I said flatly. "Would you?" "Of course not," he answered. The "Dr.'s" hair remained an unmolested tangle of Brillo.

A penciled note—in a hand that surely never won more than a D minus for penmanship—was passed me by a minion who hung on for an answer to carry back to my top sergeant, the note's author. Awaited was my "permission" for him to enter the sacred confines. I laughed out loud. Would I say no to God? In no time at all my top sergeant, a bull who had checked his horns at the entrance, minced in demurely. And stared. For half an hour the most stupid man in the world stood transfixed by the most intelligent. Then he clapped me on the shoulder and rested his hand there for support until the resolution exploded through his taut lips: "Jeezus, Reinhardt! You know only the greatest fuckin' people!" With that, he turned on his heels and departed.

"Lights?" The lights were ready. "Camera?" The camera was ready and the moment-before-shooting demand for "QUIET!" was roared out—but the star had vanished. Where to? Something told me Albert Einstein was in the act of proving that the only motion exceeding the velocity of light was his beeline for salami when his sister wasn't around to nag him. So to the mess hall to track him down, take the salami sandwich out of his unresisting hand and trot him, now a shamefaced lamb caught nibbling an illicit vine, back to the set. Once there, he gave us no further problem. He was a good, a damn good trouper. But even a perfect performer has his tiny frailties. Einstein's was a pronunciation of English totally incomprehensible to the Anglo-Saxon ear. Particularly obscure was his rendition of the word "such." Uncurled from his tongue, it invariably came out "sooooch." The bray of GI laughter echoed warningly in my ear—the GI audience destined for Einstein's "sooooch." Loath as I was to curb his uninhibited delivery, I felt I had to steer him straight. He took it in no way amiss: "Of course," he replied with a confident smile, "theoretically I know it must be 'such.' But practically it will always be 'sooooch.' "

It was well into evening by the time we had finished shooting him from all possible angles. Any actor would have found it an exceedingly long, fatiguing day. Any star would, as a matter of course, have had a Cadillac, a

Lincoln Continental, possibly a Rolls or Bentley waiting outside the studio to transport him home. Yet, when I told Einstein that I would drive him back to Princeton, he was surprised. "But it is so late and so far for you," he protested. "It is better I take the train." It might have been "so late" and "so far" in his considerate opinion. But not for me, not for the immense pleasure I looked forward to in having him all to myself again for the next two hours.

The problem was: Would the same pleasure be his if I pestered him with questions again? En route, by way of breaking the ice, I told him a joke that more or less summed up what my attitude toward relativity had been before my enlightening morning session with him: " 'Everything,' some Minsk sage pontificates, 'is relative. If you sit with a bare behind on a hot stove for two seconds, it feels like two hours. If you're two hours with a ravishing woman, it feels like two seconds.' To which one of his listeners heckles: 'And with this Einstein went to America?' " My story amused him. In fact, he said, of all the variations he had heard of it over the years he always liked mine the best. Then my lesson was resumed.

The drive was almost over. I wondered why he had not mentioned a word about my father's death all day. Surely he had heard or read about it. Strange, I thought, that he should have talked about him with such warmth on our other meetings and, suddenly, become so indifferent. We pulled up at his house. I started to get out of the car to open the door for him, but was held back by a speech spilled out without preamble: "A man like your father," he said, "the world will not see again so soon." Then he reminded me of the first conversation we had in his study about the degree of fame achieved by a scientist depending on the interest aroused by the importance of questions he happened to pose himself and added: "In the arts—the theatre—it is no different. I'm sure there are other directors no less competent than your father. But what made him outstanding—made his 'fame'—was that he fulfilled important demands he'd made on himself which—even in the layman's eyes—revolutionized the theatre." He shook my hand, let himself out and was gone, scurrying stiff-boned up the stairs with a haste that left me forgotten on the sagging seat of my secondhand Buick.

But he left me a king. A king, I realized, with a stab of guilt, whose consort had a hot dinner waiting on the hot plate for him. At the first pay station, I telephoned my queen. "Darling," I said, "now *please* hold your horses! I have terrific news. Einstein has just finished explaining the entire theory of relativity to me!" From the other end came a greedy intake of breath, then a shrewd command: "Come right home and don't tell anybody!" I reflected that the hordes lying in wait on the dark road to snatch at my secret could be dealt with by the little finger of my left hand, but decided to keep the thought to myself.

Back in the Gladstone, over roast beef risen from the ashes, I explained to Silvia word for word what Einstein had explained to me. Her mouth fell open. "You mean," she said, "that's *all*? It's that simple?" "It's that simple," I answered. The next morning she shook me awake to announce that she had been robbed. An incubus, she claimed, had crawled into her head during the night and carried off every last shred of the theory of relativity. Would I tell her everything all over again? Please. I looked at her sharply. A delaying action. I didn't know how to break the news that we were bankrupt. All I could remember was sitting in a carton.

A large part of Eleonora von Mendelssohn's possessions abroad was restored to her. But restitution of material things came too late to bolster her interest in life. For with increased addiction to drugs she had found the avenue to almost total escape from it. All that, from time to time, returned her to the pain of living were the problems of an adored brother, Francesco, who found *his* escape by going insane. In her apartment on the Upper East Side of New York, which she shared with homosexuals, she became the victim of their lovers' quarrels, sordid scenes and abortive suicide leaps to the pavement from her window, which, though touching her only peripherally, left her morose and despairing. In 1953 she was found dead in her bed. An ether-soaked cloth placed firmly over her nostrils had ended her life at the age of fifty-three.

Helene Thimig was the first of the Reinhardts to return to Europe and to the German theatre, where she played with all her former distinction. In Salzburg she both directed and acted in Max Reinhardt's revived *Jedermann* and in Vienna taught in the Max Reinhardt Seminar—efforts which earned her the title of "professor" in her own right. In the last year of her life (1973), at the age of eighty-four, she wrote a book about her husband, entitled *How Max Reinhardt Lived*—the one thing her pages do not describe. The lyrical subtitle, "A Hand's Breadth Above the Ground," would be apter had her text left her subject at that elevation, instead of transporting him—a wide-eyed innocent—into the clouds. Half vaguely eulogistic biography, half euphoric autobiography, her work reveals little of the joys and woes, stormy successes and failures, thoughts, dreams and disappointments that made the man. Having met him after he had passed his zenith, after his years of young, seething ambition had gentled, it is perhaps understandable that she lived with her own legend of Max Reinhardt and that, in remembering him, added still another to the cycle.

With travel possible again, my mother, indignantly resisting advancing age and infirmity, bundled back and forth between the New World and the Old, not happy about her reduced status in either, not about the small parts I wrote into my Hollywood films for her and not about her few-and-far-between engagements on German stages. But no matter where she was, this "pure" Aryan did not refrain from loud and lasting condemnation of her German compatriots—a brother-in-law included—who had opened their arms to Nazism. On her last visit to California, she was struck by a car while crossing Sunset Boulevard at an unlit intersection in Brentwood and dragged several hundred feet in the dark before the vehicle was stopped by horrified spectators. The X rays I looked at in a Catholic hospital in Santa Monica where she had been taken showed seventeen fractures. To the doctors who examined her it was incomprehensible that she should still be alive. How little they understood her will. For six weeks she remained a medical puzzlement. But her strength—not her will—was unequal to two grueling operations on her broken body.

Conscious and incorruptible to the last minute, she steadfastly refused the ministrations pressed on her by an attending priest. All her life, she poked at him acidly from her deathbed, she had questioned the validity of a Hereafter. Moreover, both his approach and his timing were faulty, because while *he* was staying, *she* was going and, therefore, in a very short while, would be in a better position than he to determine what the next life was all about. Not, she smiled, that she approached it with sanguine expectation. She distrusted myths. Facts—and facing them head on—were what she believed in. The Hereafter was not a fact to her. Not yet. It was not the moment for me to step in and remind her of the one fact she had never faced—that, in the prime of her life, she had lost Max Reinhardt irretrievably—and that through this single lapse from her intelligent behavior pattern she had become an obsessive crusader of a doomed cause who, in the crusading, neglected her talent, forgot her beauty and lost the fruits they entitled her to. She was seventy-eight when she died. When I went through her personal effects, I found yellowing bundles of "Beloved Else" letters from "Your Faithful Forever Max," faded photographs of him and newspaper clippings which followed him from the day he rejected her until the day he died.

The fountain of appreciation for Wolfgang's "gentlemanly" and "professional" qualities, telegraphically spouted by J. L. Warner since my father's illness, did not long survive my father. Neither did Wolfgang's new-old job at Warner Brothers. Back again on the treadmill of job hunting, hanging on, hunting again, he found one that led him to Europe, to less ego-lacerating associates than the brothers Warner and eventually to the production of a German cornball movie that had its heyday and would have been long forgotten had it not been bought and adapted for Broadway by Rodgers and Hammerstein and, thereafter, made into a film by Twentieth-Century Fox with the title *Sound of Music,* grossing ninety million dollars and giving him an annuity for life.

Helen Goes to Troy was reactivated in the late spring of 1944 through the cross-purpose efforts of the New Opera Company and my own. We opened at the Alvin Theatre on West Fifty-second Street to loud hosannas and record-breaking-run prophecies from the press. We closed three months later. "Weather" being the standard alibi for flops, we cursed the sweltering days and blamed lack of air conditioning at the Alvin for our untimely demise. My unexpressed opinion was that elements other than environmental had doomed us before we ever set foot into the Alvin: Superb musician though Korngold was, he was too operatic for Broadway operetta without the curb of Reinhardt; I, a full-time sergeant, was no match as part-time producer pushing a hip, breezy Offenbach against Madame Irion's all-out push for warmed-over nineteenth-century opéra bouffe; charming, lovely soprano Jarmila Novotna was too ladylike a replacement for sexy, spirited Leonora Corbett; but most dooming of all, with Max Reinhardt gone, William S. Paley's pledge of twenty thousand dollars was gone too. To fill the gap Meehan, Baker and I fell back on our after-dinner turn as performing monkeys in upper-crust drawing rooms. In one of the upperest the money, to our amazement, was practically thrust upon us by a Belgian baron. He was the owner of a magnificent art collection whose sustenance was provided by his generous American wife. But his collector's passion was occasionally fixed on objects neither subsidized by his wife nor appropriate for hanging on his walls. His most recent acquisition, a doe-eyed, doe-brained chorus girl, he wanted to hang on *us.* Not that we had any quarrel with a twenty-thousand-dollar doe playing Venus, a role in Reinhardt's *La Belle Hélène* taxed with no greater effort than stripping before Paris and thereby winning the golden apple over Juno and Minerva. It was just our bad luck that the baron had a double standard about exhibiting his treasures. While the nudes on his walls were there for any art-hungry eye to feast on, his nude lady friend being ogled hungrily on a Broadway stage was *out*! Our costume designer averted a dangerous crisis by encapsulating the goddess of love in a see-through-proof, neck-to-ankle undergarment which left her—when her floating draperies were cast aside—as erotic as a kiddy in woolly jammers toddling in for a night-night kiss. The baron was satisfied. The gentlemen in the front rows were not.

Helen's folding ended my soldier-boy flirtation with Broadway the heartbreaker. It left me sadder, but wiser; more important, it kept me from pursuing my ambition to live with the stage as the true love of my life—an ambition conflicting sharply with my determination to prevent the father-and-son comparisons critics sharpen their teeth on. On my discharge from the Army, I headed—without a backward glance—for the less problematic arms of the courtesan Hollywood. All was not unadulterated joy by any means, but, at least, as a motion-picture maker I invited slightly less critical invective for being my father's disappointing son, instead of his twin in artistic perfection, and went on about my own business of producing and directing films.

One of them, *The Red Badge of Courage*, became a cause célèbre set off by a series of weekly articles about it, appearing in *The New Yorker* magazine. Ostensibly, the writer of them was reporting on—covering step by step, with all its tragicomic ramifications—the making of a movie. In point of fact, her reportage about this American Civil War film was a sly and purposeful exposure of the civil war *behind* its scenes, which was tearing MGM apart. Inadvertently, she thrust me into the role of a traitor by quoting my statement that the studio was run like the British Empire (with similar effect) and with its executives, whom I named and ranked, bumbling around in corresponding cabinet posts. The loudest cry of outrage was wrung from our general manager—recently relegated to the shelf—when he read I had compared him to a minister without portfolio. Nothing I said placated him, not even my enumeration of the distinguished Englishmen who, in this position, had glorified their country's history. He didn't know what a portfolio was, but resented being without one. And his instinct was right: One of the first heads to fall when MGM started crumbling was his. I didn't wait for my turn. As the last of the family, I returned to Europe. But not for good. A man with two loves—in Europe a passionate American and in America a passionate European—cannot tarry too long with one.

It is my, admittedly biased, filial opinion that the well-timed death of my father spared him the futile effort of having to adapt himself, in his seventies, to life in post–World War II America, a country so different from the one he had dazzled as a visiting celebrity, indeed one that had stopped being dazzled by his presence as soon as he had adopted it as his home; spared him an awkward, anticlimactic return to an Old World no longer his in substance or manners.

These are the thoughts that accompany me when I accompany "Prince"

Paris (the four-legged version) on his "tours," when, unceremoniously parting company with me, he disappears into the woods after a pheasant, a squirrel, a hare or—delight of delights—a frisky young deer. I call commandingly and am irritated that he ignores me. Although, by now, I should know an actor only responds to direction when it suits him. While I wait, I wonder about the *sum total* of my father's life. I see a dozen lives in one. Dominant in all I see infinite love given and received in equal measure. I hear a conversation of his with Rudolf Kommer—that "at once good and evil spirit of eternal negation" (my father quoting Faust's description of Mephisto in Goethe's play)—in which Kommer said to him: "I must tell you, Herr Professor, ninety percent of the things you have done in your life were wrong." And I hear my father's reply: "Possibly. But, my dear Herr Kommer, it's for the remaining ten percent I live." Could it be this terse rejoinder is the answer to my quest for the sum total of his life? Ten percent? Was it enough? The eyes of uncoercible Paris (just returned) say, oh yes! He sits at my feet, a stick in his mouth, looks up at me contritely, challengingly, full of love and ardent mischief. No other actor could equal the multiplexity of these emotions in a single look. Unless there were a Max Reinhardt near to draw it from him magically, as he had from many another Puck—in another epilogue:

> If we shadows have offended,
> Think but this, and all is mended,
> That you have but slumb'red here
> While these visions did appear.
> And this weak and idle theme,
> No more yielding but a dream,
> Gentles, do not reprehend:
> If you pardon, we will mend.
> And, as I am an honest Puck,
> If we have unearned luck
> Now to 'scape the serpent's tongue,
> We will make amends ere long;
> Else the Puck a liar call:
> So, good night unto you all.
> Give me your hands, if we be friends,
> And Robin shall restore amends.

Index

A NOTE ABOUT THE AUTHOR

Gottfried Reinhardt, the younger son of Max Reinhardt, was born in Berlin on March 20, 1913 and educated at the French *Gymnasium*. While a student at the University of Berlin he began his career in theatrical production and mounted the première, in 1931, of Erich Kastner's *Pünktchen and Anton*. In 1932 he left Germany for America. After working as Ernst Lubitsch's assistant in Hollywood, he spent twenty years at Metro-Goldwyn-Mayer as script writer and then producer of, among others, *Comrade X, Rage in Heaven, Two-Faced Woman, The Red Badge of Courage* and *Town without Pity*. On Broadway, he wrote the books for both *Rosalinda* and *Helen Goes to Troy*. Since the fifties, he has also directed and produced both plays and films in Europe.

He divides his time between California and Salzburg, Austria.

A NOTE ON THE TYPE

The text of this book was set in Electra, a type face designed by William Addison Dwiggins for the Mergenthaler Linotype Company and first made available in 1935. Electra cannot be classified as either "modern" or "old-style." It is not based on any historical model, and hence does not echo any particular period or style of type design. It avoids the extreme contrast between thick and thin elements that marks most modern faces, and is without eccentricities that catch the eye and interfere with reading. In general, Electra is a simple, readable typeface that attempts to give a feeling of fluidity, power, and speed.

W. A. Dwiggins (1880–1956) began an association with the Mergenthaler Linotype Company in 1929 and over the next twenty-seven years designed a number of book types, including the Metro, Electra, Caledonia, Eldorado, and Falcon.

Composed by Maryland Linotype Composition Company, Inc., Baltimore, Maryland.
Black and white illustrations printed by the Murray Printing Company, Forge Village, Massachusetts.
Printed and bound by Haddon Craftsmen, Scranton, Pennsylvania.
Book design by Margaret M. Wagner.